DESK TOP PUBLISHING

DESK TOP PUBLISHING

Including latest versions of

WINDOWS
PHOTOSHOP
PAGEMAKER
CORELDRAW
ADOBE ILLUSTRATOR

Dinesh Maidasani
B.A., Dip. Comp. Sc.

FIREWALL MEDIA
(An Imprint of Laxmi Publications Pvt. Ltd.)
BANGALORE • CHENNAI • COCHIN • GUWAHATI • HYDERABAD
JALANDHAR • KOLKATA • LUCKNOW • MUMBAI • PATNA
RANCHI • NEW DELHI

Published by :

FIREWALL MEDIA

(An Imprint of Laxmi Publications Pvt. Ltd.)
113, Golden House, Daryaganj,
New Delhi-110002

Phone : 011-43 53 25 00
Fax : 011-43 53 25 28

www.laxmipublications.com
info@laxmipublications.com

Price : ₹ **225.00** *Only.*

First Edition : 2002, *Second Edition* : 2006
Reprint : 2007, 2012

OFFICES

✆ **Bangalore**	080-26 75 69 30	✆ **Chennai**	044-24 34 47 26
✆ **Cochin**	0484-237 70 04, 405 13 03	✆ **Guwahati**	0361-251 36 69, 251 38 81
✆ **Hyderabad**	040-24 65 23 33	✆ **Jalandhar**	0181-222 12 72
✆ **Kolkata**	033-22 27 43 84	✆ **Lucknow**	0522-220 99 16
✆ **Mumbai**	022-24 91 54 15, 24 92 78 69	✆ **Patna**	0612-230 00 97
✆ **Ranchi**	0651-220 44 60		

FDE-2829-225-DESK TOP PUBLISHING-MAI
Typeset at : Goswami Printers, Delhi.

C—4931/012/03
Printed at : Sanjeev Offset Printers, Delhi.

Contents

1 Introduction to Windows XP

Windows XP

The XP stands for experience. The name Windows XP represents Microsoft's focus on enabling end-to-end experience, unlocking the power of the PC and empowering users to make the most of their computer experience in the simplest way possible. With Windows XP Microsoft is extending the power of the PC to devices, web services and applications that enable the bradest set of experiences.

Exploring Desktop of Windows XP

As was in the earlier version of Windows, Windows XP too has a familiar desktop from where you can launch your programs using their shortcuts. A Windows XP desktop is shown here with all the relative icons. You may or may not have the same desktop on computer. But, it will be quite similar.

Windows XP and there are few which are optional and are created by the users according to their likings.

Icons

Icon is a graphic presentation of a window element. Icons are of four types which are as follows:

Disk Drive Icons

These type of Icons represents the Drives of the computer. For example: Drive3½ Floppy A:, Hard Disk drive, CD Drive, etc.

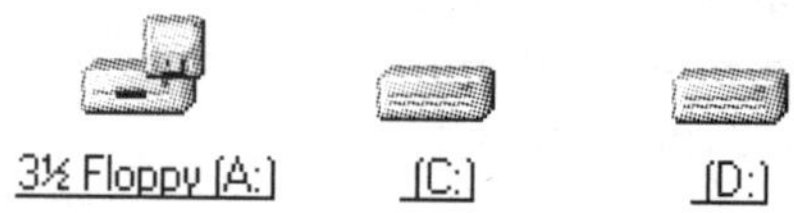

Application Icons

Application Icons means the software package which are used to run various programs. For Example: MS-Office, MS-Word, MS-Excel, MS- Access, PageMaker, CorelDraw etc.

Shortcut Icons

Shortcut Icons are created by using the option from Desktop/New/Shortcut.

Document Icons

You can create a graphical representation of any document.

Among the permanent ones on the desktop are: **My Computer**, **Recycle Bin**, **My Documents**, etc.

Before we go into details of all these and see how they help us in working, we explore the other parts of the desktop. At the bottom most left corner of the desktop is the **Start** button. By pressing it you can launch the following options.

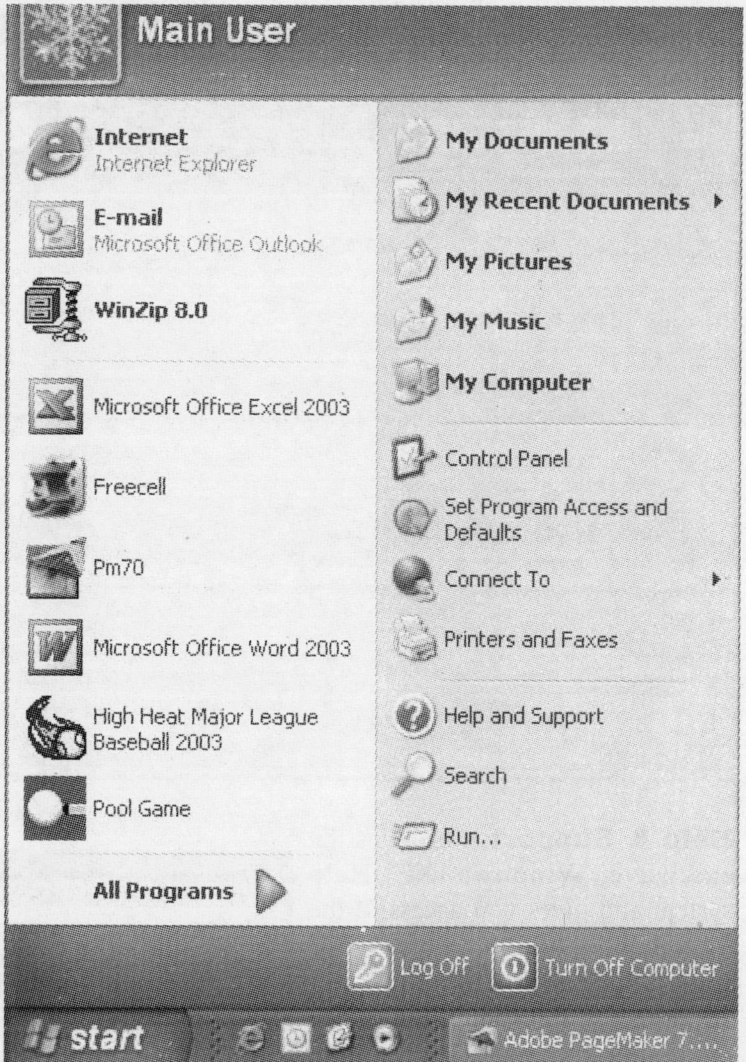

For those of you who have used earlier versions of Windows, this would look very different from the earlier ones. The main difference being that it is in 2 cols.

Internet: It opens up Internet Explorer version 6.0 for you to access Internet.

e-mail: If opens up Outlook Express for you to send and receive e-mail.

All Programs : It gives you access to all programs loaded in your computer. You can start these programs by just clicking at them.

Next we have a list of the various programs which have been recently used. So you may have something different from this.

Now, coming to the second column we have,

My Documents: It gives you the list of documents which you have stored in My Documents.

My Recent Documents: It gives you access to the last 15 documents opened.

My Pictures: It gives you the list of pictures stored by you in your computer.

My Music: It gives you the list of music files stored in the computer.

My Computer: You can access My Computer from here.

My Network Places: It gives the list of web sites you have accessed to recently.

Control Panel: You can access to Control Panel from here.

Set Program Access and Defaults: It allows you to access the various tools which you may have to use to access the various defaults.

Connect To: It provides access to connecting you to your own connection or show all the connections available in the computer.

Printers and Faxes: It shows you the various printers and faxes connected to your computer.

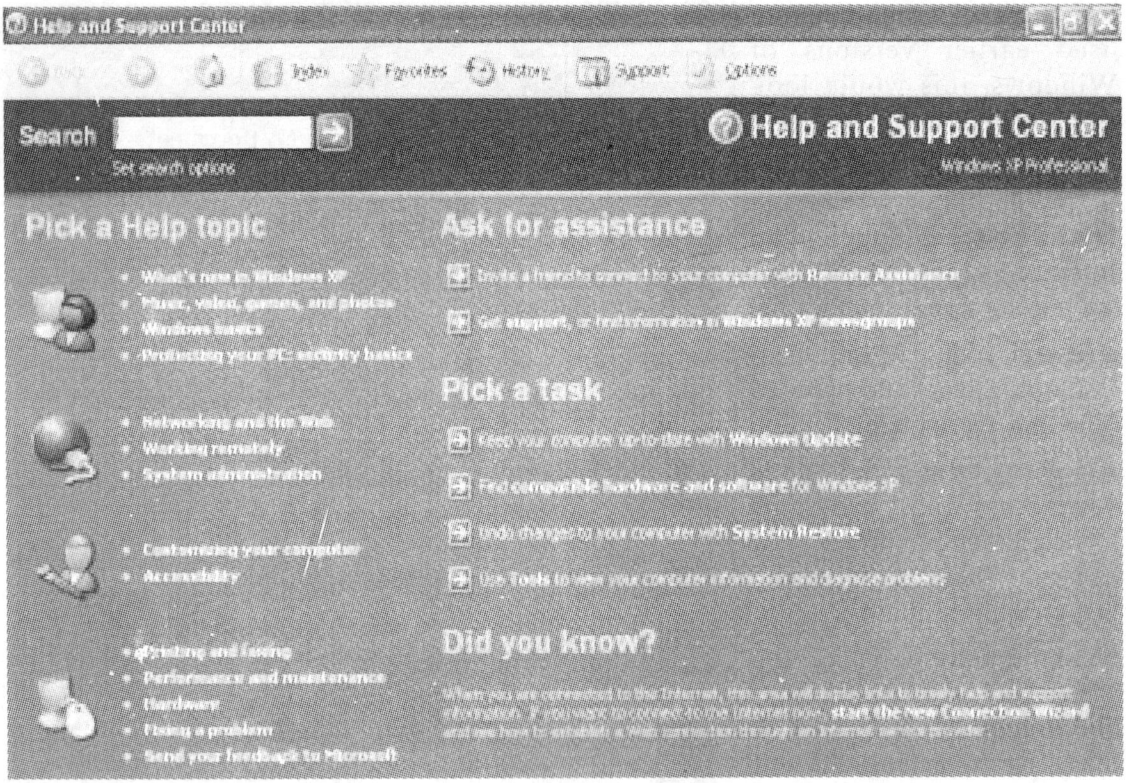

Help & Support: It opens the extensive Windows XP Help system and gives you access to the Troubleshooting.

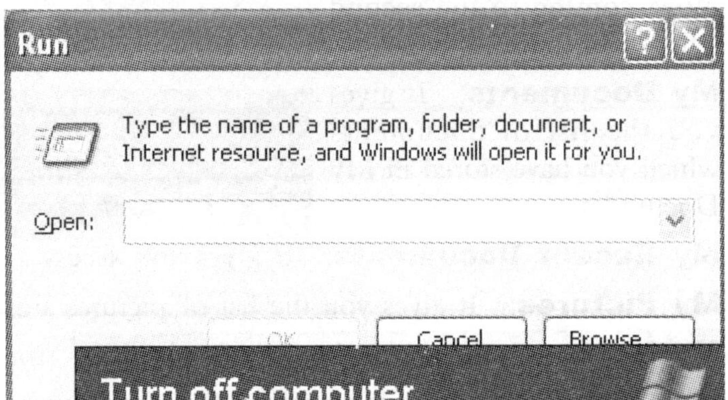

Search: This allows you to search for a file or folder.

Run: Allows you to run a particular program using a dialog box.

Log Off..: It logs off the system quickly so that you can log back with a different user profile or so that another user can log on.

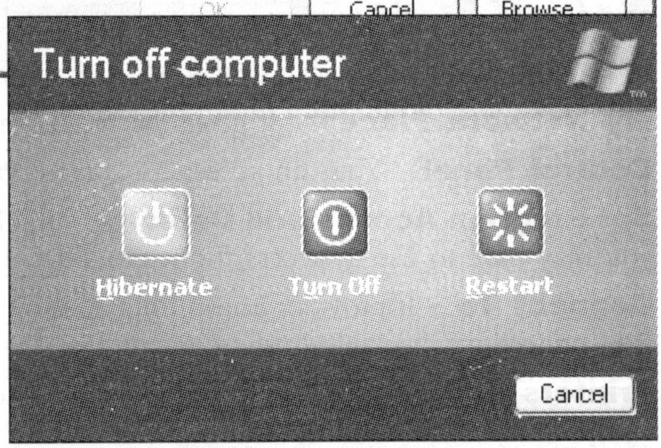

Turn Off: This gives rise to a dialog box, which asks you what you want to do. The options are:

Hibernate: Alternate to Standby

Turn off: To turn off the computer

Restart: To restart the computer

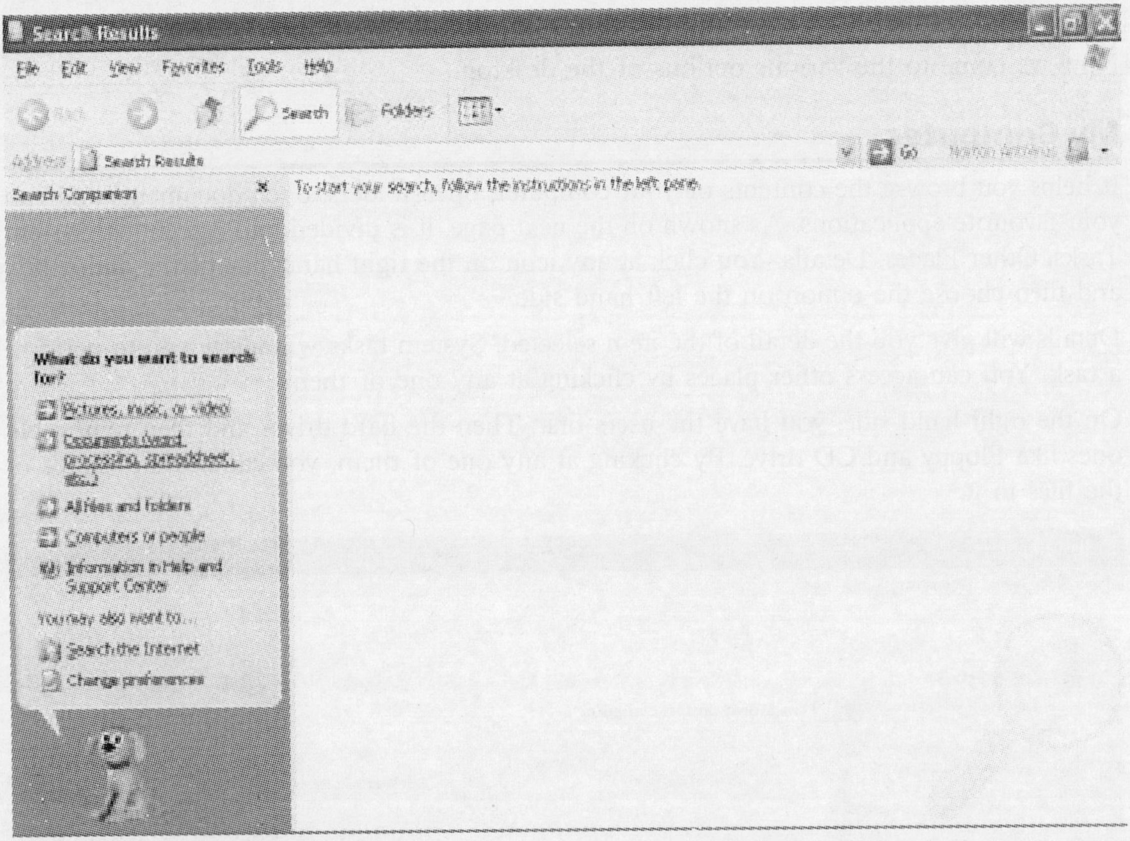

Exploring the Taskbar

It the bottom key line on the desktop. Please refer to the earlier figure of desktop for the details. Starting with the right most corner, we see the following:

Quick Launch Toolbar: Various icons here are the ones used for launching different programs. You have an option to put these icons here for the programs which you often use.

Running Tasks: When you have a program running in your system, its name will be reflected here on this taskbar to show that this program is open.

Scheduled Tasks: It shows you tasks which are scheduled to be performed at various times. You will read about them later.

Date and Time: It shows you the date and time of the system.

Now we come to the various options of the desktop.

My Computer

It helps you browse the contents of your computer, open folders, open documents and run your favourite applications. As shown on the next page, it is divided into 3 sections, System Tasks, Other Places, Details. You click at any icon on the right hand side of the dialog box and then choose the option on the left hand side.

Details will give you the detail of the item selected. System tasks will allow you to perform a task. You can access other places by clicking at any one of them.

On the right hand side, you have the users first. Then the hard drives and then removable ones like Floppy and CD drive. By clicking at any one of them, you can see the details of the files in it.

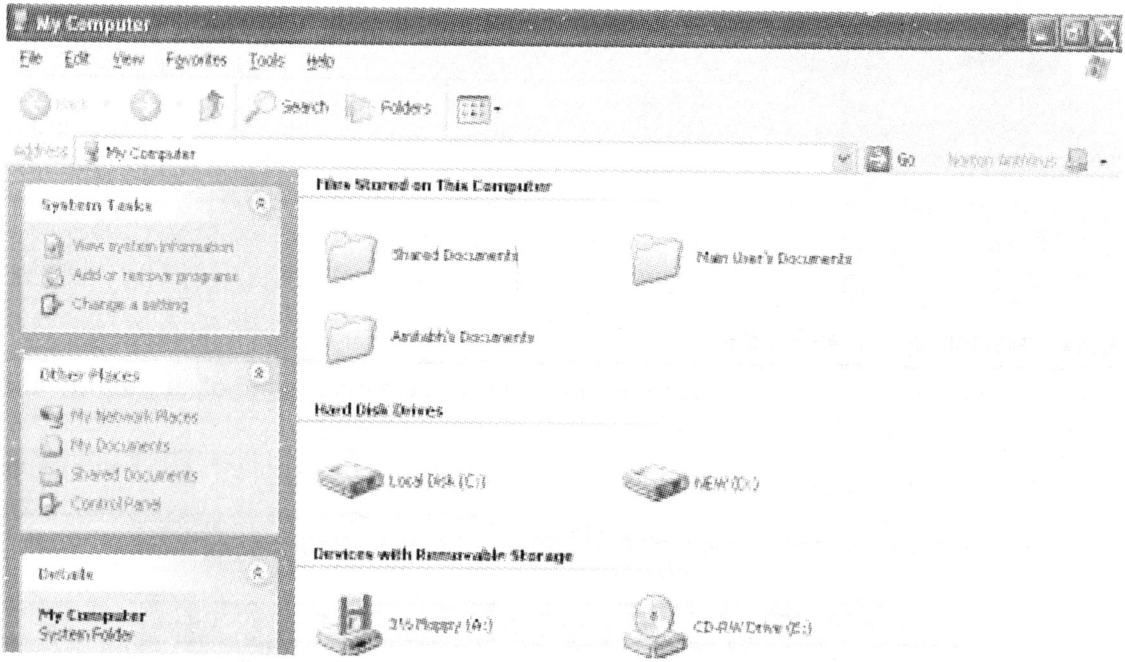

Contents of the Drive C are also shown on the next page.

The buttons on the top are useful for going and coming back to the various folders. Seeing the various views of the files, etc.

Now let us see how **My Computer** is used for copying of files.

Copying of Files

Supposing you have to copy a file from floppy disk to the hard disk. As in the previous case click at the icon of floppy drive A to get the open folder. Also open the folder of hard disk and the particular folder where you want the file to be copied. You will have to click the icon of **My Computer** again for this.

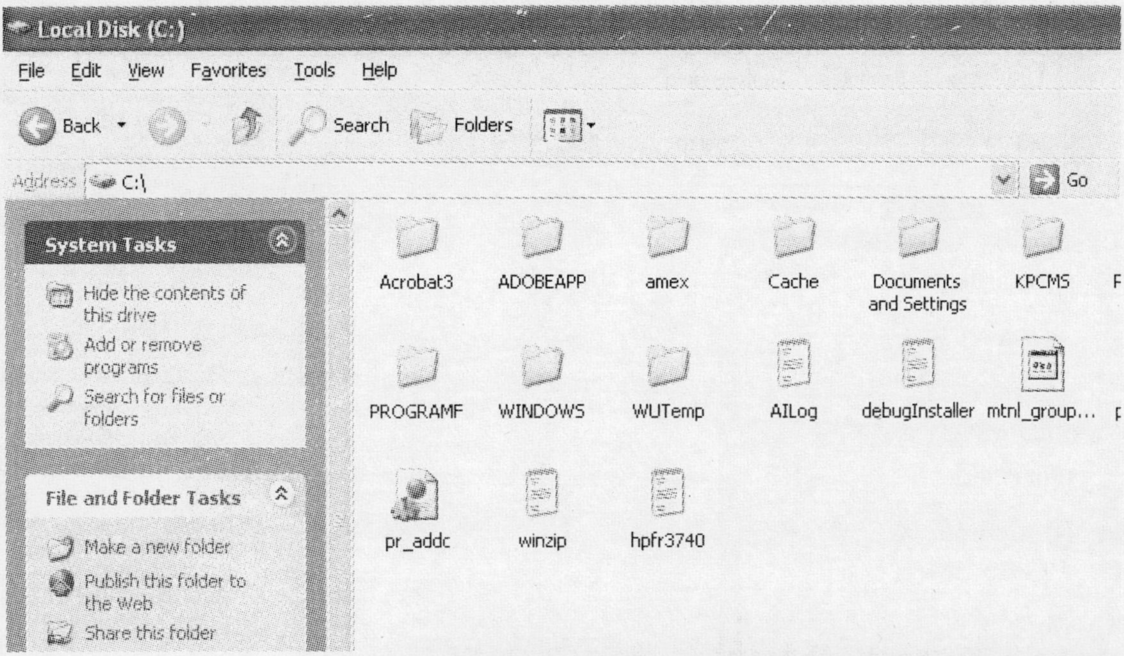

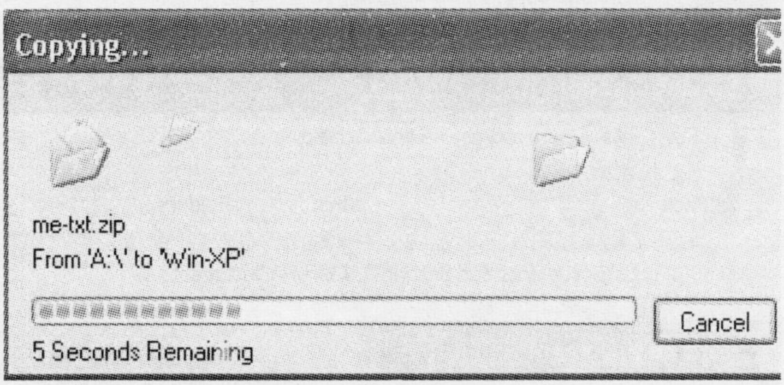

Now that both the folders of hard disk and floppy drive are open and you can see the file icon, which you want to copy to the hard disk. Just click this and drag it to drop in the folder of the hard disk. You will see the copying start. Once the file has been copied, this small dialog box will vanish and the file would be seen in both hard disk and the floppy drive.

However, if you want to copy without leaving the copy of the file in the source, press **Control Key** and then click the mouse to drag the file. This will copy the file and not leave the copy behind.

Recycle Bin

It is like a dust bin of the computer. All the deleted files are transferred here. You can in fact open this folder to see the files present in it. If you want at any stage to retrace any file, you can do it, if it is present in the **Recycle Bin**. However, if you choose to empty the recycle bin and delete the files altogether, then you cannot restore any of the file.

My Documents

This folder contains all your files which you have created and saved in it. Irrespective of the program, you can click the files to open them. The relative program will be launched automatically.

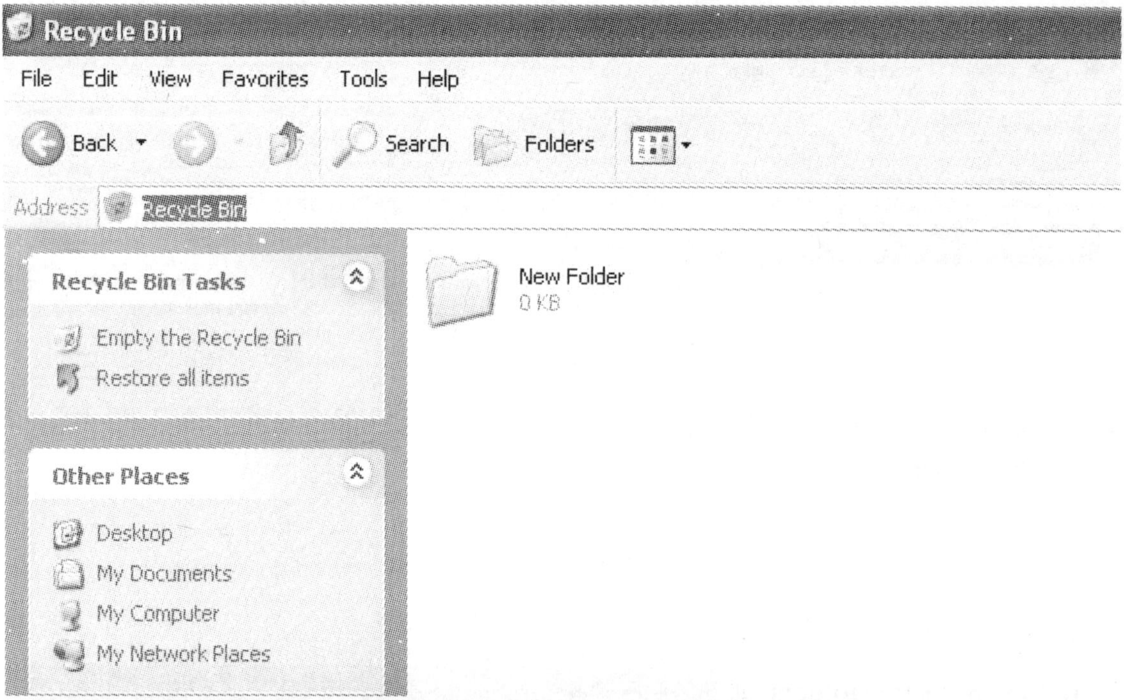
Recycle Bin
File Edit View Favorites Tools Help
Back Search Folders
Address Recycle Bin
Recycle Bin Tasks
Empty the Recycle Bin
Restore all items
Other Places
Desktop
My Documents
My Computer
My Network Places
New Folder
0 KB

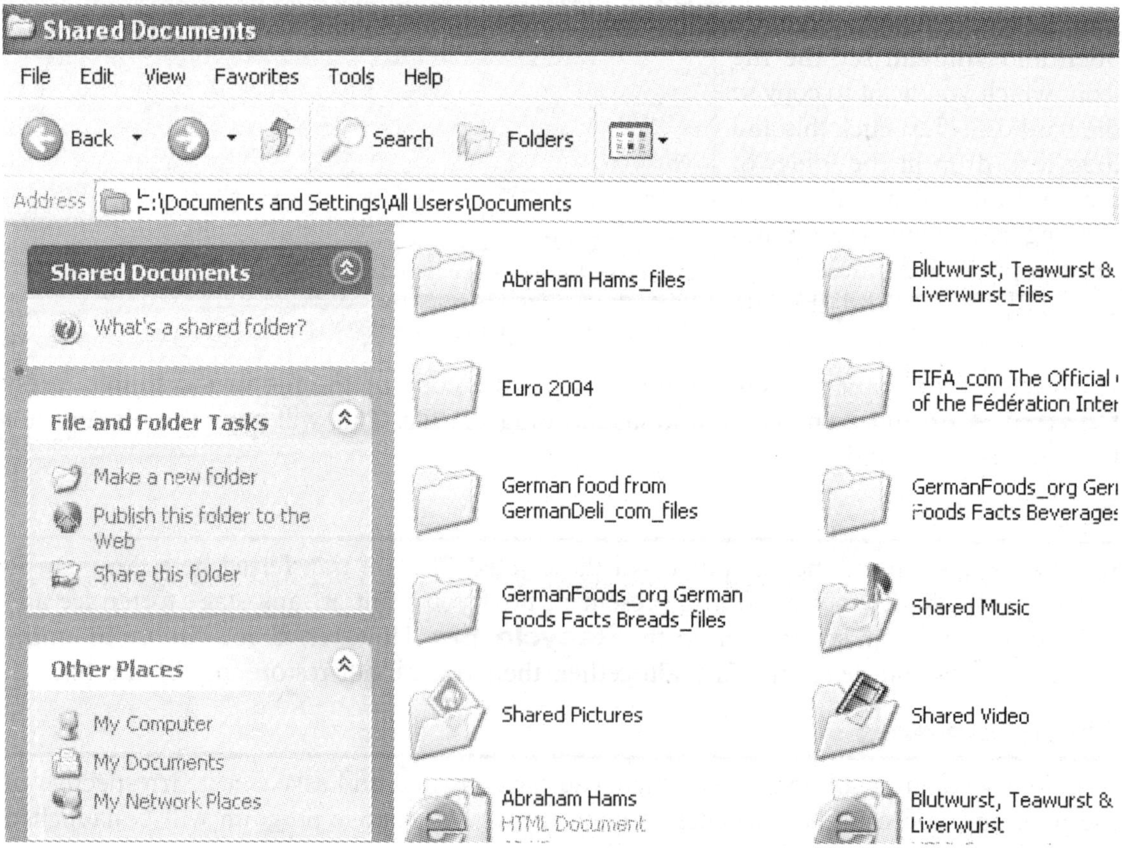
Shared Documents
File Edit View Favorites Tools Help
Back Search Folders
Address C:\Documents and Settings\All Users\Documents
Shared Documents
What's a shared folder?
File and Folder Tasks
Make a new folder
Publish this folder to the Web
Share this folder
Other Places
My Computer
My Documents
My Network Places
Abraham Hams_files
Blutwurst, Teawurst & Liverwurst_files
Euro 2004
German food from GermanDeli_com_files
GermanFoods_org German Foods Facts Breads_files
Shared Music
Shared Pictures
Shared Video
Abraham Hams
HTML Document
Blutwurst, Teawurst & Liverwurst

So far we have talked about shortcuts or icons on the desktop. But, we have not told you how they are created.

Creating Shortcuts

Supposing you have a program loaded into the computer and you are quite often using it. So you would like to have a shortcut for it. For example, I use **PageMaker**, quite often, so I have created a shortcut for this and it is available on the desktop.

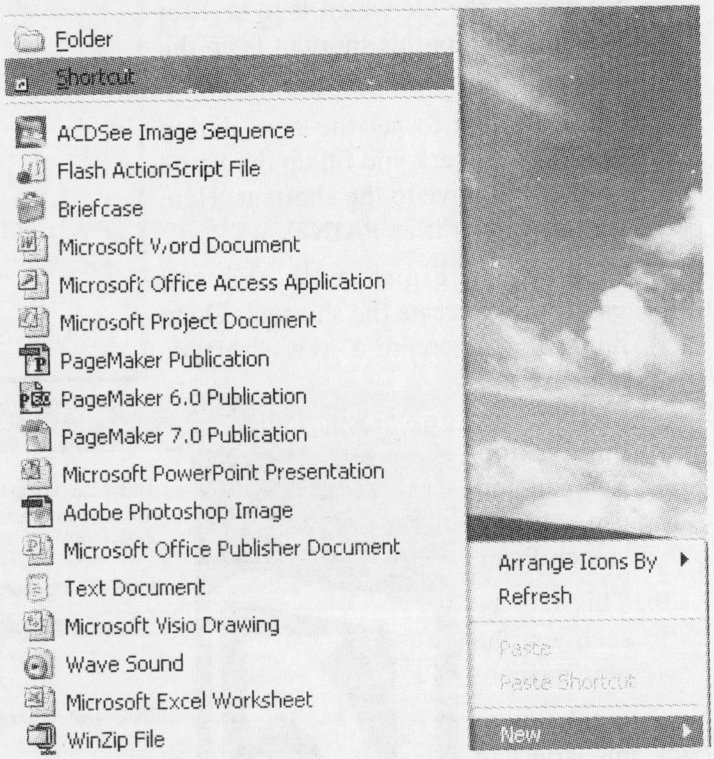

Supposing you are using a program called **Paint** quite often during your use of the computer. You would like to create a shortcut for it. Lets see how it is created.

For this you follow the steps here.

1. Minimize all your opened programs.
2. Click at the right button of the mouse on the desktop to get a menu, as shown.
3. Click at New to get the new menu, as shown. Click at Shortcut to create one.
4. This will give rise to a dialog box, as shown. Side by side, you will notice that it has created a new folder with New Shortcut as the name.

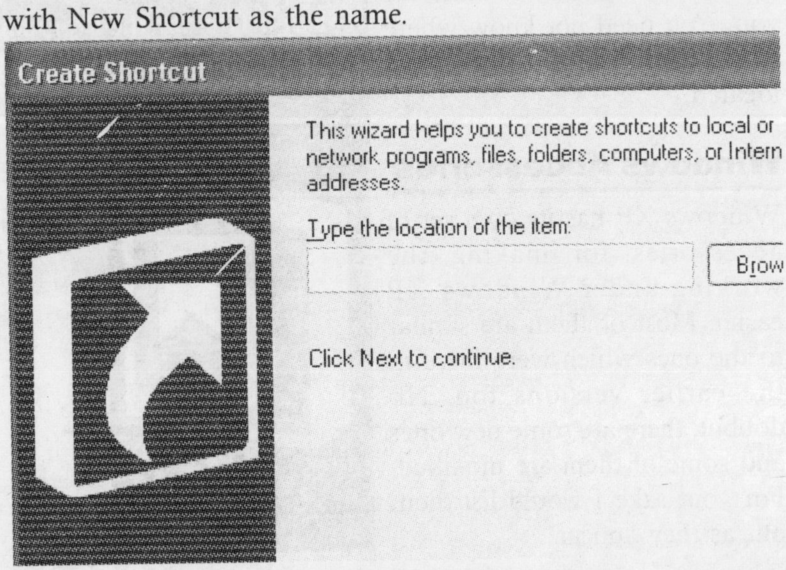

5. Click at the browse button to locate the file associated with the new shortcut. In our case it will be Paint or Paintbrush. In this case, as the picture shows that the file is available in the Windows folder under the name Paint.

   Once selected it will be filled up in the

File name column. Click it to open it. This will lead us back to the main dialog box of Create Shortcut.

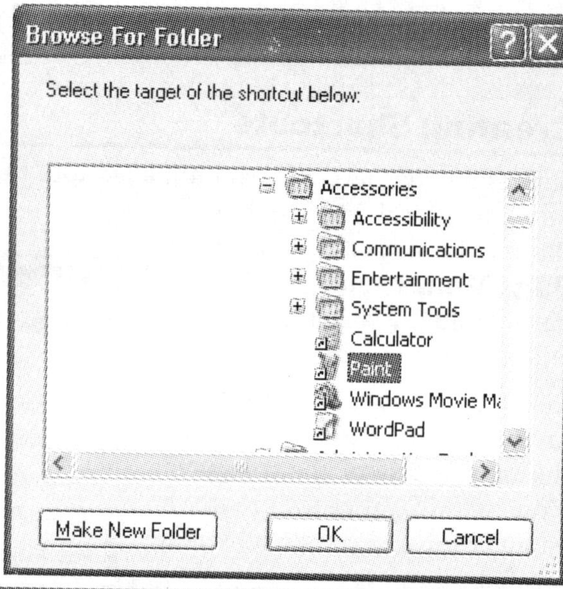

6. You will now see that the command line has been filled up with the exact location of the file which is to be Run for launching of this shortcut from the desktop.
7. Click at Next to get the next dialog box. This will ask you fill up the name you want to give to the shortcut. Here we have given it as PAINT.
8. Clicking at Finish will end the procedure to create the shortcut. Once done, it will create a new shortcut named PAINT on the desktop. You can now use it to launch Paint.

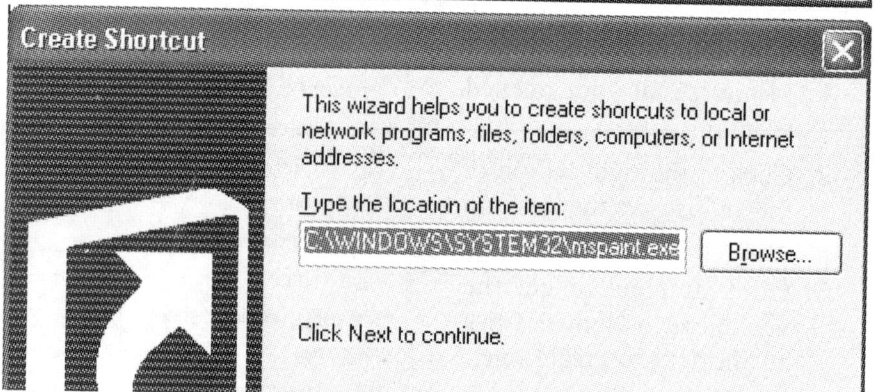

9. This can be seen on the next page.

You just have to click this icon and Paint software would start for you. You need not know where in the hard disk, this software is located.

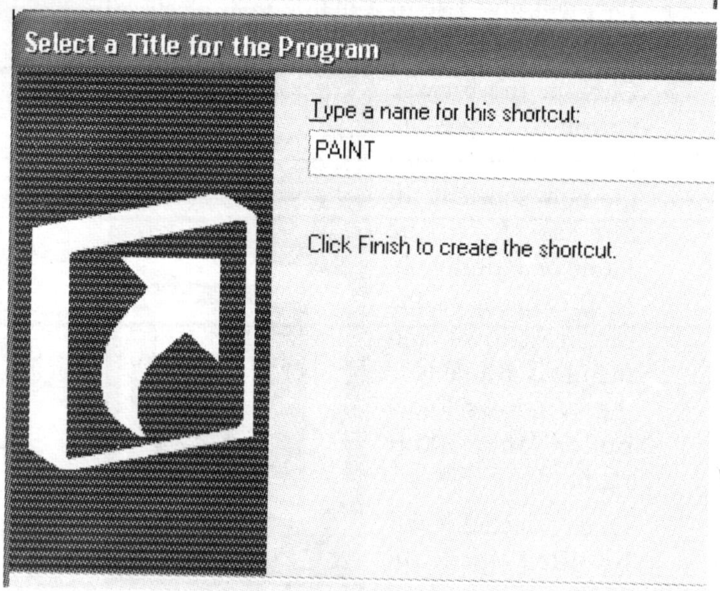

Windows Accessories

Windows XP has its own set of accessories for making the working under Windows XP easier. Most of them are similar to the ones which were there in the earlier versions too. No doubut, there are some new ones and some of them are modified. For your sake I would list them out as they appear.

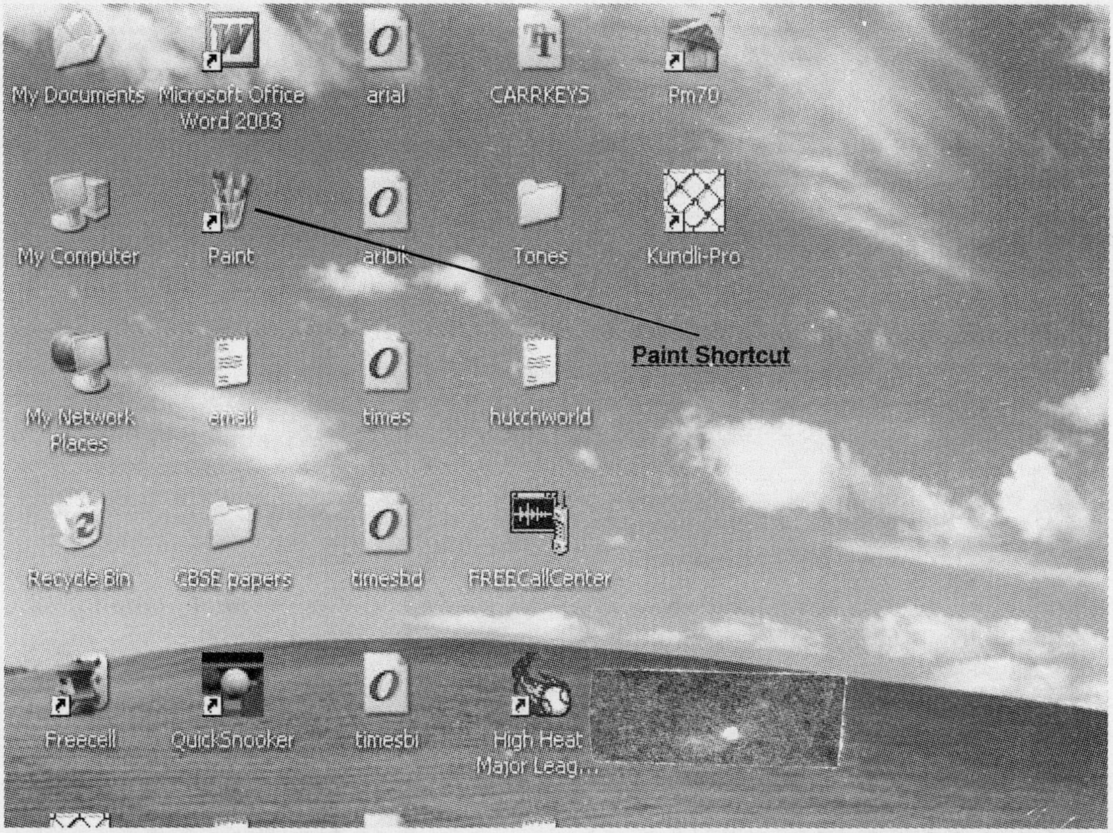

Accessing Accessories

Accessories can be accessed from **Start Menu** and **Programs**. As you can see there are various heads in Accessories, each giving rise to a set of options. Then there are options which are independent of categories.

These can be listed as:

Accessibility — Accessibility Wizard
— Magnifier
— Narrator
— On Screen Keyboard
— Utility Manager

Communications — Fax
— Hyper Terminal
— Network Connections
— Network Setup Wizard
— New Connection Wizard
— Remote Desktop Connection
— Wireless Network Setup Wizard

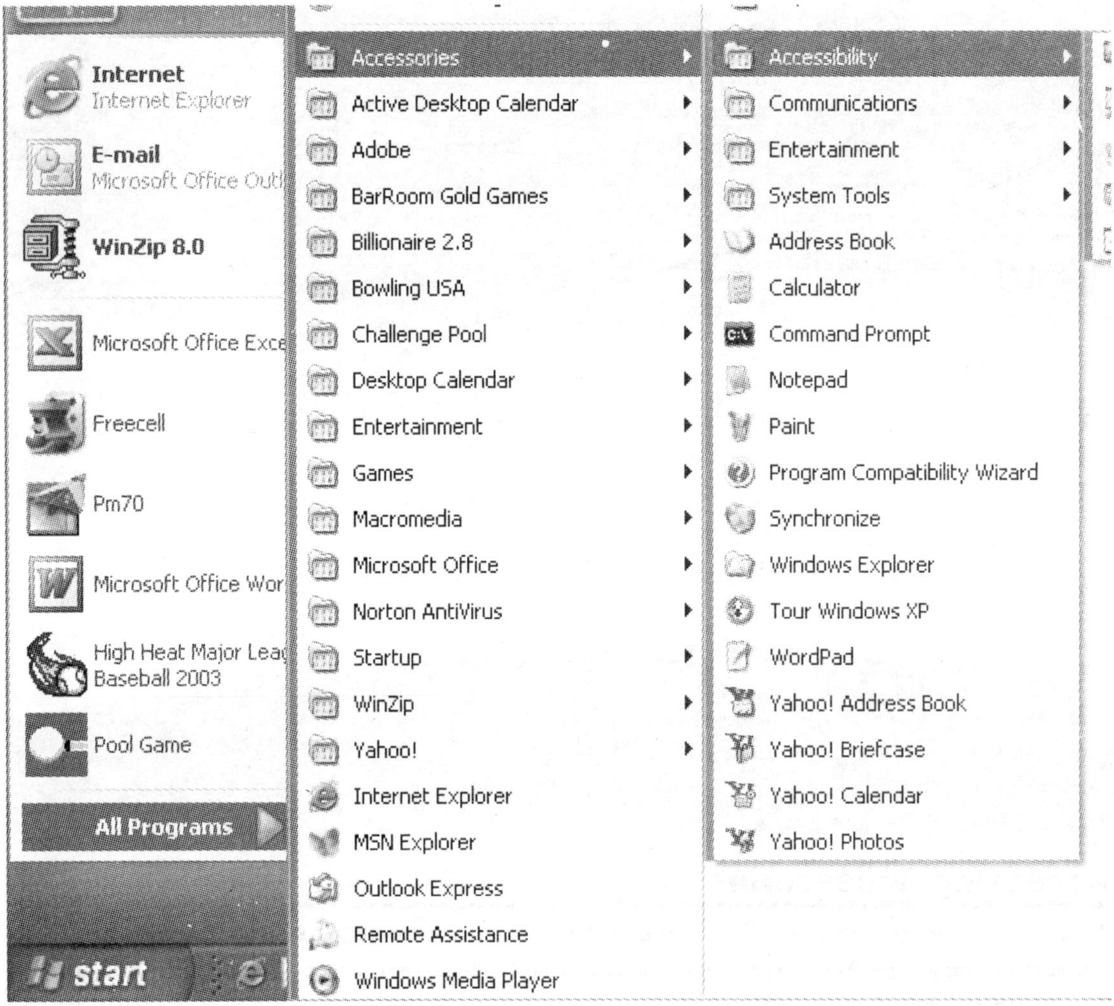

Entertainment — CD Player
— Sound Recorder
— Volume Control
— Windows Media Player

System Tools — Backup
— Character Map
— Disk Cleanup
— Disk Deframenter
— Files and Settings Transfer Wizard
— Scheduled Tasks
— Security Center
— System-Information
— System Restore

Address Book

Calculator

Command Prompt

NotePad

Paint

Program Compatibility Wizard

Synchronize

Windows Explorer

Tour Windows XP

Word Pad

Let us see each one of these individually.

Accessibility

Accessibility Wizard

This Wizard takes you to different options which allow you to set the Windows according to your needs.

Magnifier

If you are having problem in seeing the things on the screen and would like them to be magnified for you to see them clearly, then this is the right option for you. Using this you can select the magnification level and then wherever you take your mouse the matter underneath it will be magnified. You can use it with both text and graphics.

Narrator

This is a text-to-speech program that can help people with low vision set up their own

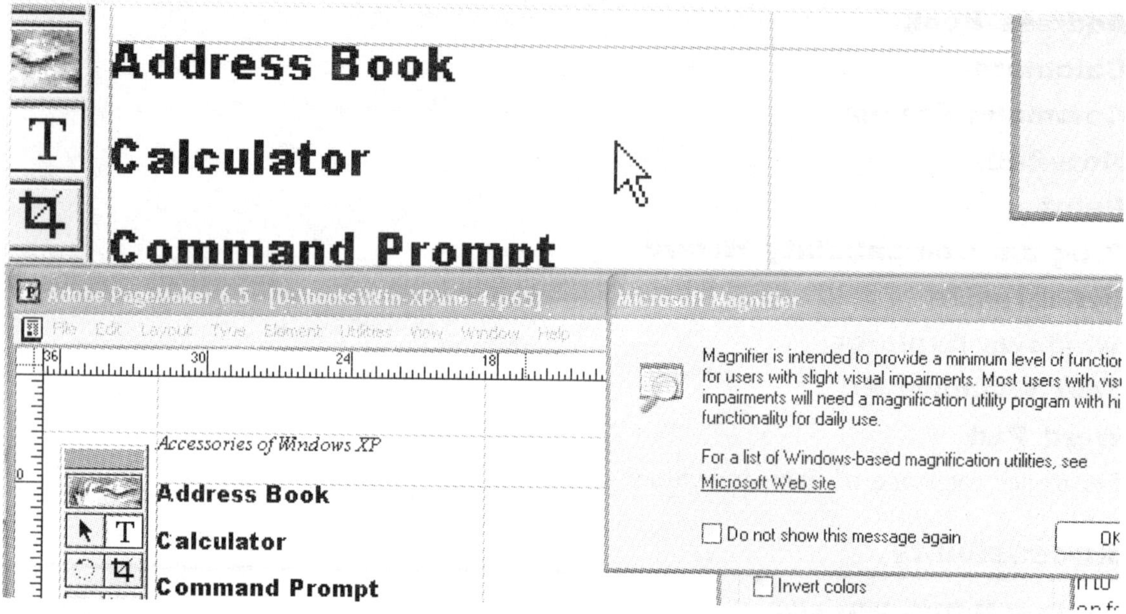

computers or use other people's computers. Narrator might not perform well with some programs and only speaks in English.

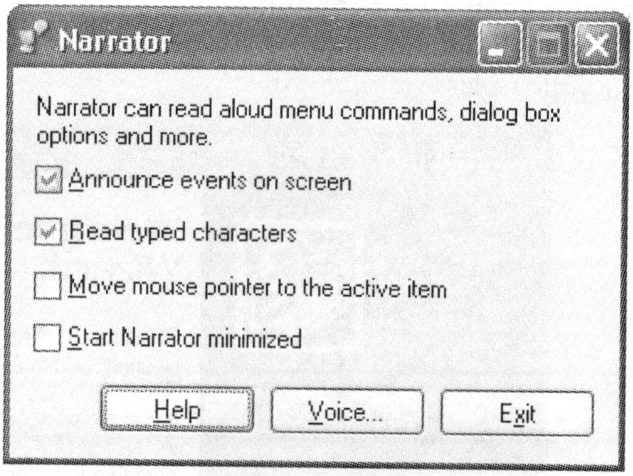

On Screen Keyboard

It gives you keyboard on the screen and you can make use of it for typing, if by any chance your keyboard is not working or giving errors.

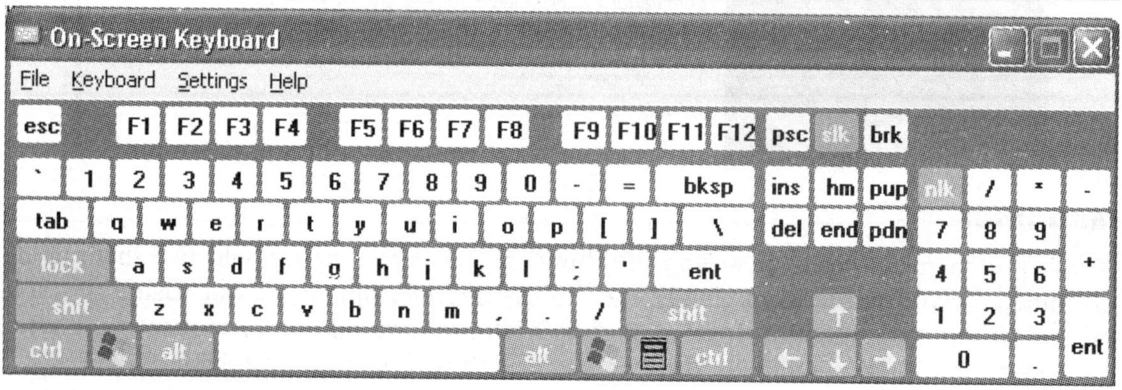

Utility Manager

It manages the activities of the various options of the Accessibility options.

Communications

Fax

If you have Fax software installed into your system, then this would help you send and received Fax.

Hyper Terminal

You can use HyperTerminal to send and receive files, or to connect to computer bulletin boards and other information programs. You can also use HyperTerminal and a modem to connect to a remote computer, even if the remote computer is not running Windows.

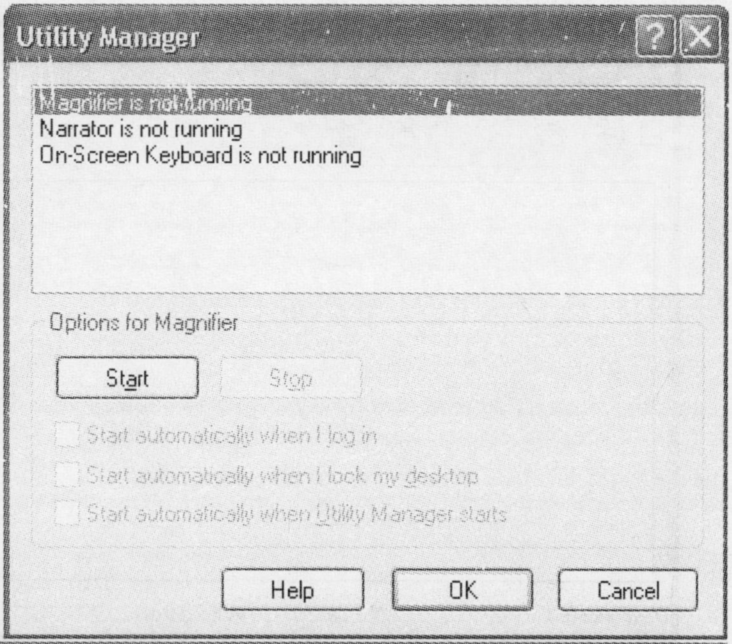

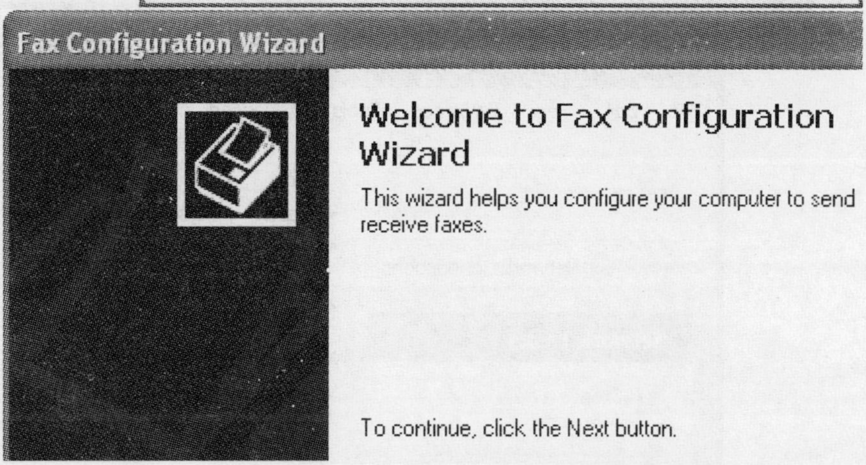

Network Connections

This command shows you the type of networking connections your computer has.

Network Setup Wizard

This wizard will guide you through various aspects of setting up networking on your own.

New Connection Wizard

Another wizard which will guide you to set your internet or networking connection.

Remote Desktop Connection

This command connects to a computer's desktop from a remote location and run applications as if you were sitting at its console.

Internet Connection Wizard

Definitely bound to a hit with the users, specially who are planning to have their internet connection set up. This wizard will guide you through the complete setup and have the connection made for you.

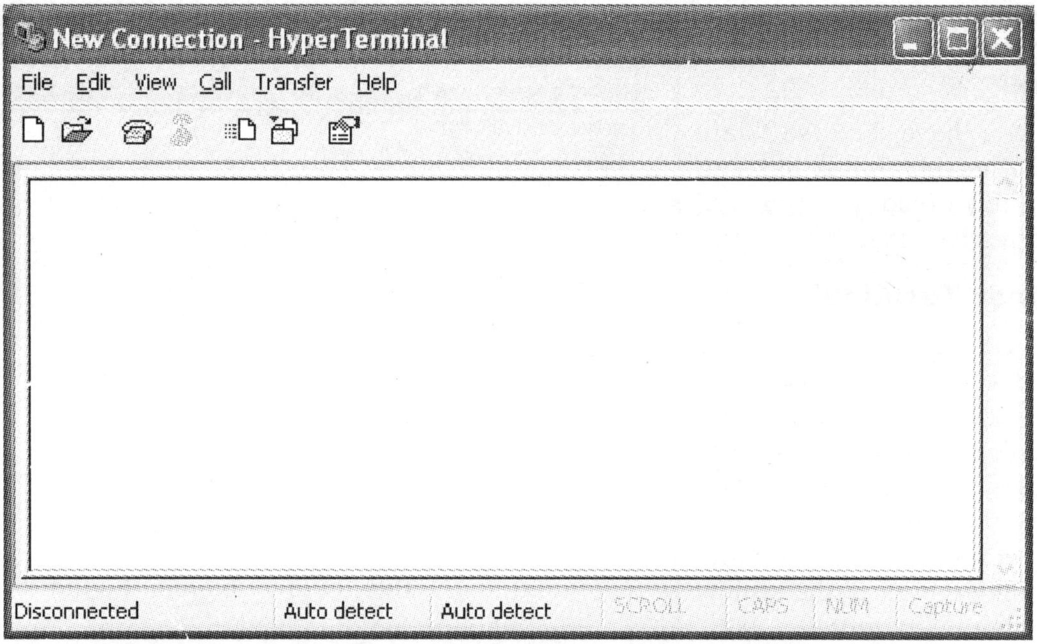

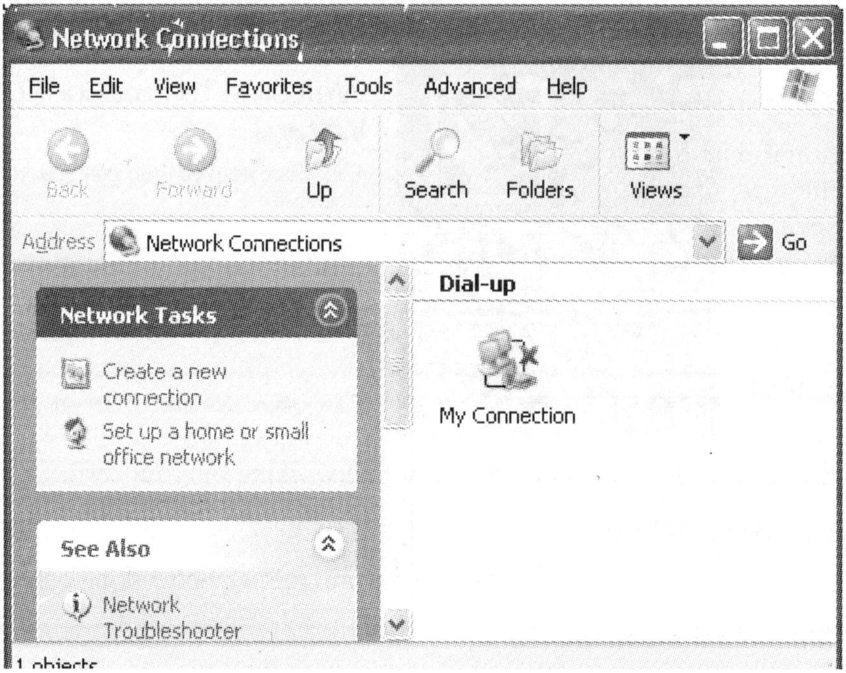

NetMeeting

This option allows you to communicate with others over the Internet or your local intranet. Using this you can Talk to others; Use video to see others and let others see you; Share applications and documents with others; Collaborate with others in shared applications; Send files to others; Draw with others in a shared whiteboard and Send messages to others in chat.

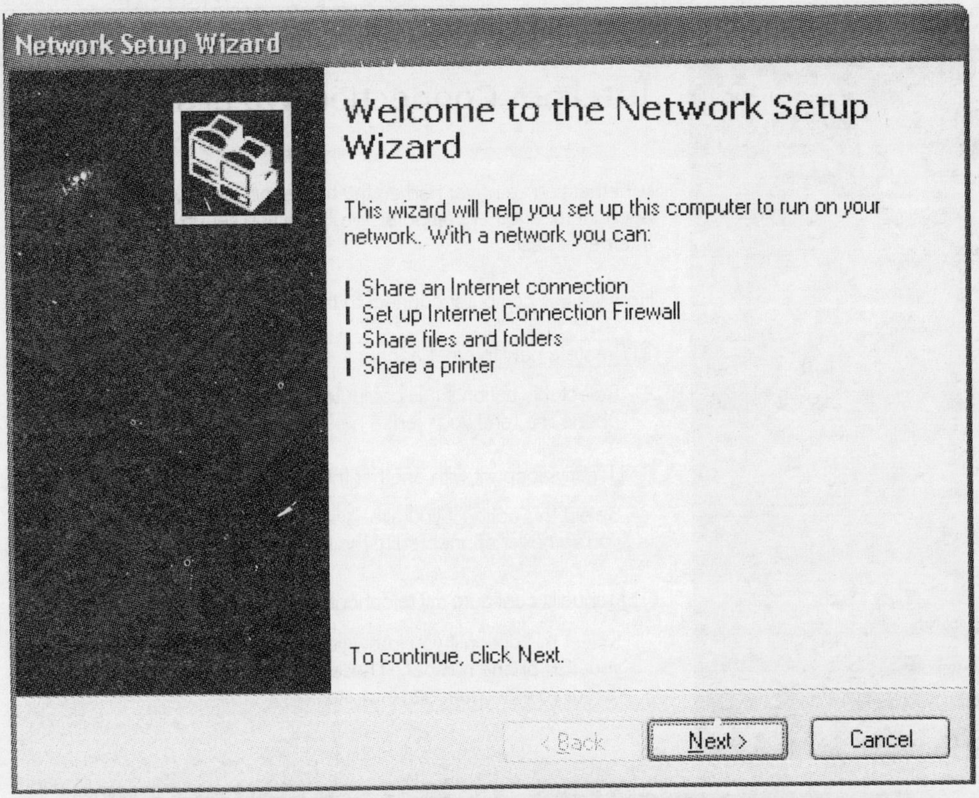
Network Setup Wizard
Welcome to the Network Setup Wizard
This wizard will help you set up this computer to run on your network. With a network you can:
Share an Internet connection
Set up Internet Connection Firewall
Share files and folders
Share a printer
To continue, click Next.
< Back
Next >
Cancel

New Connection Wizard
Welcome to the New Connection Wizard
This wizard helps you:
Connect to the Internet.
Connect to a private network, such as your workplace network.
Set up a home or small office network.

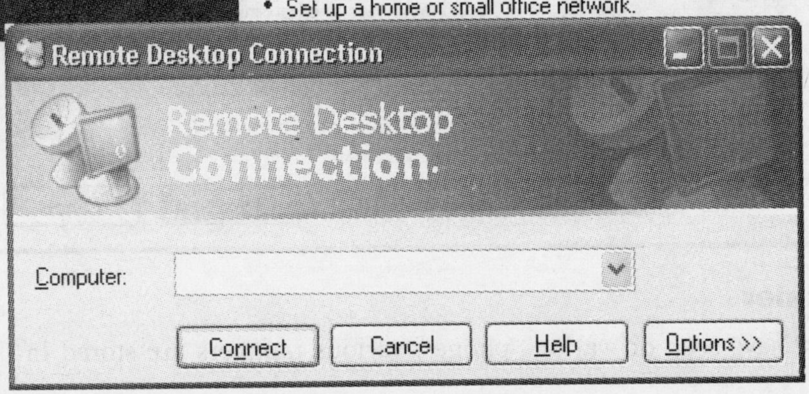
Remote Desktop Connection
Remote Desktop
Connection
Computer:
Connect
Cancel
Help
Options >>

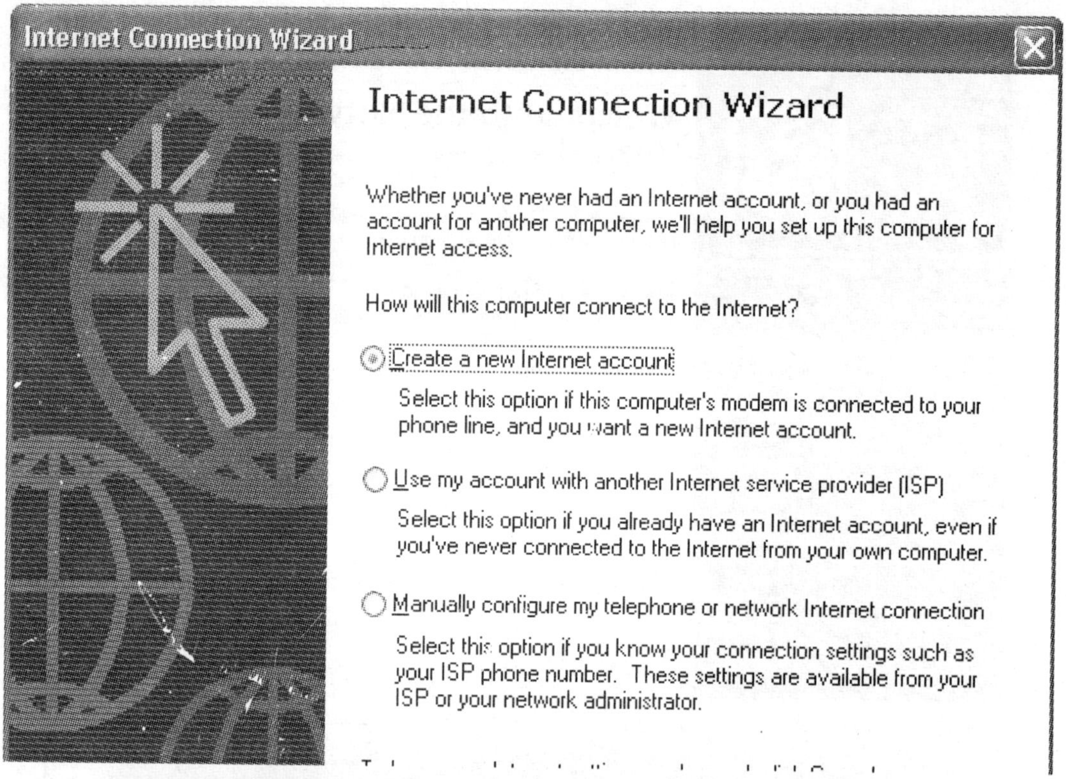

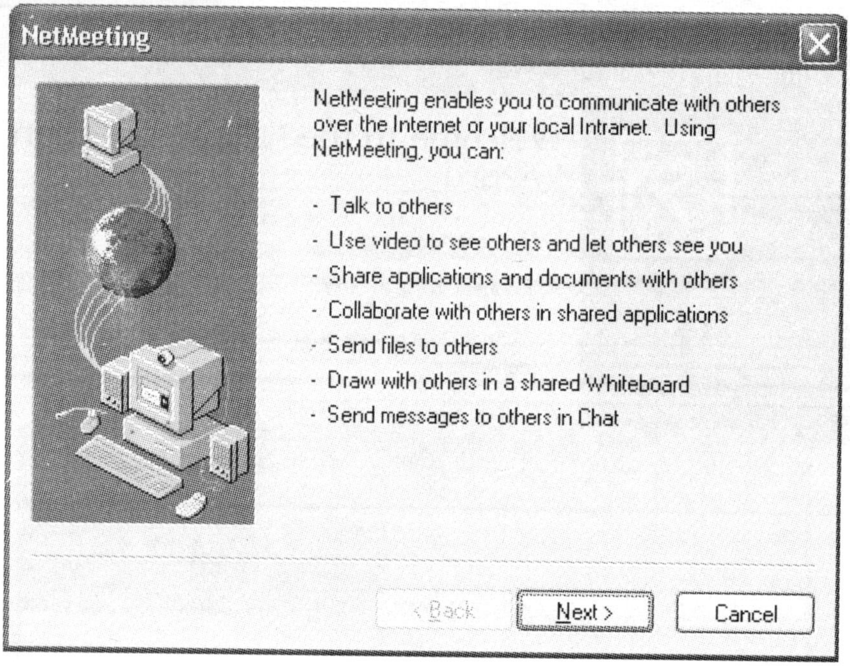

Phone Dialer

As you must have seen on various phones, various numbers are stored in the phone for speed dialling. Similarly here you store the numbers which you have to dial occasionally, so that they can be dialled by just pressing a single digit number.

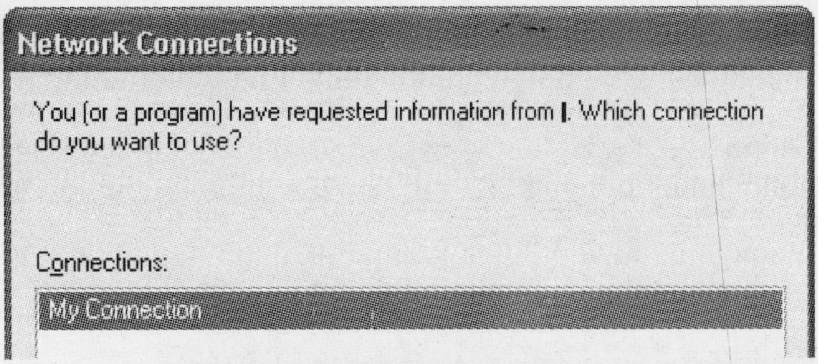

Entertainment

CD Player

This allows you to play your audio CDs and listen to music.

Sound Recorder

This allows you to record your voice or music too. Of course, you must have the multimedia kit attached to your computer for doing that.

Volume Control

If you want a sophisticated volume control to listen to your music, then this option is for you. You can your adjustment here according to your likings.

Windows Media Player

A really advanced version of the media player has been included in Windows Me. You can use it play **animated files** (.avi) created by Video for Windows. It can also be used for **sound files** (.wav), **MIDI files** (.mid and .rmi), or your audio CDs.

System Tools

This category of accessories are there to enhance the working of the computer with different tools which not only speed up the computer but also keeps the system clean of any unwanted elements.

Backup

This option allows you to backup your files from hard disk to a removable media.

Character Map

This option helps you view the various characters of the fonts available in your Windows. After seeing the format of the character, you can decide whether to use it or not.

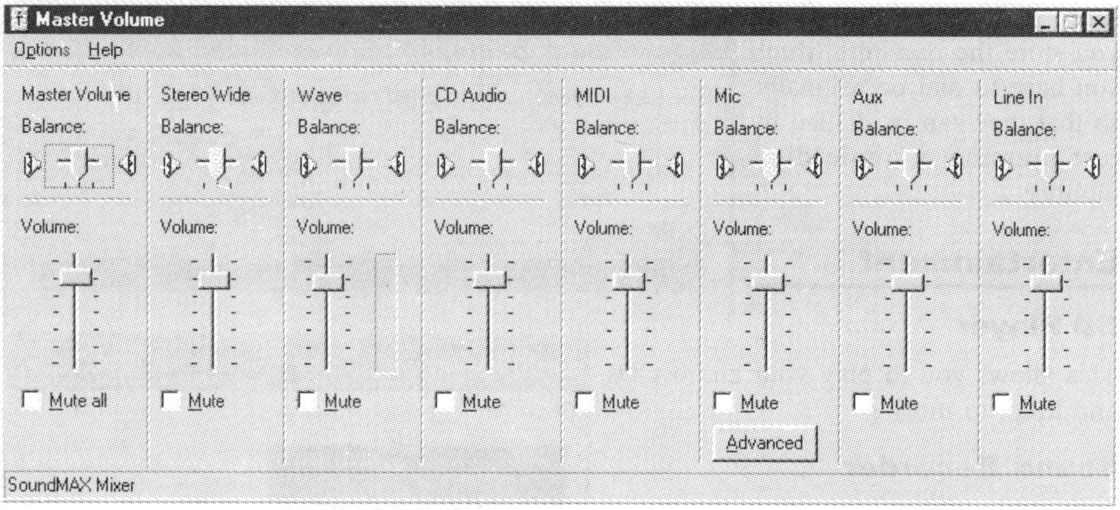
Master Volume
Options Help
Master Volume
Stereo Wide
Wave
CD Audio
MIDI
Mic
Aux
Line In
Balance:
Volume:
Mute all
Mute
Advanced
SoundMAX Mixer

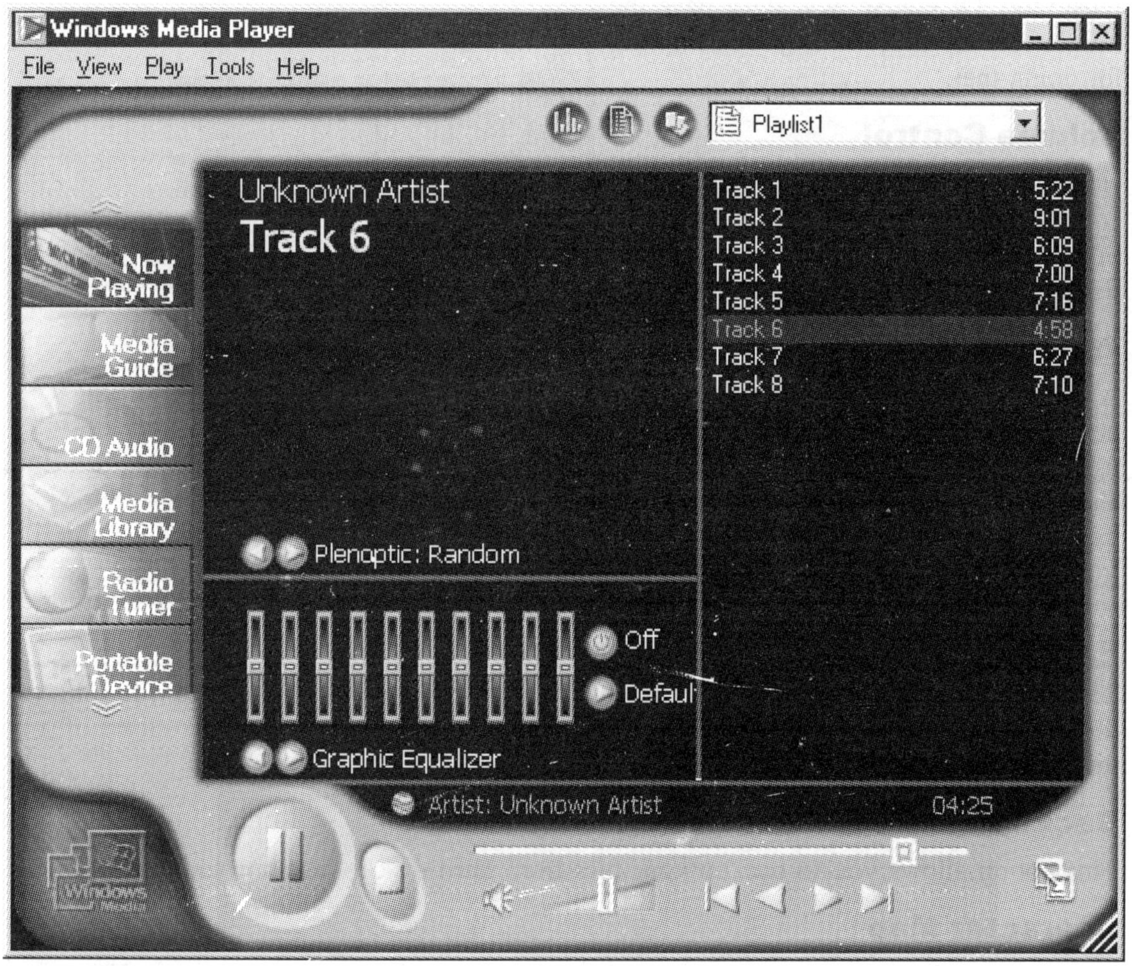
Windows Media Player
File View Play Tools Help
Playlist1
Unknown Artist
Track 6
Now Playing
Media Guide
CD Audio
Media Library
Radio Tuner
Portable Device
Track 1 5:22
Track 2 9:01
Track 3 6:09
Track 4 7:00
Track 5 7:16
Track 6 4:58
Track 7 6:27
Track 8 7:10
Plenoptic: Random
Off
Default
Graphic Equalizer
Artist: Unknown Artist
04:25

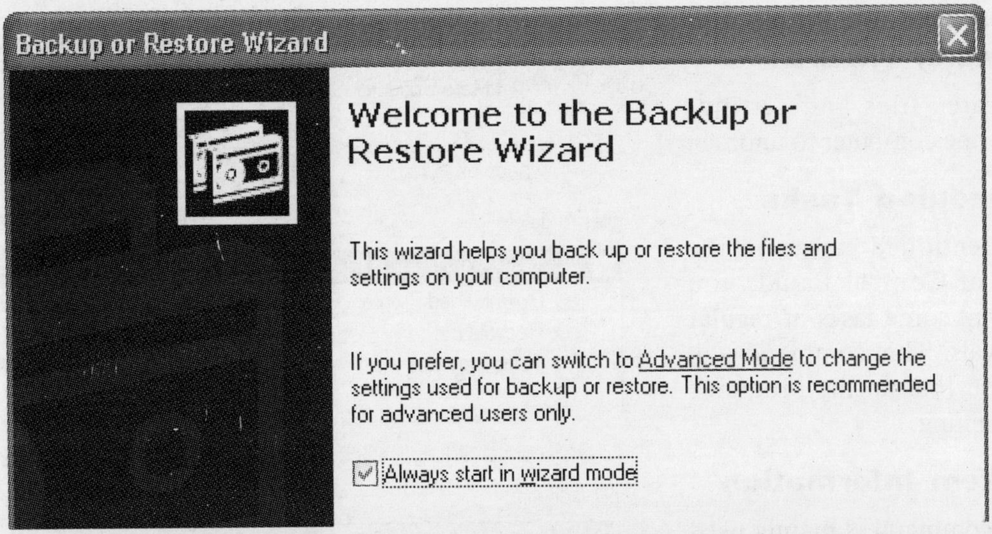

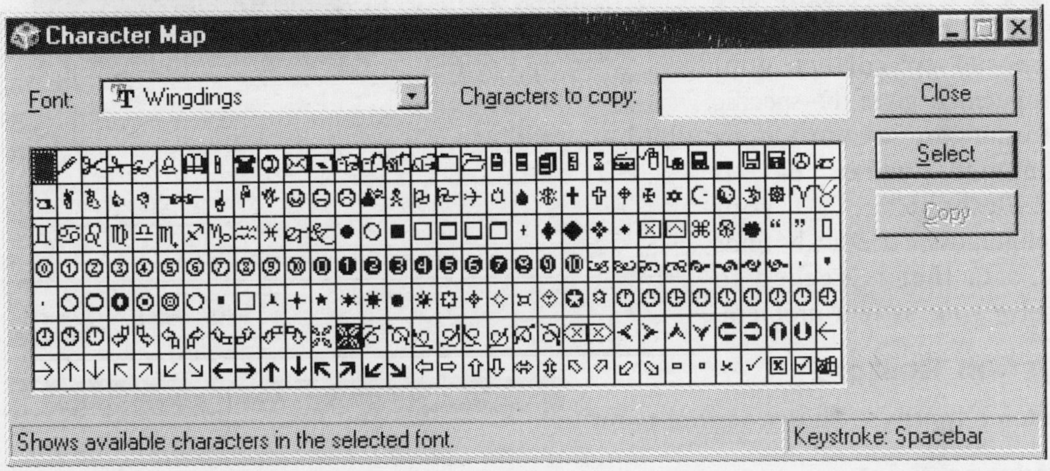

Disk Cleanup

The Windows operating system creates a mass of temporary files and cached files—all designed to speed up the performance of the graphical interface. These files do a pretty good job but, often do not get deleted when they should be. This results in a lot of files cluttered up on your hard drive. When you run Disk Cleanup, it checks for files that can be safely deleted and then presents a list of such files.

Disk Deframenter

While writing files on hard disk, Windows keeps the files at random and keeps track of its position using FAT. This results in having the files placed in hard disk, quite staggered. This command, which was there even in DOS, does the job of housekeeping and puts the files on one side and the blank space in the hard disk on the other side. This results in speeding up the activity of the hard disk. It is advised that once you run Disk Deframenter, you must run Disk Cleanup after it.

Files and Settings Transfer Wizard

Migrates files and settings from one computer to another.

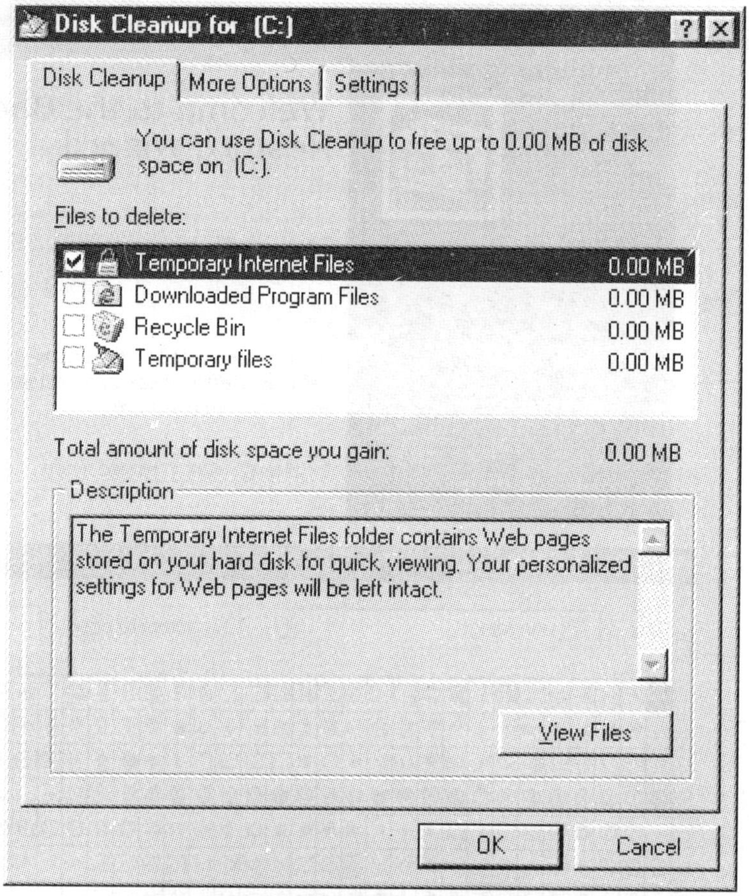

Scheduled Tasks

As mentioned earlier in the case of Control Panel, you can run some tasks at regular intervals. This command will let you line up the programs for running.

System Information

This command is mainly used by the people who are supposed to correct your computer. It gives the specific information about your computer when he is troubleshooting your configuration. It quickly finds the data that is needed to resolve your system problem.

System Restore

Restores system to chosen restore point.

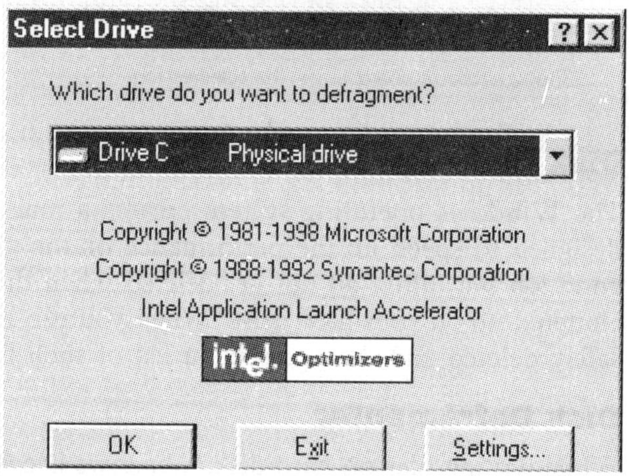

Address Book

Those of you who are familiar with the working of Outlook Express know what the Address Book is. This is actually a database where you store the name, address, e-mail number of your people whom you connect very often.

Calculator

Windows XP gives you the choice of both Standard and Scientific calculator for doing the calculations while working on the computer. A Scientific calculator is shown.

Command Prompt

Something which would make the users of MS DOS happy. Using this you can run your DOS programs.

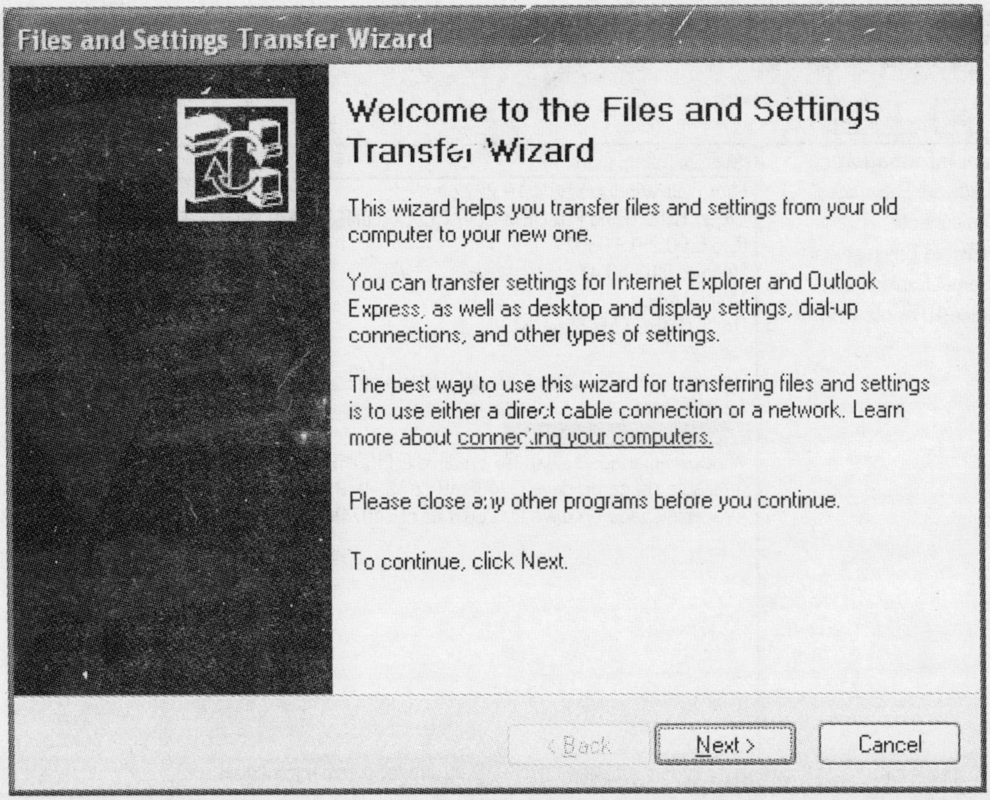

Files and Settings Transfer Wizard
Welcome to the Files and Settings Transfer Wizard
This wizard helps you transfer files and settings from your old computer to your new one.
You can transfer settings for Internet Explorer and Outlook Express, as well as desktop and display settings, dial-up connections, and other types of settings.
The best way to use this wizard for transferring files and settings is to use either a direct cable connection or a network. Learn more about connecting your computers.
Please close any other programs before you continue.
To continue, click Next.
< Back
Next >
Cancel

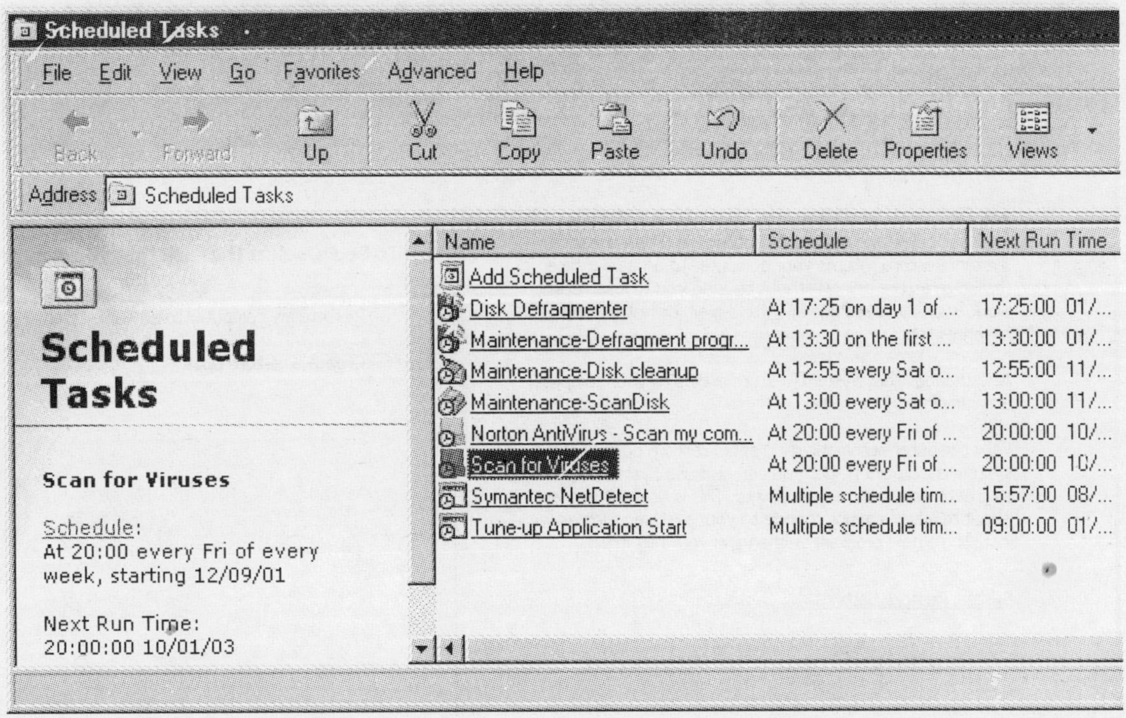

Scheduled Tasks
File Edit View Go Favorites Advanced Help
Back Forward Up Cut Copy Paste Undo Delete Properties Views
Address Scheduled Tasks
Scheduled Tasks
Scan for Viruses
Schedule:
At 20:00 every Fri of every week, starting 12/09/01
Next Run Time:
20:00:00 10/01/03
Name | Schedule | Next Run Time
Add Scheduled Task
Disk Defragmenter | At 17:25 on day 1 of ... | 17:25:00 01/...
Maintenance-Defragment progr... | At 13:30 on the first ... | 13:30:00 01/...
Maintenance-Disk cleanup | At 12:55 every Sat o... | 12:55:00 11/...
Maintenance-ScanDisk | At 13:00 every Sat o... | 13:00:00 11/...
Norton AntiVirus - Scan my com... | At 20:00 every Fri of ... | 20:00:00 10/...
Scan for Viruses | At 20:00 every Fri of ... | 20:00:00 10/...
Symantec NetDetect | Multiple schedule tim... | 15:57:00 08/...
Tune-up Application Start | Multiple schedule tim... | 09:00:00 01/...

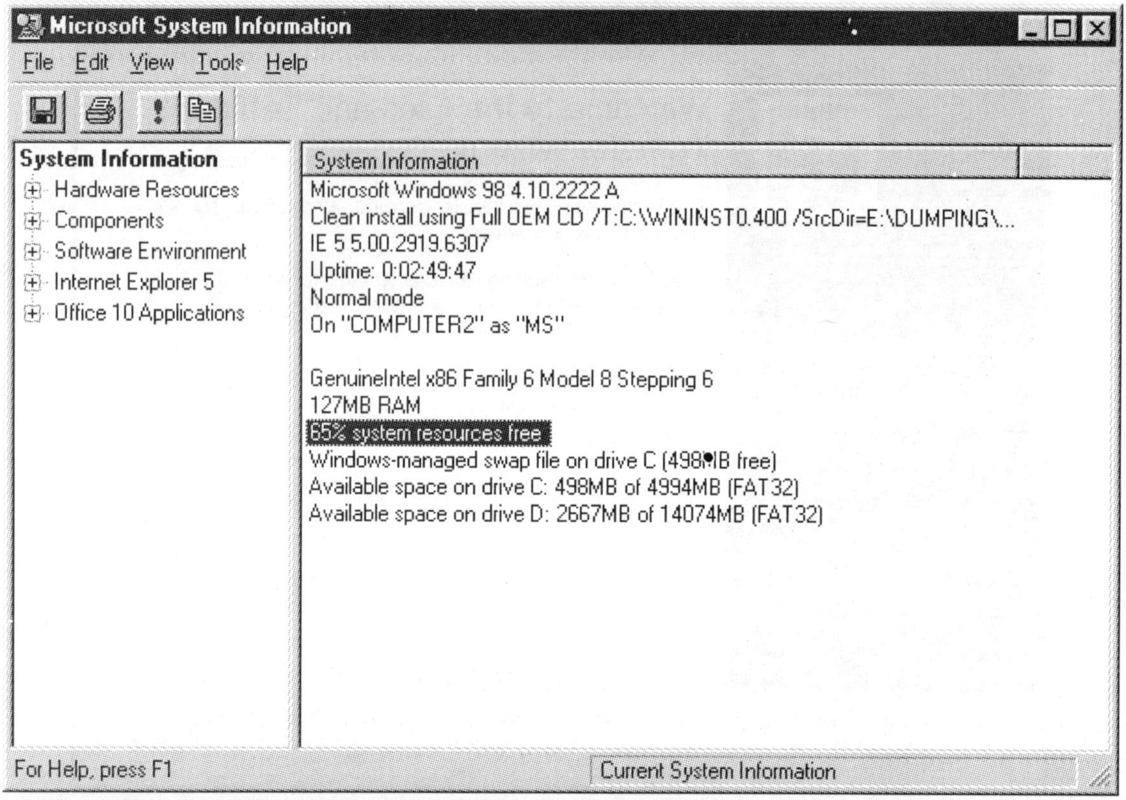
Microsoft System Information
File Edit View Tools Help
System Information
Hardware Resources
Components
Software Environment
Internet Explorer 5
Office 10 Applications
System Information
Microsoft Windows 98 4.10.2222 A
Clean install using Full OEM CD /T:C:\WININST0.400 /SrcDir=E:\DUMPING\...
IE 5 5.00.2919.6307
Uptime: 0:02:49:47
Normal mode
On "COMPUTER2" as "MS"
GenuineIntel x86 Family 6 Model 8 Stepping 6
127MB RAM
65% system resources free
Windows-managed swap file on drive C (498MB free)
Available space on drive C: 498MB of 4994MB (FAT32)
Available space on drive D: 2667MB of 14074MB (FAT32)
For Help, press F1
Current System Information

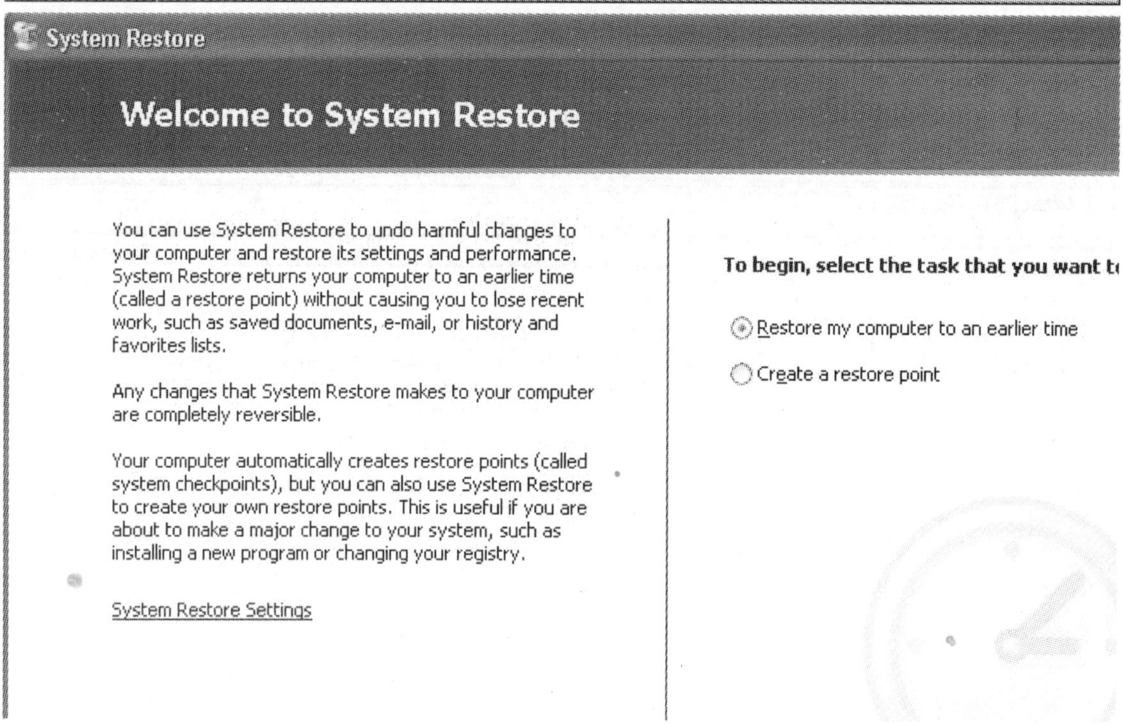
System Restore
Welcome to System Restore
You can use System Restore to undo harmful changes to your computer and restore its settings and performance. System Restore returns your computer to an earlier time (called a restore point) without causing you to lose recent work, such as saved documents, e-mail, or history and favorites lists.
Any changes that System Restore makes to your computer are completely reversible.
Your computer automatically creates restore points (called system checkpoints), but you can also use System Restore to create your own restore points. This is useful if you are about to make a major change to your system, such as installing a new program or changing your registry.
System Restore Settings
To begin, select the task that you want t
Restore my computer to an earlier time
Create a restore point

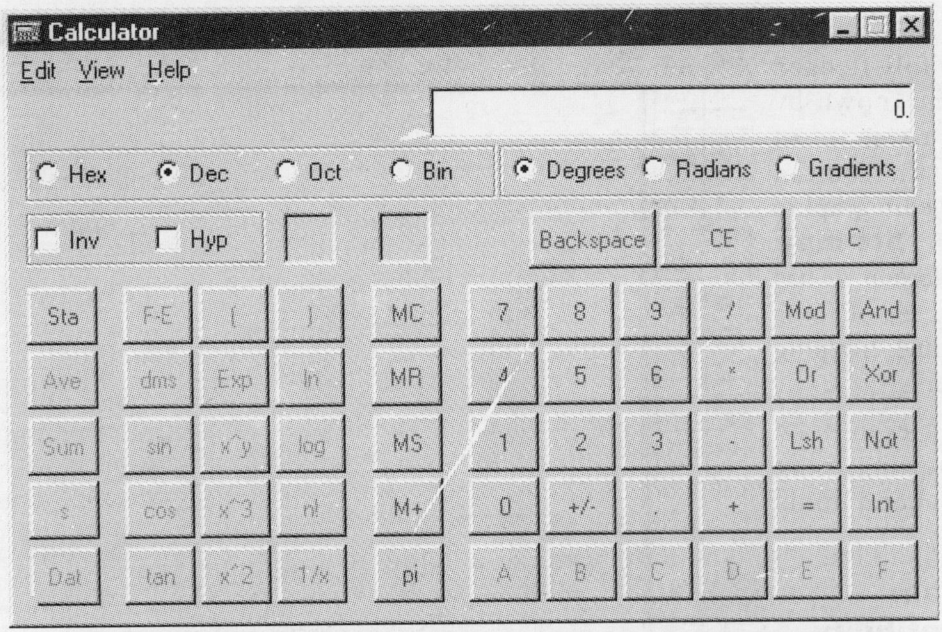

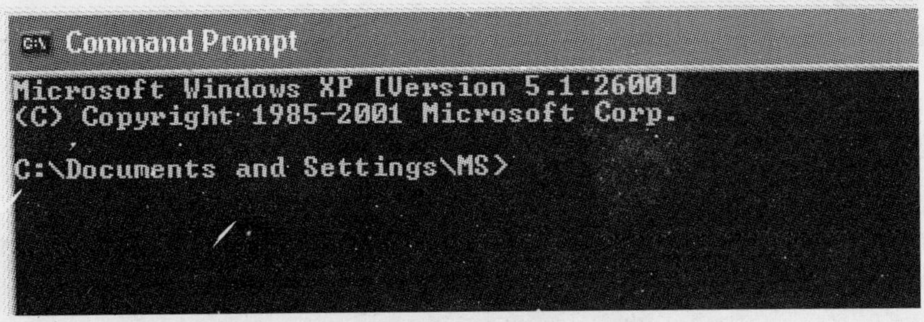

NotePad

It is a simple text editor with quite a number of features of a good word processor. It can be used as a stop-gap word processor for viewing text files.

Paint

It is a full fledged program known by the name of Paintbrush. You can create, edit graphic files in **bit-map** (.bmp) format. It has its own set of tools for editing, cropping of pictures.

You can even draw your drawing using the freehand tools available.

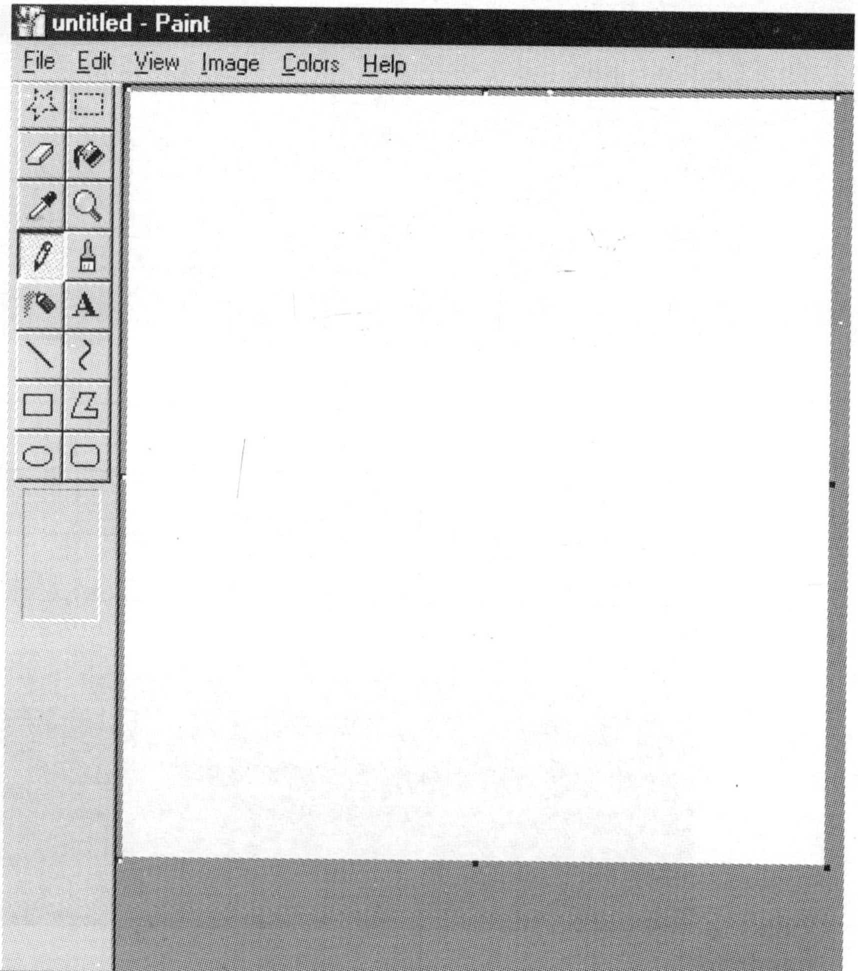

Program Compatibility Wizard

Starts the Program Compatability Wizard which helps you configure older programs to run on Windows XP.

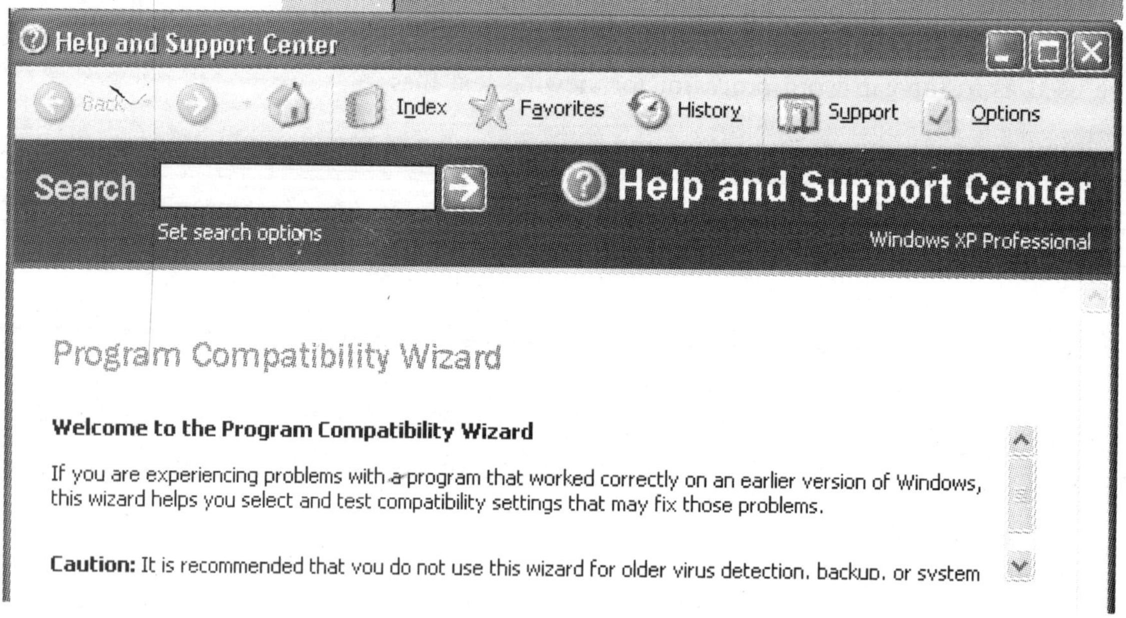

Synchronize

With this you can ensure that the data on which you are working is completely up to date and totally synchronizes with the current data on the network.

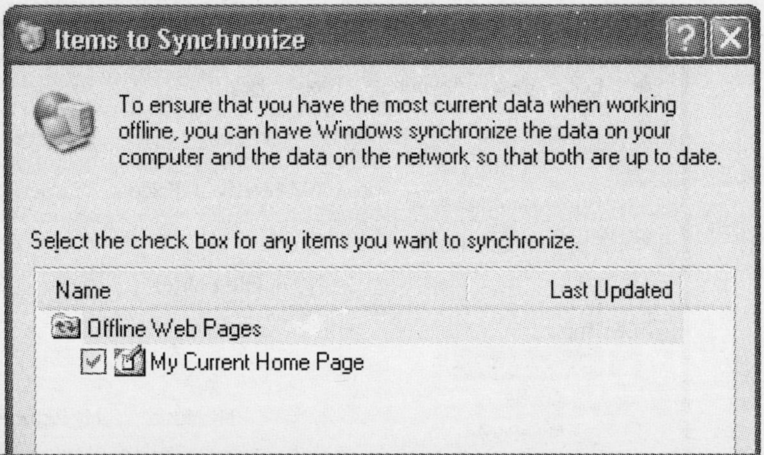

Tour Windows XP

This animation tour of Windows XP options is a must for every one whether using Windows for the first time for hundreth time. You must run it once to see what Windows XP has to offer.

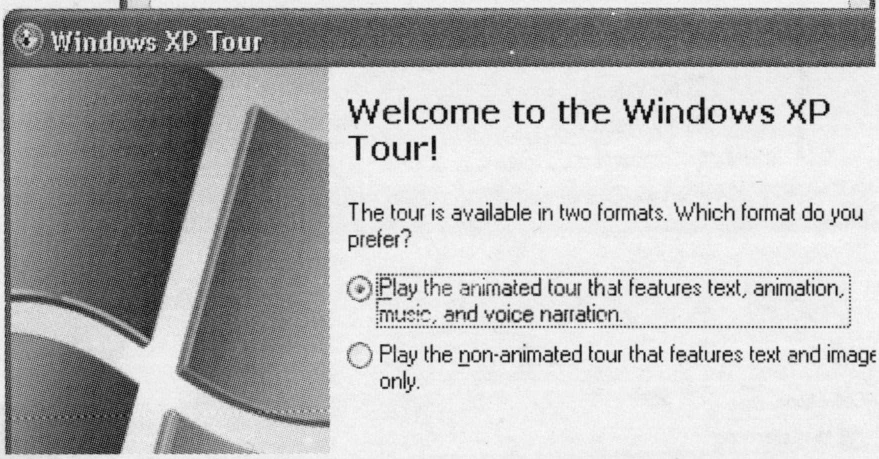

Windows Explorer

It offers you the easiest way of viewing folders, files and other resources located on your machine. The default Explorer is a two-pane window. When you click on an item in the left window pane, the right pane displays the contents. You can choose different viewing options from the View menu, the two options, small icons and details are shown on the next page.

For moving files from one folder to another, you can open more than one window of the Windows Explorer and then drag & drop.

One notable change here is that Windows XP's Explorer automatically seggregates the files based on its applications and lists them together with their parent program as heading. For example, all HTML files would be listed together with heading as HTML files, etc.

Windows Movie Maker

Turn your computer into an audio and video editing center! You can use Microsoft Windows Movie Maker to edit audio and video sequences from sources such as camcorders or digital cameras. You can create movies to share with family and friends, save images of important events, or enable distance learning. You can even create a slide show using your own pictures or pictures you import to your computer.

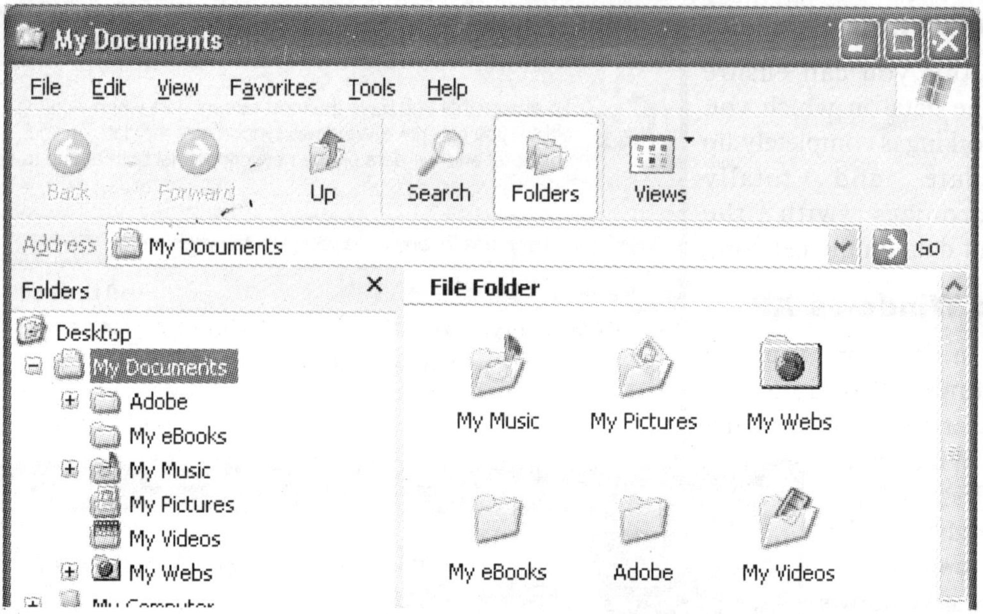
My Documents
File
Edit
View
Favorites
Tools
Help
Back
Forward
Up
Search
Folders
Views
Address
My Documents
Go
Folders
File Folder
Desktop
My Documents
Adobe
My eBooks
My Music
My Pictures
My Videos
My Webs
My Music
My Pictures
My Webs
My eBooks
Adobe
My Videos

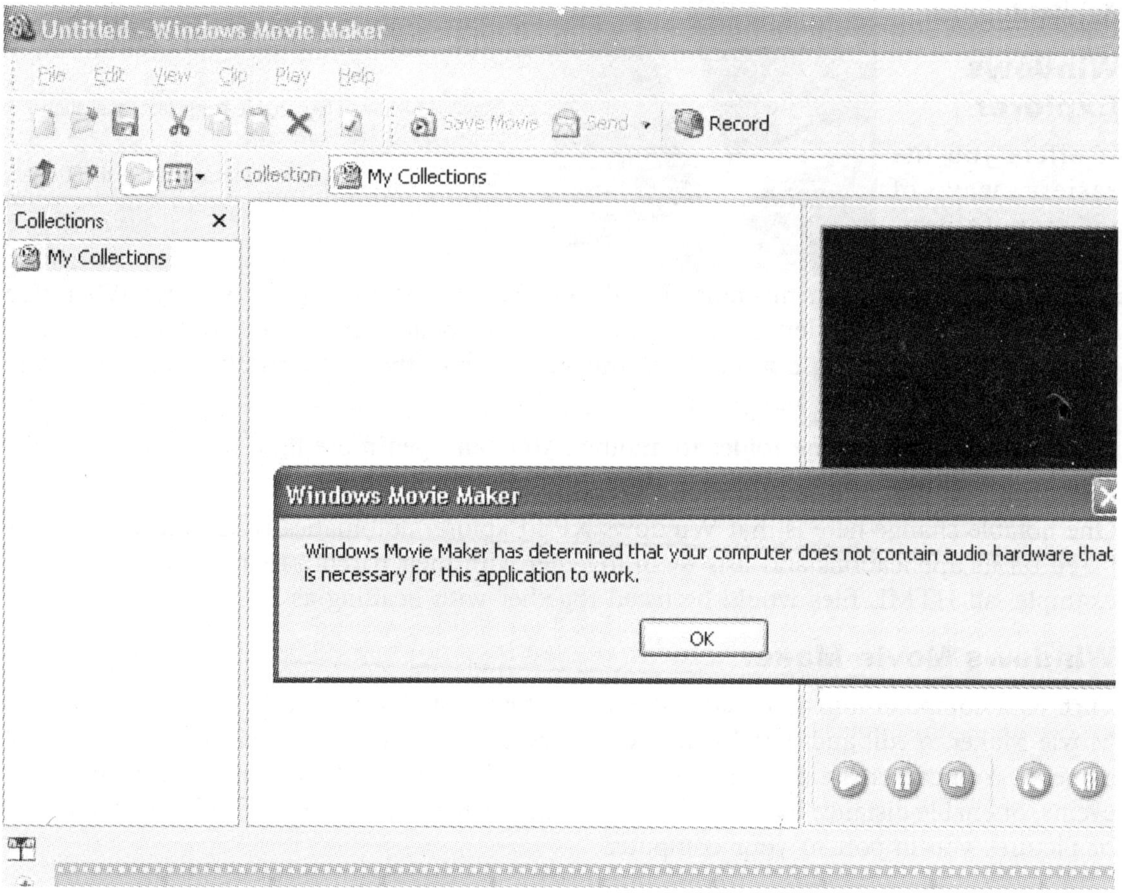
Untitled - Windows Movie Maker
File
Edit
View
Clip
Play
Help
Save Movie
Send
Record
Collection
My Collections
Collections
My Collections
Windows Movie Maker
Windows Movie Maker has determined that your computer does not contain audio hardware that is necessary for this application to work.
OK

Word Pad

It is another simple word processing program. Though better than the Note Pad, it is still falls short of a full fledged word processing software.

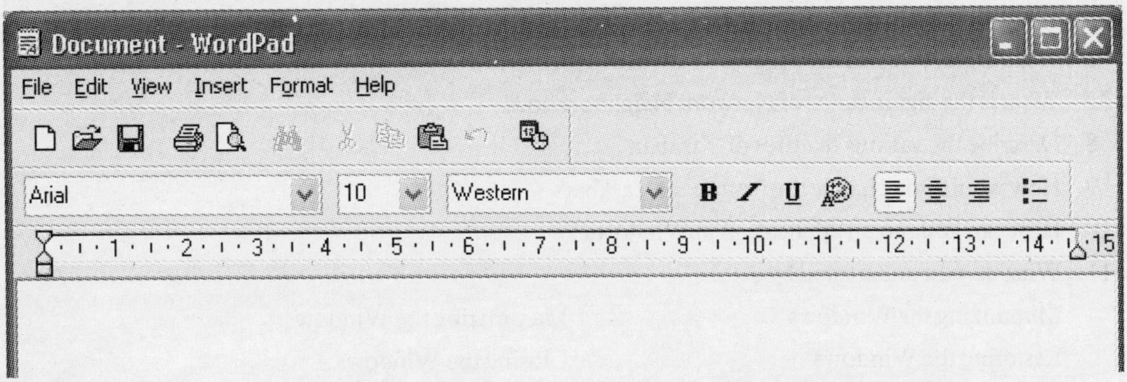

Games

Now we see what all is available under the Accessories of Windows XP and can use them whenever required. But, hold on, have we missed something. In all the previous versions of Windows, Games were part of the Accessories. But, this time, Windows XP has taken it out and created a separate folder for it. What's more it has added few new games also to it. I am covering them here since the die hard fans of games would come looking for them here.

Games

As mentioned above a separate folder has been created in Windows XP for games.

Various games are:

Classic Hearts

Classic Solitaire

Freecell

Internet Backgammon

Internet Checkers

Internet Hearts

Internet Reversi

Internet Spades

Minesweeper

Pinball

Spider Solitaire

For playing the internet games like Backgammon, Spades, etc., you need to connect to Internet before playing the game.

Descriptive Type Questions

1. How would you start Windows 98?

2. Describe the various items on the desktop of Windows 98.
3. What type of icons are there on the desktop?
4. What all is available on the Start button?
5. What all is there in My Computer?
6. What is Recycle Bin used for?
7. What is the significance of Network Neighborhood?
8. Describe the various features of Taskbar.
9. How would you change the features of Taskbar?
10. How can you run an application in Windows?
11. What do you understand by:

    Minimizing the Windows — Maximizing the Windows

    Restoring the Windows — Closing the Windows
12. What is the function of Windows Explorer?
13. How would you do the following using Windows Explorer?

    Rename a file — Copy a file

    Create a folder — Delete a file

    Move a file
14. Describe the various components of a Windows dialog box.
15. What is the purpose of Disk clean up?
16. For what purpose do you use Disk Defragmenter?
17. Which accessory would you use to connect computers?
18. How would you access the various accessories of the Windows?
19. Describe the various Internet tools.
20. Which all games are there in Windows?
21. How would you schedule various tasks for maintainance?
22. How would you control the volume of the CDPlayer?
23. If you have a Video CD, how would you run it on your computer?
24. How would you see the shape of various fonts under Windows?
25. If you have to dial from your computer, what would you use?
26. If you have to create a drawing, which program would you use?
27. To clean up your hard disk, which program would you use?
28. How would you connect various computers using Windows?
29. How and when was Windows was first introduced?
30. What are the main features of Windows 95?
31. What are the main features of Windows 98?

2 Introduction to Photoshop

Photoshop—An Introduction

Photoshop is a software for image processing. With this you can manipulate your picture, either scanned or otherwise inserted, to such an extent that you would sometimes forget which picture you started off with. But, this is not the only purpose of the software, you can use it create better looking pictures and art works with text and other graphics to beat any other similar software in the market.

Creating a File in Photoshop

As mentioned above, in Photoshop you create various type of art works using both graphics and text. The starting method is very similar what it is in most of the windows based software. Just click at New in the File menu and you have the blank page to work on. On this page you can add graphics and text which you want to. In case you have already created one, you would naturally like to open it, for that you need to open the existing file. For that you will use the command called Open, read on.

Opening An Existing File

Once created a Photoshop file is saved in the hard disk and can be called any time. For this you would you the command called Open from the file menu and then choose your file from the list of files listed in the dialog box. Once opened you can work on the file and then save it again. For saving, you need to do the following:

Saving the File

In Photoshop, you would save the file as you would do in any other software, using the keyboard option of Ctrl + S, or clicking at Save in the File menu. Using Save As you can save the file in any other format which your software supports.

Menu commands of Photoshop

Various commands in the menus are given here:

File menu

New: The New command lets you create a blank, untitled Photoshop image. You can also use this command to create a new image with the exact same pixel dimensions as an image or selection that has been copied to the Clipboard.

Open: It allows you to open an existing file from either the hard disk or other media attached to the computer, floppy drive, CD drive, etc. This also gives rise to a dialog box, from where you can select the file, which you want to open.

Browse: This command allows you to browse through files before opening them.

Open As: It allows you to open a file in another format.

Open Recent: It allows you to open a recently opened file.

Close: It allows you to close the current Photoshop file.

Save: It saves the current Photoshop file.

Save As: It allows you to save the current file under a new name or overwrite the current file.

Save for Web: It allows you to save the current file as a Web page.

Revert: This command is used to restore the most recently saved version of your file deleting all changes made since the last time you saved it.

Place: This command is used to place the text into the file.

Import: This command is active only if you have the scanner attached to your computer. This will help you in getting the scanned picture into the file.

Export: Using this command you can export the selected text of the publication into a document file in the format selected by you.

Manage Workflow: In a colour managed workflow, each colour model must have a working space associated with it. At times you may want to customize the RGB or CMYK working space to reflect a workflow that uses a particular output or display device.

Automate: The Automate commands simplify complex tasks by combining them into one or more dialog boxes. Photoshop includes the following commands (third-party companies may provide additional commands as well):

- Conditional Mode Change changes the color mode of a document to the mode you specify, based on the original mode of the document. By recording this command in an action, you can ensure that any actions that require an image to be in a specific color mode do not generate unwanted error messages.
- Contact Sheet produces a series of thumbnail previews on a single sheet from the files in the selected folder. Make sure that the images are closed before applying this command.
- Fit Image fits the current image to the width and height you specify, without changing its aspect ratio. This will resample the image, changing the amount of data in the image.
- Multi-Page PDF to PSD converts each page of the PDF document you select to a separate Photoshop file.

File Info: Adobe Photoshop supports the information standard developed by the Newspaper Association of America (NAA) and the International Press Telecommunications Council (IPTC) to identify transmitted text and images. This standard includes entries for captions, keywords, categories, credits, and origins. The captions and keyword entries can also be searched by some third-party image browsers.

Page Setup: You can define here various options for your new photoshop file.

Print with Preview: You can change the various options by seeing the preview before printing.

Print: This gives rise to a dialog box, where you can set the options for printing the publication.

Print One Copy: You can print one copy of the image on the screen.

Jump to: This gives you the option to jump to another program your choice.

Exit: Closes your session with Photoshop 6.

Edit menu

Undo/Redo: This command is used to reverse the last action taken by you. However, you can't undo all the actions. If the action can be reversed, the command read Undo on the Edit menu and names the action such as Undo Pasting. If the action cannot be reversed the command is off and thus can be read as cannot Undo. After you have do undo, you can Redo too if it is allowed.

Step Forward: This command is used to move a step forward in the motion.

Step Backward: This command is used to trace back the step in the motion

Cut: This command is used to cut the selected text or graphics from your file and keep it available for pasting it later to any other place in the same file or any other file or even any other software which supports the clipboard text.

Copy: This command is also used to copy the selected text or graphics from your file and keep it available for pasting it later. Only difference it has from Cut command is that it leaves the original text as it is whereas in the case of Cut the original text is lost. When you have more than one publication open, you can copy objects between publications without using the Clipboard. Select an object in one publication, drag it to position in the other publication window and release the mouse button to create a copy.

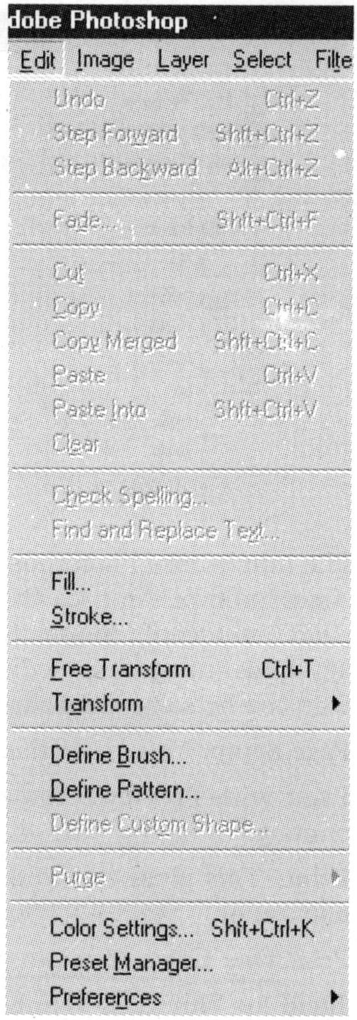

Copy Merged: This command makes a merged copy of all the visible layers in the selected area.

Paste: This command is used to place the selected text or graphics from clipboard, where the text using the above Cut or Copy command has been kept.

Paste Into: This command pastes a cut or copied selection inside another selection in the same image or different image. The source selection is pasted onto a new layer, and the destination selection border is converted into a layer mask.

Clear: This command is used to delete the current selection from your file without storing it in the **Clipboard:** This has the same effect as pressing Delete or Backspace.

Check Spelling: This is one of the new command of Photoshop 7 and allows you to spell check the text in your drawings using the in-built dictionary.

Find and Replace Text: Another of the new commands of Photoshop 7, which allows you to find particular text and replace it with another.

Fill: This command is used to fill foreground and background colour.

Stroke: Photoshop provides a variety of ways to fill a selection or a layer with colors, images, or patterns. You can also paint a border around a selection or a layer using the Stroke command. To increase the contrast between your image and the surrounding work canvas, you can fill the canvas with a specified color.

Free Transform: When an image is resampled, Adobe Photoshop uses an interpolation method to assign color values to any new pixels based on the color values of existing pixels in the image. The more sophisticated the method, the more quality and detail from the original image are preserved.

Transform: You can use rulers and guides to lay out your work, and you can copy and move selections within an image and between applications. You can also transform objects using specific transformations or using the transform bounding box.

Define Brush: You can define a brush setting here.

Define Pattern: The pattern you define here is repeated as tiles within the selection. Each new pattern replaces the current pattern. If you want to reuse patterns, save a file of swatches for defining patterns. You can also use the pattern stamp tool to paint with a pattern.

Define Custom Shape: This command allows you to select a custom shape from the options bar.

Purge: The Purge command permanently clears from memory the operation stored by the command or buffer, and cannot be undone. Use the Purge command when information held in memory is so large, Photoshop cannot perform the next operation.

Color Settings: The settings in these dialog boxes are used for the following:

- To convert images between standard color modes (such as from RGB to CMYK).
- When opening an RGB, Grayscale, or CMYK file, to compare the file's color space to the color space defined in the appropriate Setup dialog box. If the two color spaces are not the same, you can convert the file.
- When viewing a file on-screen, to convert the file to the monitor's color space. This only affects the display, not the file—Photoshop assumes that the file's true color space is the one defined in the appropriate Setup dialog box.

Preset Manager: This command allows you to preset a set of gradients to be used later and called.

Preferences: Unlike the one of Photoshop 6, this command now has more than one options.

Image menu

Mode: The modes available under Photoshop's this command are: Bitmap; Grayscale; RGB Color; Indexed Color; CMYK Color; Dutone; Lab Color; Multichannel

Adjustments: This command is used to adjust the various colours of your image. You will read more about them later.

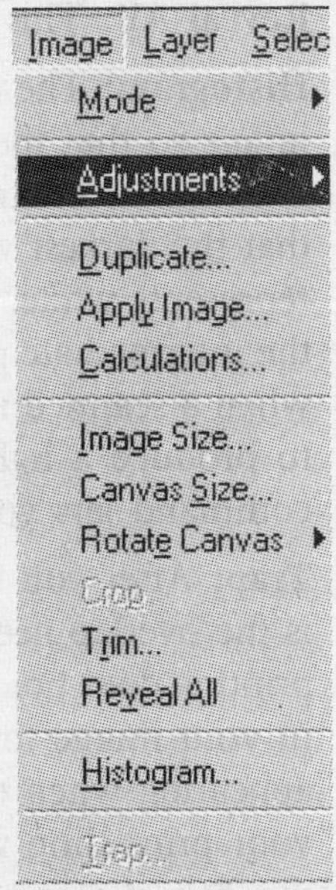

Duplicate: You can copy an entire image (including all layers, layer masks, and channels) into available memory without saving to disk by using the Duplicate command or by dragging and dropping.

Apply Image: The Apply Image command lets you blend one image's layer and channel (the source) with a layer and channel of the active image (the destination).

Calculations: The Calculations command lets you blend two individual channels from one or more source images. You can then apply the results to a new image or to a new channel or selection in the active image. You cannot apply the Calculations command to composite channels.

Image Size: When preparing images for online distribution (on a Web site, for example), it's useful to specify image size in terms of the pixel dimensions. Keep in mind that changing pixel dimensions affects not only the size of an image on-screen but also its image quality and its printed characteristics—either its printed dimensions or its image resolution.

Canvas Size: The Canvas Size command lets you add or remove work space around an existing image. You can crop an image by decreasing the canvas area. Added canvas appears in the same color or transparency as the background.

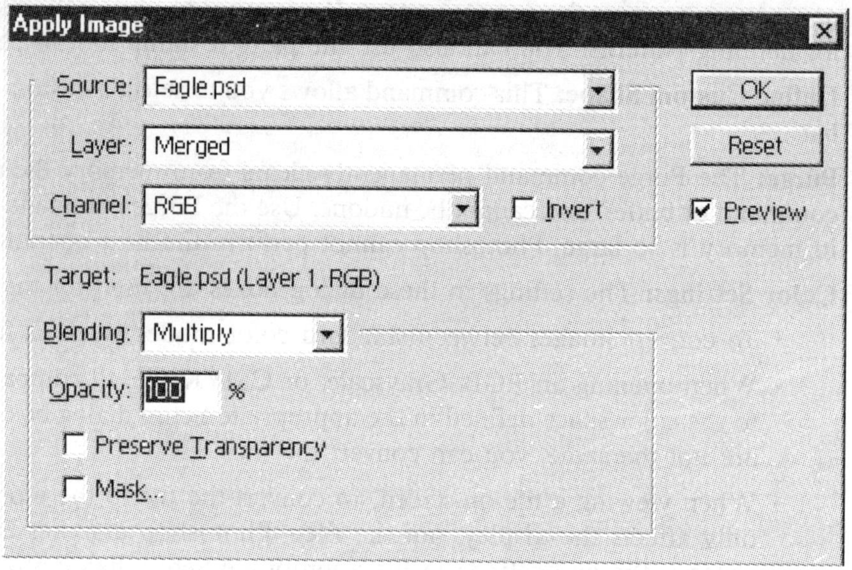

Rotate Canvas: The Rotate Canvas commands let you rotate or flip the entire image. It does not work on individual layers or parts of layers, paths, or selection borders.

Crop: Photoshop provides two ways to crop an image:

- The Image > Crop command discards the area outside of a rectangular selection and keeps the same resolution as the original.
- The crop tool lets you crop an image by dragging over the area you want to keep. The advantage of using the crop tool is that you can rotate and resample the area as you crop.

Trim: This command is used to discard a border area around the edge of the image, based on transparency or edge colour.

Reveal All: This command is used to reveal all images on the screen.

Histogram: The Equalize command redistributes the brightness values of the pixels in an image so that they more evenly represent the entire range of brightness levels. When you choose this command, Photoshop finds the brightest and darkest values in the image so that the darkest value represents black (or as close to it as possible) and the brightest value represents white. Photoshop then attempts to equalize the brightness—that is, to distribute the intermediate pixel values evenly throughout the grayscale. You might use this command when a scanned image appears darker than the original and you want to balance the values to produce a lighter image. Using the Equalize command together with the Histogram command lets you see before-and-after brightness comparisons.

Trap: After you have converted the image to CMYK, you can adjust the color trap. Trap is the overlap needed to ensure that a slight misalignment or movement of the plates while printing does not affect the final appearance of the print job. If any distinctly different colors in your image touch, you may need to overprint them slightly to prevent tiny gaps from appearing when the image is printed. This technique is known as trapping. In most cases, your print shop will determine if trapping is needed and tell you what values to enter in the Trap dialog box.

Layer menu

New: This command creates a new layer which can be via Copy or Cut menu.

Duplicate Layer: This command duplicates the selected layer.

Delete: This command deletes the selected picture, layer, etc.

Layer Properties: The layer properties allow you to lock layers of an image so that they cannot be changed.

Layer Styles: When applying layer styles, you can specify a number of common options for each effect. Various options of the layer styles are shown below and on next few pages.

New Fill Layers: A new layer is added with the optional fill selected by you.

New Adjustment Layer: A new layer is added with the option selected by you. Various available options are: Levels, Curves, Color Balance, Brightness/Contrast, Hue/Saturation, Selective Color, Channel Mixer, Gradient Map, Invert, Threshold and Posterize.

Change Layer Content: This command allows you to change the contents of a layer.

Layer Content Options: This command allows you to change the various options of a layer.

Type: This command is used to create type in a layer.

Rasterize: This command is used to rasterize the image in the layer.

New Layer Based Slice: When you create a slice from a layer, the slice area encompasses all the pixel data in the layer. If you edit the layer's content, the slice area automatically adjusts to encompass the new pixels.

Add Layer Mask: In the Layers palette, a layer mask appears as an additional thumbnail to the right of the layer thumbnail. This thumbnail represents the grayscale (alpha) channel created by Adobe Photoshop when you add the layer mask.

Enable Layer Mask: By default, the layer mask channel appear in the image. You can view and edit the contents of the mask by using this command.

Add Vector Mask: A vector mask creates a sharp-edged shape on a layer and is useful any time you want to add a design element with clean, defined edges. Once you create a layer with a vector mask, you can apply one or more layer styles to it, edit them if needed, and instantly have a usable button, panel, or other Web design element.

Enable Vector Mask: By default, the layer mask channel appear in the image. You can view and edit the contents of the mask by using this command.

Add Layer Clipping Path: A layer clipping path allows you to clip a layer using resolution independent hard edges created by the pen or shape tools.

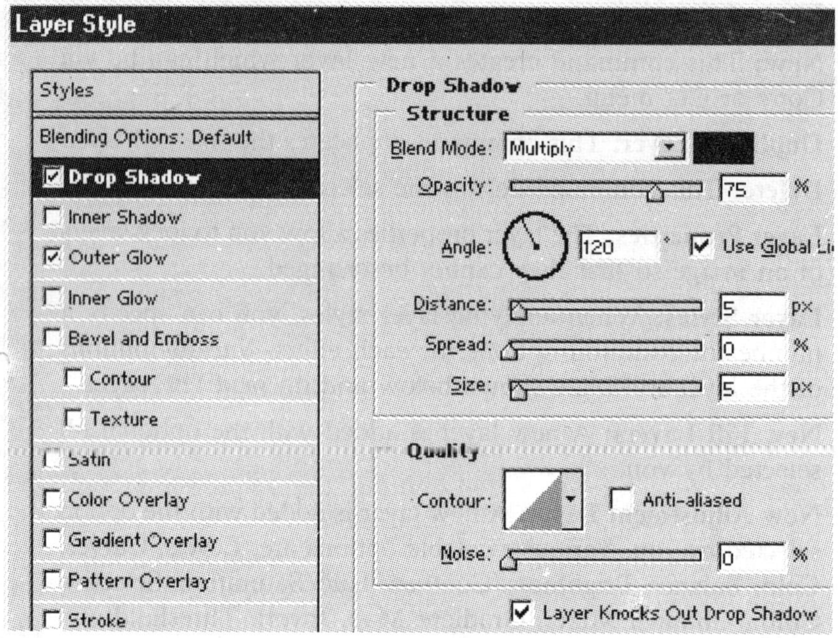

Group with Previous: This command allows you to group the selected layer with the previous grouped layers.

Ungroup: This command ungroups the layers grouped together by the above command.

Arrange: This command is used for the followings:

- Bring to Front to make the layer the topmost layer.
- Bring Forward to move the layer one level up in the stacking order.
- Send Backward to move the layer one level down in the stacking order.
- Send to Back to make the layer the bottommost layer in the image (except for the background).

Align Linked: This command is used for the followings:

- To align a single layer to a selection, make the layer active.
- To align multiple layers to a selection or to the active layer, link together two or more layers.
- To distribute multiple layers, link together three or more layers.
- Top to align the topmost pixel on the linked layers to the topmost pixel on the active layer or the topmost edge of the selection border.
- Vertical Center to align the vertical centermost pixel on the linked layers to the vertical centermost pixel on the active layer or the vertical center of the selection border.
- Bottom to align the bottommost pixel on the linked layers to the bottommost pixel on the active layer or the bottommost edge of the selection border.
- Left to align the leftmost pixel on the linked layers to the leftmost pixel on the active layer or the leftmost edge of the selection border.
- Horizontal Center to align the horizontal centermost pixel on the linked layers to

the horizontal centermost pixel on the active layer or the horizontal center of the selection border.

- Right to align the rightmost pixel on the linked layers to the rightmost pixel on the active layer or the rightmost edge of the selection border.

Distribute Linked: This command allows you to position the contents of linked layers at evenly spaced intervals.

Lock All Layers in Set: This command locks all the layers in the particular set.

Merge Layers: This command allows you to merge two or more layers.

Merge Visible: This command makes sure that the merged layers are visible.

Flatten Image: In a flattened image, all visible layers are merged into the background, greatly reducing file size. Flattening an image discards all hidden layers and fills the remaining transparent areas with white. In most cases, you won't want to flatten a file until you have finished editing individual layers.

Matting: When you move or paste an anti-aliased selection, some of the pixels surrounding the selection border are included with the selection. This can result in a fringe or halo around the edges of the pasted selection. These three Matting commands let you edit these unwanted edge pixels:

Select menu

All: This command selects all the items on the screen.

Deselect: This command deselects the items already selected.

Reselect: You can reselect the items deselected above.

Inverse: The inverted command inverts the colours in an image. You might use this command to make a positive black-and-white image negative or to make a positive from a scanned black-and-white negative.

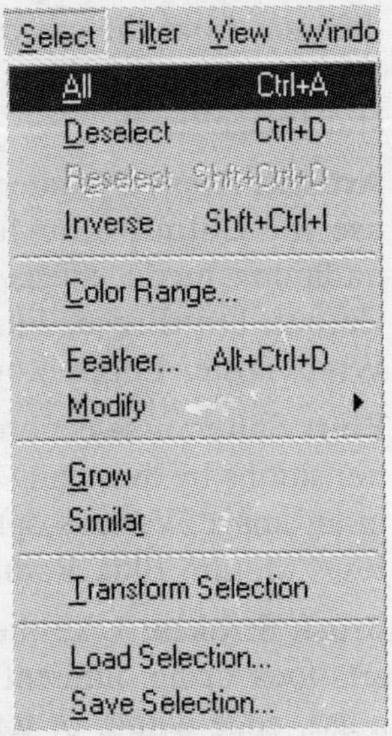

Colour Range: The Color Range command selects a specified color or color subset within an existing selection or an entire image. If you want to replace a selection, be sure to deselect everything before applying this command.

Feather: You can define feathering for the marquee, lasso, polygon lasso, or magnetic lasso tool as you use the tool, or you can add feathering to an existing selection. Feathering effects become apparent when you move, cut, or copy the selection.

Modify: You can use the following Select commands to increase or decrease the pixels in an existing selection.

Grow: Grow and Similar commands are used to expand a selection to include areas similar in color.

Transform Selection: The Free Transform command lets you use the Scale, Rotate, Skew, Distort, and Perspective commands without having to select them from the menu. To access the various transformation modes, you use different shortcut keys as you drag the handles of the transform bounding box.

Load Selection: When you have finished modifying an alpha channel or simply want to use a previously saved selection, you can load the selection into the image.

Save Selection: You create a new alpha channel as a mask. For example, you can create a gradient fill in a blank channel, and then use it as a mask. Or you can save a selection to either a new or existing channel.

Filter menu

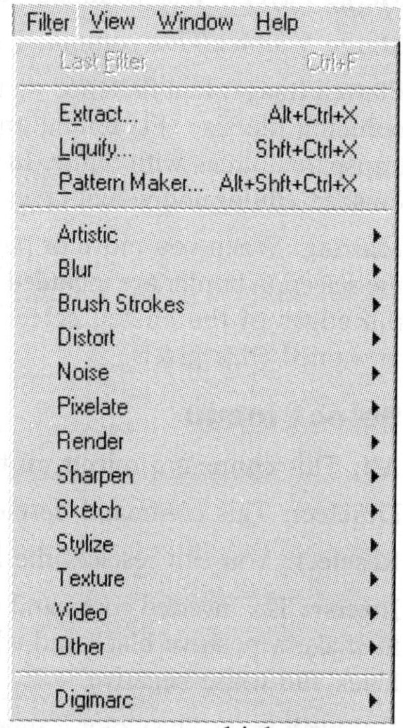

Last Filter: This command allows you to call the last filter used.

Extract: The Extract command provides a sophisticated way to isolate a foreground object and erase its background on a layer. Even objects with wispy, intricate, or undefinable edges may be clipped from their backgrounds with a minimum of manual work.

Liquify: Several tools in the Liquify dialog box distort the brush area when you hold down the mouse button or drag. The distortion is concentrated at the center of the brush area, and the effect intensifies as you hold down the mouse button or repeatedly drag over an area.

Pattern Maker: The Pattern Maker lets you create an infinite variety of patterns based on a selection or the contents of the Clipboard. Because the pattern is based on the pixels in a sample, it shares visual characteristics with the sample. For example, if you sample an image of grass, the Pattern Maker generates a tileable pattern that is different from the sample but still appears to be grass. You can generate multiple patterns from the same sample, and save pattern tiles as preset patterns for future use in Photoshop and ImageReady.

Artistic: Apply a painterly or special effect for a fine-arts or commercial project. For example, use the Cutout filter for collages or type treatment. These filters replicate natural or traditional media effects. Various options available under this command are: Coloured Pencil, Cutout, Dry Brush, Film Grain, Fresco, Neon Glow, Paint Daubs, Palette Knife, Plastic Wrap, Poster Edges, Rough Pastels, Smudge Stick, Sponge, Underpainting and Watercolor.

Blur: Soften a selection or an image. Blur filters are useful for retouching. They smooth transitions by averaging the pixels next to the hard edges of defined lines and shaded areas in an image. Various options available under this command are: Blur, Blur More, Gaussian Blur, Motion Blur, Radial Blur, Smart Blur.

Brush Strokes: Like the Artistic filters, the Brush Strokes filters give a painterly or fine-arts look using different brush and ink stroke effects. Some of the filters add grain, paint, noise, edge detail, or texture to an image for a pointlist effect. Various options available under this command are: Accented Edges, Angled Strokes, Crosshatch, Dark Strokes, Ink Outlines, Spatter, Sprayed Strokes and Sumi-e.

Distort: Geometrically distort an image, creating 3-D or other reshaping effects. Note that these filters can be very memory intensive. This command has the following options: Diffuse Glow, Displace, Glass, Ocean Ripple, Pinch, Polar Coordinates, Ripple, Shear, Spherize, Twirl, Wave and ZigZag.

Noise: Add or remove noise, or pixels with randomly distributed color levels. This helps to blend a selection into the surrounding pixels. Noise filters can create unusual textures or remove problem areas, such as dust and scratches, from an image. The Add Noise filter can be used to reduce banding in feathered selections or graduated fills or to give a more realistic look to heavily retouched areas. This command has the following options: Add Noise, Despeckle, Dust & Scratches and Median.

Pixelate: Sharply define a selection by clumping pixels of similar color values in cells. This command has the following options: Color Halftone, Crystallize, Facet, Fragment, Mezzotint, Mosaic and Pointillize.

Render: Create 3-D shapes, cloud patterns, refraction patterns, and simulated light reflections in an image. You can also manipulate objects in 3-D space, create 3-D objects (cubes, spheres, and cylinders), and create texture fills from grayscale files to produce 3-D-like effects for lighting. This command has the following options: 3D Transform, Clouds, Difference Clouds, Lens Flare, Lighting Effects and Texture Fill.

Sharpen: Focus blurry images by increasing the contrast of adjacent pixels. They include the Sharpen Edges and Unsharp Mask filters, which find and sharpen areas where significant color changes occur (such as at the edges). The Unsharp Mask filter is commonly used for high-end color correction This command has the following options: Sharpen, Sharpen Edges, Sharpen More and Unsharp Mask.

Sharpen

Original Sharpen Edges

Sketch: Add texture to images, often for a 3-D effect. The filters also are useful for creating a fine-arts or hand-drawn look. Many of the Sketch filters use the foreground and background color as they redraw the image. Various options under this command are: Bas Relief, Chalk & Charcoal, Charcoal, Chrome, Conte Crayon, Graphic Pen, Halftone Pattern, Note Paper, Photocopy, Plaster, Reticulation, Stamp, Torn Edges and Water Paper.

Stylize: Produce a painted or impressionistic effect on a selection by displacing pixels and by finding and heightening contrast in an image. After using filters like Find Edges and Trace Contour that highlight edges, you can apply the Invert command to outline the edges of a color image with colored lines or to outline the edges of a grayscale image with white lines. Various options under this command are: Diffuse, Emboss, Extrude, Find Edges, Glowing Edges, Solarize, Tiles, Trace Contour and Wind.

Texture: Give images the appearance of depth or substance, or to add an organic look. Various options under this command are: Craquelure, Grain, Mosaic Tiles, Patchwork, Stained Glass and Texturizer.

Video: Include the NTSC (National Television Standards Committee) Colors filter, which restricts the gamut of colors to those acceptable for television reproduction, and the De-Interlace filter, which smooths moving images captured on video. This command has the following options: De-Interlace and NTSC Colors.

Other: Let you create your own filters, use filters to modify masks, offset a selection within an image, and make quick color adjustments. This command has the following options: Custom, DitherBox, High Pass, Maximum, Minimum and Offset.

Digimarc: Embed a digital watermark into an image to store copyright information. This command has the following options: Embed Watermark and Read Watermark.

View menu

Proof Setup: Select this command to choose the output display that you want to simulate:

- **Custom:** To soft proof colours as displayed on a specific output device.
- **Working CYMK:** To soft-proof colours using the current CYMK working space.
- **Working Cyan Plate, Working Magenta Plate, Working Yellow Plate, Working Black Plate, or Working CMY Plate:** To soft-proof specific CYMK ink colour using the current CYMK working space.
- **Windows RGB:** To soft-proof colours using either a standard Windows monitor as the proof profile space that you want to simulate.
- **Monitor RGB:** To soft-proof colours using your current monitor colour space as the proof profile space.
- **Simulate Paper:** To preview the specific shade of white exhibited by the print medium.
- **Simulate Ink Black:** To preview the amount of black pigment absorbed by the print medium.

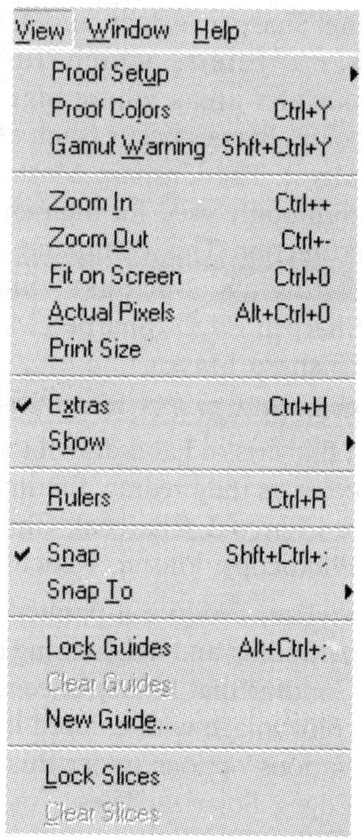

Proof Colours: Use this command to toggle the soft-proof display on or off.

Gamut Warning: The gamut is the range of colors that can be displayed or printed in a color system. A color that can be displayed in RGB or HSB models may be out-of-gamut, and therefore unprintable, for your CMYK setting. Photoshop automatically brings all colors into gamut when you convert an image to CMYK. But you might want to identify the out-of-gamut colors in an image or correct them manually before converting to CMYK.

Zoom In Select the zoom tool, and click the area you want to magnify. Each click magnifies the image to the next preset percentage, centering the display around the point you click. At maximum magnification, the center of the zoom tool appears empty.

Zoom Out Select the zoom tool. Hold down Alt (Windows) or Option (Mac OS) to activate the zoom-out tool, and click the area of the image you want to reduce. Each click reduces the view to the previous preset percentage.

Fit on Screen: These options scale both the view and the window size to match the monitor size.

Actual Pixels: This command displays the image at 100%.

Print Size: The magnification of the image is adjusted to display its approximate printed size, as specified in the Print Size section of the Image Size dialog box.

Extras: This command allows you to show all images on the screen.

Show: From here you can select the various options to be seen on the screen.

Rules: Shows or hides rulers on the screen.

Snap: This command snaps the various guides on the screen.

Snap To: From the sub-menu you can select the various guides which you want to snap to.

Lock Guides: This command locks all the column and ruler guides so that you cannot move them accidentally.

Clear Guides: This command clears all guides from the screen.

New Guide: This command allows you to have a new guide on the screen.

Lock Slices: Using this command you can lock the varies slices on the screen.

Clear Slices: The above locked slices can be unlocked using this command.

Window menu

Documents: It has the following commands under it.

- **Cascade:** This command opens another window of the current image.
- **Tile:** Using this command you can see on the screen more than one image.
- **Arrange Icons:** This command arranges icons on the screen.
- **Close All:** This command closes all the open windows on the screen.
- **New Window:** This command opens a new window of the screen image.

Workspace: This command allows you to save the current workspace.

Tools: Hides/Shows the tools dialog box on the screen.

Options: Hides/Shows the various options on the screen.

File Browser: It brings the File Browser dialog box on the screen.

Navigator: Hides/Shows the Navigator dialog box on the screen.

Info: Hides/Shows the Info dialog box on the screen..

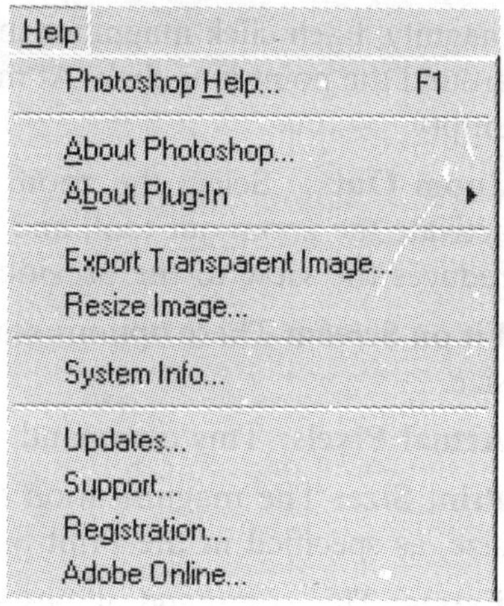

Colour: Hides/Shows the Color dialog box on the screen.

Swatches: Hides/Shows the Swatches dialog box on the screen.

Styles: Hides/Shows the Styles dialog box on the screen.

History: Hides/Shows the History dialog box on the screen.

Actions: Hides/Shows the Actions dialog box on the screen.

Layers: Hides/Shows the Layers dialog box on the screen.

Channels: Hides/Shows the Channels dialog box on the screen..

Paths: Hides/Shows the Paths dialog box on the screen.

Brushes: Hides/Shows the brushes dialog box on the screen.

Show Character: Hides/Shows the Character dialog box on the screen.

Show Paragraph: Hides/Shows the Paragraph dialog box on the screen..

Hide Status Bar: Hides/Shows the Status bar on the screen.

Help menu

This menu has the various options which help you in case you want to know more about any command.

Using Tools

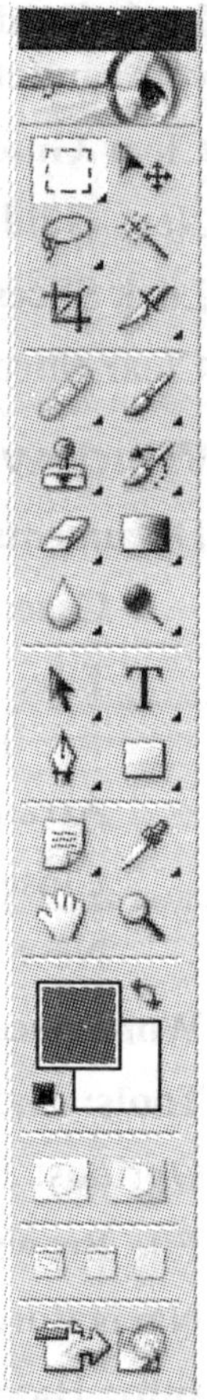

Photoshop has lots of tools to work with. These tools are available on the left side of the screen in the form of a toolbar, as shown here. These tools are for various purposes such as Selection, Painting, and Drawing, Erasing, etc. For each tool when selected you would see the various options on the top of the toolbar in the form of another toolbar.

Let us see how these tools one by one.

Rectangular Marquees

This is the first tool on the toolbar. If pressed it gives rise to the various tools available under it.

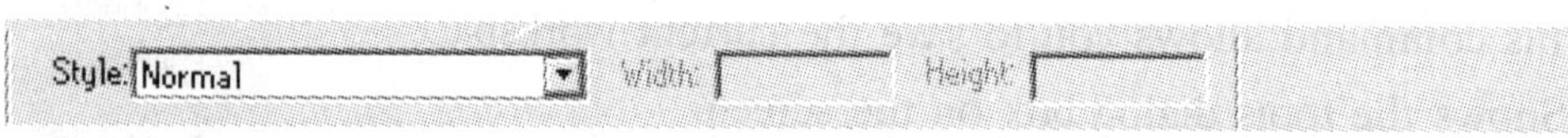

Click the Marquee tool in the toolbox. Move the tool over the blank canvas of your file and see the result. You can create a rectangular marquee with it as shown here.

Various type of styles which can be used are Normal, Constrained Aspect Ratio,

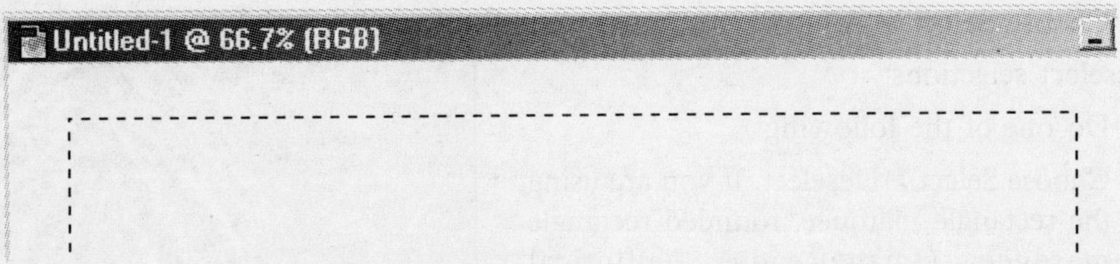

and Fixed Size. If you press and hold Shift key after you have made your first selection before you click again, you can make additional selections.

Move Tool

This tool is used to move the objects from one place to another. Click the Move tool in the toolbox. It gives rise to various options of the tool on screen, as shown here.

The move tool lets you drag a selection or layer to a new location in the image. With the Info palette open, you can track the exact distance of the move.

To specify move tool options:

1. Select the move tool.
2. Select any of the following:

   Select Pixel Doubling to speed the preview of the move tool's effect by temporarily doubling the size of the pixels in the preview. This option has no effect on the pixels in the file; it simply provides faster previews with the tool. Auto Select Layer to select the topmost layer that has pixels under the move tool, rather than the selected layer.

To move a selection or layer:

1. Select the move tool.

To activate the move tool when another tool is selected, hold down Ctrl.

1. Do one of the following:

   Move the pointer inside the selection border, and drag the selection to a new position. If you have selected multiple areas, all move as you drag. Select the layer you want to move. Then drag the layer to a new position.

Lasso Tool

These tools are used when you have to select irregular shapes. Using the Lasso tool to select an object requires a steady hand and good hand-eye coordination, as well as a clean mouse and mousepad or trackball. When selected it gives rise to the following options on the screen.

To select all pixels on a layer within the canvas boundaries:

1. Select the layer in the Layers palette.

2. Choose Select > All.

To deselect selections:

1. Do one of the following:

   Choose Select > Deselect. If you are using the rectangle marquee, rounded rectangle marquee (ImageReady), elliptical marquee, or lasso tool, click anywhere in the image outside the selected area.

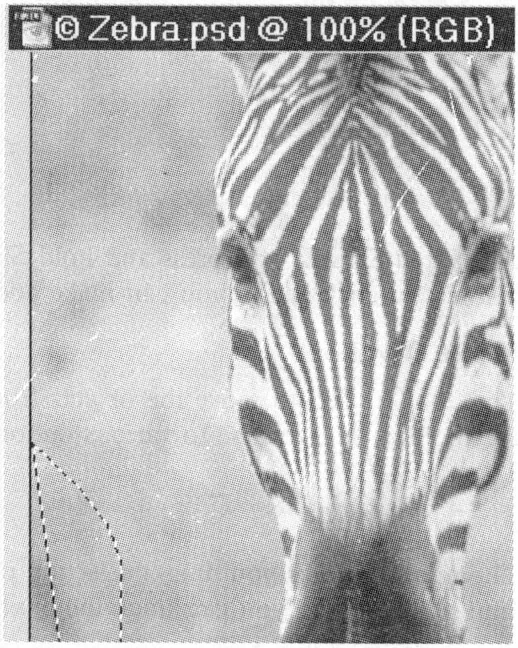

Magic Wand Tool

This tool is little different from the other selection tools. The Magic Wand selects pixels somewhat differently, it selects them based on colour values. This enables you to cut foreground objects, out of the background.

When selected it gives rise to the following options.

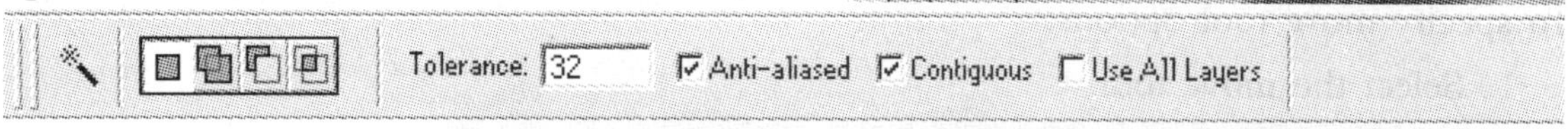

You cannot use the magic wand tool on an image in Bitmap mode.

To use the magic wand tool:

1. Select the magic wand tool.
2. In the options bar, specify a selection option. You can create a new selection, add to, subtract from, or restrict the selection. The magic wand cursor changes indicating which option is selected.
3. For Tolerance, enter a value in pixels, ranging

from 0 to 255. Enter a low value to select colors very similar to the pixel you click or a higher value to select a broader range of colors.

4. To define a smooth edge, select Anti-aliased.
5. To select all areas using the same colors, select Contiguous. Otherwise only the adjacent pixels will be selected.
6. To select colors using data from all the visible layers, select Use All Layers. Otherwise, the magic wand tool selects colors from the active layer only.
7. In the image, click the color you want to select. All adjacent pixels within the tolerance range are selected.

Cropping Tool

This tool helps you in getting rid of unwanted parts of the picture. It forms part of the marquee tools submenu. You can also crop by making a selection with the rectangular marquee and then using the menu command Image, Crop to crop the image. When selected this tool gives the following options.

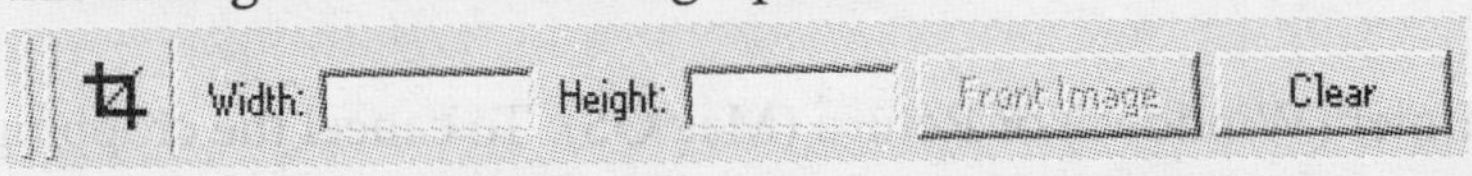

You can use the following methods to crop images:

— Use the Crop command or the crop tool set to Delete to discard the area outside of a rectangular selection. Use the Crop command or the crop tool set to Hidden or Hide to hide the area outside of a rectangular selection. Use this feature when creating animations with elements that move from offscreen into the live image area.

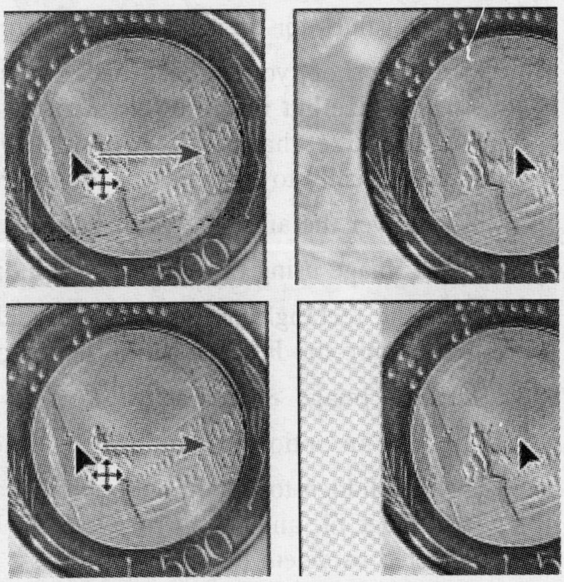

— An image with the Crop command applied using the Hidden option and repositioned using the move tool.

— An image with the Crop command applied using the Delete option and repositioned using the move tool.

— Use the Trim command to discard a border area around the edge of the image, based on transparency or edge color.

— When using the crop tool, you can rotate the selected area before you perform the cropping operation. You can also specify a fixed size for the target image created from the cropped selection.

To use the crop tool:

1. Select the crop tool.
2. In the options bar, select an option to remove the cropped area:

   Delete to permanently discard the cropped area. Hide to hide the cropped area but preserve the area in the image file.
3. Drag over the part of the image you want to keep.

   When you release the mouse button, the crop marquee appears as a bounding box with handles at the corners and sides.
4. Adjust the crop marquee:

   To move the marquee to another position, position the pointer inside the bounding box and drag. To scale the marquee, drag a handle. To constrain the proportions, hold down Shift as you drag a corner handle. To rotate the marquee, position the pointer outside the bounding box (the pointer turns into a curved arrow), and drag. To adjust the point around which the marquee is rotated, drag the circle at the center of the bounding box.
5. To crop the image, press Enter (Windows) or Return (Mac OS). To cancel the cropping operation, press Esc.

To specify the size of the cropped area:

1. Select the crop tool.
2. In the options bar, select Fixed Target Size.
3. To begin with the size values of the current image, click Front Image.
4. Enter values for the size you want for the cropped area.

   In Photoshop, you can also set the resolution you want for the cropped area. If you specify size but not resolution, the resolution changes automatically to compensate for the size change. If you specify resolution but not size, the size changes automatically to compensate for the resolution change.
5. Drag over the area you want to keep with the crop tool, and then press Enter.

To crop an image using the Crop command:

1. Use the rectangle marquee tool to select the part of the image you want to keep. Make sure the Feather option in the options bar is set to 0 pixels.
2. Choose Image > Crop.
3. Choose an option to hide or delete the cropped area:

   Select Hidden to hide the cropped areas of the image. The cropped areas are still in the image file and can be made visible by moving the layer with the move tool. Select Deleted to delete the cropped areas.
4. Click OK.

To crop an image using the Trim command:

1. Choose Image > Trim.
2. Crop the border:

   Select Transparent Pixels to remove an area of transparent pixels from the image. Select Top Left Pixel Color to remove an area the color of the upper left pixel from the image. Select Bottom Right Pixel Color to remove an area the color of the lower right pixel from the image.
3. Select one or more areas of the image to be trimmed: Top, Bottom, Left, or Right.
4. Click OK.

Slice Tool

You can create user-slices with the slice tool, from a layer, from a selection (ImageReady), or from guides (ImageReady). When you create a slice from a layer, the slice area encompasses all the pixel data in the layer. If you edit the layer's content, the slice area automatically adjusts to encompass the new pixels.

When selected it gives rise to the following options:

When defining an area for use as a rollover, place the rollover element on a separate layer, and create a slice from that layer. If you apply an effect to the layer—such as a drop shadow or glow—to create a rollover state, the slice automatically adjusts to encompass the new pixels.

To create a slice with the slice tool:

1. Select the slice tool. Any existing slices automatically display in the document window.
2. Choose a style setting in the options bar:

   Normal to determine slice proportions by dragging. Constrained Aspect Ratio to set a height-to-width ratio. Enter whole numbers or decimals for the aspect ratio. For example, to create a slice twice as wide as it is high, enter 2 for the width and 1 for the height. Fixed Size to specify the slice's height and width. Enter pixel values in whole numbers.
3. Drag over the area where you want to create a slice. Hold down Shift as you drag to constrain the slice to a square. Hold down Alt to draw from the center.

To create a slice from a layer:

1. Select a layer in the Layers palette.
2. Do one of the following: Choose Layer > Make Slice From Layer.

The Airbrush Tool

The airbrush tool applies gradual tones (including sprays of color) to an image, simulating traditional airbrush techniques. The edges of the stroke are more diffused than those created with the paintbrush tool. The pressure setting for the airbrush tool controls how quickly the spray of paint is applied. If you hold down the mouse button without dragging, you can build up color.

When selected it gives rise to the following options.

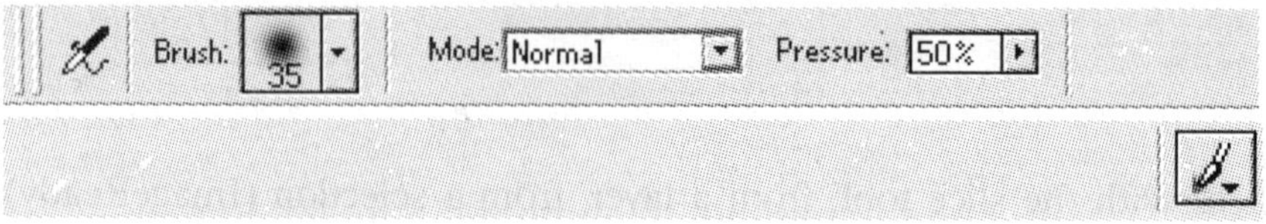

To use a painting brush:

1. Specify a foreground color.
2. Select airbrush tool.
3. Choose a size for the brush from the brush menu in the options bar. If a brush is too large to fit in the menu, it appears as a smaller brush with a number indicating the actual diameter in pixels.
4. Specify a blending mode to control how painting affects existing pixels in the image.
5. Specify pressure for the airbrush tool.
6. Specify the rate at which a brush stroke fades dynamically.
7. Drag in the image to paint.

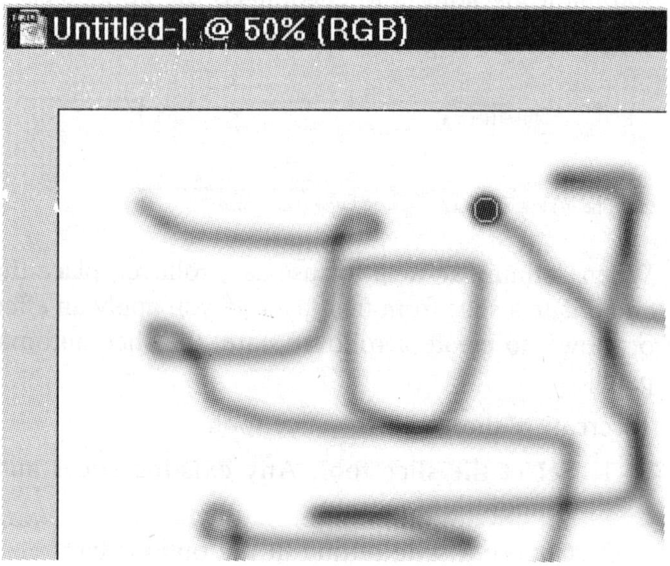

Paintbrush Tool

This tool is the most important of all brush tools in Photoshop. It is quite similar to the Airbrush but here the paint is applied quite evenly.

The paintbrush tool creates soft strokes of color.

When selected it gives rise to the following options.

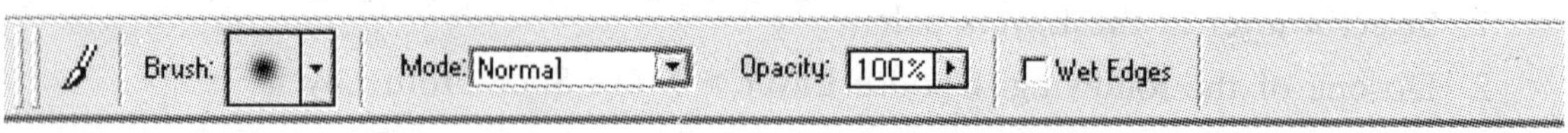

To use a paintbrush tool:

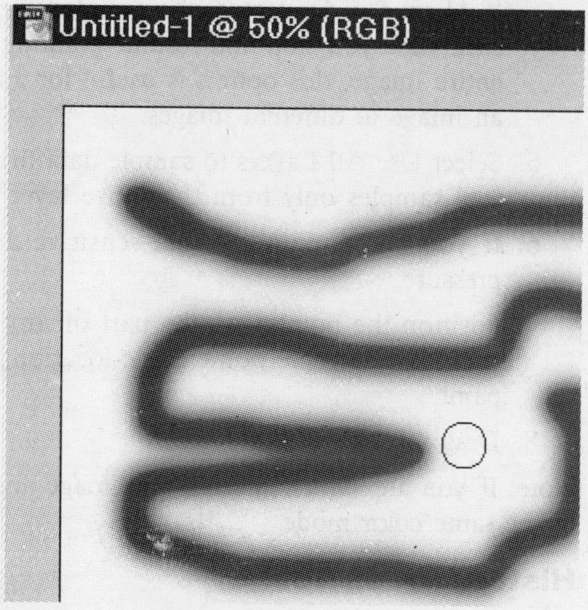

1. Specify a foreground color.
2. Select the paintbrush tool.
3. Choose a size for the brush from the brush menu in the options bar. If a brush is too large to fit in the menu, it appears as a smaller brush with a number indicating the actual diameter in pixels.
4. Specify a blending mode to control how painting affects existing pixels in the image.
5. Specify opacity for the paintbrush.
6. Set additional options:

   For the paintbrush tool, select Wet Edges to paint with a watercolor effect. The paint builds up along the edges of the brush stroke.
7. Specify the rate at which a brush stroke fades dynamically.
8. Drag in the image to paint.

To draw a straight line with one of the painting tools, click a starting point in the image. Then hold down Shift, and click an ending point.

Clone Stamp Tool

The clone stamp tool takes a sample of an image, which you can then apply over another image or part of the same image. Each stroke of the tool paints on more of the sample. Cross hairs mark the original sampling point.

When selected this gives the following options:

To use the clone stamp tool:

1. Select the clone stamp tool.
2. Choose a size for the brush from the brushes menu in the options bar. If a brush is too large to fit in the menu, it appears as a smaller brush with a number indicating the actual diameter in pixels.
3. Specify a blending mode and opacity.
4. Select Aligned to apply the entire sampled area once, regardless of how many times you stop and resume painting. This option is useful when you want to use different sized brushes to paint an image. You can also use the Aligned option to duplicate two halves of a single image and place them at different locations.

If Aligned is deselected, the sampled area is applied from the initial sampling point each time you stop and resume painting. Because the clone stamp tool samples the entire image, this option is useful for applying multiple copies of the same part of an image to different images.

5. Select Use All Layers to sample data from all visible layers. If this is deselected, the tool samples only from the active layer.
6. If you are using a pressure-sensitive drawing tablet, specify the effects of stylus pressure.
7. Position the pointer on the part of any open image you want to sample, and Alt-click. This sample point is the location from which the image is duplicated as you paint.
8. Drag to paint with the tool.

Note: If you are sampling from one image and applying to another, both images must be in the same color mode.

History Brush Tool

The history brush tool lets you paint a copy of one state or snapshot of an image into the current image window. This tool makes a copy, or sample, of the image and then paints with it. For example, you might make a snapshot of a change you made with a painting tool or filter. After undoing the change to the image, you could use the history brush tool to apply the change selectively to areas of the image. Unless you select a merged snapshot, the history brush tool paints from a layer in the selected state to the same layer in another state.

The history brush tool works similarly to the clone stamp tool, but on any state or snapshot of the image, not just the current one. When selected it gives rise to the following options:

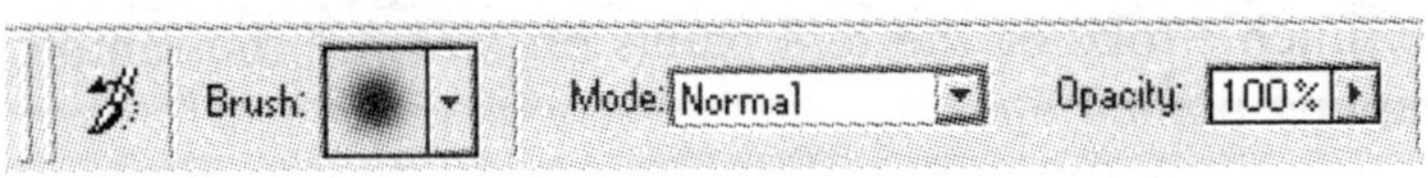

To paint with a state or snapshot of an image:

1. Select the history brush tool.
2. Specify the opacity and blending mode.
3. Choose a brush size.
4. If desired, select Impressionist to paint with an "impressionistic" copy of the source state or snapshot. This option drags and smears the pixels as you paint.
5. In the History palette, click the left column of the state or snapshot to use as the source for the history brush tool.
6. Drag to paint with the history brush tool.

Eraser Tools

You can also use the eraser to return the affected area to a state selected in the History palette.

When selected it gives the following options:

To use the eraser tool:

1. Select the eraser tool (icon).
2. Choose a size for the brush from the brush menu in the options bar. If a brush is too large to fit in the menu, it appears as a smaller brush with a number indicating the actual diameter in pixels.

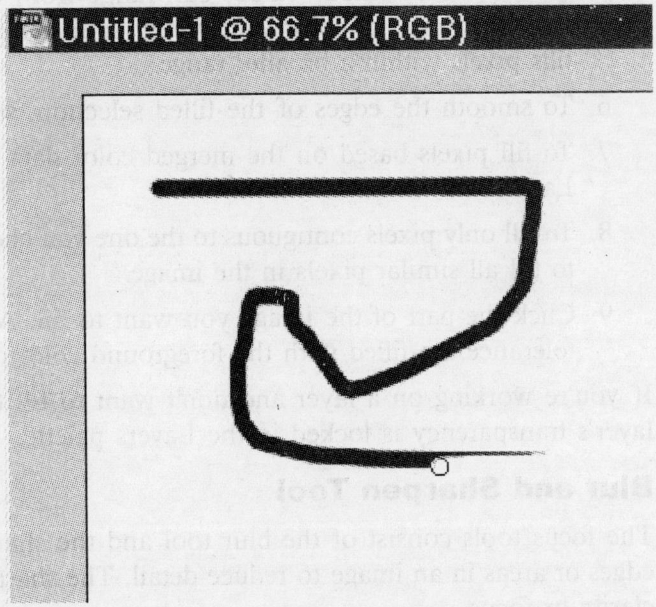

3. Choose the tool type you want to use as an eraser—paintbrush, airbrush, pencil, or block.
4. Specify an opacity to define the strength of the erasure. An opacity of 100% erases pixels to complete transparency. A lower opacity erases pixels to partial transparency.
5. If you're using the paintbrush eraser, select Wet Edges to paint with a watercolor effect. When this is selected, the erased effect builds up along the edges of the brush stroke.
6. To erase to a saved state or snapshot of the image, select Erase to History. To use the eraser tool in Erase to History mode, hold down Alt as you drag in the image.
7. Specify how a brush strokes fades dynamically.
8. Drag through the area you want to erase.

Paint Bucket Tool

The paint bucket tool fills adjacent pixels that are similar in color value to the pixels you click.

When selected it gives rise to the following options:

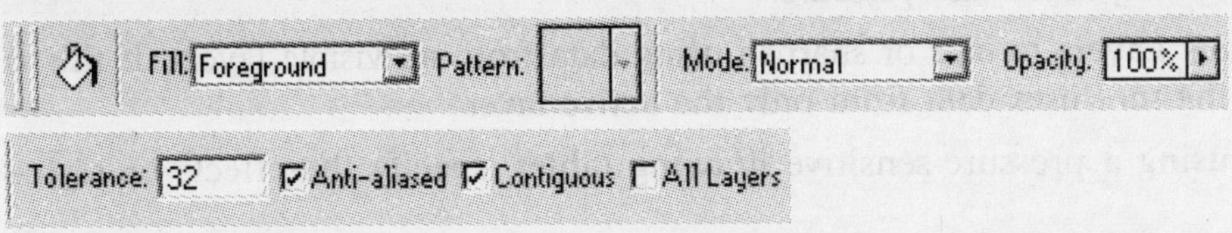

The paint bucket tool cannot be used with images in Bitmap mode.

To use the paint bucket tool:

1. Specify a foreground color.
2. Select the paint bucket tool.
3. Specify whether to fill the selection with the foreground color or with a pattern.
4. Specify a blending mode and opacity for the paint. (See Setting options for painting and editing.)
5. Enter the tolerance for the fill. The tolerance defines how similar in color a pixel must be to be filled. Values can range from 0 to 255. A low tolerance fills pixels within a range of color values very similar to the pixel you click. A high tolerance fills pixels within a broader range.
6. To smooth the edges of the filled selection, select Anti-aliased.
7. To fill pixels based on the merged color data from all visible layers, select Use All Layers.
8. To fill only pixels contiguous to the one you click, select Contiguous; leave unselected to fill all similar pixels in the image.
9. Click the part of the image you want to fill. All adjacent pixels within the specified tolerance are filled with the foreground color or pattern.

If you're working on a layer and don't want to fill transparent areas, make sure that the layer's transparency is locked in the Layers palette.

Blur and Sharpen Tool

The focus tools consist of the blur tool and the sharpen tool. The blur tool softens hard edges or areas in an image to reduce detail. The sharpen tool focuses soft edges to increase clarity or focus.

When Blur tool is selected you get the following options:

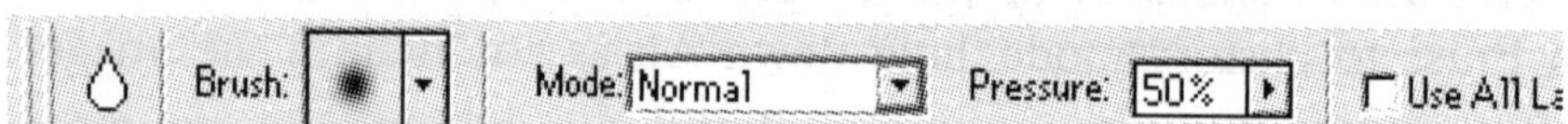

To use the blur or sharpen tool:

1. Select the blur tool or sharpen tool.
2. Choose a size for the brush from the brushes menu in the options bar. If a brush is too large to fit in the menu, it appears as a smaller brush with a number indicating the actual diameter in pixels.
3. Specify a blending mode and pressure.
4. Select Use All Layers to blur or sharpen using data from all visible layers. If this is deselected, the tool uses data from only the active layer.
5. If you are using a pressure-sensitive drawing tablet, specify the effects of stylus pressure.
6. Drag over the part of the image you want to blur or sharpen.

Dodge Tool

The toning tools consist of the dodge tool and the burn tool. Used to lighten or darken areas of the image, the dodge and burn tools are based on a traditional photographer's technique for regulating exposure on specific areas of a print. Photographers hold back light to lighten an area on the print (dodging) or increase the exposure to darken areas on a print (burning).

When selected it gives rise to the following options:

To use the dodge or burn tool:

1. Select the dodge tool or burn tool.
2. Choose a size for the brush from the brushes menu in the options bar. If a brush is too large to fit in the menu, it appears as a smaller brush with a number indicating the actual diameter in pixels.
3. Select what to change in the image:

   Midtones to change the middle range of grays. Shadows to change the dark areas. Highlights to change the light areas.
4. Specify the exposure for the tool.
5. If you are using a pressure-sensitive drawing tablet, specify the effects of stylus pressure.
6. Drag over the part of the image you want to modify.

Path Component Selection Tool

Since there are two different types of data in your image, rasterized and vector, you need to use separate sets of tools to make each type of selection. You can select pixels or make non-pixel selections. When you select pixels, you are selecting resolution dependent information in the image. Additionally, you can also select resolution independent paths and vector objects (or layer masks) in an image using the vector selection tools.

You can select paths and vector objects by clicking with the path component selection tool or the direct selection tool. Selecting a path or segment displays all of the anchor points on the selected portion, including any direction lines and direction points if the selected segment is curved. Direction points appear as filled circles, selected anchor points as filled squares, and unselected anchor points as hollow squares.

When selected this gives rise to the following options:

To select a path or vector object:

1. Select the path name in the Paths palette, or select the layer containing the vector object in the Layers palette.
2. Do one of the following:

   To select the entire path or subpath, select the path component selection tool (icon), and click anywhere inside the path. If the path consists of several subpaths, only the subpath under the pointer is selected.

   To display the bounding box along with the selected path, select Show Bounding Box in the options bar.

   To select a segment of the path, select the direct selection tool, and click one of the segment's anchor points or drag a marquee over part of the segment.

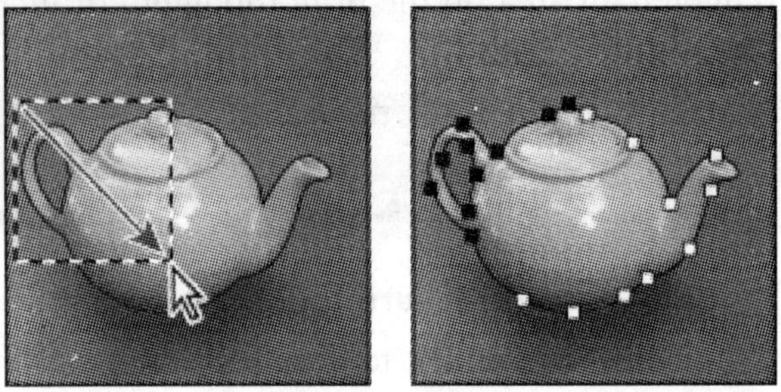

Marquee-drag to select segments.

   Marquee-drag to select segments. When the direct selection tool is selected, you can select the entire path or subpath by holding down Alt and clicking inside the path.
3. To add selections, select the path component selection tool or the direct selection tool, then hold down Shift while selecting additional paths or segments. To activate the direct selection tool when any other tool is selected, position the pointer over an anchor point, and press Ctrl .

To add, subtract, restrict, or invert the filled areas in selections:

1. Using the path component selection tool, choose one of the following options in the options bar, then drag a marquee to select existing path areas.

   Add to Path Area adds the area in the new selection. Subtract from Path Area removes the overlapping area in a new selection from the existing path selection. Restrict Path Area, restricts the area to the overlapped range of the new selection and the existing path selection. Invert Path Area, inverts the overlap area of the new path selection within the new selection.

Type Tool

You can insert new text, change existing text, and delete text in type layers.

When selected this tool gives rise to the following options:

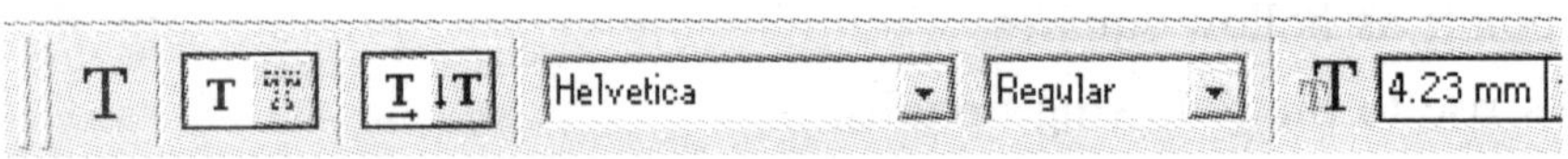

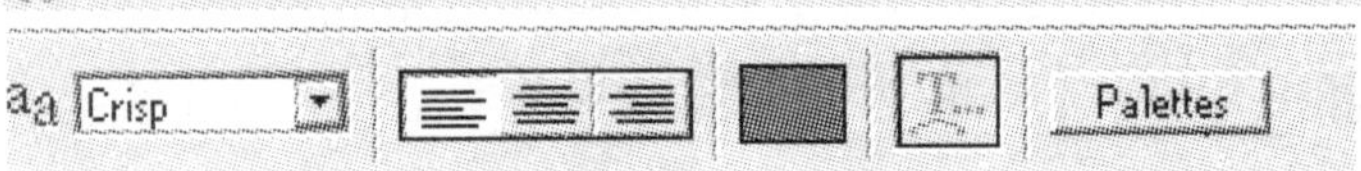

To edit text in a type layer:

1. Select the type tool.

2. Select the type layer in the Layers palette or click in the text to automatically select a type layer.
3. Position the cursor in the text and do one of the following:

   Click to set the insertion point. Select one or more characters you want to edit.
4. Enter text as desired.
5. Commit the changes to the type layer.

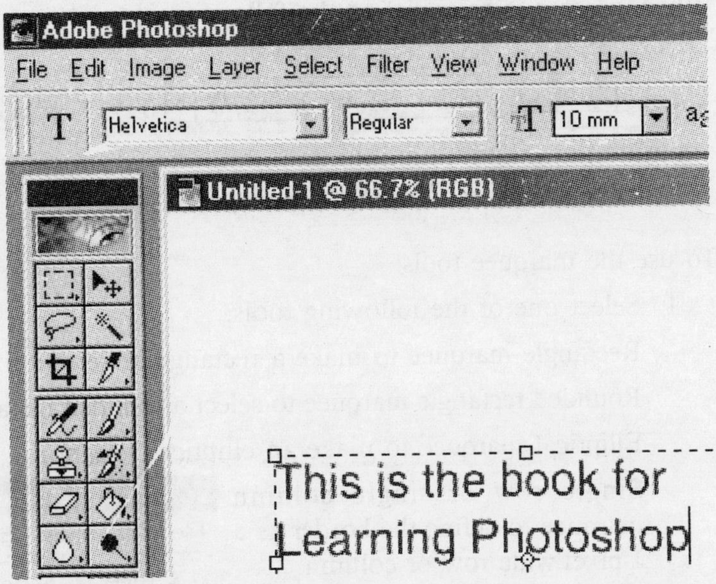

Pen Tool

The Info palette displays information about the color values beneath the pointer and, depending on the tool in use, other useful measurements.

It is used to draw various curvical lines on the screen.

Various shown by the tool when selected are:

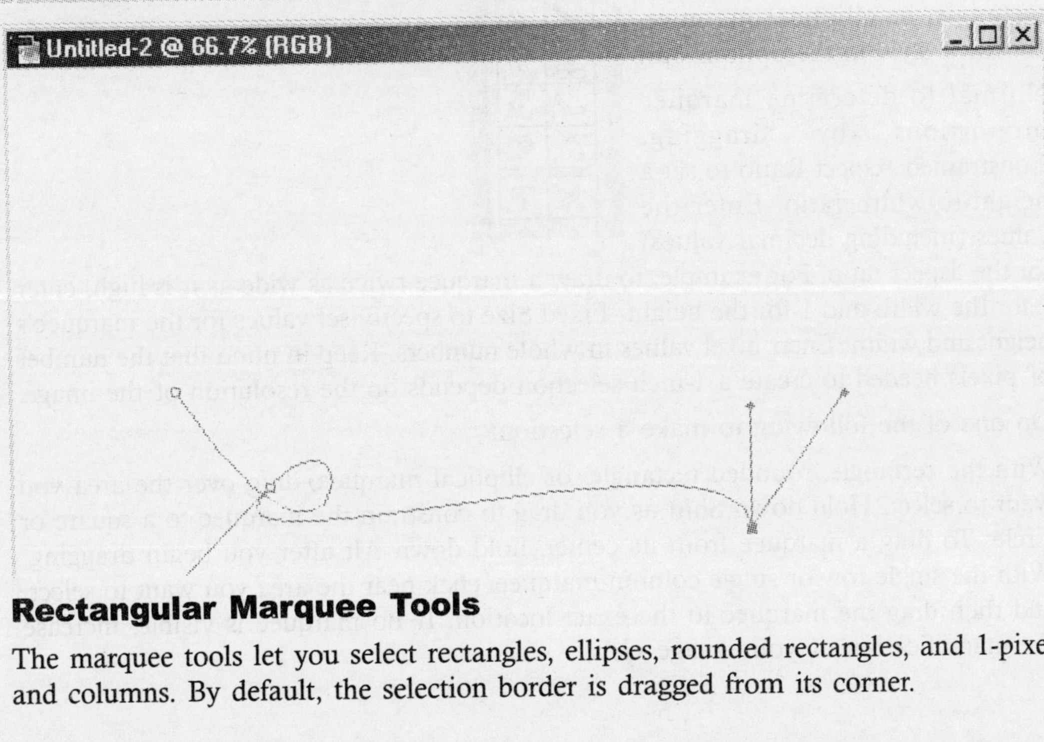

Rectangular Marquee Tools

The marquee tools let you select rectangles, ellipses, rounded rectangles, and 1-pixel rows and columns. By default, the selection border is dragged from its corner.

When selected it gives rise to the following options.

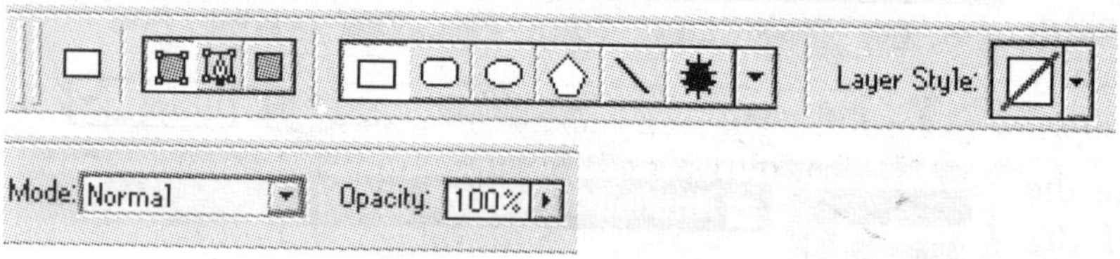

To use the marquee tools:

1. Select one of the following tools:

   Rectangle marquee to make a rectangular selection.

   Rounded rectangle marquee to select a rounded rectangle such as a Web-page button.

   Elliptical marquee to make an elliptical selection.

   Single row or single column marquee to define the border as a 1-pixel-wide row or column.

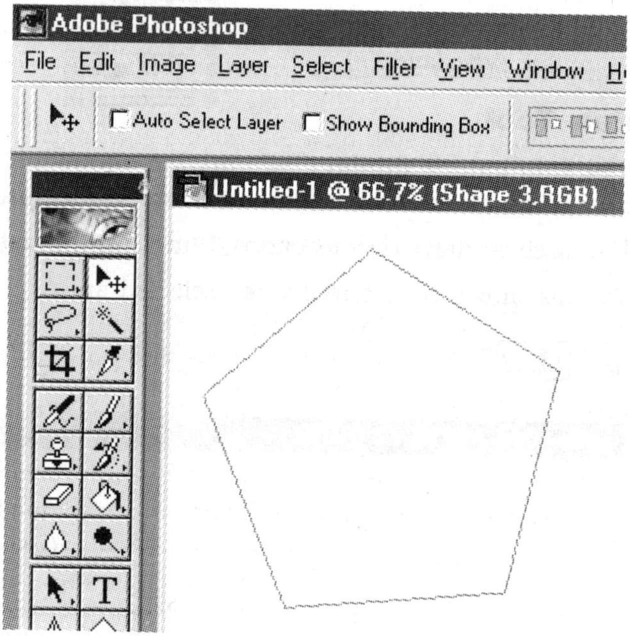

2. In the options bar, specify a selection option.
3. In the options bar, specify a feathering setting. Turn anti-aliasing on or off for the rounded rectangle or elliptical marquee.
4. For the rectangle, rounded rectangle, or elliptical marquee, choose a style in the options bar:

   Normal to determine marquee proportions by dragging. Constrained Aspect Ratio to set a height-to-width ratio. Enter the values (including decimal values) for the aspect ratio. For example, to draw a marquee twice as wide as it is high, enter 2 for the width and 1 for the height. Fixed Size to specify set values for the marquee's height and width. Enter pixel values in whole numbers. Keep in mind that the number of pixels needed to create a 1-inch selection depends on the resolution of the image.
5. Do one of the following to make a selection:

   With the rectangle, rounded rectangle, or elliptical marquee, drag over the area you want to select. Hold down Shift as you drag to constrain the marquee to a square or circle. To drag a marquee from its center, hold down Alt after you begin dragging. With the single row or single column marquee, click near the area you want to select, and then drag the marquee to the exact location. If no marquee is visible, increase the magnification of your image view.

Notes Tool

This tool is used to write notes on the image. This note is only visible and would not be printed while printing.

When selected this gives rise to the following options.

As is clear from above you can select font, colour, size, etc, for the note text from here.

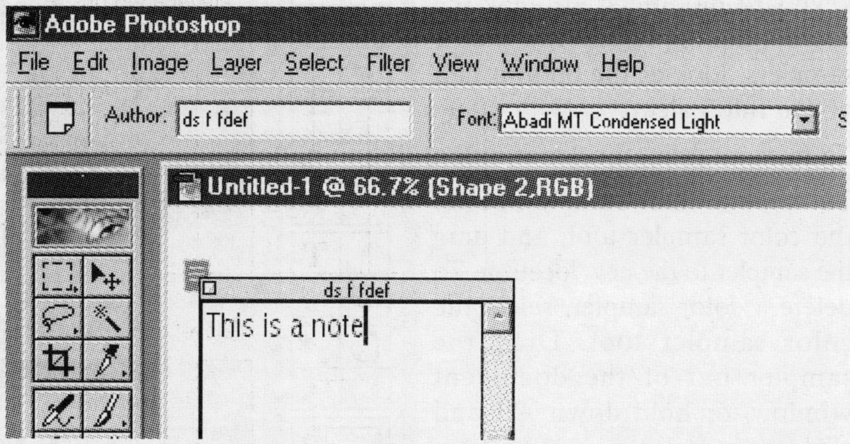

Eyedropper Tool

You can view the color of a single area using the eyedropper tool, or you can use up to four color samplers to display color information for one or more locations in the image. These samplers are saved in the image, so you can refer to them repeatedly as you work, even if you close and reopen the image.

When selected it gives rise to the following options.

To use the Info palette and the eyedropper or color sampler tool to see color values:

1. Choose Window > Show Info to open the Info palette.
2. Select the eyedropper tool or color sampler tool, and choose what to sample from the pop-up menu in the eyedropper or color sampler tool options:

   Point Sample to read the value of a single pixel. 3 by 3 Average to read the average value of a 3-by-3 pixel area. 5 by 5 Average to read the average value of a 5-by-5 pixel area.
3. If you selected the color sampler tool, place up to four color samplers on the image. Click where you want to place a sampler.
4. Open a color adjustment dialog box.
5. Make your adjustments in the dialog box, and before applying them, view the before and after color values in the Info palette:

To view color values using the eyedropper tool, move the pointer over the area of the image you want to examine. Opening a color adjustment dialog box activates the eyedropper tool outside the dialog box. You still have access to the scroll controls and to the hand and zoom tools when using keyboard modifiers. To view the color values under the color samplers, look at the bottom half of the Info palette.

To move or delete a color sampler:

To move a color sampler, select the color sampler tool, and drag the sampler to the new location. To delete a color sampler, select the color sampler tool. Drag the sampler out of the document window, or hold down Alt and click the sampler.

To change the display of color sampler information in the Info palette:

To display or hide color sampler information in the Info palette, choose Show Color Samplers or Hide Color Samplers from the palette menu. To change the color space in which a color sampler displays values, move the pointer onto the color sampler icon in the Info palette, hold down the mouse button, and choose another color space from the menu.

To use the eyedropper tool and Color palette to see color values:

1. Choose Window > Show Color to open the Color palette.
2. Open a color adjustment dialog box. This activates the eyedropper tool outside the dialog box.
3. Click the pixel you want to check in the image.
4. Make the adjustments in the dialog box, and before applying them, view the adjusted color values in the Color palette.

Hand Tool

This tool is used if the entire image is not visible in the document window, you can navigate to bring another area of the image into view. In Photoshop, you can also use the Navigator palette to quickly change the view of an image.

When selected this gives the following options:

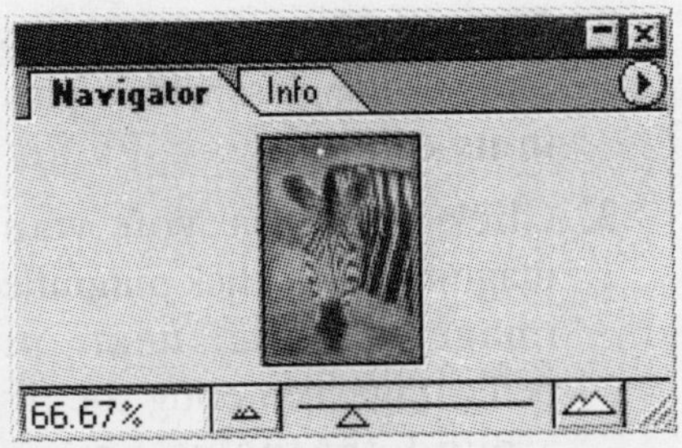

To view another area of an image:

Do one of the following:

1. Use the window scroll bars. Select the hand tool and drag to pan over the image.

To use the hand tool while another tool is selected, hold down the spacebar as you drag in the image.

To move the view of an image using the Navigator palette (Photoshop):

1. Choose Window > Show Navigator.
2. Do one of the following:

   Drag the view box in the thumbnail of the image, which represents the boundaries of the image window. Click in the thumbnail of the image. The new view includes the area you click.

To change the color of the Navigator palette view box:

1. Choose Palette Options from the Navigator palette menu.
2. Choose a color:

   To use a preset color, choose an option for Color. To specify a different color, click the color box, and choose a color as described in Using the Adobe Color Picker.

3. Click OK.

Zoom Tool

You can magnify or reduce your view using various methods. The window's title bar displays the zoom percentage (unless the window is too small for the display to fit), as does the status bar at the bottom of the window.

The options of the tool are:

The 100% view of an image displays an image as it will appear in a browser (based on the monitor resolution and the image resolution).

To zoom in, do one of the following:

1. Select the zoom tool.

2. The pointer becomes a magnifying glass with a plus sign in its center.
3. Click the area you want to magnify. Each click magnifies the image to the next preset percentage, centering the display around the point you click. When the image has reached its maximum magnification level of 6400%, the magnifying glass appears empty.
4. Choose View > Zoom In to magnify to the next preset percentage. When the image has reached its maximum magnification level, the command is dimmed.
5. Enter a magnification level in the Zoom text box at the lower left of the window.

To zoom out, do one of the following:

1. Select the zoom tool.
2. Hold down Alt to activate the zoom-out tool.
3. The pointer becomes a magnifying glass with a minus sign in its center.
4. Click the center of the area of the image you want to reduce. Each click reduces the view to the previous preset percentage. When the file has reached its maximum reduction level of 3.13%, the magnifying glass appears empty.
5. Choose View > Zoom Out to reduce to the previous preset percentage. When the image reaches its maximum reduction level, the command is dimmed. Enter a reduction level in the Zoom text box at the lower left of the window.

To magnify by dragging:

1. Select the zoom tool.
2. Drag over the part of the image you want to magnify.

   The area inside the zoom marquee is displayed at the highest possible magnification. To move the marquee around the artwork in Photoshop, begin dragging a marquee and then hold down the space bar while dragging the marquee to a new location.

To display an image at 100%, do one of the following:

1. Double-click the zoom tool.

2. Choose View > Actual Pixels.

To change the view to fit the screen, do one of the following:

1. Double-click the hand tool.
2. Choose View > Fit on Screen.

These options scale both the view and the window size to fit the available screen space. If the image is smaller than the monitor size, the image is displayed at 100%.

To automatically resize the window when magnifying or reducing the view:

With the Zoom tool active, select Resize Windows to Fit in the options bar. The window resizes when you magnify or reduce the view of the image.

When Resize Windows to Fit is deselected (the default), ImageReady maintains a constant window size regardless of the image's magnification. This can be helpful when using smaller monitors or working with tiled views.

Healing Brush Tool

Photoshop 7 has a new tool called Healing Brush Tool. This tool lets you correct imperfections, causing them to disappear into the surrounding image. Like the cloning tools, you use the healing brush tool to paint with sampled pixels from an image or pattern. However, the healing brush tool also matches the texture, lighting, and shading of the sampled pixels to the source pixels. As a result, the repaired pixels blend seamlessly into the rest of the image.

To use the healing brush tool:

1. Select the healing brush tool.
2. Click the brush sample in the options bar and set brush options in the pop-up palette:
3. If you're using a pressure-sensitive digitizing tablet, choose an option from the Size menu to vary the size of the healing brush over the course of a stroke. Choose Pen Pressure to base the variation on the pen pressure. Choose Stylus Wheel to base the variation on the position of the pen thumbwheel. Choose Off to not vary the size.

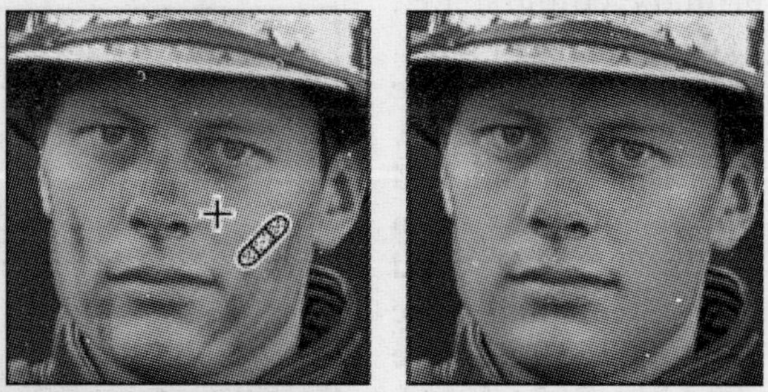

4. Choose a blending mode from the Mode pop-up menu in the options bar:
5. Choose Replace to preserve noise, film grain, and texture at the edges of the brush stroke.

Determine how you want to align the sampled pixels:

1. If you select Aligned in the options bar, you can release the mouse button without losing the current sampling point. As a result, the sampled pixels are applied continuously, no matter how many times you stop and resume painting.

2. If you deselect Aligned in the options bar, the sampled pixels are applied from the initial sampling point each time you stop and resume painting.

For the healing brush tool in sampling mode, set the sampling point by positioning the pointer in any open image and Alt-clicking (Windows).

Drag in the image.

The sampled pixels are melded with the existing pixels each time you release the mouse button. Look in the status bar to view the status of the melding process.

If there is a strong contrast at the edges of the area you want to heal, make a selection before you use the healing brush tool. The selection should be bigger than the area you want to heal but precisely follow the boundary of contrasting pixels. When you paint with the healing brush tool, the selection will prevent colors from bleeding in from the outside.

Understanding Colours

Colours are everywhere around us. But, how does one colour differ from another. There are a number of colour libraries and each one of them have different shades. There is so much to colours that it may need one book to study each one of them. Let us concentrate on what is available under Photoshop.

We would be talking about 4 different type of colour modes:

RGB (Red, Green and Blue) CYMK (Cyan, Yellow, Magenta and Black)

HSB (Hue, Saturation and Brightness) CIE Lab

Let us study them one by one.

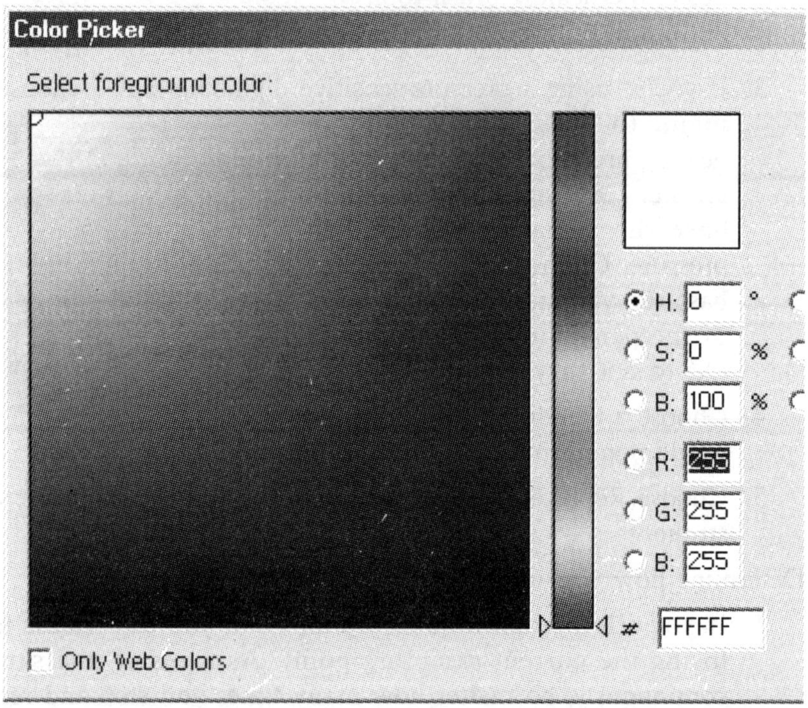

RGB Model

This is made up of three primary colours, i.e., Red, Green and Blue. Most of the colours are the mixture of all these. For example a pure Red will be 255, maximum for a colour, of Red and 0 of Green and Blue each. While the White would be 255 of each and Black would be 0 of each.

CYMK Model

As said earlier CYMK stands for Cyan, Yellow, Magenta and Black.

These 4 also make a set of combinations to form different colours. Here you have to add them according to percentages of each one of them. This set of colours are used by the high-end laser printers and are mostly used by commercial printers.

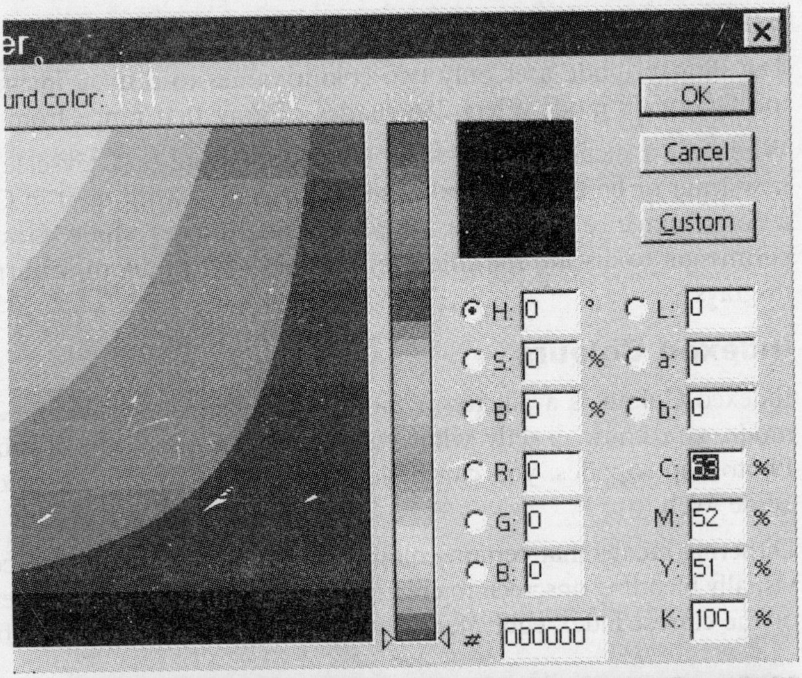

HSB Model

This is another colour combination where H stands for Hue, S for Saturation and B for Brightness. Here Hue is the basic colour from the colour wheel, which is expressed in terms of degrees from 0 to 360. It represents the position of the colour on the colour wheel.

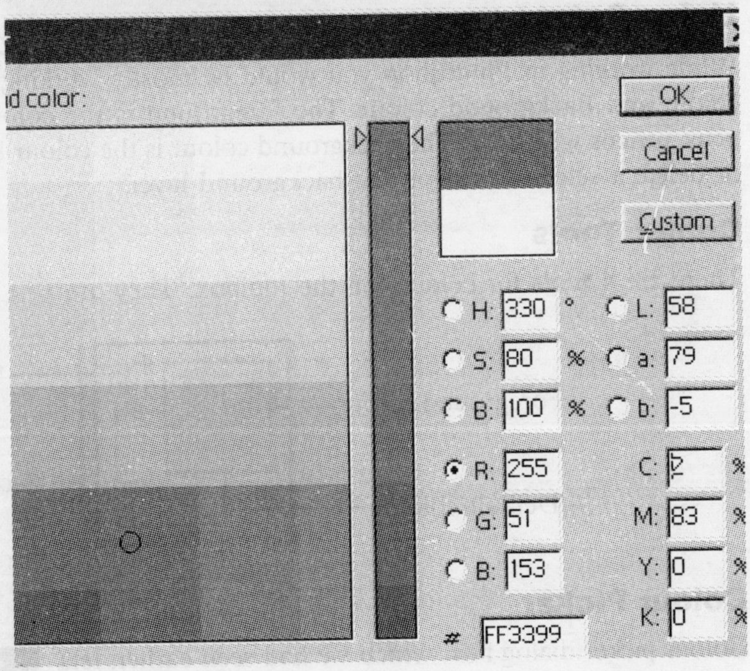

Saturation is the strength of the colour. It is measured in percentage of colour minus the amount of gray in it. Brightness is also measured in terms of percentage. It varies from 0 where it is black and to 100 where it is white.

CIE Lab

Photoshop uses the CIE mode, because its gamut is so broad, to convert from one colour model to another.

Working Models

You would be working in RGB modes mostly in Photoshop. The difference between modes and models is simple. The models are methods of defining colour. Modes are methods of working with colour based on the models. There are modes for black and white too like, Grayscale and Limited Colour work.

Bitmap and Grayscale Mode

The Bitmap mode uses only two colour values to display images—black and white, while the Grayscale mode offers 256 shades of gray that range from white to black.

Whenever a picture is printed in black and white or Grayscale, for instance, as part of a newsletter or brochure, it makes sense for you to work on it in Grayscale mode. To convert a color image to Grayscale, simply choose Image; Mode, Grayscale. You will asked for permission to discard the colour information. Click Ok to confirm, and picture is converted to grays.

Indexed Colours

Indexed Colour is a palette or rather a collection of palettes—256 to be exact. With this mode, you know exactly what you are getting, and you do not like any of the palettes Photoshop supplies, you can build your own. This type of colours are perfect for World Wide Web.

Dithering means that certain colours are combined, that is, adjacent pixels are interspersed, visually blending onscreen to create a new colour although they retain their original colour—or the closest index equivalent—when viewed at a large magnification.

Using Paints

While working in Photoshop you would be mostly working with two colours: Foreground colour and Background colour. The foreground is the colour where all your brushes and pens, pencils will work. The background colour is the colour Photoshop uses when you erase or delete a selected area on the background layer.

Colour Tools

There are 4 tools for colours on the toolbox. They are:

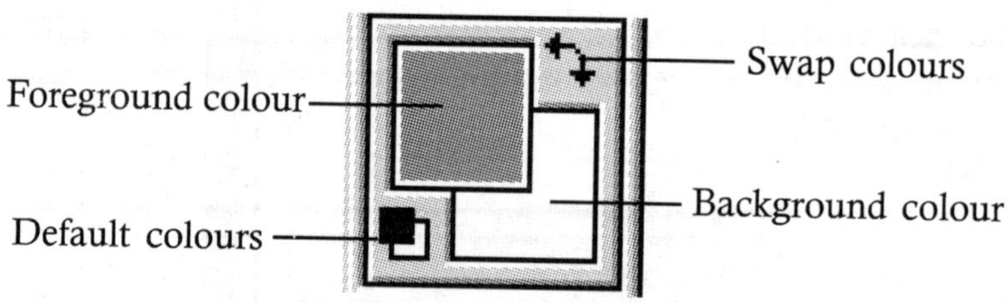

Colour Picker

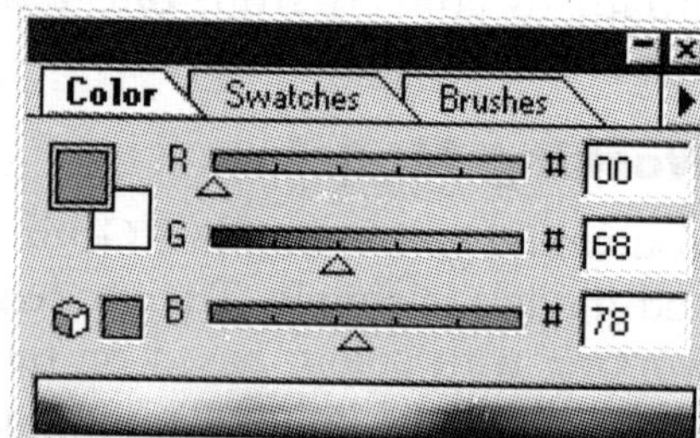

Colour picker dialog box, which we had seen earlier, lets you select a foreground or background colour in any of several ways. You can click the colour spectrum to select a colour, or drag the triangle up or down if you had rather do that.

A colour is usually a mixture of few colours. You add some Red, some Blue and maybe some Yellow and Black to make certain colour. There is no rule governing this. You can mix any quantity of any colour and make the colour which suits you.

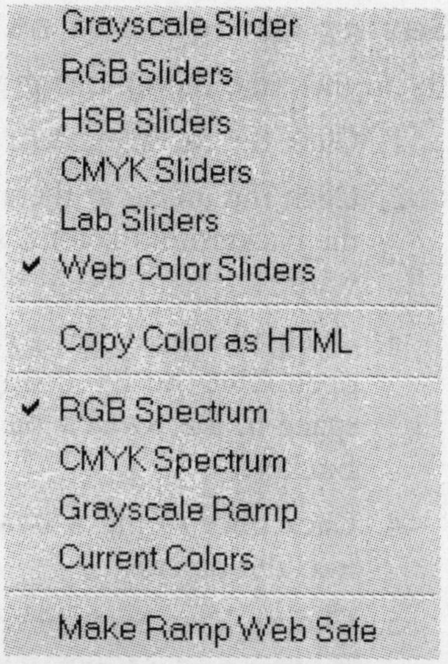

The Colour Palette

It is not that you have to work with Colour Picker only. You have Palettes too, which are as good but not that much detailed. You can leave it open on the desktop, so you can change colours without having to go through all the fuss of clicking a swatch in the toolbox, finding the colour, and then Ok your choice.

The menu also allows you to reset the colour bar at the bottom of the Palette window, according to the colour model with which you are working. By clicking at the right button on the right top of the palette. If you click Make Ramp Web Safe, the only colours displayed on the colour bar will be the 216 colours that all current Web browsers can display.

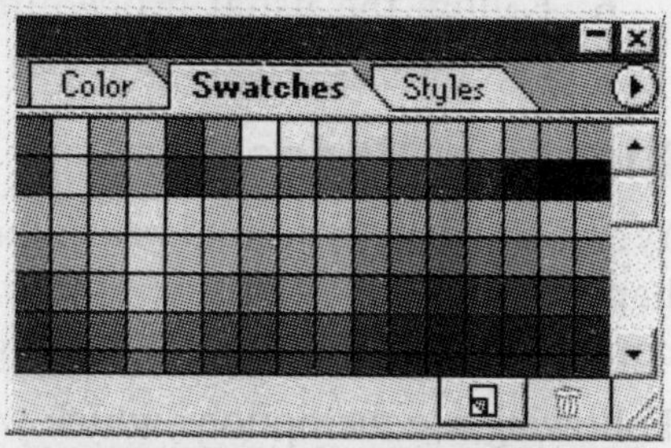

The Swatches Palette

The Swatch palette works like a box of watercolours of a child, on the screen. You simply dip your brush in any colour and start painting with it. To choose a foreground colour, simply click the one you want. To choose a background colour, press Option + click to select the colour you want to use.

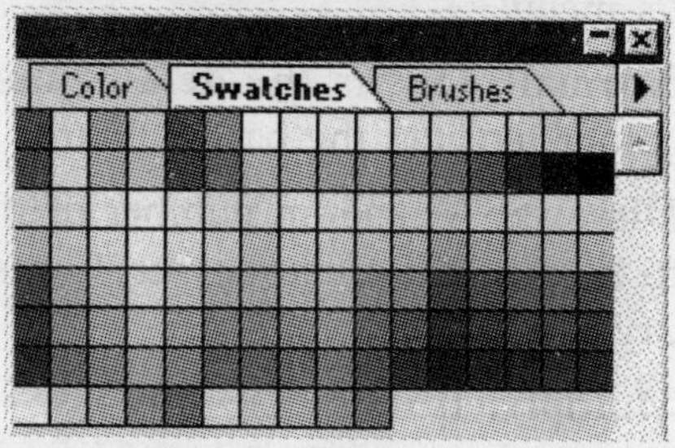

Adding New Colours

For adding a new colour to the palette, you do the following:

1. Click the foreground colour swatch in the toolbox.
2. Use the Colour Picker to select the desired colour and click Ok.
3. Open the Swatches palette.
4. Using the tab in the lower-right corner of the Swatches palette, drag the window out so that it resembles the one shown here.
5. Move your cursor into the space below the existing swatches. It changes into the Paint Bucker tool.
6. Click and the new colour is added.
7. If you press Shift, you can add the new colour anywhere you like, replacing whatever swatch you click.

Saving Foreground as a Swatch

To do this take the following steps:

1. Click the foreground or background colour with the Eyedropper tool.
2. Click the image at the spot where you want to capture the colour. If you are saving the background colour, Alt + click the colour you want.

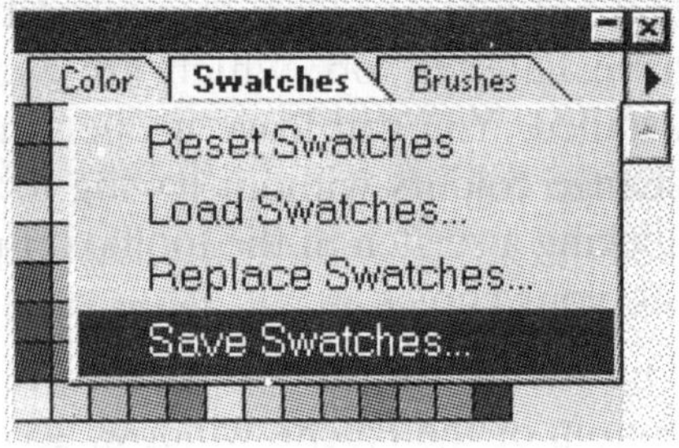

3. Open the Swatches palette, if it is not already open. Put the Eyedropper on any empty (gray) space in the Swatch palette. It turns into a Paint Bucket.
4. Click once to put a swatch of the selected colour into the palette.
5. Choose Save Swatches from the palette's pull-out menu.
6. Follow the usual procedure to name your Swatch file, and save it in Photoshop Goodies or whatever folder is convenient for you.

Blending Modes

When you place a second brush full of paint over one that has already there, different things happen, depending on the colour of the paint you are applying. In Photoshop, you can control all these factors by applying what is called Blending modes.

Following are the options which you can choose from the various paintbrush options under its menu.

Normal: This is the default mode. The blend colour replaces the base colour.

Dissolve: A random number of pixels is changed to become the blend colour. Gives a splattered or dry brush effect.

Multiply: It multiplies the base colour by blend colour, giving you a darker colour. The effect is like drawing over the picture with a magic marker.

Behind: Works only on transparent parts of a layer. You appear to be painting on the back of a sheet.

Screen: It multiplies the base colour by the inverse of the blend colour, giving you a lighter colour. The effect is like painting with bleach.

Overlay: Either multiplies or screen, depending on the base colour. Preserves the highlights and shadows of the base colour.

Hard light: Multiplies or screens the colours, depending on the blend colour. The effect is similar to shining a harsh spotlight on the image.

Soft light: Darkness or lightness depending on the blend colour. The effect is said to be similar to shining a diffused spotlight on the image. With a light blend color, it has very little effect.

Darken: Evaluates the colour information in each channel and assigns either the base colour or the blend colour, whichever is darker, as the result colour. Lighter pixels are replaced, but darker ones do not change.

Color Dodge: Brightens the base colour to reflect the blend colour.

Color Burn: Darkens the base colour to reflect the blend colour.

Lighten: Evaluates the colour information in each channel and assigns either the base colour or the blend colour, whichever is lighter, as the result colour. Darker pixels are replaced, but lighter ones do not change. This is the exact opposite of Darken.

Exclusion: Similar to the Difference mode, but with a softer effect.

Difference: Compares the brightness values in base and blend, and subtracts the lighter from the brighter.

Hue: Gives you a result combining the luminance and saturation of the base colour and the hue of the blend colour.

Saturation: It gives you a colour with the luminance and hue of the base colour and the saturation of the blend colour. Unless you reduce the saturation of the blend colour significantly, nothing shows.

Colour: Retains the luminance of the base colour with the hue and saturation of the blend colour. Useful for colouring monochrome images as it retains the gray levels.

Luminosity: Gives a result colour with the hue and saturation of the base colour and the luminance of the blend colour. Opposite effect to Colour Blend mode.

Smudges

When you blend two or more colours, it is called Smudging. You can do this in more than one way. The smudge tool looks like a finger. It is in the same toolbox compartment with the Blur and Sharpen tools. The Smudge tool picks up colour from wherever you start to drag it and moves it in the direction in which you drag.

Following are the smudges at 100%, 50% and 25%.

You can set the smudge options from the Smudge Tool Options dialog box.

The Blending modes are on a pull-down menu. This tool does not give all the Blending mode options but you can choose, aside from Normal, as shown here, Darken, Lighten, Hue, Saturation, Colour, or Luminosity. Of these Darken and Lighten modes are mostly used.

Focus Tools

These tools are : Blur, Sharpen and Smudge. They can be used to touching up an image, fixing tiny flaws, and bringing items into sharper contrast.

The options in each of these tools can be changed from the various options available under each one of them, as shown below.

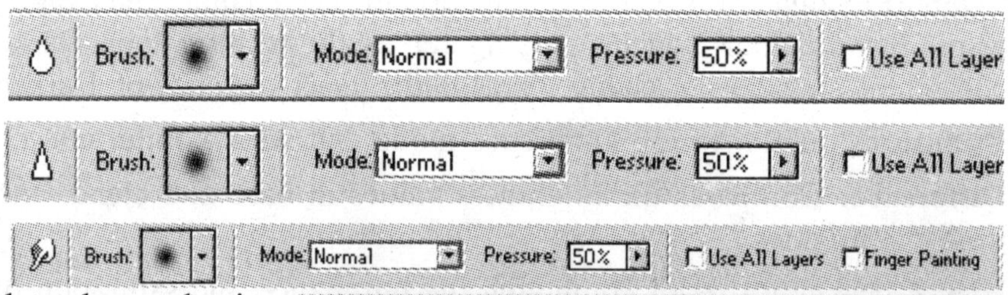

Sharpen tool can bring up the contrast to create the illusion of sharper focus, while Blur is most useful to rid the background of unwanted clutter and to de-emphasize parts of the picture that you do not want viewers to notice. Sharpening tool is the exact opposite of the Blur tool. Where the Blur tool softens pixel values, the Sharpen tool hardens them and brings them into greater relief by increasing the contrast between adjacent pixels. Sharpening is best done in very small doses. If you go over a section too much or have the pressure set too high, you can end up burning the color out of an image, which probably make it look worse than it did initially.

For doing this follow the following steps:

1. Click once on the Magnifying glass to zoom in on your picture to have the magnification around 200%.
2. Select the Blur tool. Choose a soft-edged brush shape from the Brush palette.
3. Double-click the Focus tools in the toolbox to open the Options palette.
4. Click the Options palette and type 5 to set the pressure to 50%.

5. Drag the Blur tool across the picture.
6. Switch to the Sharpen tool by pressing Shift+R. Choose a hard-edged brush. Drag it over a different part of the picture. Try to drag it along the edge of an object and note the effect.
7. Notice the Blur in first and second picture here.

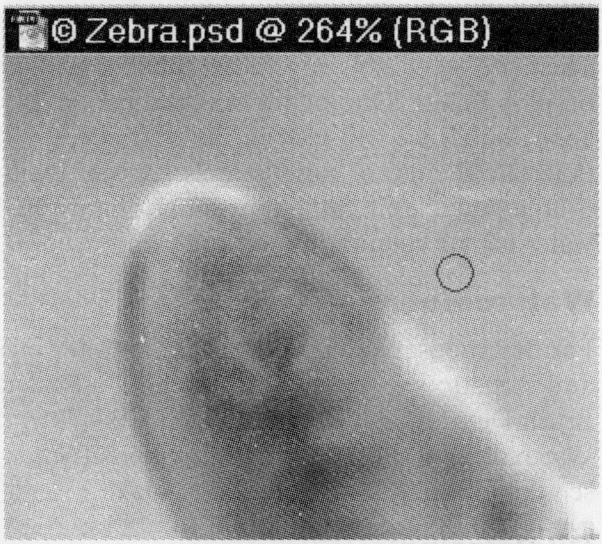

The Toning Tools

The Toning tools include the Dodge, Burn, and Sponge tools. Dodge and Burn are opposites, like Sharpen and Blur, but, instead of affecting the contrast between adjacent pixels, they either lighten or darken the area to which the tool is applied.

Dodge and Burn Tools

Dodging, is accomplished by waving a Dodge tool, usually a cardboard circle on a wire, between the projected image from the enlarger and the photographic paper. This blocks some of the light and makes the dodged area lighter when the print is developed. Burning has the opposite effect to dodging—instead of lightening a small area, it darkens the area. Here by blocking the enlarger light with your hand you can reach the area to be burned.

Inside the Tools Options palette you have the 3 choices:

Shadows

Midtones

Hightlights

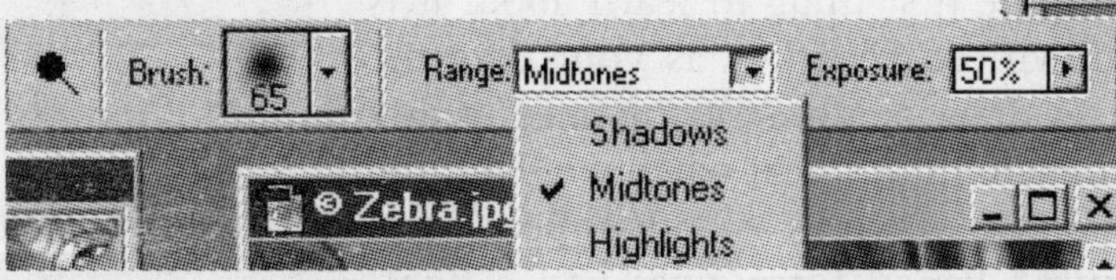

These options indicate the types of pixels that the tool will affect. If you want to adjust the shadows, such as making them lighter and leaving the lighter pixels untouched, select Shadows. The default option for the Dodge is Midtones. Select the highlights when you want to lighten already light-coloured areas, leaving the darker areas untouched.

Sponge Tools

It is also a darkroom feature. When a picture in the developing tray is not turning dark enough, or looks to be underexposed or weak in colour, the darkroom technician can often save it by sloshing some fresh, full-strength developing chemical on a sponge and rubbing it directly on the wet paint in the tray. On a colour image, it sublety increases the colour saturation in the area to which you apply it. On a grayscale image, it increases or decreases contrast by moving the grayscale level away from or toward mildly gray.

Different Media

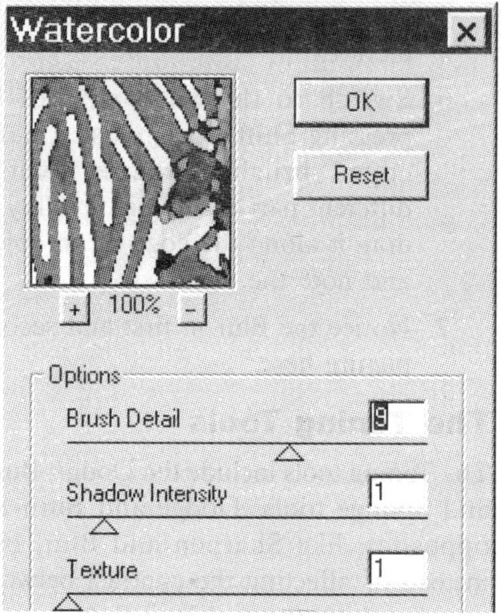

There are other tools which can enhance the looks of your image. One of them is the use of filter, about which we will read in the next chapter, the other are the use of various tools. One of them is Watercolour. You can change any picture to its water colour counterpart.

Watercolour

For this choose Watercolour from the Filter menu and Artistic submenu. You can also adjust the Brush Detail, Shadow intensity and Texture in the Watercolour dialog box. In the thumbnail you can see the effect of the changes you make.

Oil Painting

All of us know the difference between watercolour and oil colours. The base is water in first whereas it is oil in the second. For this we select the option of Underpainting from the Artistic submenu in the Filter menu. In the dialog box, select the options shown here. You can however, differ with me and choose different options and click Ok to see the effect. Underpainting actually builds the foundation of the main painting.

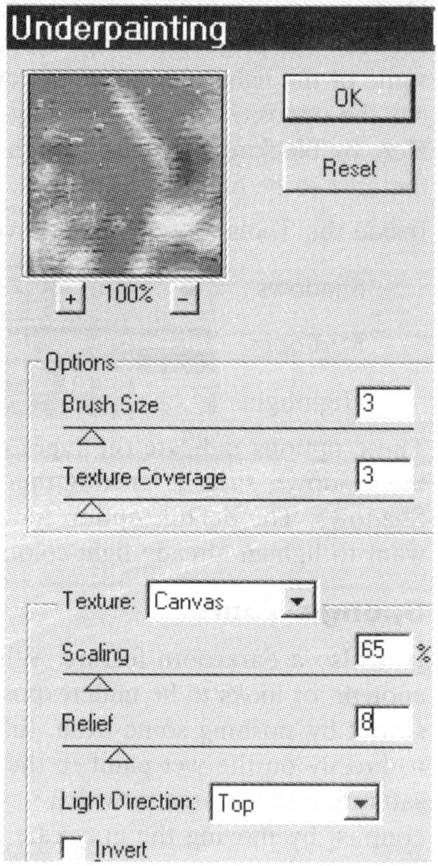

Pencil Filters

The Pencil tool has been part of every graphics program the very first ones. The first thing to learn about it is that by holding down the Shift key as your drag the pencil tool you can draw neatly straight lines at any degree. Another thing to note is that when you have the Auto Eraser function On, it works as both as pencil and eraser. The Coloured Pencil filter gives you a light, somewhat more stylized drawing from your original image. The crosshatch filter, applied to the some image retains much more of the colour and details but still looks like a pen-and-ink drawing.

Chalk and Charcoal Filters

Since early ages Chalk and Charcoal have been used to make drawings. The same has been incorporated in Photoshop too. When you apply the Chalk and Charcoal filter, which is found on the Filter menu, you will see that it reduces your pictures to three colours, using a dark gray plus the foreground and background colours that you have set in the tool window. Chalk uses the background colour and Charcoal becomes the foreground colour.

The Chalk and Charcoal dialog box has options for both Chalk and Charcoal area as well as the Stroke Pressure option. Stroke option varies from 0 to 5 whereas the others vary from 0 to 20.

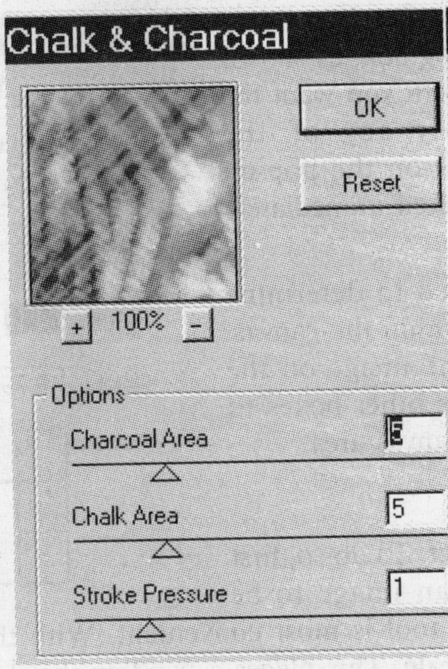

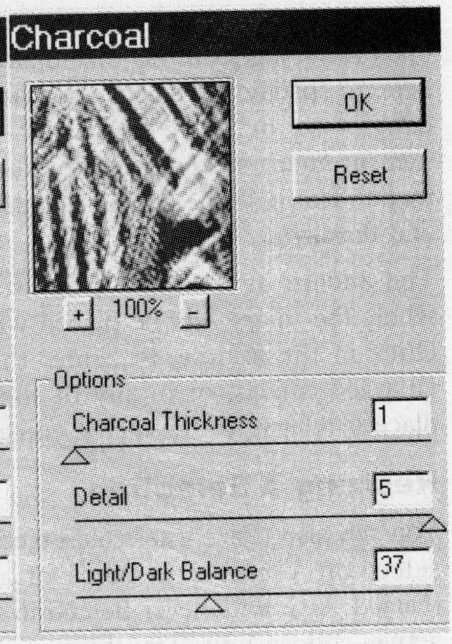

Image Handling

There will be times when you need to make an object bigger or smaller as you copy it from one picture to another. You may need to straighten a titled horizon, or even stand something upright. You may even need to make someone face left instead of him facing right.

Resizing an Image

For this we use the Image Size dialog box, as shown here. You can see the pixel dimensions in pixels or percentages. You can also see the image print size in inches, centimeters, points, picas, or columns; percentage can also be found using the pop-up menus.

When the dialog box is first opened, all the settings are to the 100% of the image. You can change this percentage to enlarge or reduce the image. But, the easiest way to do it to take the help of Constrain Properties.

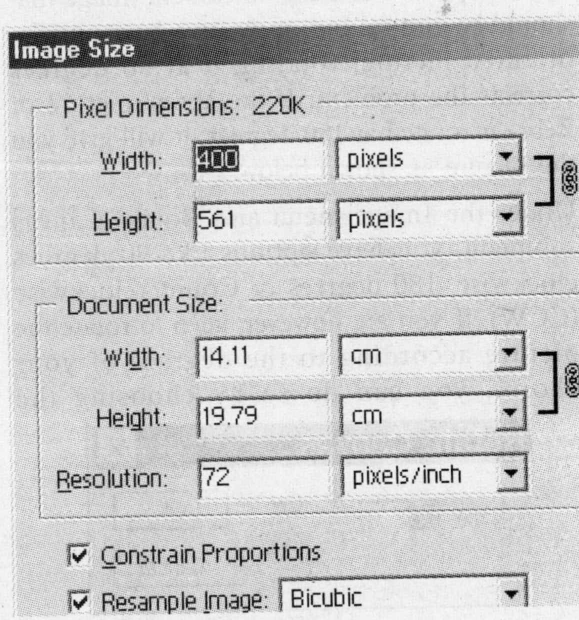

Resizing a Canvas

Resizing the canvas larger gives you extra work space around the image, instead of changing the size of the image. It is so because resizing uses the current background colour to fill in the space, be

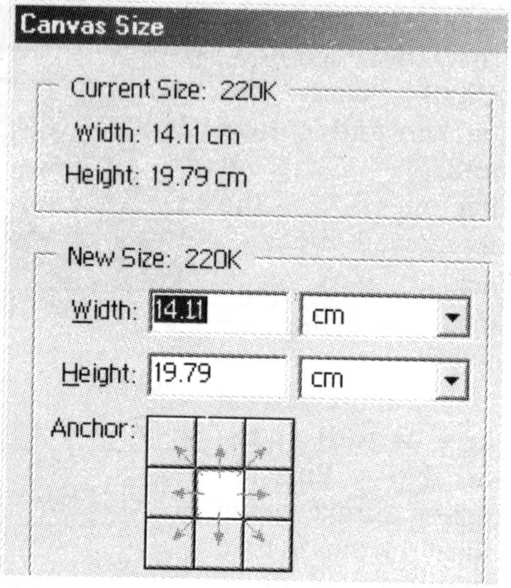

sure it is a colour you want. To resize the canvas, open the Image, Canvas Size dialog box, as shown here, to specify the height and width you want the canvas to be. You can specify any of the measurement systems you prefer on the pop-up menu. The new file size is calculated immediately and displayed.

The anchor at the bottom is used to determine where the image will be placed within the canvas. Click in the middle, to center the image on the enlarged canvas, or in any of the other boxes to place it relative to the increased canvas area.

Resizing a Selection

You can also resize a selected object. To do so, first select the object or a piece of an image to be resized. Use whichever Selection tool is most convenient. With the Selection Marquee active, choose Edit, Transform, Scale. This places a window that looks like the cropping window around your selected object. Drag on any of the corner handles on the box to change the size of the image while holding down the Shift key to maintain its proportions. If you drag on the side handles of the box, you will stretch the selection's height or width accordingly.

Rotating

There are many reasons why you might want to need to rotate an image. If you have a scanned picture or a digital camera image that should be vertical but opens as a horizontally-oriented picture, rotating it at 90 degrees corrects the problem. If the above picture of Zebra is rotated at 180 degrees, it will give you the picture as shown below.

Under the Image menu and Rotate Canvas submenu, you have options like 90 degrees clockwise, 180 degrees or Counterclockwise (CCW). If you are however, keen to rotate the picture according to the degrees of your choice, you can do so by choosing the

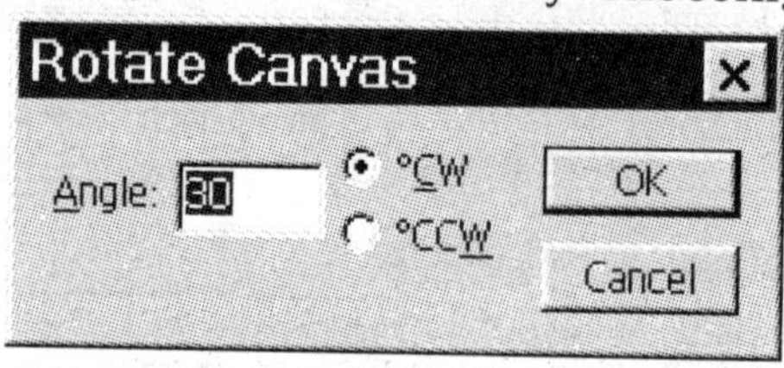

Arbitrary dialog box, also available under the same submenu. Result of this 30 degrees rotation can be seen on below.

Transforming Image Manually

This type of transformations is for those who consider themselves to be good at calculations. You have to do all the calculations and fill up the spaces according to your guess work and then click Ok.

For this you put the figures in the top row options of X and Y axis and then click Enter.

The image would be rotated according to your needs. However, if find that it is not what you wanted, just click Undo and Retry.

Using Layers and Masks

Layers are the various layers that you can create of the image or picture for the editing purposes and putting them one over the another for the final result. Masking is the method by which you can select a portion of the image or picture for editing and doing changes.

Layers

The Layers palette is where you control your layer. Be it be for creating, adding, deleting, hiding, and showing. The small versions of your images on the left of the palette are called thumbnails. Each of these small rectangles represent a separate layer.

If thumbnails are small for your liking, select the Palette Options to see more thumbnails.

Creating a New Layer

1. Using the Airbrush and your biggest brush shape, choose any light to medium colour and spray paint a large patch of colour on the canvas.

2. Look at the thumbnail called Background.
3. Click the small page icon at the bottom of the Layer palette. You have just added a layer.

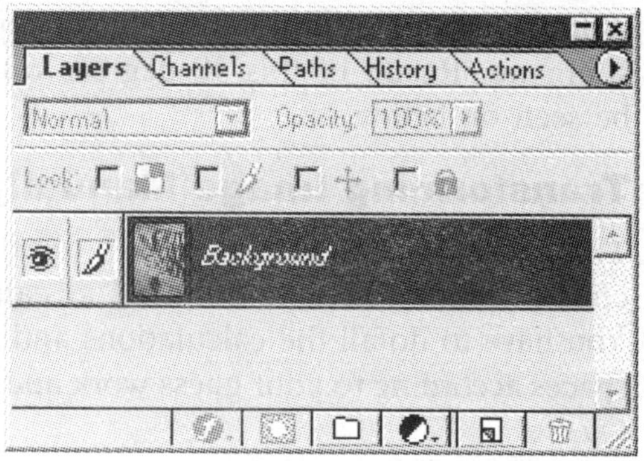

Another way of adding a new layer is by opening the menu on the right hand side of the dialog box and click at New Layer.

A new layer like above is added.

Hiding and Showing of Layers

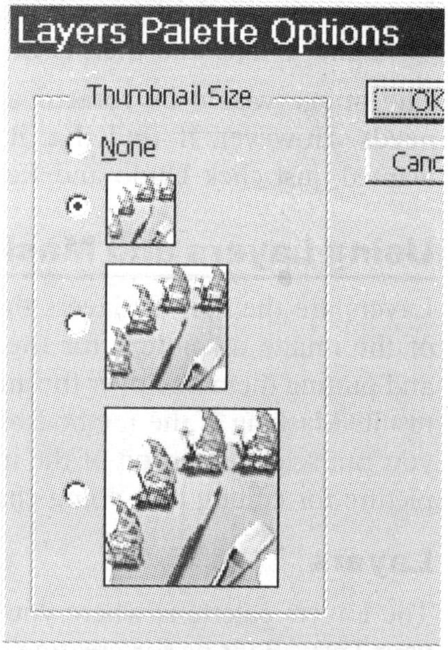

To the left of the thumbnails, you will notice small icons that resemble eyes. These indicate that a layer is visible. If you see the eye, you can see the layer. If you click the eye, however, the eye disappears and the layer becomes hidden.

In the following figure Layer 1 is hidden and the other one is shown.

Working with Multiple Layers

Whenever you are combining two or more images the elements you paste over the background image are added on separate layers. You can use the Layer palette to control precisely how these elements are combined. You can also control the Blending modes that affect how one layer appears on top of another, just as you could when painting over an image or background.

Merging Layers

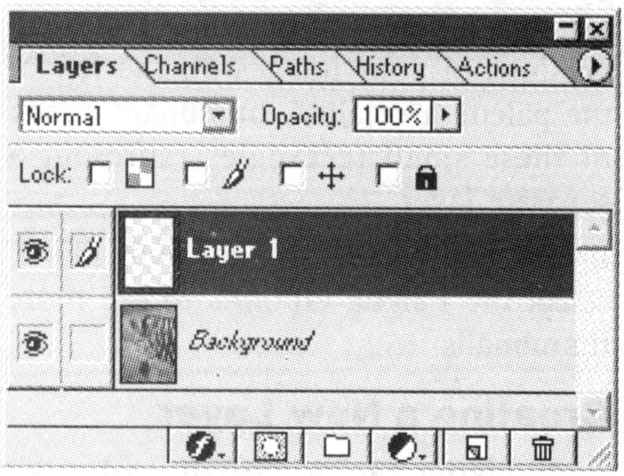

The more layers you add to an image, and more effect that you add to those layers, the larger your image file will become. There are two main factors here:

Merging — Merging groups of layers without flattening the entire image conserves memory space but still allows you to work on the layers that you have not yet finished. Merging Down merges a layer with the one directly below it. You also can merge just the visible layers choosing the appropriate Layer, Merge command.

Flattening — Flattening, on the other hand, compresses all visible layers down to one layer. Any layers that you have made invisible at the time of flattening are lost.

To flatten an image, simple choose Layer, Flatten Image, but make sure that you are done. At this point all the layers are reduced to one.

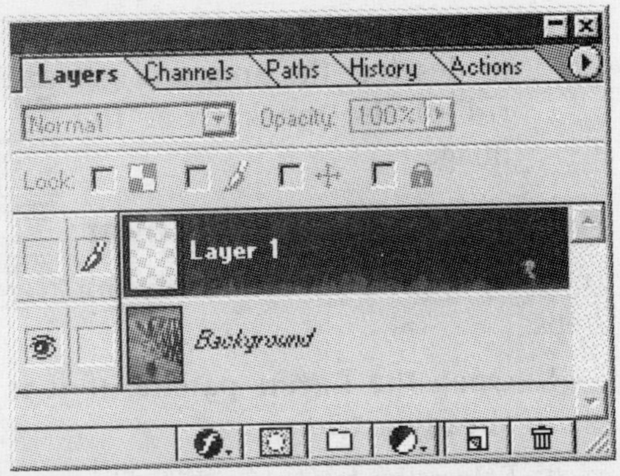

Layer Effects

A number of automated effects that you can apply to layers, shown on the next page, are available under Layer menu and Layer Style submenu. They include drop shadows, glows, beveling, and embossing, etc.

You can apply these and see the effects.

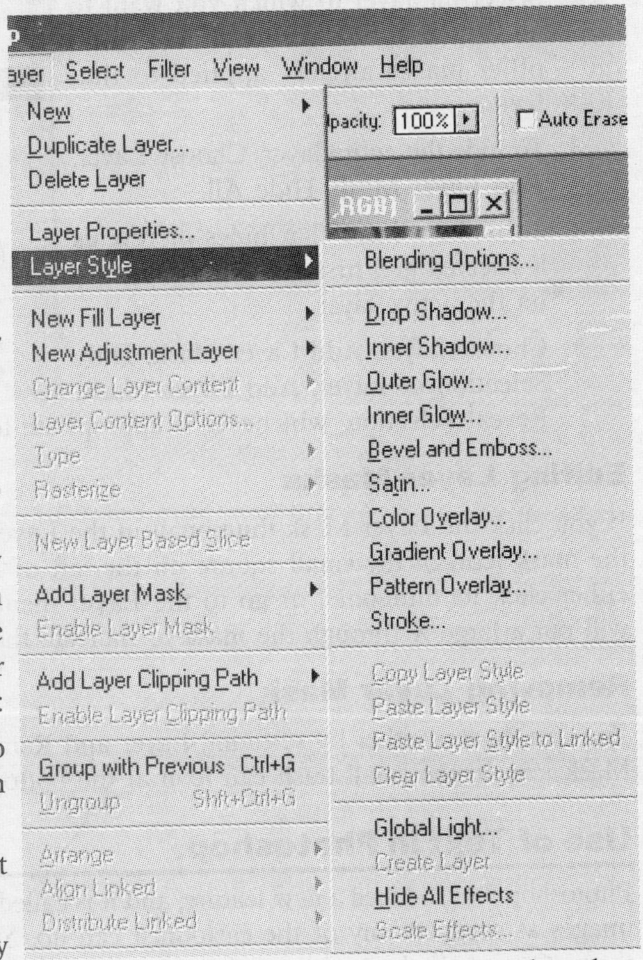

Masks

It is the selection that you make because it permits you to do something that affects only the selected area, effectively masking anything that is not selected. Masks can let you change one part of a picture without changing all of it.

Quick Mask

You can mask an image in Photoshop on your own using the Magic Wand. But, it also provides with a very easy method too. It is called Quick Mask. In this case you can see both the image and the mask at the same time. For creating a quick mask do the following:

1. You can use any selection tool to select a part of the image which you want to mask.
2. Click the Quick Mask button at the bottom of the toolbox.
3. You see a colour overlay indicating the mask on the protected area, which is to say, the area not selected.
4. If the mask needs editing, select an appropriate Paintbrush size and from the Brush palette and click the Paintbrush.
5. When the mask is edited to your satisfaction, click at the Standard Mode button to return to the original image.

6. You can now press Ctrl + D to deselect the area and get rid of the mask from the image.

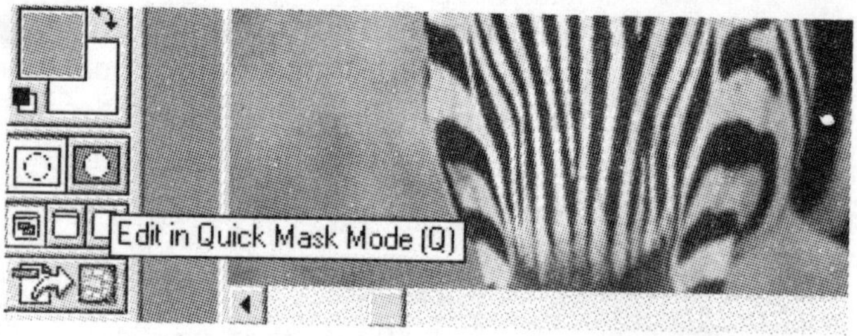

Adding Mask to the Layer

It can be done in the following steps:

1. Open the Layers palette, if it is not already active.
2. Select the layer to which you want to add a mask. Make sure there are no other masks already applied to that layer.
3. To hide the entire layer, Choose Layer, Add Layer Mask, Hide All.
4. To make a mask that hides or reveals a selected are, first make the selection on the active layer.
5. Choose Layer, Add Layer Mask, Hide Selection or Layer, Add Layer Mask, Reveal Selection, whichever is appropriate for your needs.

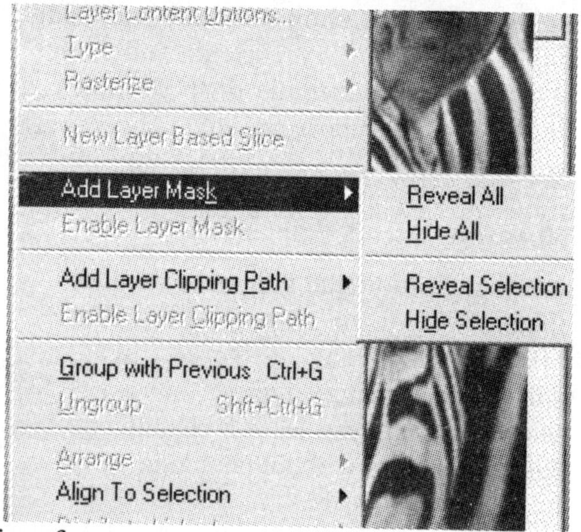

Editing Layer Masks

If you click the Layer Mask thumbnail in the Layers palette to make it active you will see the mask icon in the small square on the left of the layer thumbnail. To edit the layer, either click its thumbnail or go to the Layer menu and select Disable Layer Mask. This will put a large X through the mask to indicate that the mask is inactive.

Removing Layer Mask

You can do this either by selecting Layer and Remove Layer Mask or dragging the Layer Mask icon in the small trash can icon at the bottom of the window.

Use of Text in Photoshop

Photoshop 7 introduced a new feature, and it is called Liquify. This enables you to manipulate images as easily as any of the cartoonist can do. You can stretch, shrink, blend and wrap them. One of the best uses for this feature is to make distorted faces or caricatures.

For creating a cariature and you will need is a good picture of someone whom you know. The you can begin and use the Liquify tools in Photoshop 7 to distort the face in a fluid, painterly style. You will practive recommended movements for best results and you will learn how to protect or reconstruct parts of your image.

Manipulating Features

Instead of taking someone's photo and destroying it, I am taking a plain and simple Sunset image and distort it. You can then take your own photo and distort it. (You can even do with the photo of your teacher). The main tools that we would be using would be Bloat and Pucker.

1. Open the image Sunset.psd and choose Image/Liquify.
2. You remain in the Liquify environment for all these steps. Do not click OK until after you have completely finished with the distortions.

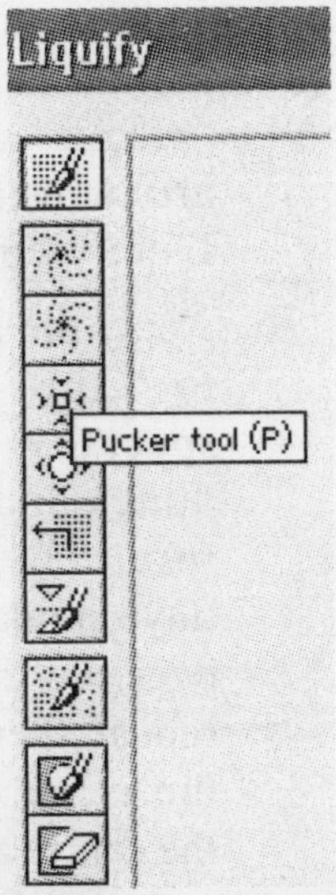

3. Select the Pucker tool and draw in a circular motion around the centre of the photo. This can be seen on the next page. For this use a Brush Size of about 60 pixels and Brush Pressure around 50%.
4. The Pucker tool makes an area smaller. For better control, use small circular movements with your styles (or mouse). This will help you reduce the area without distorting it in other ways. Change the brush Size or Brush Pressure in the Liquify dialog box as needed. Tablet users can enable the Stylus Pressure check box.
5. Liquify is not just a command, but an entire desktop environment with its own special toolbar and options. The Brush Size Pressure settings in the Tool Options section of the Liquify dialog box are completely independent of the size and pressure controls in the Photoshop options/ strip. You can use the bracket keys to alter brush size one pixel at a time (left bracket reduces brush size, right bracket increases it), but the numeric keys do not enable you to change pressure

(opacity). The hot spot for each Liquify tool is at the center of the brush. Therefore, you might want to use Preferences/Display and Cursors to make the brushes "precise" white you are working with Liquify effects.

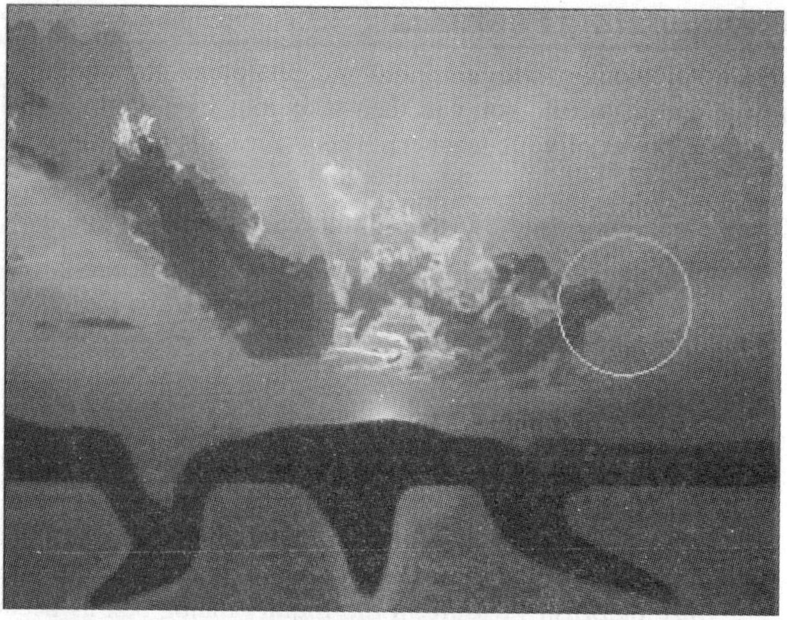

6. Apply the Bloat tool to the picture specially to the dunes and see the result. Begin with tiny circular strokes over the dunes and repeat them for all the other dunes in the centre and at the ends. Set Brush Size to about 40 pixels.
7. Enlarging the clouds first keep it from being obliterated when you bloat the center of the cloud. If the highlight on the cloud becomes too dominant, soften edges with short strokes from the Bloat tool, using very light pressure. This procedure works much more efficiently than dismissing the Liquify dialog box so that you can use the standard Blur tool.
8. Now select the Wrap tool and set the brush Size to around 80 pixels. Drag each corner of dune to the right and down. This effect can be seen on the next page
9. The brush should be large enough to spread pixels around the dunes realistically. Too small of a brush will create a thin line and too large of a brush will spread the distortion to other parts of the photo.

10. Continue using the Wrap tool, but enlarge the Brush Size to about 100 pixels. Pull all the dunes downwards creating more curves in the picture.
11. You can also pull the dunes both downwards and upwards. It is not enough to just change each feature by reducing or enlarging it. A good caricature also exaggerates the shape of the image and then creates a final effect.

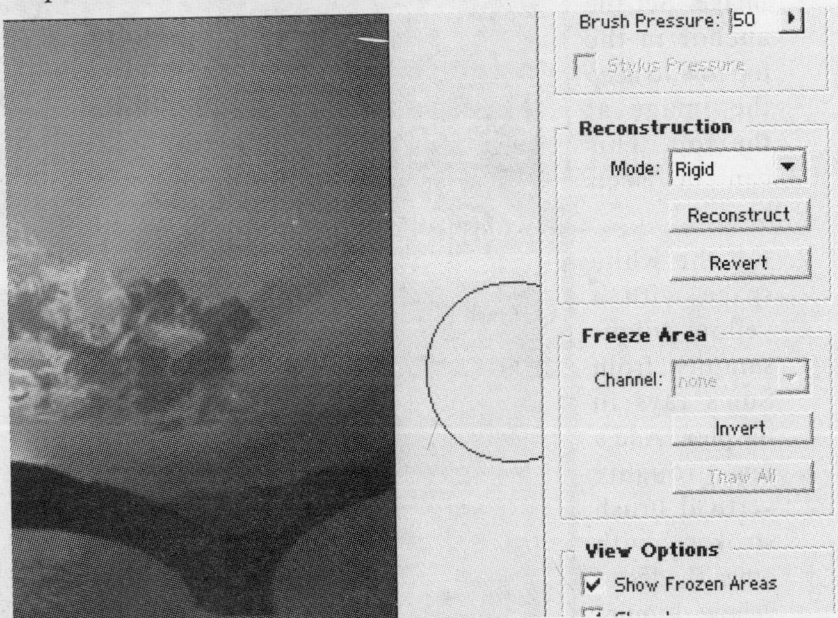

12. Photoshop's menu strip is unavailable while you are in the Liquify dialog box, but you can undo your preceding brush stroke with the usual keyboard combination Ctrl+Z.
13. Fine-time your distortions with the Reconstruct tool. Choose the Mode for Reconstruction and the size and pressure you need for best control. When you are satisfied with the results, click OK to dismiss the Liquify dialog box.
14. The Reconstruct button automatically re-creates the original pixels in the entire image, in accordance with the mode you have selected. So with Smooth mode, pressing the Reconstruct button allows the original to slowly emerge form the distortions. You can stop the process at any moment by pressing the Spacebar. Rigid and Stiff modes

reconstruct the image more quickly, but still give you time to stop the process if you like an intermediate stage.

15. Do not use the Revert button unless you want al changes to disappear instantly. Fortunately, you can undo the Revert command.

Distorting the Picture

Now we will add more space at the bottom of the image and use Liquify tools to give dunes a fluid look. You will learn to protect portions of the image you want to remain unchanged.

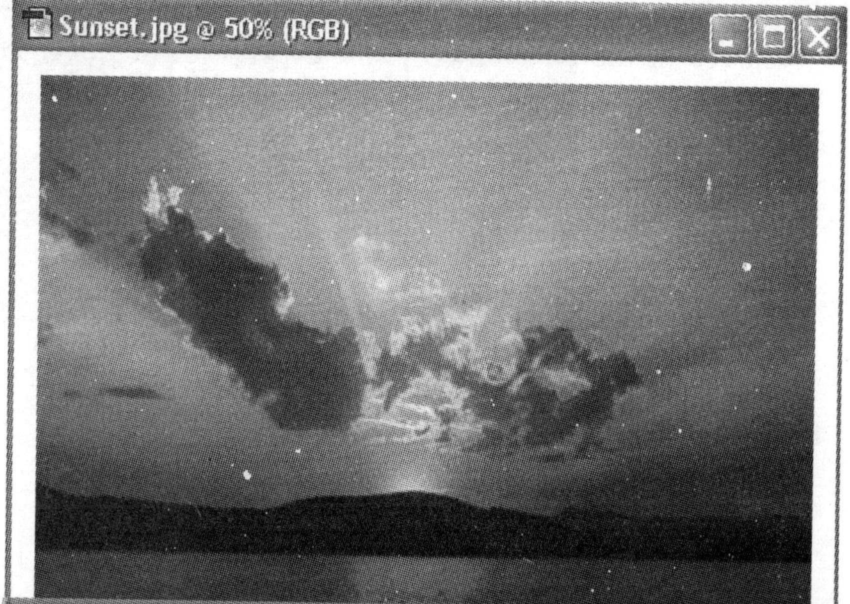

1. Use Image/ Canvas Size to add about a ½ inch of white space at the bottom of the image. Set the anchor in the top row to keep the image at the top. This can be seen here.

2. Fill the white space with a yellow colour sample from Sun's rays in the phot. Add a few roughly vertical brush strokes with other shades of yellow. Liquify effects will be added to this area.
3. You can avoid distorting areas of an image

you want to remain unchanged by using the Freeze tool in the liquefy dialog box. After you have prepared frozen areas, avoid using the Revert button, because it will undo your work with the Freeze tool as other effects. Instead, rely on the Reconstruct tool.

4. Paint over clouds and the upper part of the background with the Freeze tool. Be sure to cover all skin-tone pixels, including the dune. It is useful at this stage to keep main photo static while you work freely with other parts of the image. The Freeze tool creates a mast to protect pixels from distortion. Paint over areas you want to protect and the familiar 50% red (indicating a mask) appears to show which pixels are frozen. You can switch to the Thaw tool to release pixels from the mask. You can toggle the visibility of the mask from a check box in the View options.
5. Use the Bloat and Pucker tools with vertical strokes on the other parts of the image. A little experimentation with placement of the Bloat tool should reward you with some beautiful shading effects. Recall that you can undo any stroke.
6. The Twirl tools both respond well to circular brush strokes, as do the their neighbors, Pucker and Bloat. It does not seem to matter which direction your strokes turn. The Clockwise Twirl always produces a clockwise distortion and the Counterclockwise Twirl is true to its name as well.

Applying a Radial Blur

A Radial Blur is an effect that blurs an image in toward a center point or rotates it around a center point. The effect is similar to the photgraphy technique of making a zoom lens time exposure that creates a tunnel effect in toward the subject.

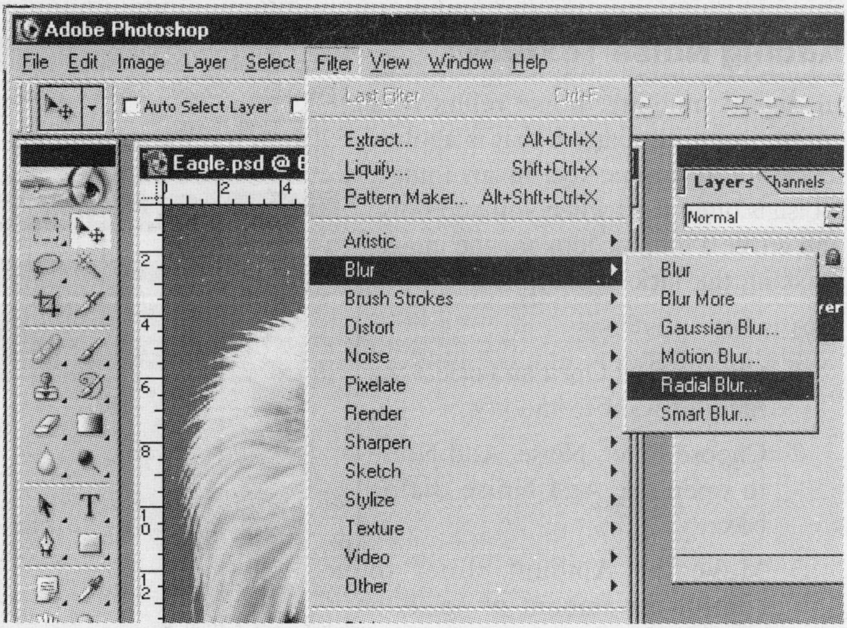

This is how it is done.

1. Choose File, Open and select the file you want to modify. Choose Filter, Blur, Radial Blur to open the Radial Blur dialog box.
2. Drag the Amount slider to control the degree of blur being applied to the image.

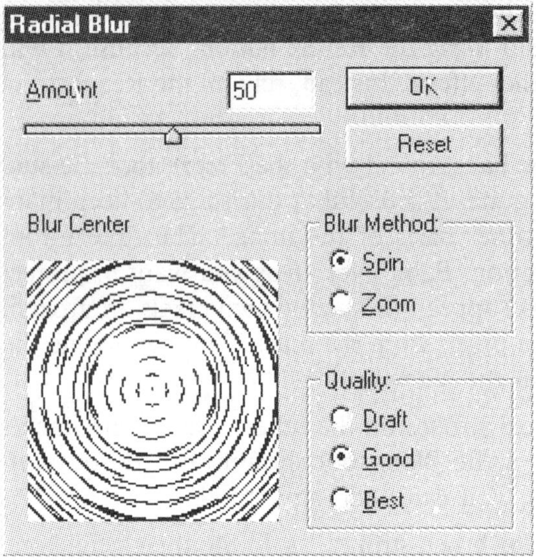

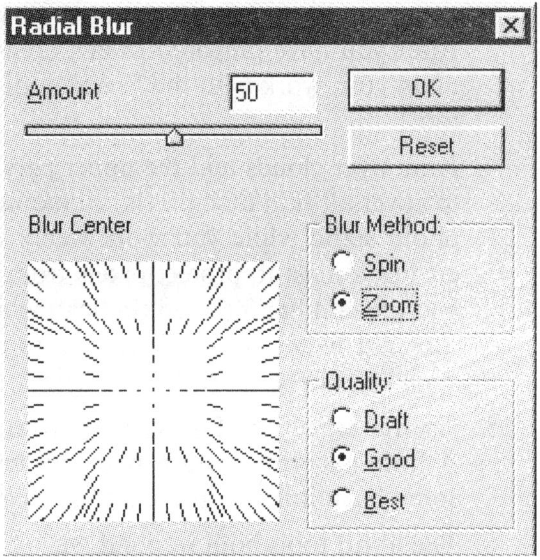

3. Select either Spin or Zoom to determine whether the blur rotates around a center point in the image or zooms straight into the image.
4. Select Draft, Good, or Best as the Quality mode, keeping in mind that the higher the quality, the longer it takes to apply the effect. Note that higher quality does not affect the file size, just the amount of time it takes to display the image.
5. Click Ok to apply the Radial Blur filter.

Adding Noise Texture

In digital imaging, noise refers to a coarse, pointillist pattern that is applied to create a graphic feel in an image. Noise is often used when you add noise and create a graphic look for the image, masking the lack of sharpness.

This is how it is done.

1. Choose File, Open and select the file you want to modify.
2. Choose Filter, Noise, Add Noise to open the Add Noise dialog box.
3. Move the Amount slider to control the amount of noise in the image. Observe the effect in both the preview window in the dialog box and in the original image area.

4. Select either the Uniform or Gaussian option to control how the effect is applied. The Gaussian option tends to mimic more closely the noise that appears on the emulsion of photographic film.

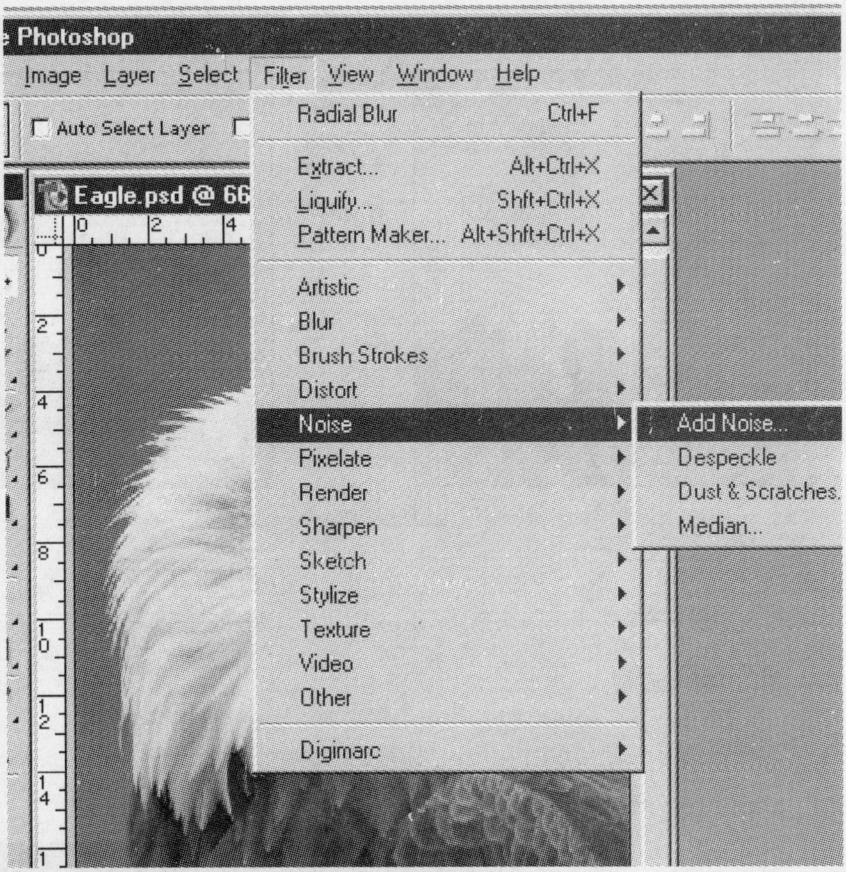

5. Enable or disable the Monochromatic check box and observe the effect this option has one the image. By default, noise is added to an image using randomly coloured pixels. These colours can be distracting in some images: the Monochromatic option adds noise using grayscale pixels.
6. Click Ok to close the Add Noise dialog box and apply the effect, as shown on the next page.

Creating Halftone Pattern

The Halftone Pattern filter creates a graphic effect that simulates a halftone screen being applied to an image. This effect reduces the image to two colours and creates a stylized graphic feel that is distinctive and unique.

The colours used for the filter are taken from the foreground and background colours, so be sure to select these colours before applying the filter.

This is how it is done.

1. Choose File, Open and select the file you want to modify.
2. Because the hafltone effect uses the foreground and background colours, you must set these colours before applying the filter. Click the Foreground colour swatch in the toolbox and choose the desired colour from the Color Picker. Click the Background colour swatch and select the second colour.

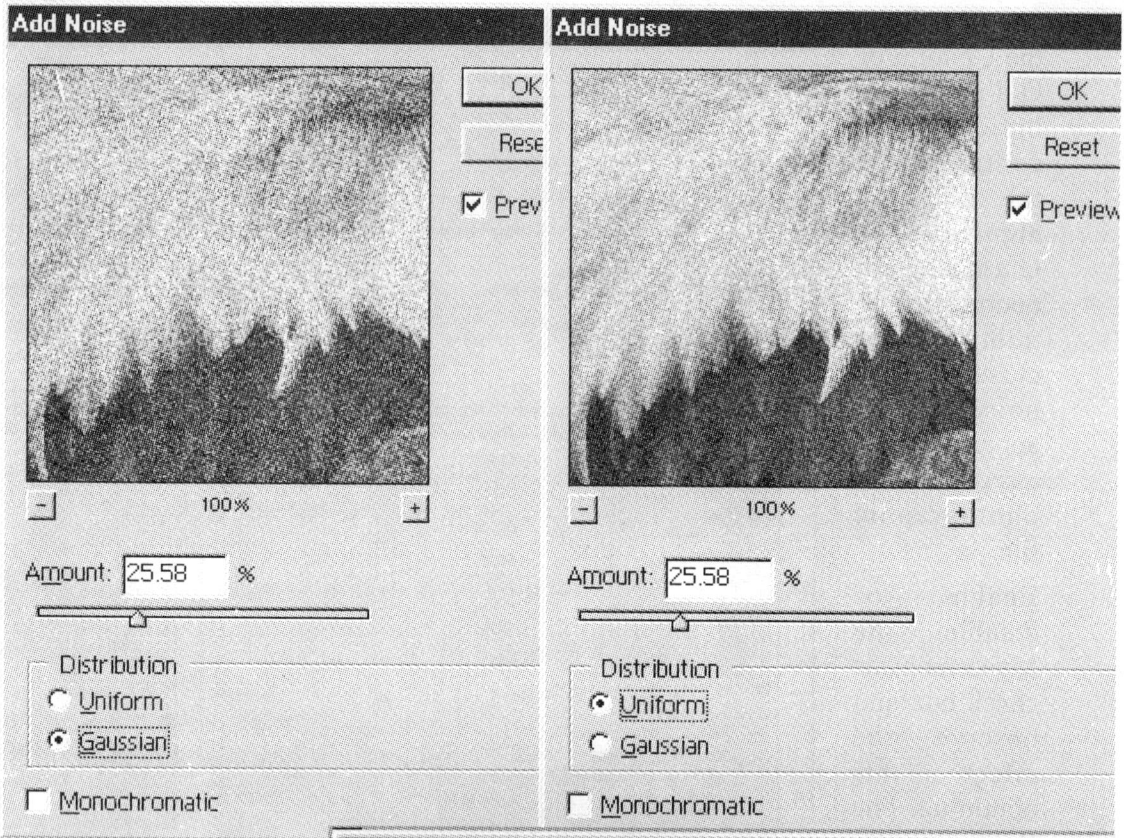

3. Choose Filters, Sketch, Halftone Pattern to open the Halftone Patern dialog box.
4. From the Pattern drop-down list box, choose Dot, Circle, or Line to determine the actual halftone pattern to be used. Observe the effect your selection has on the preview window at the top of the dialog box.
5. Adjust the Size slider to control the

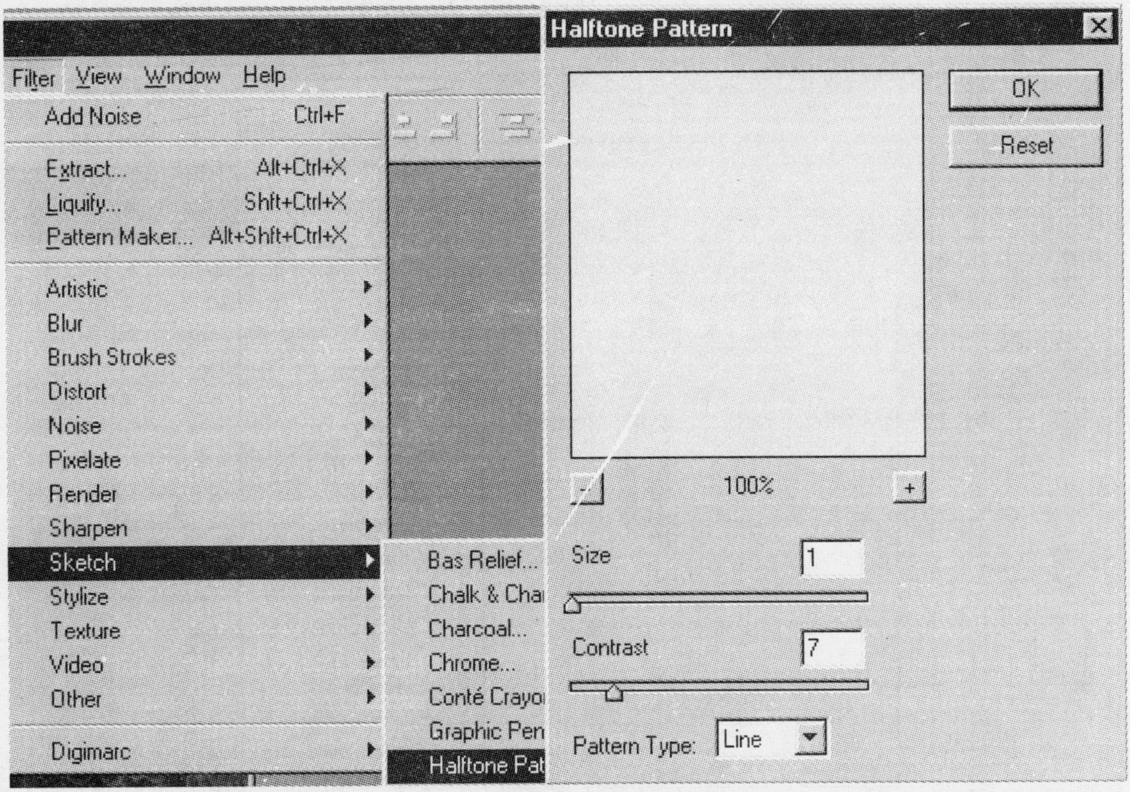

size of the halftone pattern relative to the image. Adjust the Constrast slider to control how prominently the effect is applied to the image.

6. Click Ok to close the Halftone Pattern dialog box and apply the effect to the image.

Blending Modes

Blending modes are one of the fastest ways to experiment with imaging effects in your Photoshop files. The basic function of a blending mode is to compare two sets of pixel data and combine them in different ways.

This is how it is done.

1. Select Windows menu, Layers to open the Layers palette. The Blending mode drop-down menu is at the top of palette. Hightlight a layer tile in the list and click and hold the menu to select one of the modes. The contents of the selected layer are compared with all the layers below it to achieve the result. Keep in mind that you cannot apply a blending mode to the background layer.
2. You can select any of the paint or shape tools and apply them using the blending modes. With the tool selected, select an option from the Mode menu in the Options bar. This approach to modes compares the values from the paint colour or source data, if you are using the Clone Stamp or History Brush tool, wiht the underlying image. Blending modes are available with the following tools: Airbrush, Paintbrush, Clone Stamp, History Brush, Gradient and Shape.

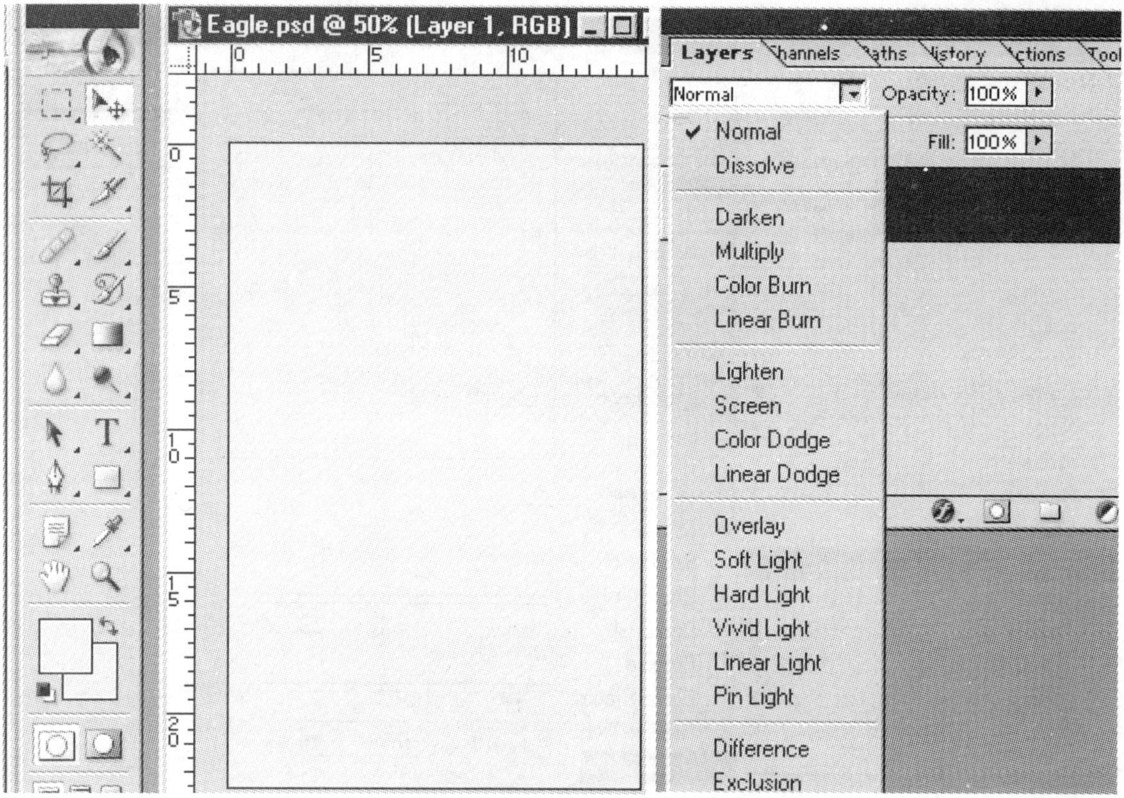

3. After applying a filter, select Edit, Fade. The Fade dialog box opens wiht an Opacity slider and a Mode menu. Select the desired mode from the menu and click Ok to apply the effect. This approach to modes compares the original image data with the results of the filter effect.

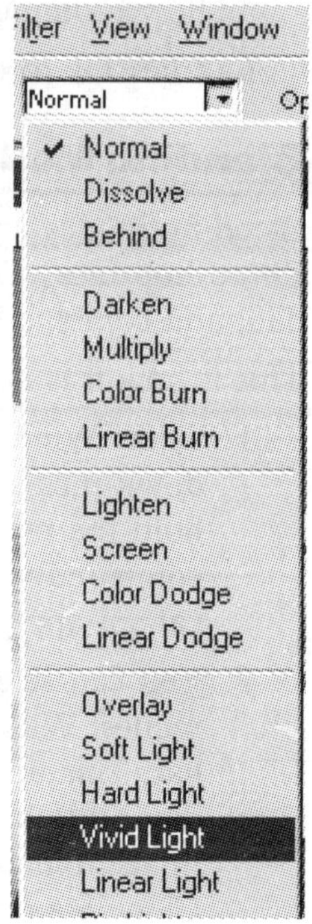

4. Select Edit, Fill to launch the Fill dialog box. Select Foreground Colour or Background Colour from the Use menu and then select the desired blending mode from the Mode menu. If you want, you can enter a percentage value in the Opacity text box to apply the mode with a degree of transparency. This approach to modes compares the current foreground or background colour with the image.

5. Select Edit, Fill to launch the Fill dialog box. Select Pattern from the Use menu and select a pattern preset from the Custom Pattern list. Choose the desired blending mode from the Mode menu. If

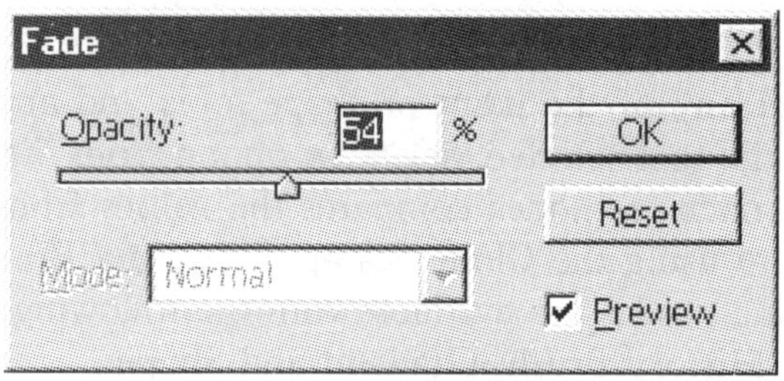

you want, enter a percentage value in the Opacity text box to apply the mode with a degree of transparency. The approach to modes compares the pattern values with the image.

6. Follow the steps to set the History source in the History palette. Then select Edit, Fill to launch the Fill dialog box. Select History from the Use menu and select the blending mode from the Mode menu. If you want, enter a percentage value in the Opacity text box to apply the mode with a degree of transparency. This approach to modes compares the selected history state with the image.

Applying Ripple Effect

The Ripple Effect, which is part of Distort filter, is used to create the look of rippling concentric circles across the image surface.

This is how it is done.

1. Choose File, Open to select the file you want to modify.
2. Choose Filter, Distort, ZigZag to open the ZigZag dialog box.
3. From the Style drop-down list, choose a distortion pattern. The pattern you choose is reflected in the wireframe preview window at the bottom of the dialog box and in the preview window at the top of the dialog box.
4. Adjust the Amount slider to control the percentage of distortion. Watch the effect of your changes in the preview windows.
5. Adjust the Ridges slider to control how many circular ridges applied in the patterns.
6. Click Ok to close the ZigZag dialog box and apply the filter and see the result here.

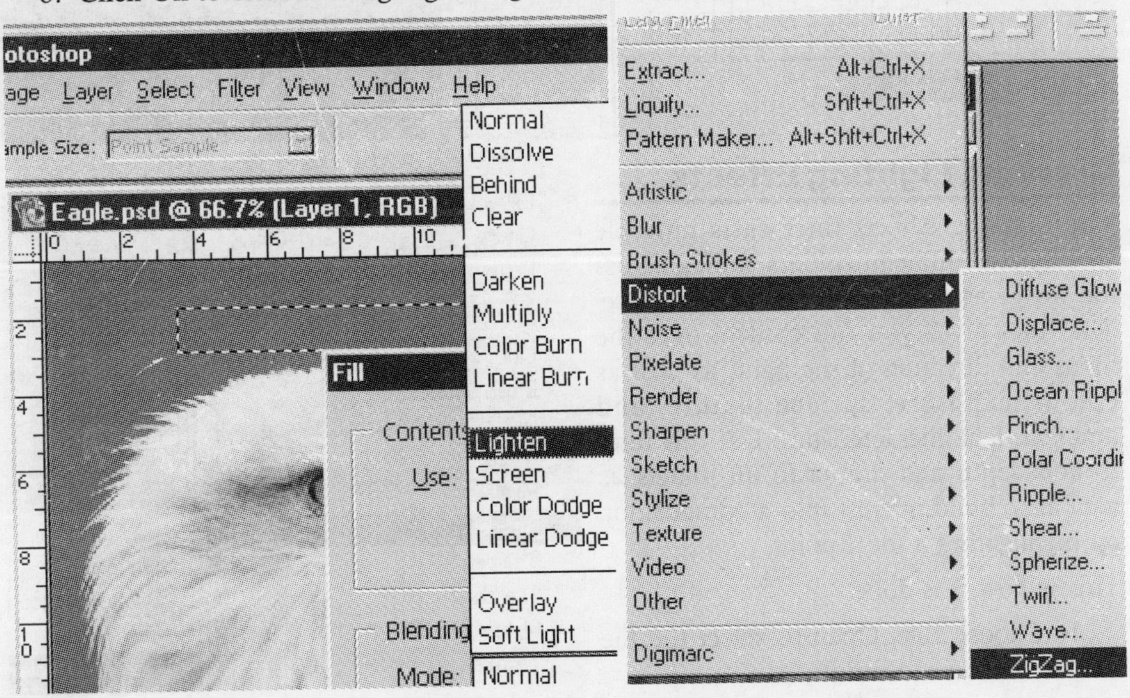

Creating Lighting Effects

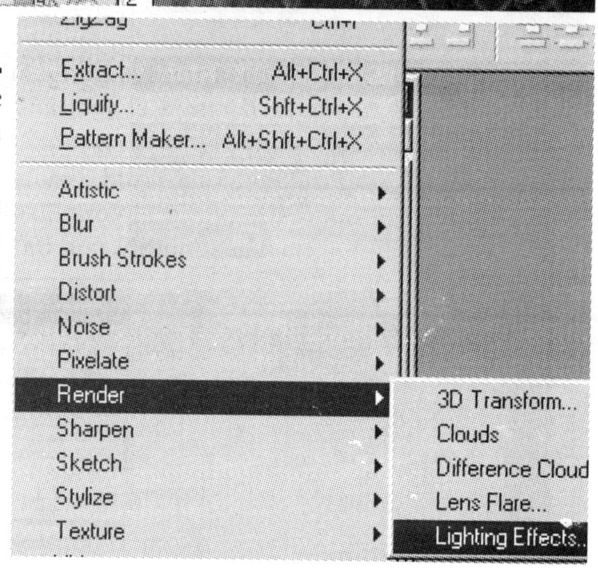

The Lighting Effects filter casts multiple spotlights of different colours, falling across the image as though it were a flat surface. The filter gives you full control over the focus and direction of the light, as well as colour, exposure, surface texture, and ambient light characteristics. Use this filter to add depth and drama to an image, as well as to build interest into a composition by highlighting a focal point.

This is how it is done.

1. Choose File, Open to select the file you want to modify.

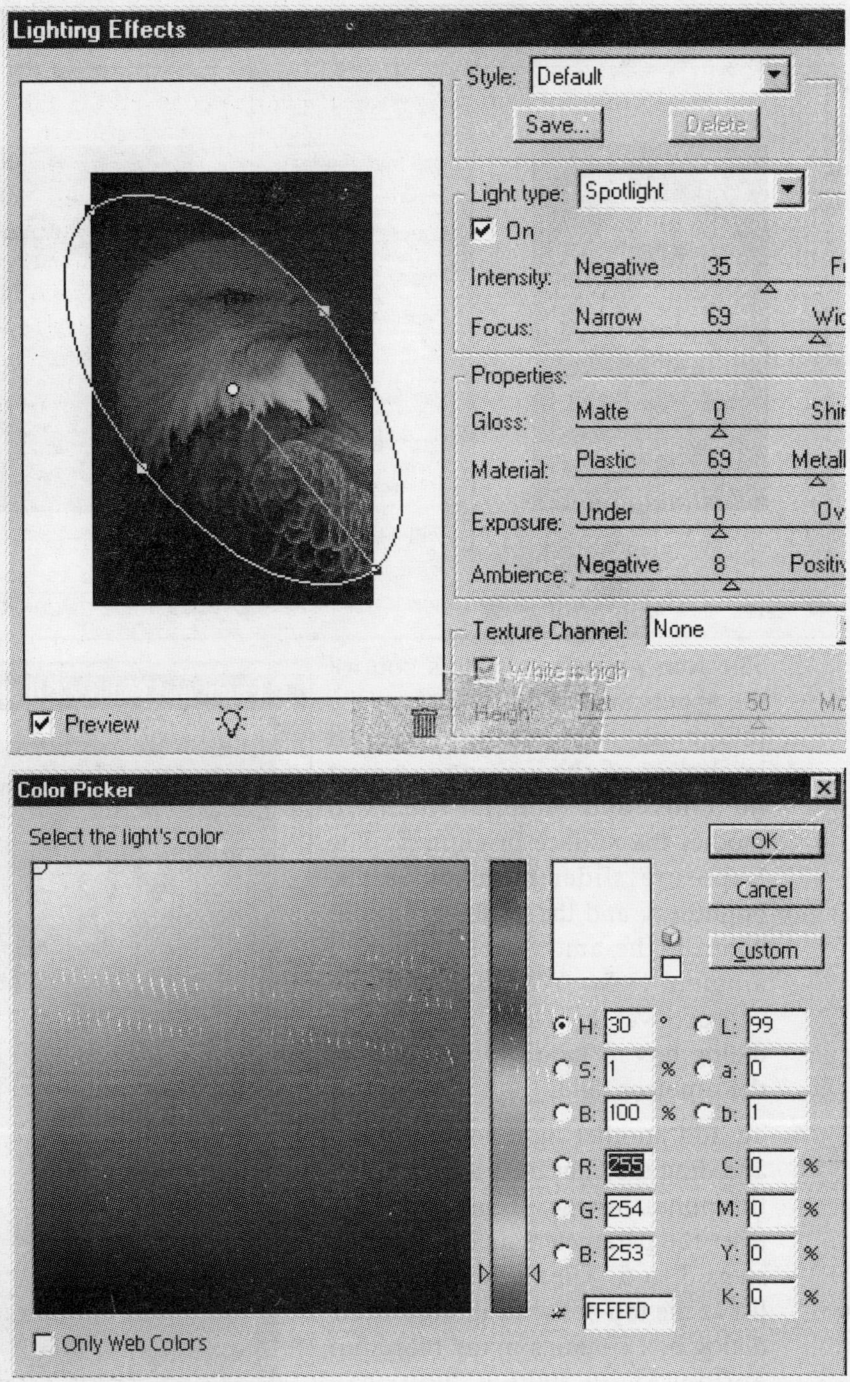

2. Choose Filter, Render, Lighting Effects to open the Lighting Effects dialog box. You will see a thumbnail of the image on the left side of the dialog box, with one spotlight already placed over the image.
3. Click and drag the center of the light to reposition the light circle in relation to the thumbnail image. Then click the point where the light source line meets the light circle and drag to move the light source. Finally, drag the handles on the light circle to widen or narrow the light beam as it is cast on the image.
4. Modify the Intensity and Focus sliders as desired to brighten the image and focus the light beam. Click the colour swatch to display the Color Picker so that you can select a colour for the light itself.

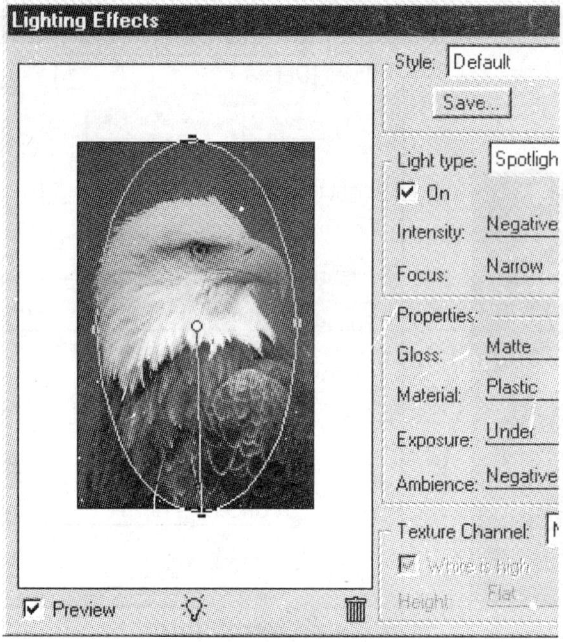

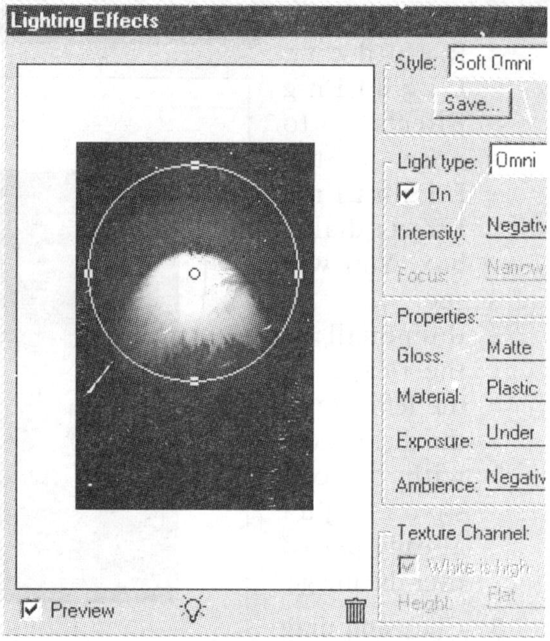

5. The four Properties sliders control the appearance of the surface of the image as well as the overall brightness of the exposure. Adjust the Gloss and Material sliders to modify the surface brightness. The Exposure slider controls image brightness, and the Ambience slider controls the amount of secondary ambient light. You can click the colour swatch in this area of the dialog box to modify the colour of the ambient light.

6. To add another light sources, click and drag the light bulb icon into the thumbnail image. Reposition and reset the parameters as described in steps 3 to 5. The Style drop-down list at the top of the Lighting Effects dialog box contains many more fun options with which you can experiment. If you want to remove a light, drag it to the trash can icon a the bottom of the dialog box. Keep in mind that you need at least one light source.

Descriptive Type Questions

1. What is Photoshop used for?
2. Describe the various file command of Photoshop.
3. Which tool would you use for moving objects from one place to another?
4. Which tool would you use to select irregular shapes?
5. How would you select pixels based on colour values?
6. Which tool is used for getting rid of unwanted parts of the picture?
7. Which tool is used to user-slices with the slice tool, from a layer, from a selection (ImageReady), or from guides (ImageReady)?
8. Which tool applies gradual tones (including sprays of color) to an image, simulating traditional airbrush techniques?
9. Which tool creates soft strokes of colors?
10. Which tool takes a sample of an image, which you can then apply over another image or part of the same image?
11. Which tool lets you paint a copy of one state or snapshot of an image into the current image window.
12. How would you erase the affected area to a state selected in the History palette?
13. Which tool fills adjacent pixels that are similar in color value to the pixels you click.
14. Which tool softens hard edges or areas in an image to reduce detail?
15. Which tool consist of the dodge tool and the burn tool?
16. How would you insert new text, change existing text, and delete text in type layers?
17. Which tool is used to write notes on the image.
18. What is the use of eyedropper tool?
19. What is hand tool used for?
20. What is zoom tool?
21. Which are the various colour modes used?
22. Which dialog box lets you select a foreground or background colour in any of several ways?
23. What is Smudging?
24. What is Sharpen tool used for?
25. What is Pencil tool used for?
26. What effect you get using the Charcoal filter?
27. Which palette allows you to control your layer?
28. How would you mask an image in Photoshop?
29. How would you distort the picture?
30. How would you apply a radial blur in Photoshop?
31. How is noise texture added?

32. How is half tone pattern created?
33. How would you blend modes?
34. How would you apply ripple effect?
35. How would you create lighting effects?
36. How would you manage multiple layers?
37. How would you remove layer mask?
38. Decribe the process of rotating an image.
39. How would you resize an image?

3 Introduction to PageMaker

Page Maker makes pages

Yes, it is true, Page Maker makes pages. The software in fact works on creation of pages. The concept here is to work on pages. You create a page according to the size required, fill it with Text and Graphics and do all the formatting required on it to make the page ready for printing. It is in fact the pre-print process, the page created in Page Maker would be printed only on the printer but in the press too, as it looks on the screen. You can design your book, magazine, brochure, etc., in Page Maker and then send it for printing to the press.

Creating a New Page

To start with, we will click at New in the File menu. This will give rise to a document setup dialog box as shown here. Now, we have to fill this box, according to our specifications. We would be creating a page of size 5 inches x 8 inches and would set the details accordingly.

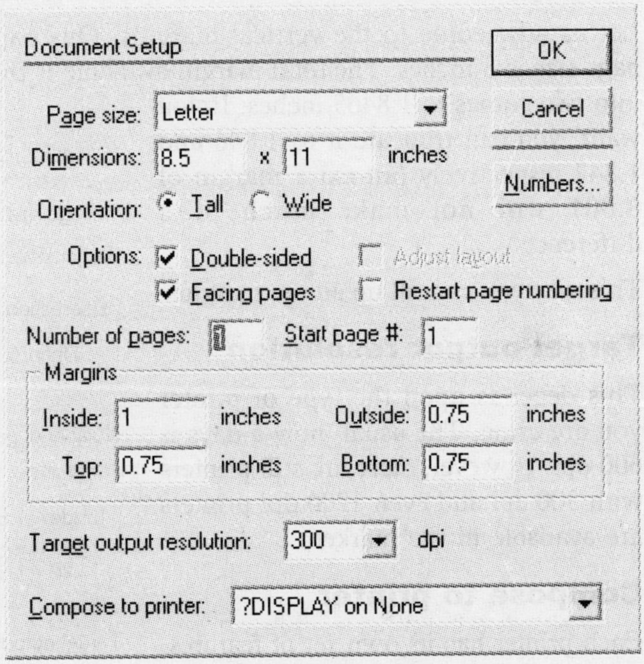

Page Size

We will stick to A4 size of paper for all our work. So click at A4 here and you will see the size of the paper being reflected in the next boxes where Dimensions of the paper are given.

Orientation

The orientation for this kind of page would be Tall. (Here it is referred as Tall and Wide instead of Portrait and Landscape).

Options

Double-sided pages when selected will create left and right pages differently. You must have noticed this difference in almost all books and pages. So select it. Facing pages option will let you see 2 pages at a time on the screen. This helps in visualizing since the book would ultimately be opened like this. We would select this too.

Number of Pages

You would always start with 1 and let the software fill up the pages later on.

Starting page

We will keep it 1 here. It is used for putting a number since your publication can be the 3rd chapter of the book and the first 50 pages have been consumed by the first two chapters, then you would like to put 51 here to start the 3rd chapter with page number 51.

Margins

Now this is tricky. You remember the layout of various pages which were shown to you in the first chapter. It was also told that the our text page should be almost in the center of the page and the margins on all sides of the text should not less than 0.5 inches.

So let us see how the dimensions of inside and outside are measured.

Our paper size width wise is 8.268 inches and the page size is 5 inches. This means that a total of 3.268 inches (8.268 - 5.0) of white space is left with us. This has to be divided equally (almost) on both sides of the page size. So if we divide 3.268 inches by 2, we get 1.634 inches. This much of space we have to leave on both left and right hand side of the paper to get our page in centre of the paper, horizontally.

So fill up 1.634 inches in both inside and outside margins.

Let us now come to the vertical margins. Our paper size here is 11.693 inches and the page size is 8 inches. The total margin available is thus 3.693 inches. This if divided equally into two comes to 1.8465 inches. If you want, you can truncate it to 1.846 and 1.847 respectively (an extra margin of 0.001 will not make much of a difference.)

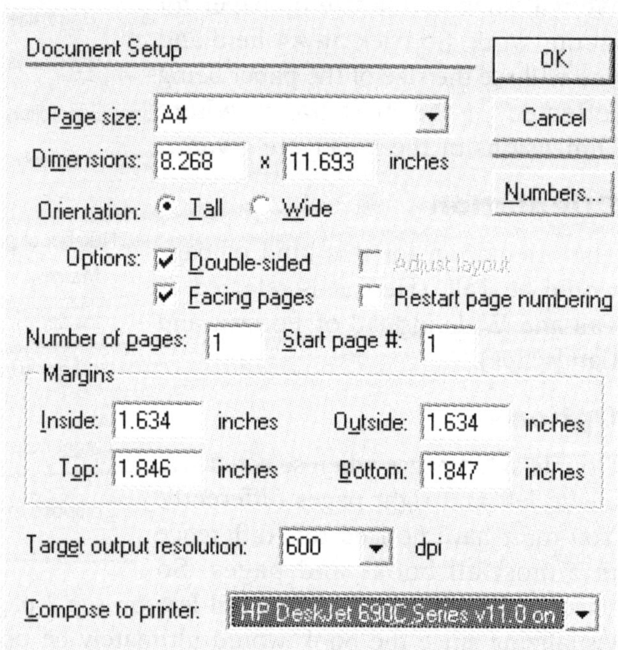

This way you can fill up all the margins.

Target output resolution

This depends upon the type of printer you are using. The usual now-a-days is 600 dpi. However, there are still printers with 300 dpi and even 1200 dpi printers are available in the market.

Compose to printer

Each printer has its own set of features. The text may or may not change if you change the target printer. So it is always better to define here the printer you are going to use. If you are not sure just choose the printer attached to your computer, which is your default printer and will be shown here in any case.

So now you have all the options ready. Fill them up and your dialog box should look like the one shown on the next page. Click at Ok to get a new desktop of PageMaker to start your work. But would it not be nice to check the accuracy of the page before starting further, since if the page size is not perfect, the rest of the story will be all wrong. For this we will be using zero option. Before this you must ensure that both the rulers are on screen, as shown on the next page.

Checking the Page Size

Click at zero position box and drag the zero cross lines to the top of the page crossing, i.e., where the horizontal and vertical lines of the page meet on the top left corner of the page. You will now see the zero on both sides of the ruler, i.e., on the top and the left. Now with one side having zero, see the right side of the page, you will see that it points to 5 inch on the top ruler.

Similarly if you see the vertical rule, the horizontal line points to 8 inch on the scale. This confirms that our page is of the size 8 inches by 5 inches. Now onwards all the work will be done on this desktop. This is the actual page which will be printed as it is, once we put it through our printer.

Remember, these lines are just indicative and will not be printed while printing this page. These lines are called the guide lines and can be placed anywhere on the screen and can be drawn by dragging the mouse button on either of the ruler, i.e., on left or on top.

Now that we have the page ready, we would like to place some text on it. There is a convention that the text is always typed in a word processing program and then it is brought into the PageMaker. It has been there since the earlier versions of the software did not have the facilities of performing the various checks on the text, which most of the word

processors have. These are: Spell checking, Find and Replace, etc. Slowly and slowly all these have been added to the PageMaker software too and can be conveniently used on the text of the PageMaker. I have a different opinion about this. Since in most of the earlier offices where it was used, there were different operators for both word processing and page making. Thus the work was always divided like this. Moreover, typing of the text in PageMaker is slow compared to word processing. Either way we assume that the text has been typed in some word processor and proceed further and place the text.

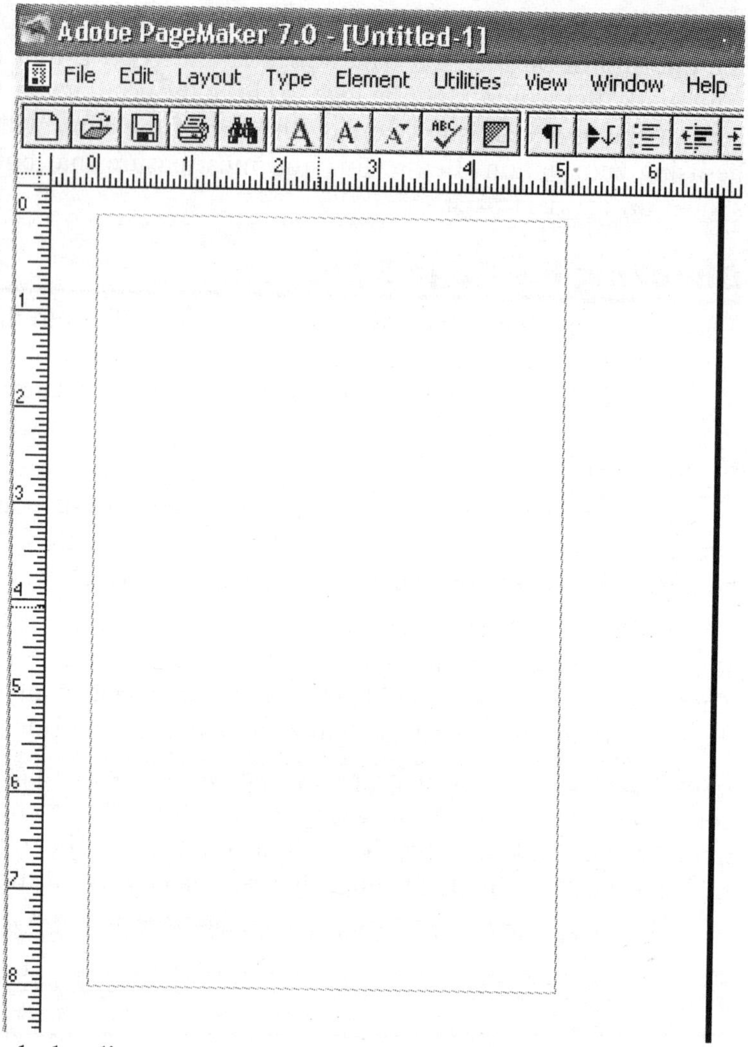

Placing the Text

Place command is under the File Menu. Once clicked it gives rise to a dialog box which asks you where the file, which you want to place, is located. Click at directory options to reach the directory where the file is located. Double Click (or click and press Ok) to place the file in your publication.

Now this file could have been keyed in any of the word processing programs, PageMaker has the filters for most of the word processors. If the text in one of the word processors for which PageMaker has in built filters, the text will be inserted as it is. If it is not able to recognize the type of word processor, it will ask for the name of the software used for creating it, as shown here. You click at one of the software listed in the dialog box on the next page.

If still it is not able to recognize, then there is no option. Either you will have to load the filter for that software or convert the text into one of the known software.

Once the text is accepted, it will be available in the form of an icon. All you have to do it to place the text within the page frame made earlier by you. There are 3 types of icons, this text can have. They are:

Manual

It allows you to place the text manually, i.e., after placing the text on one page, you will have the option of placing the remaining text on the next page.

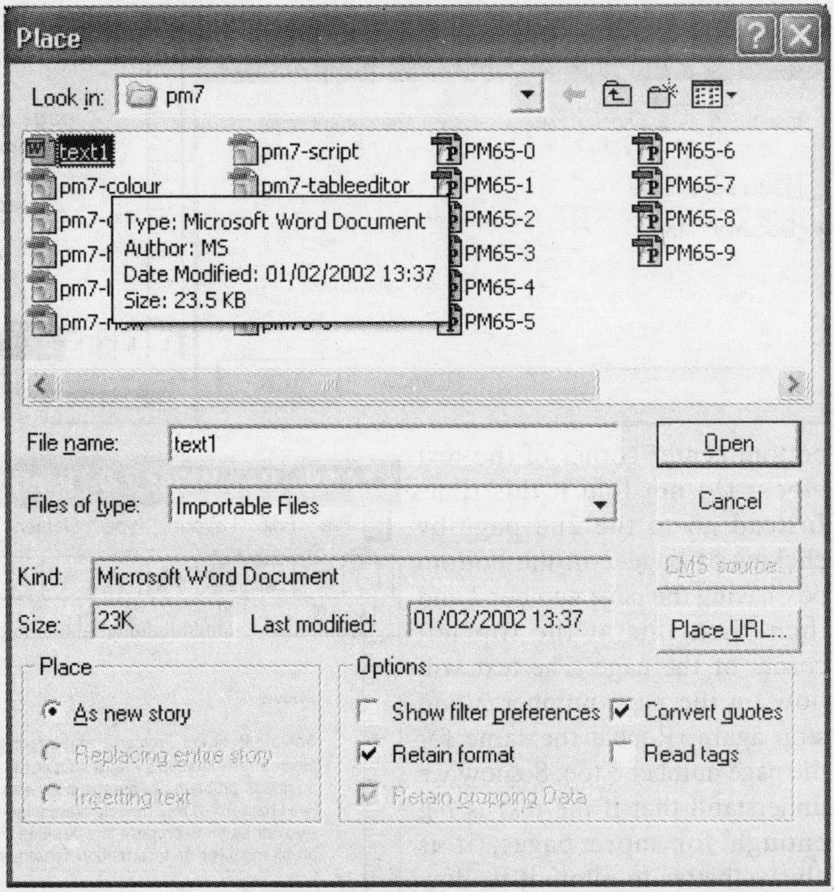

Semiautomatic

You can change the text placement from page to page in this kind.

Autoflow

Here the text will be placed automatically, placing all the text in one flow, creating more new pages on its own, till the whole text is placed.

Just click this icon at the starting point of the page, i.e., top left corner of the page, where we had put the zero edge earlier. In case you want the text to autoflow, you can change the option by clicking at autoflow in the layout menu.

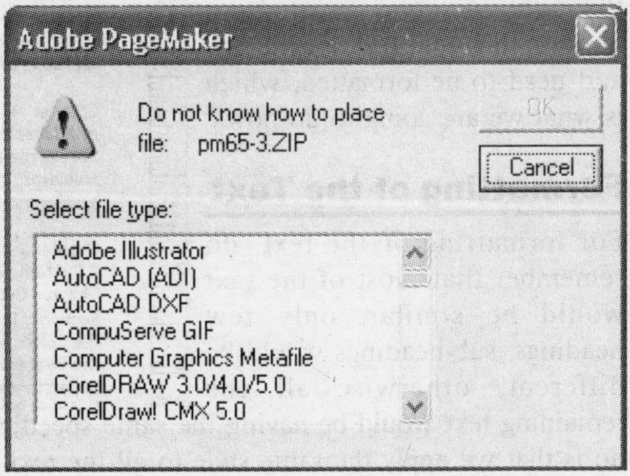

In our case, we assume that the text is enough to last 3 pages and it has stopped after placing the text on the first page. Now at this stage you have 2 options, either click the text with pointer tool and click at the autoflow tool in the layout menu. This will make the text in autoflow mode. Now pick up the bottom centre corner of the text block and slowly move it up using the mouse. The text will start folding itself. Do it till you get the whole text doled up. You will end up an autoflow icon. Click at the top corner of the page and see the text flow to the all the 3 pages.

Secondly, insert the pages manually, using the command, Insert Pages from the Layout menu. Click at Insert to insert 2 new pages. Then from the 1st page, pick up the text from the

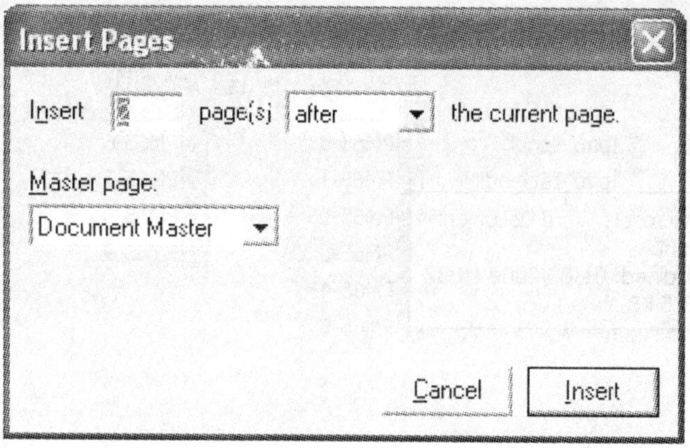

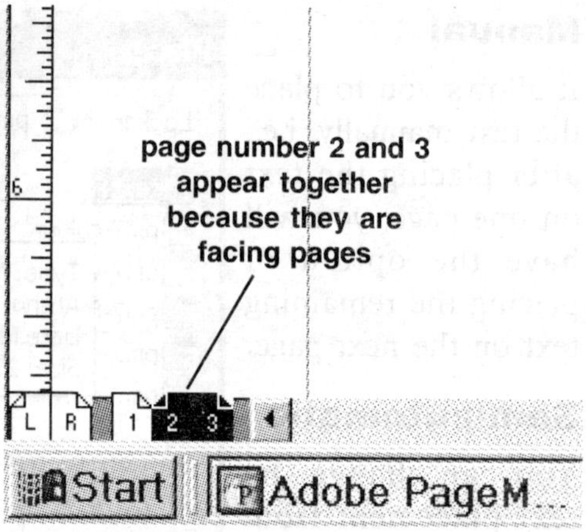

bottom center corner of the text block. Do not fold it this time. Instead go to the 2nd page by clicking at page 2 in the bottom box having the page number 2 and then click this at the top left corner of the page. The text will flow on the page number 2 and stop again. Repeat the same for the page number 3 too. So now we understand that if the text is big enough for more pages, it is always better to allow it to flow through. As you must have noticed that this text is just raw and need to be formatted, which is what we are going to do now.

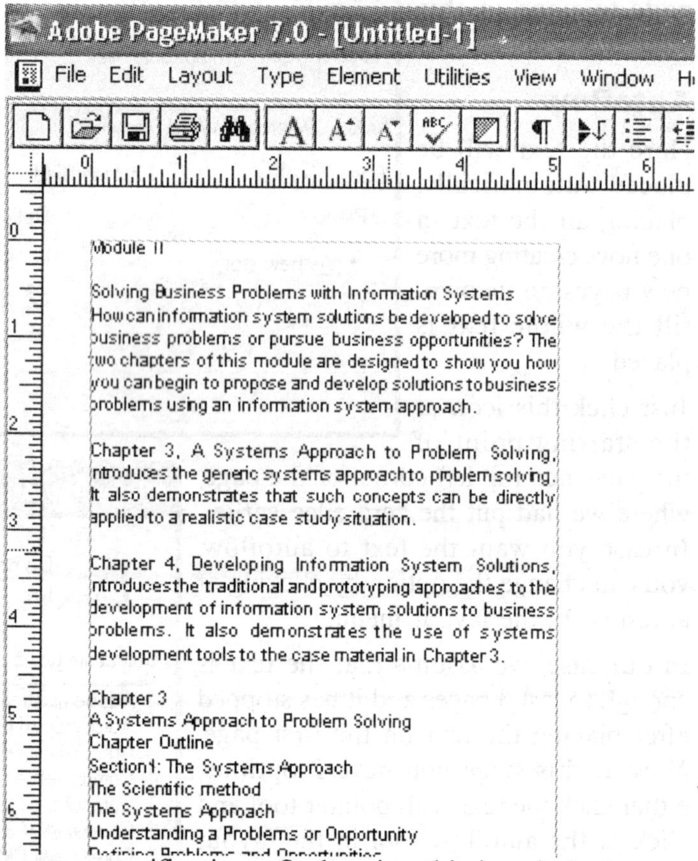

Formatting of the Text

For formatting of the text, do remember that most of the text would be similar, only few headings, sub-headings would be different, otherwise all the remaining text would be having the same specifications. So keeping this in mind what we do is that we apply the same style to all the text and then pick each heading/sub-heading manually and change them accordingly.

For formatting of the complete text, we need to select the whole text. For this we have the command called **Select All**. So place our cursor at any place within the text and call this command from Edit menu. Immediately the whole text will be highlighted from page 1 to 3. First of all we will change the font, etc., of the text. For this we have the **Character** command which is under Type menu. With the text highlighted, call this command from the type menu, a dialog box, as shown here appears.

Various options of the dialog box are:

Font

As you know font is the type style which allows us to make the font decorative or more readable, depending on what sort of text you are using. In most of the books, the font Times New Roman is used for text because of its clarity. So will also use the same.

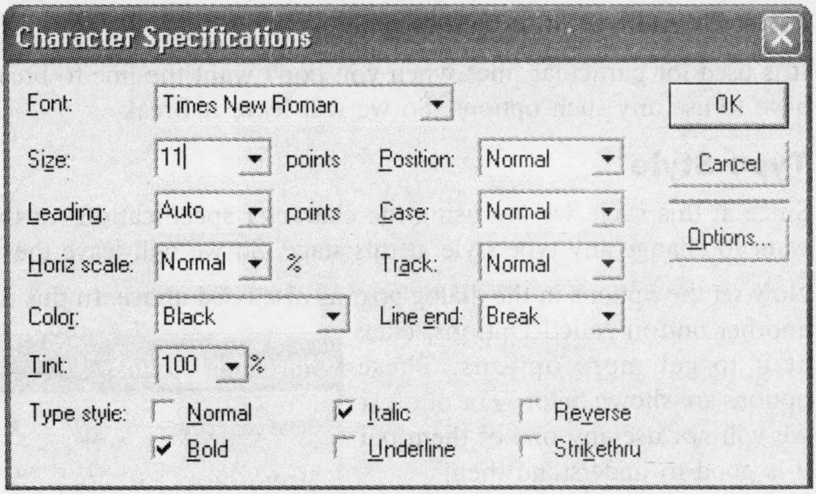

Size

This signifies the weight of the character. To most of the readers, sizes 10 to 12 are quite readable. Newspapers are mostly printed in 10 points. For our book we will have 11 points.

Leading

It is the space between the two lines, you can squeeze it to include more number of lines on a page if you want to. But, for our book, we will stick to Auto, meaning a space of about 2 point between the lines.

Horizontal scale

This is used when you have to either squeeze the text to a line or expand it to fill the space. Neither of the condition applies to our text. So we will stick to Normal.

Colour

You can choose to let you text look in a colour different from black, but, as far as our book goes, black is beautiful.

Tint

If you are not choosing colour then the question of choosing tint does not arise.

Position

Using this you can make your text Superscript or Subscript. This is used for particular characters and not for the full text, as we are doing it here. So we will leave it Normal.

Case

You can change the case of particular text, like making it ALL CAPS, SMALL CAPS, etc.

Track

This is used for fine tuning of the text. You can make the text block loose, very loose, tight or very tight. But we will keep it to Normal only.

Line Break

It is used for particular lines when you don't want the line to break. In our case we do not have to use any such options. So we will leave it Break.

Type Style

Since at this stage we are using the character specifications of the whole text, we do not want to change any type style at this stage. So we will leave the whole thing as normal.

Now set the options in the dialog box, as discussed above. In this dialog box, you will notice another button called Options, click at it to get more options. These options are shown below. For our text we will not use any one of them but it is good to understand them.

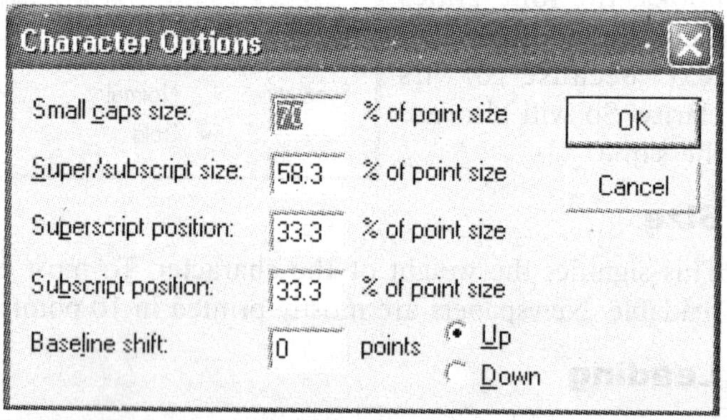

Small caps size

As we had seen above, there is an option of using small caps in the character settings. From here you can define how much height the small cap should have compared to full caps. Here the option is 70%, i.e., if the capital letter is of 10 mm, then the small cap will be of 7 mm.

Super/subscript size

This option determines how much thick the character should become once it becomes either superscript or subscript.

Superscript position

As you make the character Superscript, this option defines how much height it should go up from the normal position.

Subscript position

As you make the character Subscript, this option defines how much it should go down from the normal position.

Baseline shift

Here you can make the adjustment of setting the character up or down from the baseline. This command is useful when you have to align the text to the top instead of aligning it to the bottom, as is usually done.

So once we have set the character specifications of the whole text, click Ok in the character dialog box to register all the changes made by you. The text will remain highlighted till you click at any place outside the text. Once done your text page would look like the one shown on the next page. Next we will do the paragraph settings.

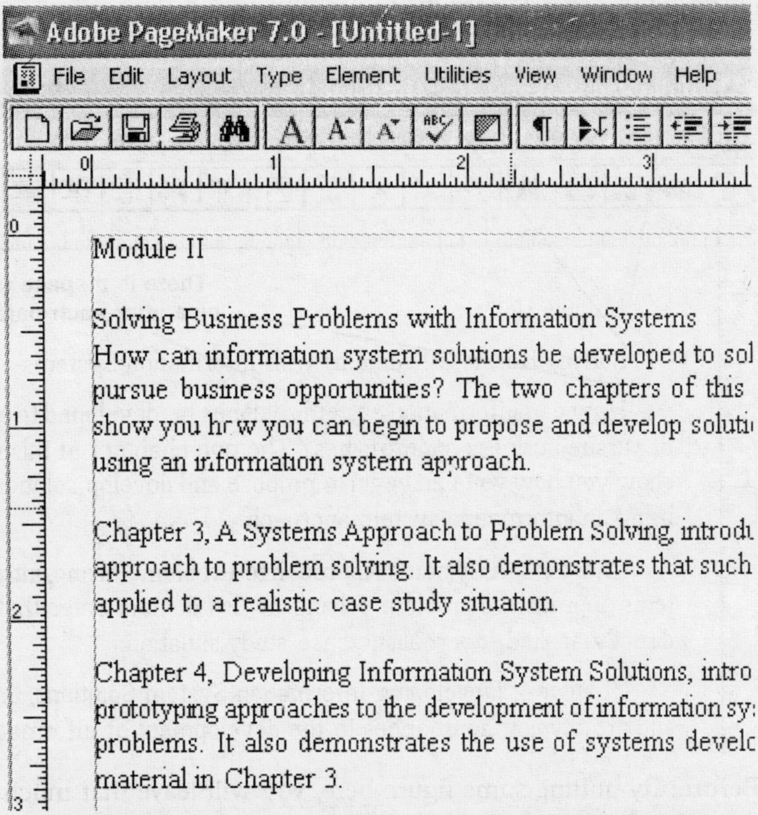

Paragraph settings

These settings are available in Paragraph dialog box which can be called by using the command **Paragraph** under the **Type** menu. As you can see from the dialog box, on next page, there are many options which can be used here. Let us see each of them. (You would notice here that the scale being used is Pica. 6 Picas make 1 inch and 1 Pica has 12 points)

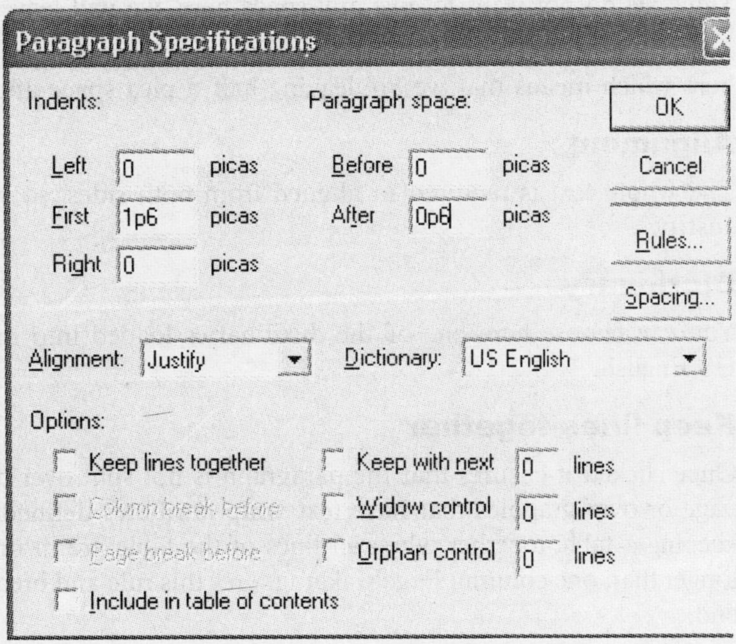

Indents

Here you will set the figures in terms of points and pica as to how much space you want to leave on all sides of your text.

Left: Here you define how much of the left indent you want to give to the paragraph. We do not want to give any indent here.

First: The amount of space you mark here will reflect in each para being given that much of space to the first line of the para. Let us give a space of one and a half pica to it.

Right: We do not want the text to shift from right alignment. So leave it at 0.

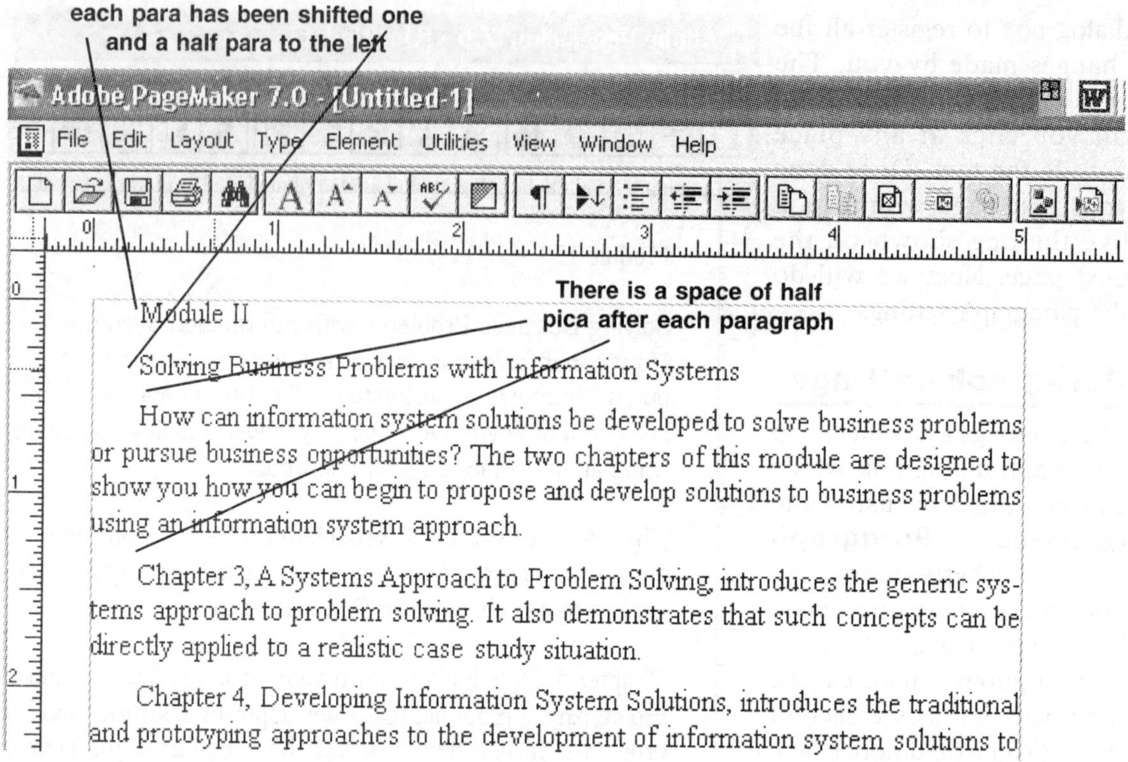

Before: By putting some figure here, you will leave that much space above each paragraph. Since we do not want to give any space here, we will leave it at 0.

After: We definitely want some space after each paragraph. So we will leave 6 point space here which means that we are leaving half a pica space after each paragraph.

Alignment

The whole text is required to aligned from both sides, so we would choose the option of Justify.

Dictionary

You can choose here one of the dictionaries loaded into the system. Here we choose the US English.

Keep lines together

Once clicked it ensures that the paragraph is not split over different columns, from page to page or over graphics that have text wrap attributes defined. This option is also useful for keeping a table together when all lines of the table are in one paragraph. If a paragraph is longer than one column, PageMaker ignores this rule and breaks the paragraph at the column end.

Column break before

This option when clicked ensures that the paragraph begins with a new column.

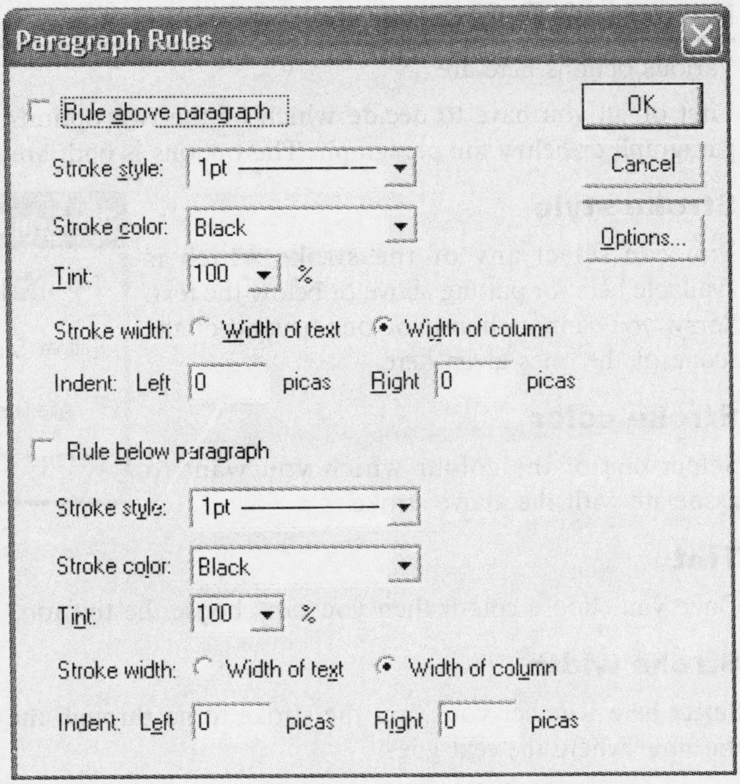

Page break before

This option when checked ensures that the paragraph begins on a new page. This is useful if you want certain heading to always start from a new page.

Keep with next 0 lines

This when clicked ensures that the last line of the paragraph is placed with a certain number of lines of the next paragraph and specify the number of lines (1, 2, 3). This option is used to keep headlines connected to their accompanying text.

Widow control 0 lines

This command specifies how many lines (up to 3) constitute a widow, when that number of lines fall at the bottom or page range, PageMaker moves the line or lines to the next column or page to eliminate the widow.

Orphan control 0 lines

This command specifies how many lines (up to 3) constitute an orphan. When that number of lines fall at the column or page, PageMaker adds one more line to the column or page to eliminate the orphan.

Include in table of contents

Once this is clicked it suggests that the paragraph or heading is to be included in the Table of Contents which will be generated later.

We will use the settings shown earlier (Remember to highlight the text before applying it) and click Ok. The next page figure shows the effect of these paragraph settings. But, this is not all to the paragraph settings. There is more to it. For that call the paragraph dialog box again and click at **Rules** to get a new dialog box.

This is used for drawing a line over or below the text. Since we are not using these options here, we have not applied them, but, it is a good idea to understand them. Very soon we would be using them, when we come to the headings of the text.

Paragraph Rules

Various options here are:

First of all you have to decide which of the two options you have to choose, rule over paragraph or below the paragraph. The options is both are similar.

Stroke style

You can select any of the stroke which is available here for putting above or below the text. Sorry, you cannot choose anyone beyond of the scope of the ones given here.

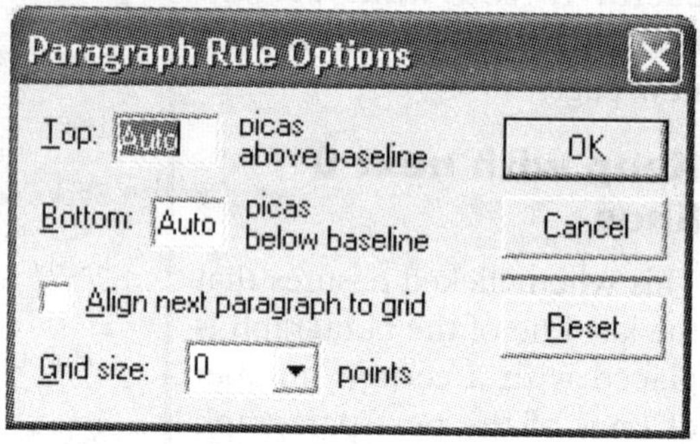

Stroke color

Select one of the colour which you want to associate with the above stroke.

Tint

Once you choose colour then you can choose the tint too.

Stroke width

Select here whether you want the stroke to go through the whole column or just stick to the limit where the text goes.

Indent

As in paragraph, you can select how much of the space you want to leave from left or right for drawing this line. This space can again be given in picas (or you can change the preferences). Within this rules dialog box, there is another dialog box, which allows to set the spacing above and below the lines.

Rulers Options

This displays the options of Rules and their placements. The dialog box is shown on the next page. This is used to specify the vertical placement of paragraph rules and to establish a leading grid that ensures the alignments of baselines across the column of text regardless of odd sized heading and inline graphic.

Rules are positioned relative to the top or bottom of the area that contains the text within its vertical spacing also called leading. Various options are:

Top

Define here the position of top rule vertically. The default setting is auto which aligns the upper edge of the rule with the top of the first line of every selected paragraph. To position the rule higher or lower, enter a measurement in top when positioned higher, the rule may increase size of the slug of the first line of text.

Bottom

Position the bottom rule vertically, the default setting is auto which aligns the bottom edge of the line along with the bottom of the slug of the last line of every selected paragraph. When the option is set to auto the rule does not change the size of the slug of the last line of text. To position the rule higher or lower enter a measurement in bottom when positioned lower, the rule will increase the size of the slug of the last line of the text.

Align next paragraph to grid

If you are creating a publication that has multiple text column you may want the baselines of the body text to align horizontally. Some attributes of heading and subheading paragraph can disrupt this alignment for the body text that follows.

Grid Size

To restore the baseline alignment of body text, grid size is set. This makes the PageMaker add extra space after the paragraph if necessary to ensure that the following paragraph is positioned on this grid.

Now we come back to another option of the paragraph menu called **Spacing**. It is very important if you have to fine tune the text spacing.

Spacing

This allows you to control the spacing attributes in word and letter space, sets the pair kerning, leading method and autoleading percentage.

Word space

The space between words, created by pressing the spacebar, is called the space band and is part of the font design. The default desired word spacing is 100% of the space band of the associated font, you can change the desired spacing to any percentage between 0% and 500%. When setting justifies text, you can create a range within which PageMaker spaces word by setting values for minimum and maximum. The range limits for minimum and maximum are 0% and 500% of the space band.

Letter space

Each letter has a natural width that includes the space around the letter. In PageMaker a letter is measured from the left edge of one letter to the edge of the next letter. This distance is called the pen advances. The default desired letter spacing is 0% that is letter with no extra spacing added to or subtracted from it. You can change the space between letters

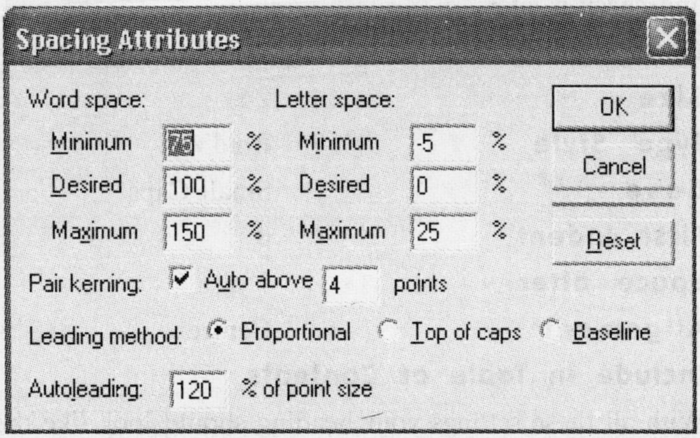

by changing the desired letter spacing. Add or subtract any percentage up to 100% of the space band.

Pair kerning

When auto is checked, PageMaker kerns, adjusts the space between a pair of characters by the amount specification in the current font. By default PageMaker kerns pairs larger than 12 points, although the effect of automatic pair kerning is less visible at small sizes. If you unchecked auto, PageMaker does not kern pairs at all.

Leading method

You can select a leading method to control the vertical spacing of text within the slug (the vertical space in which a line of text is positioned). The various options are:

Baseline: Select this to align the baseline of the text with the bottom of the slug.

Proportional: Select this to position the baseline of the text two third of the way down from the top of the slug.

Top of caps: Select this to position the baseline of the text at a distance from the top of the slug, equal to the height of the tallest ascender in the font.

Autoleading

Here you can define the autoleading in terms of the percentage of the font size. PageMaker default is 120% which means that for a text of 10 points with leading Auto will have the space between two lines of 2 points.

This finishes our quest for information about the paragraph dialog box. Now that we have set the character and paragraph settings, we proceed ahead and set the various other items of the text. First of all is the chapter number.

Setting Chapter Number

As we know that whatever matter has to be changed it has to be highlighted first. So highlight "Chapter 10" in the text. So now we will do the following settings for this. I am not explaining here how you will do that. It will be a good exercise for you to do it yourself and check it later.

Font	Arial
Size	24
Type Style	Bold
Case	Small Caps
First Indent	0
Space after	1 pica
Alignment	Centre
Include in Table of Contents	

With all these settings your heading should look like the one shown below. This was not very difficult, was it? In fact, all this when you practice will be very easy to follow and you would be able to do it without even referring to this book, expect for the keyboard shortcuts.

Now let concentrate on the chapter name or the title of the chapter "File System Interface". For this you do the following settings.

Font	Arial
Size	16
Type Style	Bold
Case	All Caps

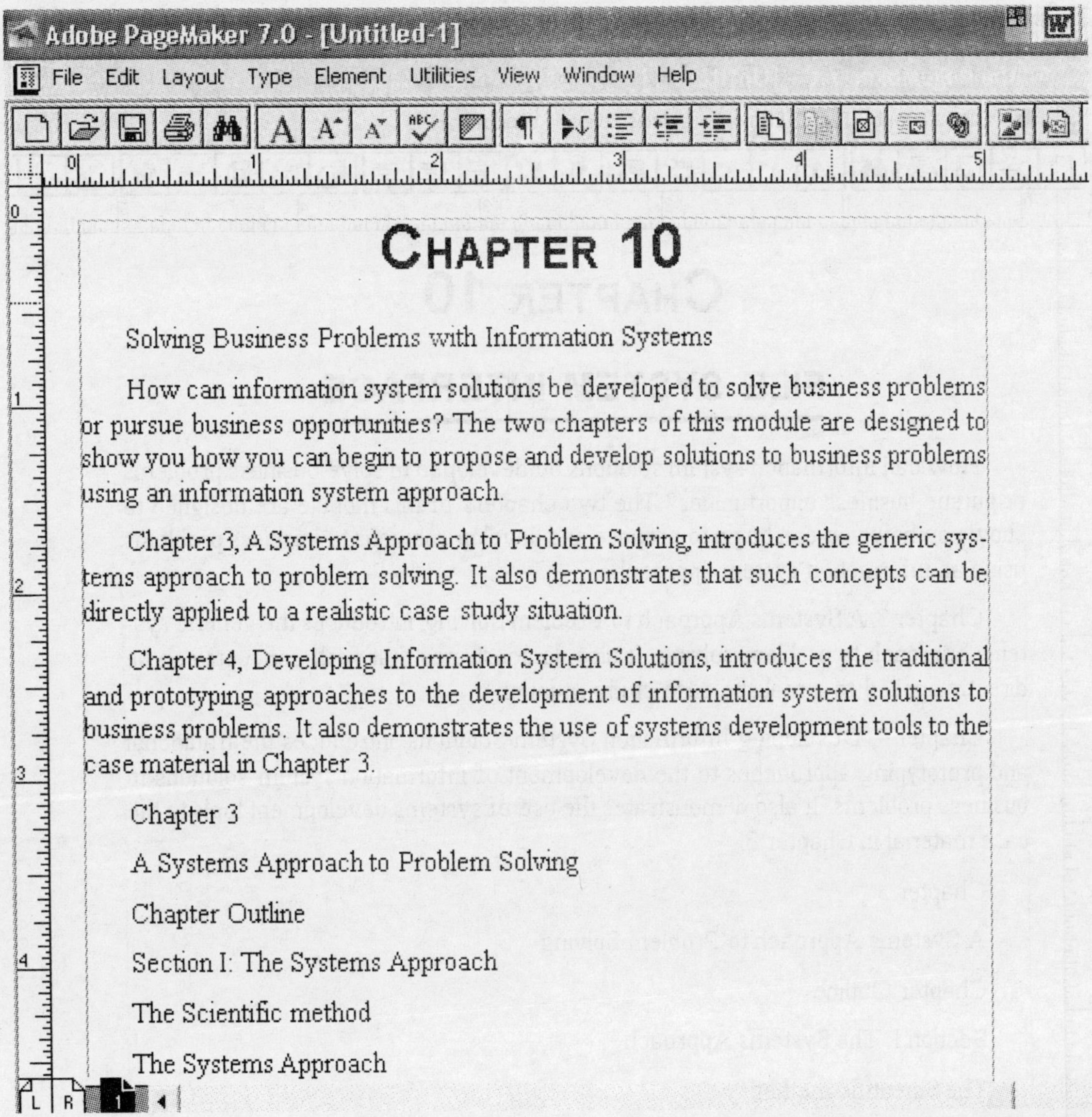

First Indent	0
Space after	1 pica
Alignment	Centre
Include in Table of Contents	
Rule below paragraph	Yes
Stroke style	2 point
Stroke width	width of text
Space below the Stroke	8 points

This can be seen in the figure shown on the next page. Next in line is the heading called

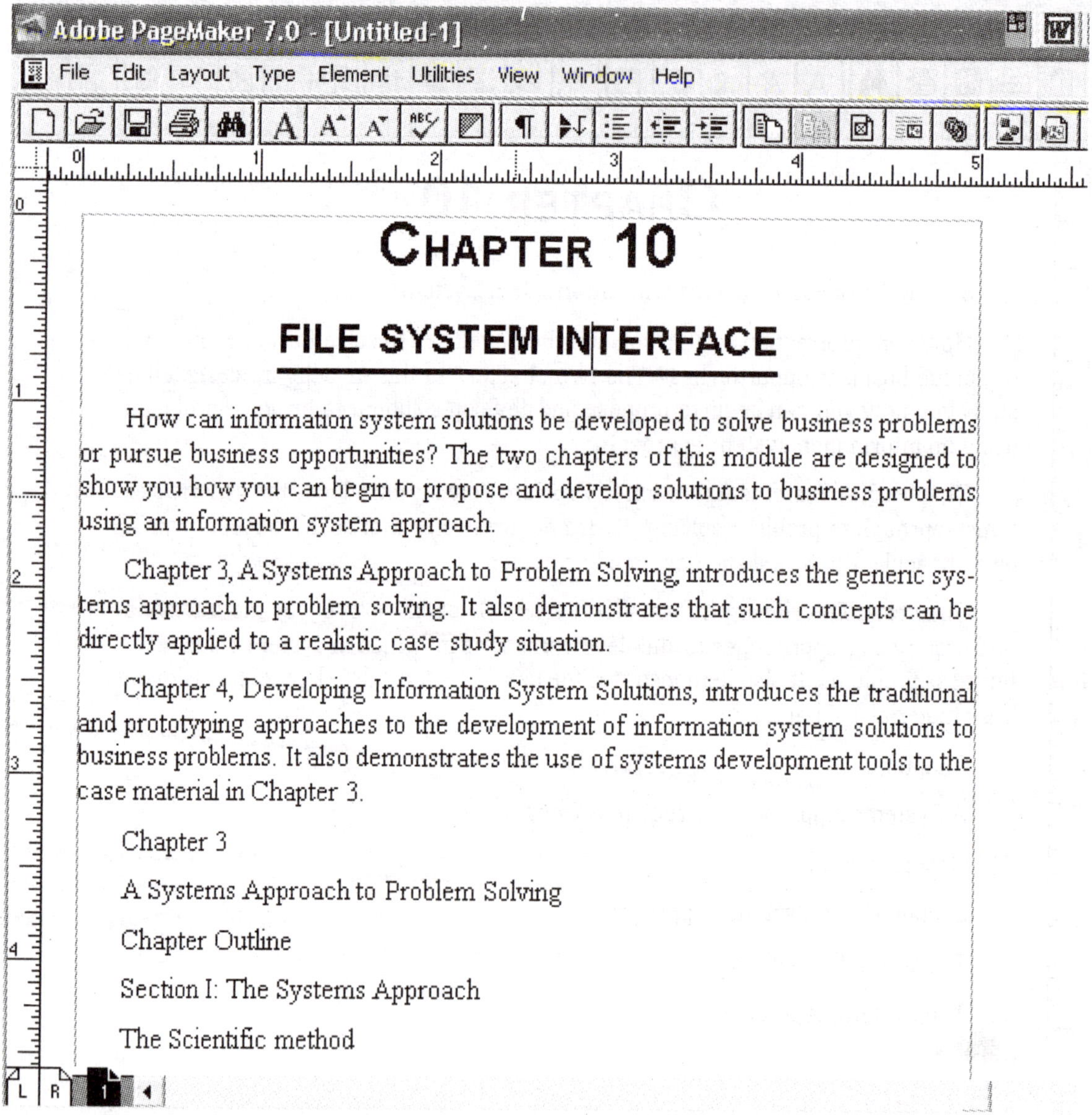

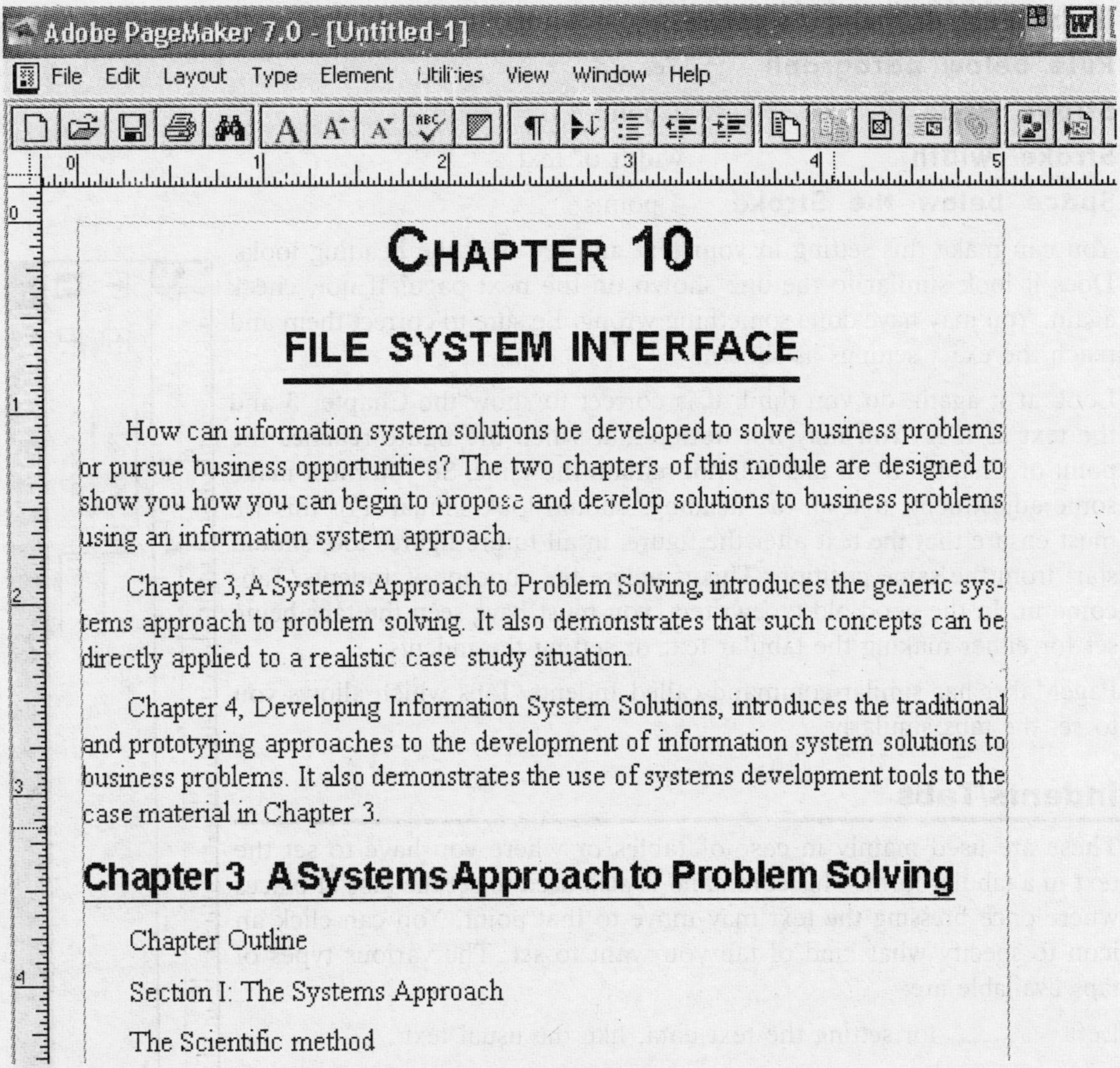

"Chapter 3 A Systems Approach to Problem Solving". For this we will be doing the following settings.

Font	Arial
Size	14
Type Style	Bold
Case	Normal
First Indent	0
Space before	4 points
Space after	8 points
Alignment	Left

Include in Table of Contents

Rule below paragraph	Yes
Stroke style	1 point
Stroke width	width of text
Space below the Stroke	4 points

You can make this setting in your text and see how the heading looks. Does it look similar to the one shown on the next page? If not, check again. You may have done something wrong. Be sure to correct them and reach the exact settings as shown.

Look at it again, do you think it is correct to show the Chapter 3 and the text as it is. You may not notice that when the figure reaches the point of Chapter 10 all this will not remain the same. So you must make some adjustment that all the headings should look similar. For this we must ensure that the text after the figure, in all future figures too, should start from the same position. This is where the concept of Indents/Tabs come in. In the good old typewriters, you must have seen the tabs being set for either making the tabular text or setting the indents.

PageMaker has similar command called Indents/Tabs which allows you to set the tabs similarly.

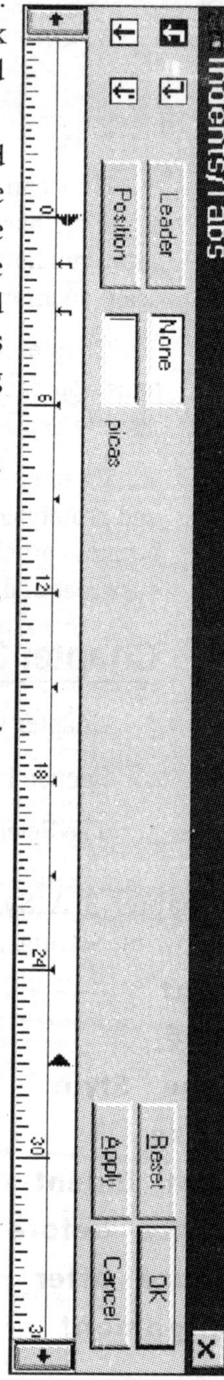

Indents/Tabs

These are used mainly in case of tables or where you have to set the text in a tabular form. This command is also used to set the tabs at places where once pressing the text may move to that point. You can click an icon to specify what kind of tab you want to set. The various types of tabs available are:

Left	for setting the text data, like the usual text.
Right	for setting the numeric data, like the amount in Rupees which you must have seen that it is allied to the right.
Centre	for setting the data which you want to centralize, mainly the headings of the tables.
Decimal	for aligning the numeric data on the basis of decimals, like the numeric data which is available in decimals.

These you can set it by clicking a point on the ruler or by choosing an option from the position box. Other options are:

Leader

This is used to specify the type of leaders you want along with the tab. The various options are in the form of dotted lines, underlines, hyphen lines, none and custom where you can set your own character to act as leader. To create a leader, click a tab icons, click the leader button to see PageMaker predefined leader and selected the leader style you want from the list. To create your own leader style, select custom and type one or two characters in the leader.

Position

This is used to specify what you want to do relative to a specific tab you can:

Add tab: It adds a tab at a position specified in the edit box.

Delete tab: It deletes the tab from a position specified in the edit box.

Move tab: It moves a selected tab from its current position to the position you type in the edit box.

Repeat tab: It repeats a tab automatically setting a series of tabs at the distances between the selected tab and the proceeding tab or the tab ruler zero point.

Reset

Once clicked it resets all the tabs and returns to the default condition.

Apply Before finally saying Ok, you can check whether your tabs have been set properly by clicking at this. This will leave the Indents/Tabs dialog box On and you can see underneath it that the tabs have been set properly. If satisfied, press Ok.

There are two very important type of indents which I must define here. They are Hanging indent and First indent.

Hanging indent

This text has been created using hanging indent. In this you select the first line to start from zero and the subsequent lines to start from the indented point. To do this first take the icon to the position where you want all the subsequent lines to begin, in this case 7 pica. Now pick up the upper portion of the icon and drag it to zero position. The upper portion of icon defined the first line. Put a left tab at 7 pica too, for the setting of the first line tab. This is called Hanging indent.

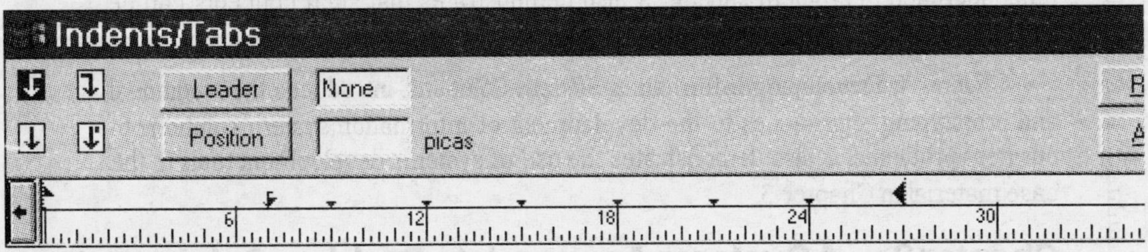

First indent

You must have seen that in some cases the first line of each para starts from a particular distance, this is called first indented para. To set this take the icon to the zero point. Pick up the top half of the icon and drag it to the point where you want to set the first line indent.

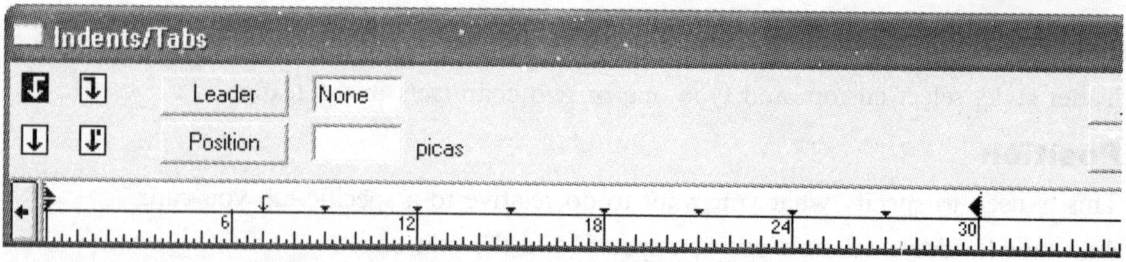

Coming back to our problem, we will set the indents in our heading using these options. Incidentally, Indents/Tabs dialog box can be generated by clicking at Indents/Tabs under the Type menu. Since the Chapter 3 to say 3 or more will not take more than one and a half pica, we will for the safe side put the left indent at seven pica on the heading.

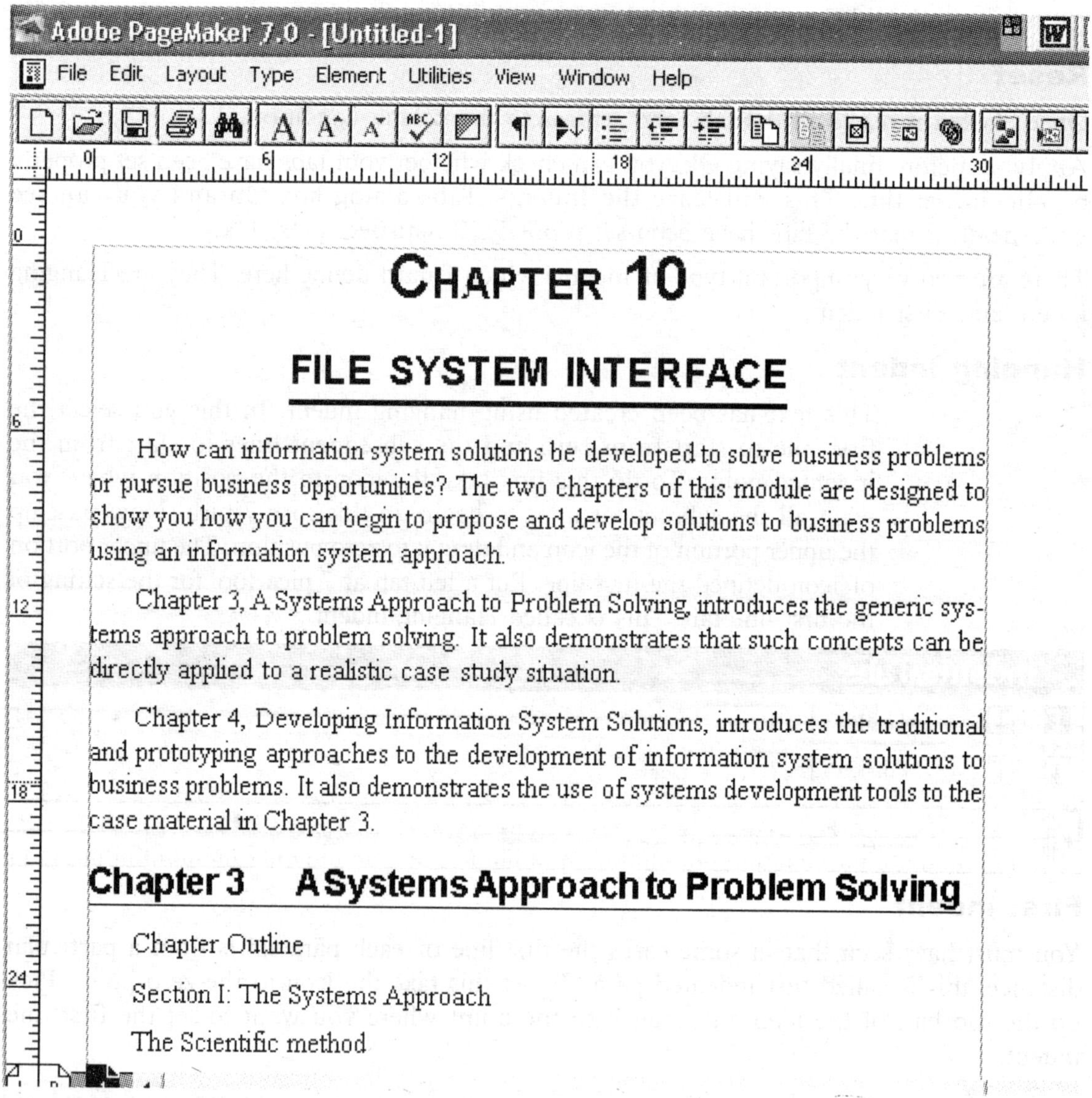

Set this indent on the heading "Chapter 3 A Systems Approach to Problem Solving". Now press tab between 3 and the text "A System......". Notice the change. But first see the tab set at three pica in the Indent/Tab dialog box.

But all we going to do this for each and every headings. You think it is possible to remember all these settings of the headings for full 200 to 300 pages of the text. You are bound to make some mistake somewhere. To avoid this kind of thing, we have what are called as Styles. You set styles and be assured that all the chapters have the same kind of styles.

Styles

For this we have the command called **Define Styles**, available under Type menu. Once called it gives rise to a dialog box as shown on the next page. You can add new style sheet to a publication by:

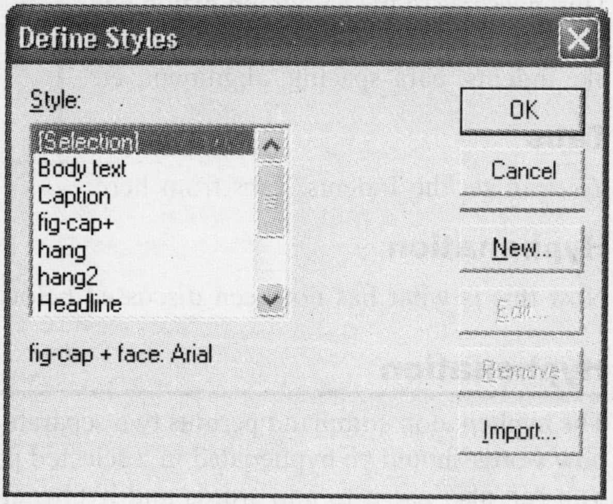

- Define style from scratch using the formatting of a selected paragraph.
- Defining a new style on one of the active publications existing styles.
- Copying an existing style sheet from another publication.
- Importing word processed document with style sheet attached.

You can add a new style to your publication style sheet at any time while you are working on your publication. Once you have added a new style to the style sheet, that style appears on the style palette.

Style sheet dialog box has the following commands:

Style

PageMaker initially supplies a list of styles which can be used. You can select any one of the same by clicking it and changing its parameters.

New/Edit

Choose one of these depending upon whether you want to edit the existing one or create a new one. A quick way to create a new style is to base it on an existing one. This style will have to be selected before you click new.

Remove

Select the style which you want to remove and press remove, this particular style is deleted.

Import

You can copy all the styles of a particular publication from another PageMaker publication or template.

Once you select one of the them, New or Edit. It gives rise to a new dialog box, as shown here. In the case of new, you have to give a name here. It also shows you the settings already made to give you a brief idea of what is stored under this style. On the right hand panel, you have the 4 settings:

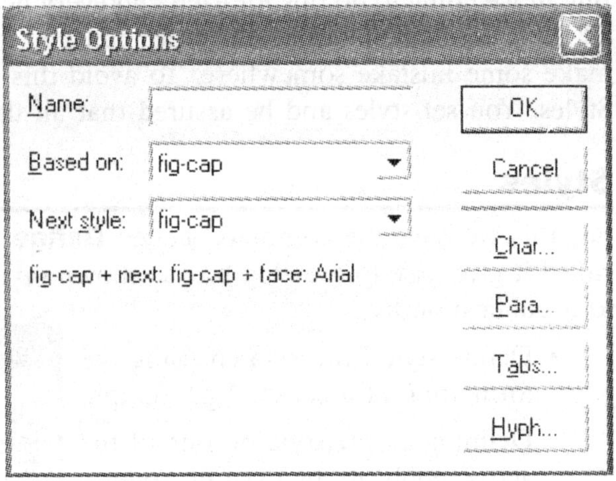

Character

Clicking at it gives rise to the character dialog box, which we had discussed earlier. You can set the various options here like, Font, Size, Leading, etc.

Paragraph

This gives rise to the paragraph dialog box, where you can set the paragraph settings like indents, para spacing, alignment, etc.

Tabs

You can set the Indents/Tabs from here.

Hyphenation

Now this is what has not been discussed before. Let us discuss this first.

Hyphenation

The hyphenation command permits two separate operations. Its main purpose is to determine how words should be hyphenated in a selected paragraph or paragraphs of a particular style. You can also use it to add words and hyphenation instruction to your user dictionary.

When you click at the hyphenation the dialog box appears which has the following options.

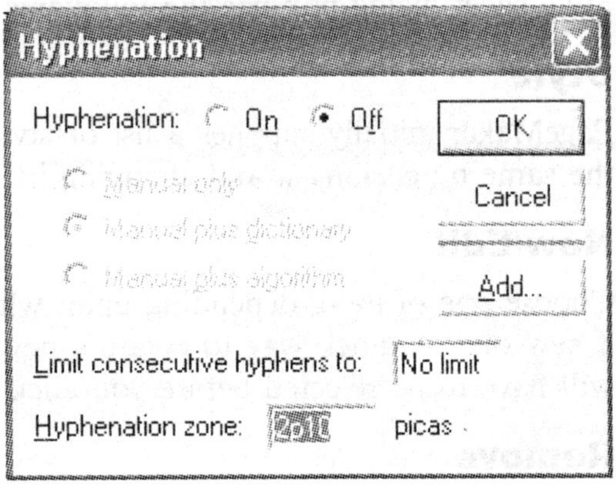

Hyphenation

Select to have the hyphenation ON or OFF. If off, select one of the following option.

Manual only: Select this option if you want a discretion hyphenation. A discretional hyphen is that which you insert manually where you want a word to break, if it falls within the hyphenation zone. To insert discretional hyphenation in story editor or layout view, press Ctrl + Shift + hyphen window where you want the word to be hyphenation.

Manual plus dictionary: Select this option to hyphenate words containing discretionary hyphens as well as words in the online dictionary, raking of possible hyphenation breaks. In case we have both the discretional hyphen and dictionary one, the discretionary hyphen prevails over.

Manual plus algorithm: This provides for greater flexibility for hyphenation. Words may be hyphenated by discretionary hyphens, dictionary or by the hyphenation algorithm. This algorithm permits hyphenation break in words not found in the Page Maker dictionary or the user dictionary.

Limit consecutive hyphens to

You can define the limit of hyphenated words that occur in consecutive lines in a paragraph by using this command. You can enter number from 1 to 255 or type nolimits.

Hyphenation zone

Determines the amount of space in which hyphenation can occur at the end of each line for unjustified text. Page Maker applies the desired word spacing and built-in letter spacing. If the last word in the line does not fill and that word starts to the left of the hyphenation zone, PageMaker tries to hyphenate that word. In general, the larger the hyphenation zone, the more ragged the right margin of text will be. The smaller the zone, the more hyphenation will occur. This option has no effect on justified text.

Add

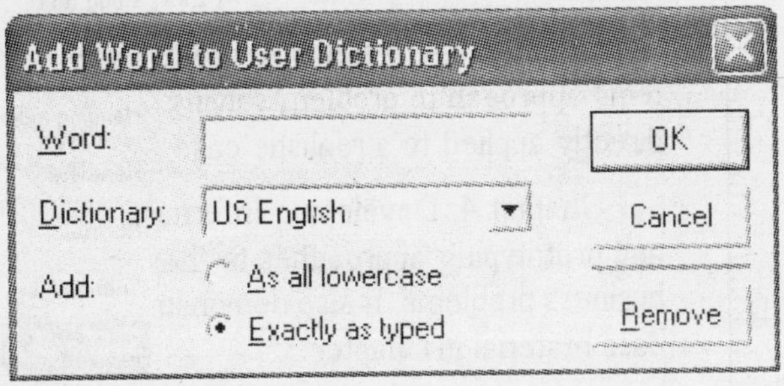

This displays the add word dialog box for:

- Selecting which dictionary you want to modify.
- Add or change hyphenation breaks for a word.
- Add word to or remove words from the dictionary.

If the word you add, already exists in the dictionary, the new hyphenation breaks and capabilities replace the previous ones. This finishes our introduction to the Hyphenation command. Now we know how to use it. If you want that no word should break in your text, choose the option of OFF.

Now we know about the all the options of the Styles dialog box. Click each one of them, one by one and fill up their respective data. For example, for the Body text, you fill the details, which you had filled up for the complete text, as on earlier page for the character and on next page for the paragraph settings. Similarly you can change the options for Caption and Headline and make them the ones which we had selected for the Chapter number and Chapter headings. The heading options can be set in the option named Subhead 1 and so on.

When you have finished all the settings. Click Ok to record all the styles. Now all you have to do is to apply them. Call the styles sheet on the screen from the Window menu. By picking up paragraph one by one, you can apply the styles as shown next. You must have noticed that we have not given any folio number to our pages in the publication. For this we have to understand the concept of master pages again. As was said earlier that master pages lie at the bottom left of the publication, but what are these master pages and where are they used, let us see.

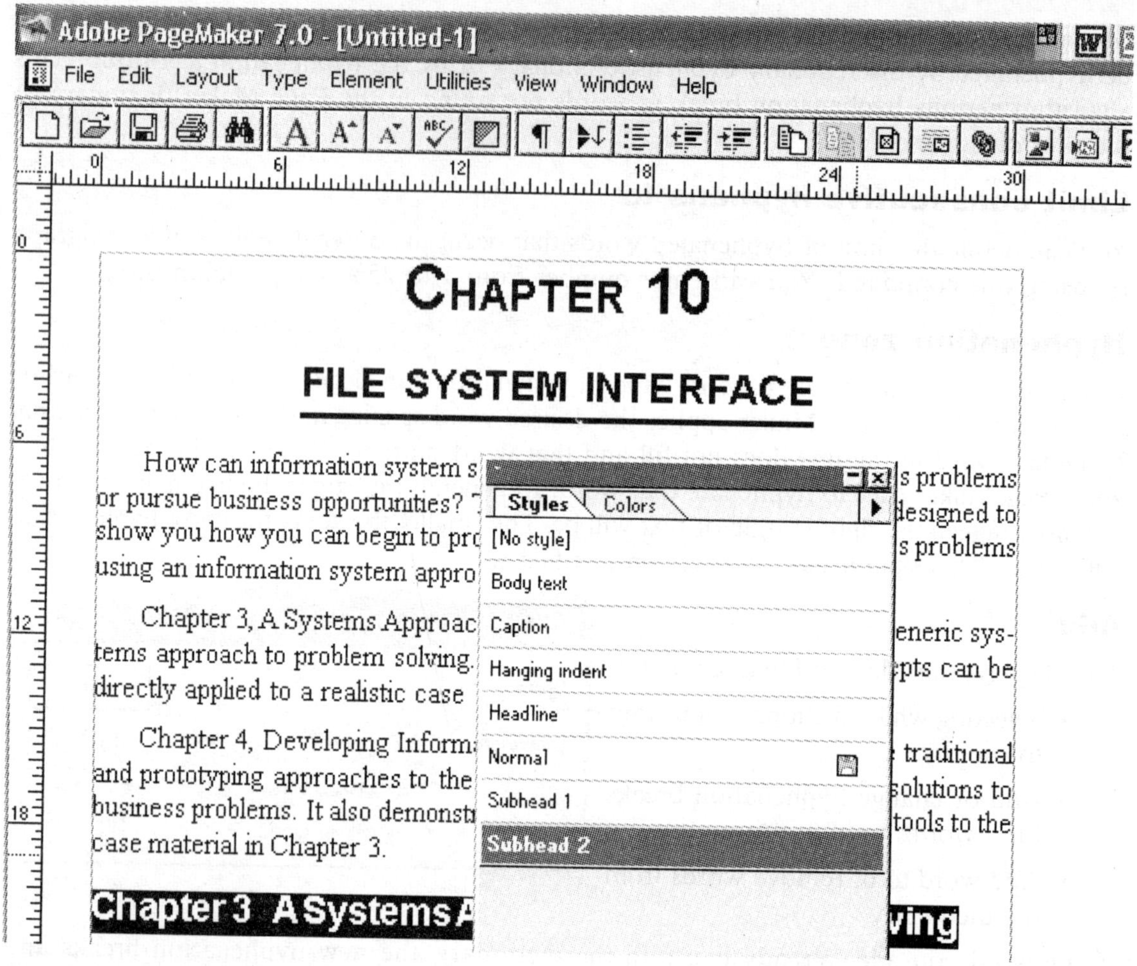

Master Pages

Whatever we put at the master pages gets reflected at all the pages in the publication. So what we do is, put whatever is common to all pages, on the master pages. This includes Headers and Footers. Sometimes while making invoices, we put the invoice matter on the master page and type the current bill on the regular pages. Even for typing the routine office correspondence, we sometimes make the letterhead on the master page, so that it need not be typed on all pages.

Header and Footers

Header is what you put on the top of each page of the book. Footer is what you put at the bottom of the page. In this book, you would notice that I have put header on the top. You can even put it on the bottom to make them Footer instead of Header.

Page Numbering

It follows a very defined pattern. I would not call it a rule, but would like to call it a

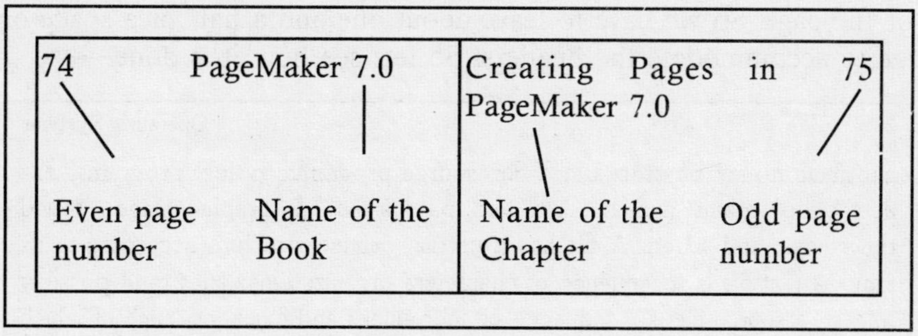

convention. Given above is the format of the page you are looking at. Now you know what comes where, but how to create it, is the problem. For this click at the master page location, to see the master pages on the screen. You will see a blank page format side-by-side as seen above. With the help of the mouse click at any place in the page format and type the name of the chapter. Click this with the pointer tool and drag its corner to the left top of the right hand page format.

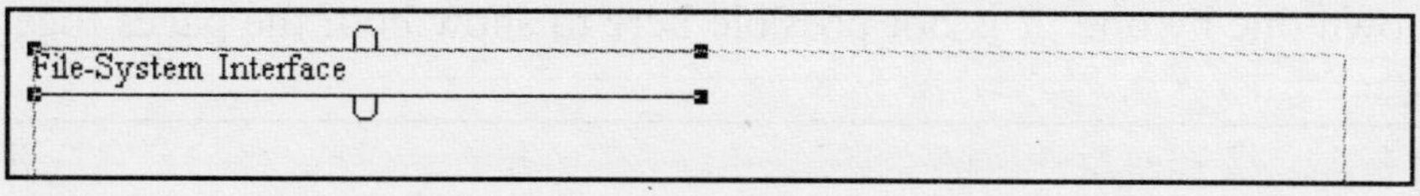

Click it with the text tool and format it according to the requirements. For a book whose text is of the size of 11 points, the folio text can be of 9-10 points. So you can choose it to be in 10 points. Again using the pointer tool click at the text to form a block of text. Drag the right corners of the text block to make it half of the page size, as shown above.

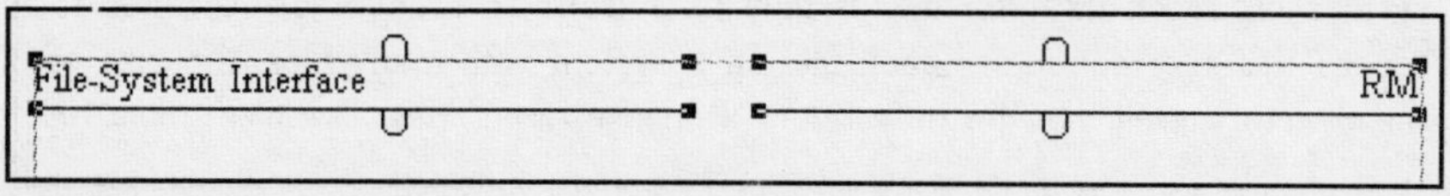

Again click at any place inside the page block to get cursor for typing. Type **Ctl+Alt+P**, to get a symbol **PB** on the page. This is the indicator of the page number on the master page. Make it 10 points Times New Roman as above but make it right aligned by **Ctrl+Shift+R**. Now drag it to the right corner of the right hand side of the master page, as shown below, after making the block as half.

Similarly for the left hand page, type Ctl+Alt+P for the page number on the left hand corner and the book name for the right hand side of the left hand page. So now when you see the left hand page of the master page, you will see something like this. Do not worry about **RM** becoming **LM** on this page, it the indicator that this is Left Master (LM) and the other is Right Master (RM). Now open the page 2-3 of the publication and see the effect these headers. Oh God, what happened. The text of the header and text matter of the page 2 and 3 has been mixed up. This is so since we did not make provision for having the header

on the top of the page. So we have to leave about one and a half pica space on the top of the each page to accommodate the headers. So lets see how it is done.

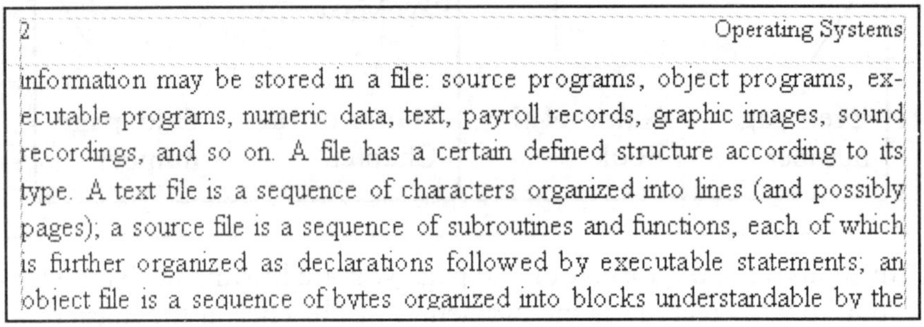

2 Operating Systems

information may be stored in a file: source programs, object programs, executable programs, numeric data, text, payroll records, graphic images, sound recordings, and so on. A file has a certain defined structure according to its type. A text file is a sequence of characters organized into lines (and possibly pages); a source file is a sequence of subroutines and functions, each of which is further organized as declarations followed by executable statements; an object file is a sequence of bytes organized into blocks understandable by the

On the master page put a guide at one and a half pica from the top. This is our indication that the text would start from this line downwards. Now what you will have to do is that you will have to drag the text on page number 2 and 3 downwards by one and a half pica to make the header look like the one shown here. Due to constraints in page size, both pages are shown one by one. It is not possible here to show both the pages together on this and next page.

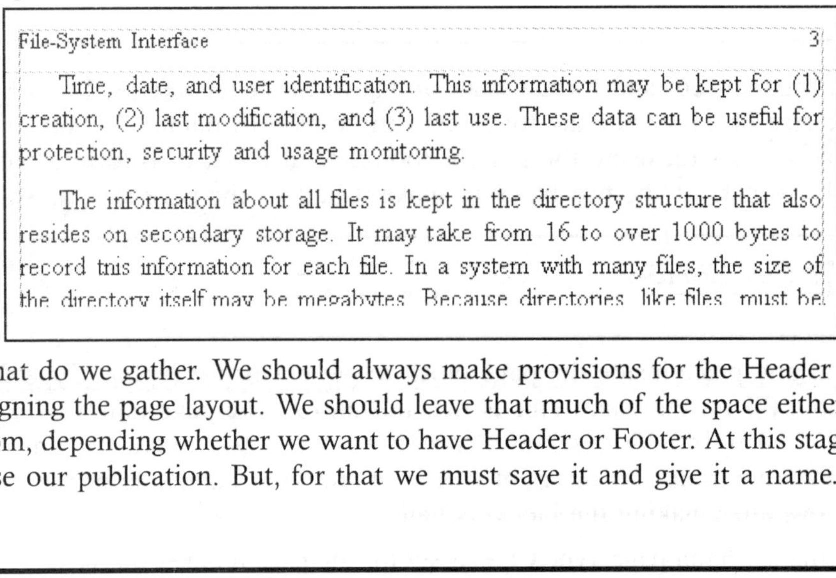

File-System Interface 3

Time, date, and user identification. This information may be kept for (1) creation, (2) last modification, and (3) last use. These data can be useful for protection, security and usage monitoring.

The information about all files is kept in the directory structure that also resides on secondary storage. It may take from 16 to over 1000 bytes to record tnis information for each file. In a system with many files, the size of the directory itself may be megabytes. Because directories, like files, must be

So now what do we gather. We should always make provisions for the Header and Footer, before designing the page layout. We should leave that much of the space either on the top or on bottom, depending whether we want to have Header or Footer. At this stage we would like to close our publication. But, for that we must save it and give it a name.

Saving

It is a natural command, since whatever you do on computer, you must save it to preserve for the future. So first time when you give the save command **Ctrl+S**, PageMaker will ask you to give a name to your file. It is totally optional, where you want to save the file in your directory. Select the name which you want to give to your publication, its location, etc., before giving the save command, to get the save dialog box, as shown here. Once saved the file would be stored in the hard disk and can be called whenever required.

Closing of the Publication

When you feel that you have finished your work with the file, close the publication using the **Close** command from the File menu.

Editing Pages in PageMaker

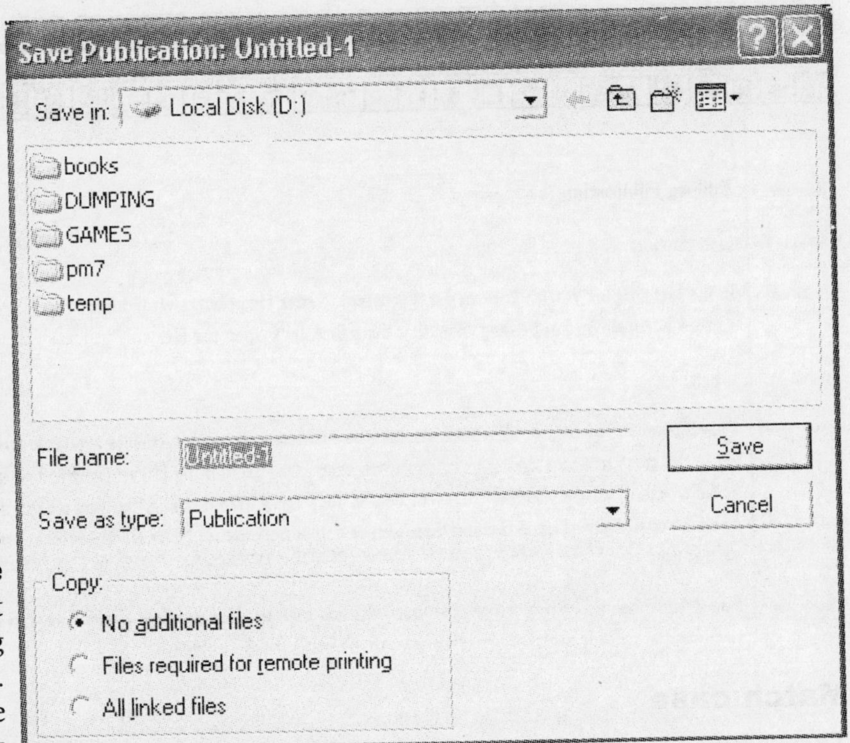

Earlier we learned how to create a page in PageMaker. Now we would learn to edit it. But, first thing first, let's open the file.

Open

PageMaker's **Open** is no different from various other open commands. It is available under **File** menu. Once clicked it gives rise to a dialog box, as shown here. You click at the file you want to open. This file will be opened in the position, where you has closed it, i.e., at the page where it was when you closed it. Remember, you can even open a copy of the original file and then save it with a new name. Now let us perform our various other commands on this file.

PageMaker has its own word processing, which is built-in. This is called **Story Editor** in PageMaker. You can perform the various word processing operations using these commands.

Story Editor

Click your text with text tool anywhere in the text and press **Ctrl + E** to get into the story editor mode. As you can see from the figure below, changing to story editor, the **Layout** menu has become the **Story** menu. It has commands which are applicable to story editor only. Not only this, the text is also displayed with the style name on the left hand side for easy reference.

Now we will perform the various word processing options on this text while still in the story editor mode. The first and foremost is the **Find** command.

Find

This command is used to find a particular word in the text. This command can be called from the **Utilities** menu. Once the dialog box, as shown here, comes on the screen, you can type in the word which you want to search. Then by clicking at **Find**, you will be able to start the search.

Various options of the dialog box are:

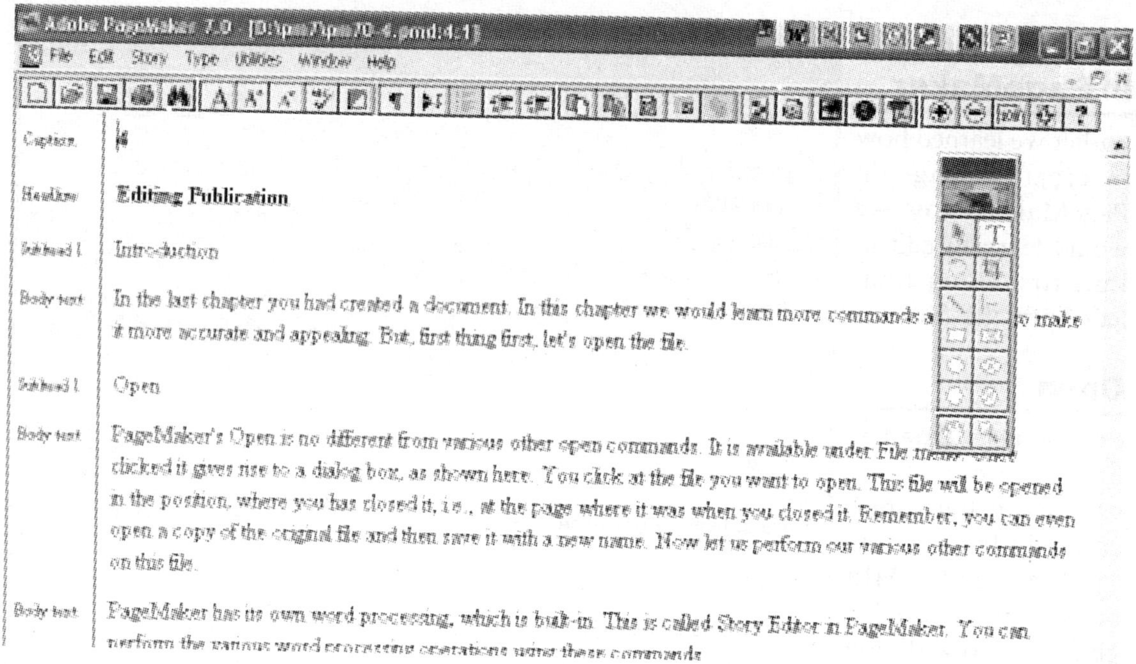

Match case

This command is used when you have the word which exactly matches the case of the word typed in the box.

Whole word

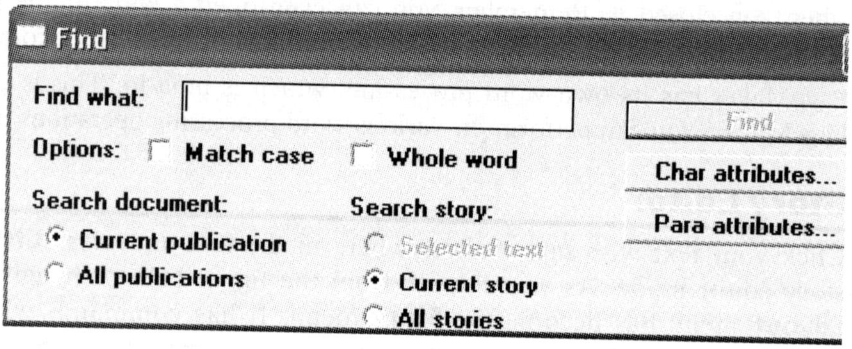

Sometimes you are looking for a word maybe "Ta" as a single word. If you do not click this then all the words starting with "Ta" will also be selected.

Search document

This has the following options:

Current publication: The search will be performed in the current open publication only.

All publications: The search will be performed in all the publications which are open.

Search story

This has the following options

Selected text: It is possible that you may have highlighted some text from which you want to find this particular word.

Current story: Instead of highlighting some text, you can search for the word in the whole story.

All stories: There may be more than one stories in the publication. This option will search in all the stories of the publication.

The second part of this command is **Change**, where you find something and change it with another.

Change

This command is used when you have to replace one word with another. Supposing due to the change of name of the city called *Bombay* to *Mumbai*, it has become necessary to make the same change in your publication which has the word extensively used. Now, it is not possible to find out each occurrence of the word and change it manually. So, this command comes in handy. All the various options of the **Find** command and valid here too, like the options of match case, whole word, etc.

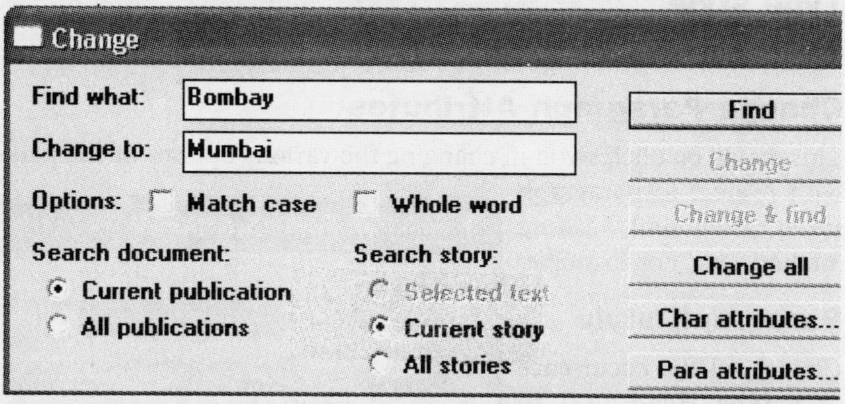

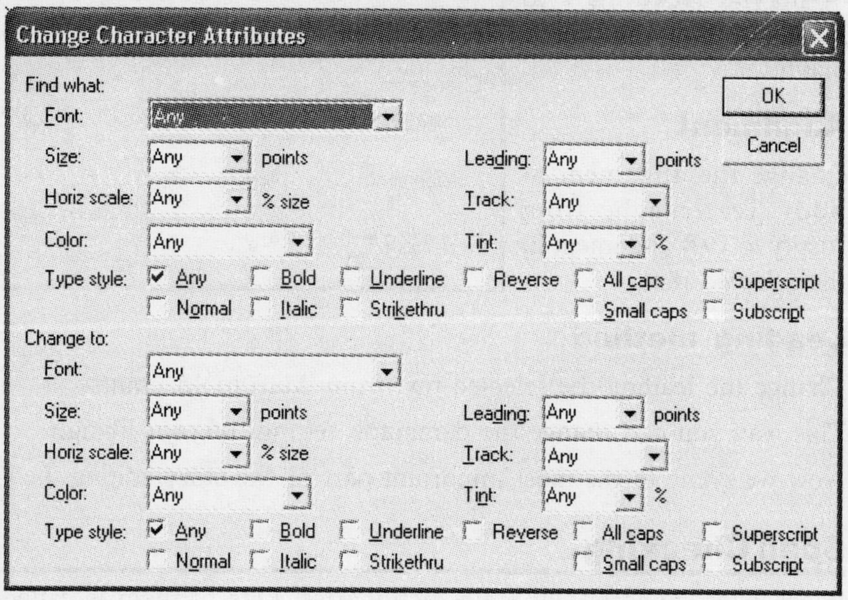

You have the option of changing all at one go by clicking **Change All**. Otherwise click at **Change** and it will change one by one. Le me discuss here the two other options which I had not discussed under Find. These are **Char attributes** and **Para attributes**.

Change Character Attributes

This dialog box helps you in changing character properties using the other options as well.

You can change with respect to fonts, sizes, types, etc. But remember for this both your fields of **Find what** and **Change to** in the opening **Find** dialog box should be blank. For example,

Font

Change all Arial font to Times New Roman font. For this change Find what Font to Arial and Change to Font to Times New Roman.

Size

Change all occurrence of 14 points size to 12 point size.

Type style

Change all occurrence of Bold to Normal.

Change Paragraph Attributes

This dialog box helps you in changing the various options of the paragraph. You can change with respect to paragraph styles, alignment, leading method, etc. For example,

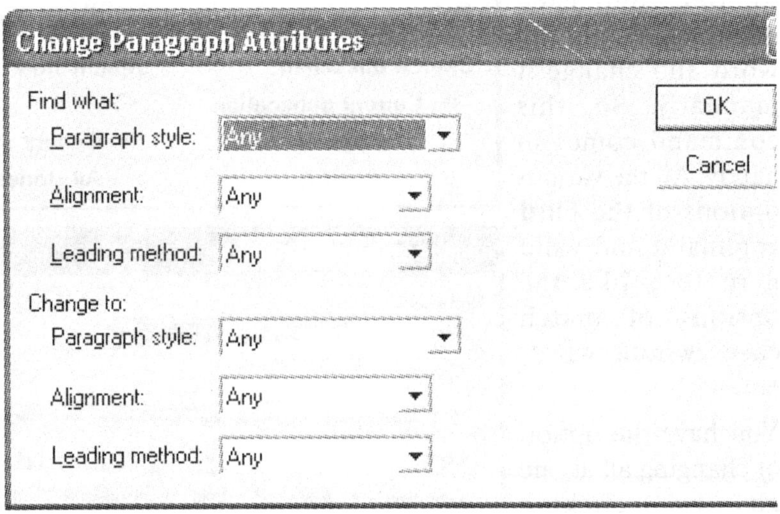

Paragraph style

Change all the occurrence of maybe Heading 1 to Heading 2 as the case maybe.

Alignment

Change the alignment of Body Text maybe from Justify to Left alignment in the selected text.

Leading method

Change the leading the selected text from Auto to 15 points.

This way you can change the paragraph settings of your liking.

Now we come to the most important part of the story editing, i.e., spell checking.

Spell Checking

PageMaker supports two main dictionaries. One of them is called **UK English** and the other one is called **US English**. While installing the software you have the option of installing either one of the two or maybe you can install both of them. But, preferably for a publication, you will use either one of them.

When you spell check your document, each word of your document is compared with the corresponding words in the dictionary. If not found in dictionary, it is pointed out as an error. Then the choice is yours whether to accept the word as it is or make the change according to the changes suggested by the software.

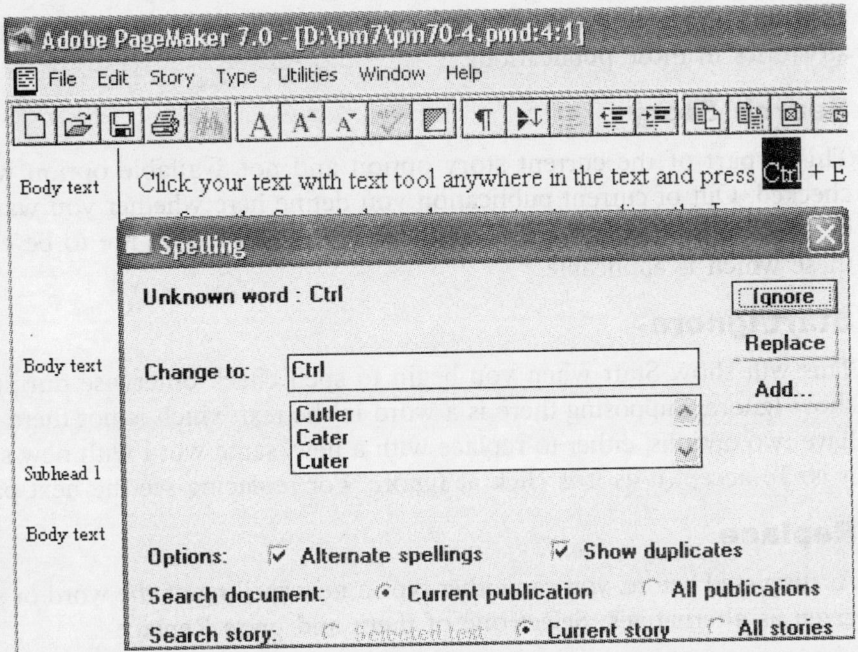

For checking the whole document, your cursor should be at the starting point of the text. However, if you want a particular part of the text to be spell checked, then select this text before entering the story editor and then start the spell checking. The **Spelling** command is available under the Utilities menu. Once initiated it will give rise to a dialog box, where you just have to click **Start** to start the spell checking. Once a wrong word is found the spell checking dialog box, as shown here, will be displayed.

This dialog box has the following options:

Change to

PageMaker displays the word which is not there in the dictionary with which it is comparing. In this box either you type the word you think is the corrected version of the word not found or alternatively, you can click from the possible words given in the box below for suggestions. After selecting, click it twice to make sure that the word fills the box of change to before replacing.

Alternate spellings

These words are provided from the dictionary to give suggestions regarding words. If however, you do not want them to appear, select the options accordingly for this can definitely speed up the spell checking.

Show duplicates

It is possible that the text may contain duplicate words like text text. PageMaker will show them but not delete them. The choice is totally yours to drop one of them or not. Similar to above, you can speed up spell checking by keeping it off.

Search document

In this option you specify whether you want the current publication to be spell checked or all open publications. If you search all open publications, PageMaker automatically searches all stories in those publications.

Search Story

This is part of the current story option and not available option wherein all stories are checked. Out of current publication you define here whether you want the Selected text to be checked or Current story to be checked or All stories are to be checked. Select one of these which is applicable.

Start/Ignore

This will show Start when you begin to spell check otherwise during the checking it will show Ignore. Supposing there is a word in the text which is not there in the dictionary, you have two options, either to replace with a new/same word with new spelling or accept it as it is. To accept it as it is click at Ignore. For replacing see the next para.

Replace

As discussed before, you can either type a new spelling of the word or select from the option given as alternatives. Select one of them and press Replace

Add

Opens the add word to user dictionary dialog box in which you specify the word you want to add to or remove from the dictionary. If a word is displayed in the Change to edit box PageMaker displays it in the word edit box otherwise the word box is empty, ready for you to type in the word you want to add.

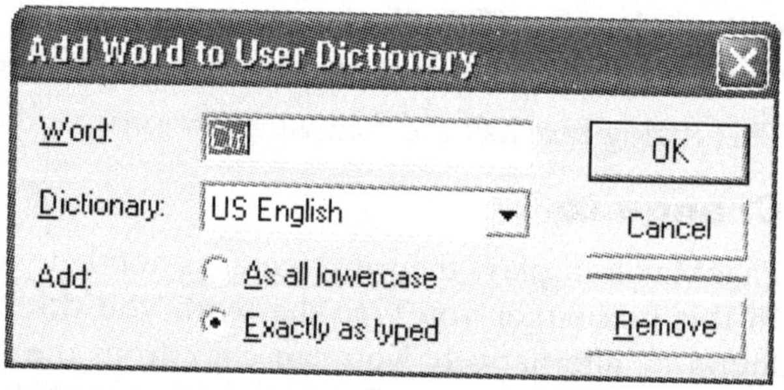

Word: This box displays the word which come from the previous menu of being not there in the Dictionary.

Dictionary: PageMaker adds the word in the word edit box to the dictionary you select.

Add all lowercase: Click this to add the word to the dictionary in a generic form that will match that word with any ordinary capitalization pattern, so PageMaker will highlight only spelling errors not capitalization errors.

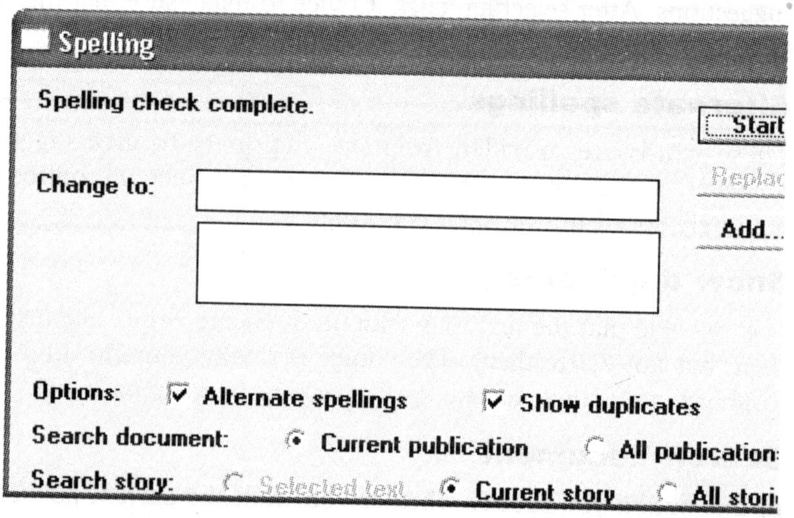

Exactly as typed: Click this to highlight words if they do not match the entry exactly as typed.

Once all the word have been corrected and spell checked, PageMaker will inform you so. With this we end the story editor session, so you can come back to the page layout by again pressing **Ctrl+E**.

But, this is not the end of editing. There are other editing commands which are very commonly used in all the word processors. These are **Cut**, **Copy**, **Paste**, etc. Let us see how these commands are used.

Cut

This command is used to cut the selected text or graphics from your file and keep it available for pasting it later to any other place in the same file or any other file or even any other software which supports the clipboard text.

To select an independent graphic to cut, use the pointer tool. To select text or an inline graphic, use either the pointer tool or the text tool, keeping in mind the following guidelines:

— Use the pointer tool to select an entire text block, maintaining its type specifications and line length. Cutting and pasting a text block by text tool turns it into a separate story.

— Use the text tool to select a range of text to cut.

When you use the pointer tool to cut an entire text block from a page, the space that was occupied by the block remains blank. When you use the text tool to cut all or part of a text block, PageMaker automatically closes the gap. When you cut an inline graphic or an independent graphic with text wrapped around it, the text fills the space which graphic occupied.

Copy

This command is also used to copy the selected text or graphics from your file and keep it available for pasting it later. Only difference it has from **Cut** command is that it leaves the original text as it is whereas in the case of **Cut** the original text is lost.

When you have more than one publication open, you can copy objects between publications without using the **Clipboard**. Select an object in one publication, drag it to position in the other publication window and release the mouse button to create a copy.

Paste

This command is used to place the selected text or graphics from clipboard, where the text using the above **Cut** or **Copy** command has been kept. You can paste text and graphics using either the pointer tool or the text tool, depending on how you want the pasted object to be incorporated into your publication.

When you use the pointer for pasting, the location of a pasted object is determined by its original position on the screen, if it is visible. The object is pasted at a slight offset from that position, if it is not visible, PageMaker places the object in the centre of the visible page. To paste an object at its original position, press **Shift** as you choose paste from the edit menu.

Text pasted using the pointer tool becomes a separate text block. This text is not thread to the other text in the publication and it retains the formatting it had when cut or copied. A graphic pasted with the pointer tool is independent and is not tied to the text surrounding it.

Paste Multiple

This command is just an extension of above mentioned **Paste** command wherein instead of pasting from the clipboard matter once, you can paste it as many times as you want by defining the number of copies you want and their placement too.

Method of pasting is also similar to paste command, i.e., when to choose the pointer tool and when to choose the text tool. Various options available under this dialog box are:

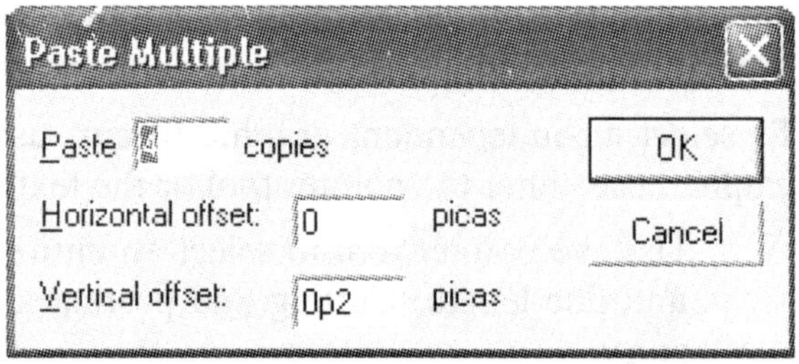

Paste

You can specify here the number of copies you want to paste.

Horizontal offset

You can specify here the horizontal distance between each of the pasted objects or group of objects. This option is not available when multiple pasting with the text too.

Vertical offset

You can specify the vertical distance between each copy of the paste object or group of objects. This option is also not available when multiple pasting with the text tool.

You can even enter positive or negative value in horizontal offset and vertical offset. Positive number offset copies from left to right and from top to bottom relative to the original object. Negative number offset copies from right to left and from bottom to top. You cannot undo this command.

Working with Columns

You can divide the page of the publication into different columns of equal size. You can create columns of unequal length by pulling guides to the required place. However, the text flow from previous page, i.e., **Autoflow** does not recognise this option and does

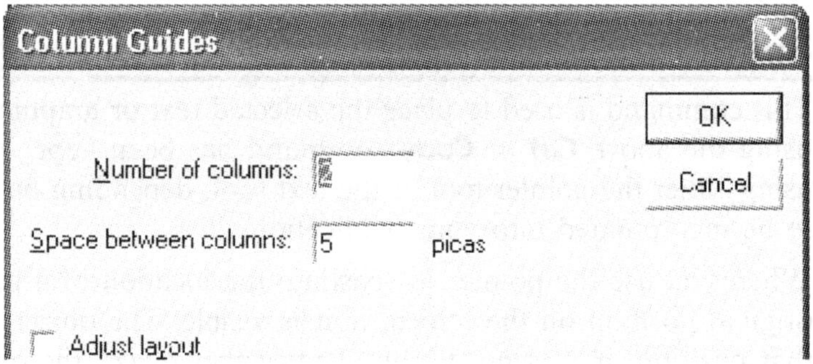

not flow the text in unequal columns. The maximum number of columns that you can create on a page are 20.

If not defined the page is counted to have 1 column, so that the number of column which you should mention here using the column guides should be minimum 2.

Number of columns

Specify here the number of columns you want on the page.

Space between columns

Specify the amount of space you want to leave between the two columns.

If you have to have a full publication divided into the columns, it is advised to have the columns made on the master page itself so that you do not have to set the guides on all pages. This is where I come back to the page layout of setting two pages on one A4 paper, which was briefly introduced to you on page 15 of this book. In this case too, we will divide the A4 page into 2 columns each forming a page. As you would remember the paper size of A4 is 11.693 inches by 8.268 inches. Out of this we will make two pages of 7 inches by 4 inches and leave enough space for cutting on all sides.

We will select out **Document Setup** as follows:

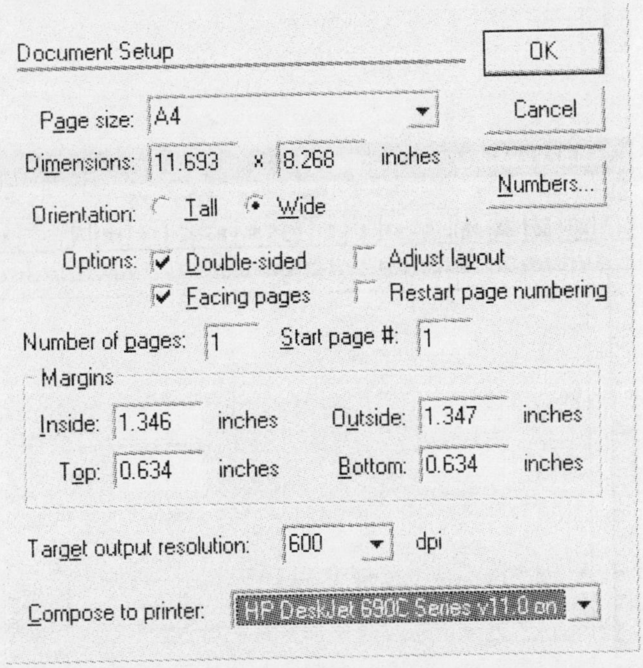

As you would have noticed that we have left space of 1.346 inches and 1.347 inches on both sides respectively. This would leave you with a space of 9 inches on the horizontal side. On the vertical side, the space of 0.634 inches on both sides would leave the vertical page size of 7 inches. Once clicked the above document setup would leave you with a page layout as shown on the next page.

Now that you have a page size of 9 x 7 inches. All you have to do is to divide the page horizontally into 2 and this can be done easily by using the command of Column guides.

Just call **Column guides** and divide the page into 2 column with

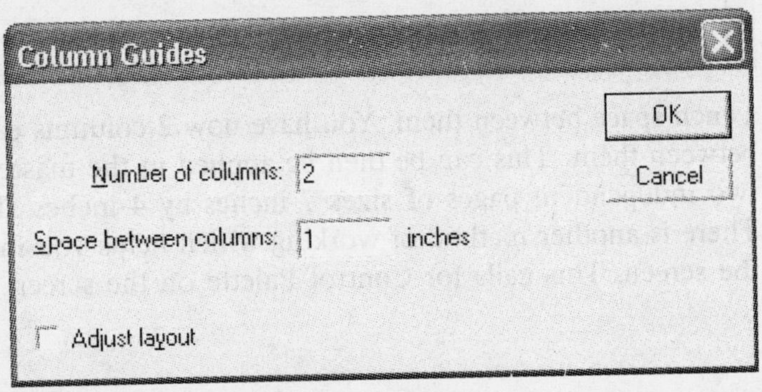

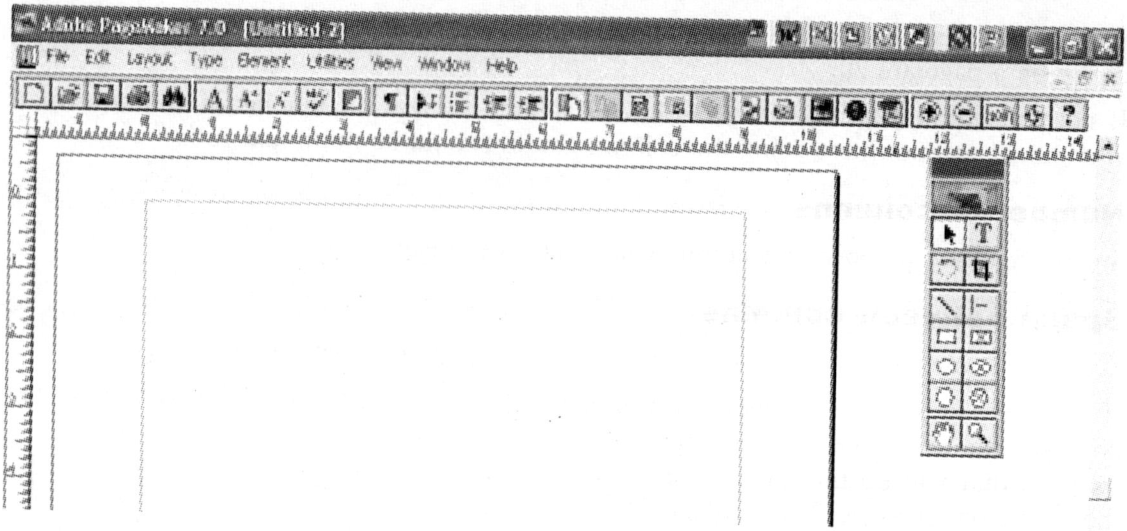

1 inch space between them. You have now 2 columns each of 4 inches and 1 inch space in between them. This can be then be applied in the master page and you have the page with two independent pages of sizes 7 inches by 4 inches. This can be seen on the next page. There is another method of working which helps you in putting most of the commands on the screen. This calls for Control Palette on the screen.

Control Palette

This command available under Window menu displays the control palette, as shown here. This can be used to format text & graphics and to trace the movements of the cursor & positions of objects on publication pages. The Control palette displays different options depending on the object or the tool selected.

Manipulating objects

You can use Control palette options to manipulate objects on the page. You can move, resize, rotate, skew or reflect graphic objects and text blocks and crop imported graphics, as well as measure their size and position on the page. The Control palette numerically tracks changes to selected objects, much as the dotted lines in the rulers track the movement of the cursor. The Control palette displays values accurately to 1/20 of a point. In contrast, the rulers display ¼ point increments at 400% view.

Formatting text

When you are using the text tool in layout view or when you are working in story editor, you can use the Control palette to format text. In either case, you can switch the Control palette between two views:

Character view It lets you change character attributes.

Paragraph view It lets you change paragraph attributes.

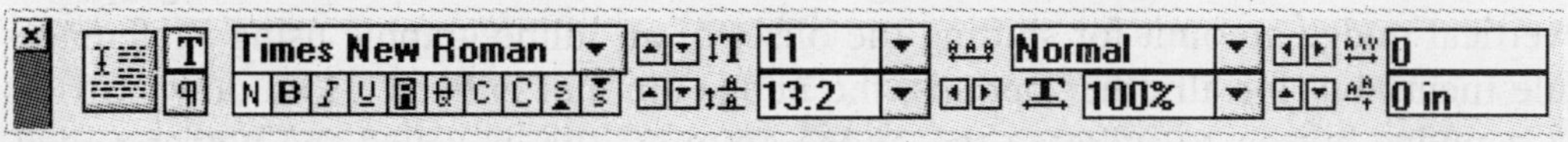

Character View

To format one or more selected character in your text, use character view. Character attributes such as font, type style, and type size display on the Control palette when the text tool is selected (or when you are working in the story editor) and you click the Character view button.

Paragraph View

To format one or more selected paragraph, use paragraph view. Paragraph attributes such as styles, alignment and indents display on the Control palette when the text tool is selected (or when you are working in story editor) and you click the Paragraph view button.

Changing and applying palette settings

You can change settings on the Control palette in several different ways. Depending on the option, you change settings by:

Clicking a mouse

The effect of clicking a button depends on the option.

Typing an entry

When you change a Control palette setting by typing a number, PageMaker displays an alert message if the number is invalid. For example, you can't rotate an object more than 360 degrees.

When you change a setting by typing a word, for example, a font or paragraph style, PageMaker compares the available options to match the characters you are typing.

When you change a setting by typing an entry, you must click the Apply button or press Enter to apply the change to the selected text or object.

Performing arithmetic

You can add to, subtract from, multiply or divide any existing value for an option by typing a mathematical expression into the edit box.

Selecting from a list

When you change a setting by selecting a list option, PageMaker applies the change immediately.

Using the Nudge buttons

Nudge buttons are located next to most options on the Control palette that have a numerical value. Clicking a nudge button increases or decreases the value for an option by a set amount. When you change a setting by clicking on a nudge button, PageMaker applies the change immediately.

You can set the horizontal and vertical nudge amount for the Position and Sizing options and the vertical nudge amount for shifting the offset of an inline graphic using Preferences on the File menu, but for all other options, the nudge amount is fixed. Hold down Ctrl as you click a nudge button to increase the nudge amount; this is called the power nudge. Power nudge is the nudge amount multiplied ten times.

Changing the options

By default, options on the Control palette use the measurement and vertical ruler defaults set for the publication. However, you can use a different unit of measure for a particular measurement, such as paragraph indents or the dimensions of an object. Activate a numeric option, and then Shift + F11 (Windows) to cycle through the units of measure available for the option.

Using the keyboard

You can use the Control palette to modify graphics and text blocks without removing yours hands from the keyboard.

Control palette options available with an object selected

Apply button

Click to modify selected objects after you type numeric values for one or more options.

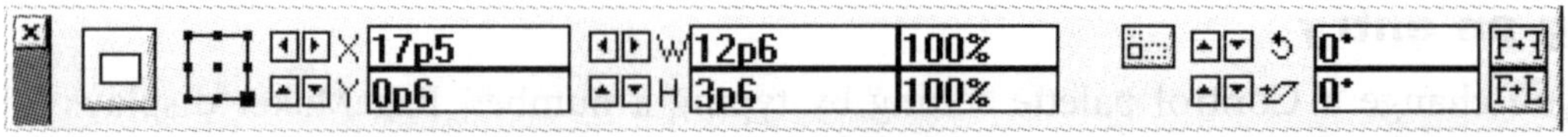

Clicking a button or selecting an option from a list automatically applies your changes. PageMaker implements all changes entered on the palette that are not yet applied. The appearance of the Apply button changes depending on the selected object. If you have no object selected, the button displays the icon for the tool currently selected. If you have several objects selected, the Apply button displays an icon representing several objects.

Proxy

The Proxy represents the selected object. The reference point on the Proxy represents the point you are manipulating on the object; the X and Y coordinates displayed in the position option are those of the active reference point. You can change the reference point by clicking a different reference point on the proxy or by clicking or dragging a different handle on the object.

When the reference point is a box, the reference point remains stationary and modifications are measured from it. When the reference point is an arrow, the reference point moves as the object is modified. To change between a box and an arrow, click the active reference point. To select a reference point, activate the proxy and then press the arrow keys. Alternatively, select a reference point by pressing a number on the numeric keypad.

When NumLock is on, the numbers 1-9 on the numeric keypad, each correspond to a point on the proxy. The 5 key corresponds to the center reference point and the 7 key corresponds to the upper-left reference point.

Position

Displays the X and Y coordinate values of the reference point on pointer, relative to the current rulers. If your reference point is the upper-left corner and you are positioning a rectangle, X and Y reflect the coordinates of the upper-left corner of that rectangle.

If you are drawing a rectangle, X and Y reflect the coordinates where you pressed the mouse button when you began to draw. When you select multiple objects, X and Y reflect the reference point for the rectangular area defined by the outside edge of all selected objects. You can also move or resize a selected object by changing the values in Position option.

Nudge amount is 0.01 inches or as set in the Preferences dialog box.

Allowable values

You cannot enter a value that positions any part of an object outside the pasteboard. When resizing, you cannot enter a value that creates a horizontal or vertical dimension that is zero or negative.

Sizing option

Displays the width W and height H of the selected object or cropping rectangle. PageMaker displays only one size for lines, which is line length L. When the reference point appears as an arrow, the specified values resize the object or cropping rectangle by repositioning the reference point.

Nudge amount is 0.01 inches or as set in the Preference dialog box.

Allowable values

Maximum size of a graphic is 45.51 inches (116 cms). Maximum size of a text block is 2.75 inches (58 cms). You cannot enter a value that positions any part of an object outside the pasteboard or that creates a horizontal or vertical dimension that is zero or negative.

Percentage scaling

It displays the percentage changed from the original size. This option is available for scaling objects drawn with the PageMaker drawing tools or images placed on the page.

When the reference point appears as a box, the specified values resize the object from the reference point or when the reference point appears as an arrow, the specified values resize the object by repositioning the reference point.

If you scale an object drawn in PageMaker, the percentage of original size reflects the original size only during the current editing session. If you deselect the object and then select the object again, 100% is displayed for both options. PageMaker always remembers the original size of imported graphic objects.

When the reference point appears as a box, the reference point remains stationary and PageMaker applies the specified percentages from the reference point outward. When the reference point appears as an arrow, PageMaker applies the specified percentages by repositioning the reference point to stretch or shrink the object.

Allowable values

You cannot enter a value that positions any part of an object outside the pasteboard or that creates a horizontal or vertical dimension that is zero or negative.

Scaling and Cropping

This option indicates the way you are resizing a graphic. When you select an imported graphic using the pointer tool, PageMaker highlights the Scaling button. When you select an imported graphic using the cropping tool, PageMaker highlights the Cropping button. Whichever tool you select, you can click either button to determine how to resize the graphic.

Proportional scaling

When you scale an object, use this option to specify whether you want to change an object's height and width independently or maintain its original proportions. When the option is turned on, PageMaker maintains the original proportion of height to width when you resize a graphic. When you resize proportionally, the values for the percentage options change in tandem, regardless of which one you enter values in. When this option is turned off, you scale the object's height and width independently.

Printer resolution scaling

When you scale a bitmap graphic, i.e., with TIFF extension and so on, turn this option on to scale the image so that its resolution is compatible with the target printer resolution in the Document Setup dialog box to be same as magic stretch.

Rotating

Rotates the selected object using the reference point on the proxy.

When the reference point is a box, the option rotates an object around the reference point. When the reference point is an arrow, the option rotates an object by moving the reference point.

Positive numbers rotate the object counter clockwise; negative numbers clockwise. When you rotate an object more than 10 degrees but less than 350 degrees, the proxy rotates to approximate the rotation of the object and the reference points on the proxy remain the same in relation to the selected object.

Skewing

It skews the selected object horizontally in relation to the selected reference point on the proxy. When reference point is a box, the object is skewed from the reference point. When the reference point is an arrow, the object is skewed by moving the reference point. Positive numbers move the top edge of the object to the right and negative numbers move the top edge of the object to the left.

Now we know how to use the Control palette. We come back to our book for which we had placed text and done some editing on it like spell checking etc. Now we perform more commands on it. One of them is called Book and is used to combine the various publications of a particular book.

Book

Use this command to create a list of publications to be treated as a single document called a **Book**. You can work with each publication in the book separately too or you can tell PageMaker to perform certain tasks showing or creating an index, creating a table of contents, or printing the entire book in one go. This command can be called from **Utilities** menu. Book publication list dialog box lets you create a book list and control the page numbering of the publication in that list. The options of the dialog box are discussed below:

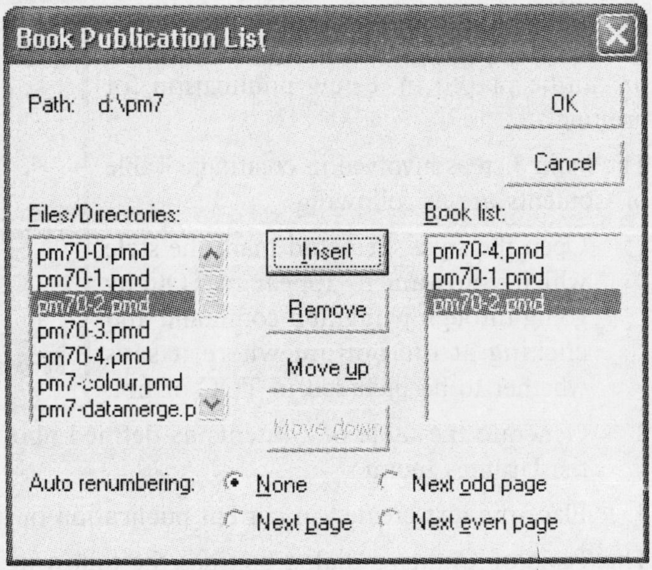

Insert

Add the publication selected in the list box on the left to the book list on the right. You can also double click the publication name in the left list box to add it to the book list. To update this list you rename a publication or move it to a new location on your hard disk. Remove the publication you renamed or moved and insert the new version into the book list.

Remove

Use this to remove the selected publication from the book list.

Move up/Move down

The command moves the selected publication up or down one position in the book list. This becomes necessary when you have to make sure that the page numbering in the publications is not to be disturbed and their sequence remains the same.

Auto renumbering

PageMaker repaginates and prints the publication of the book in the order they appear in the book list. You can choose the options as following:

None: Do not renumber the pages.

New page: The next publication in the Book should start from the next page of the previous publication entry.

Next odd/even page: Certain books have the style of starting all new chapters from the next odd page or next even page, use this option for the same.

One of the commands which works on Book is **Table of Contents**, let us see how it uses it.

Table of Contents

This command is used to generate Table of Contents (TOC). This can be created for a single publication or a number of publications if the book list is used. The created TOC is in the form of a new text story which can be placed on any page of the current publication or can be placed in a new publication for printing.

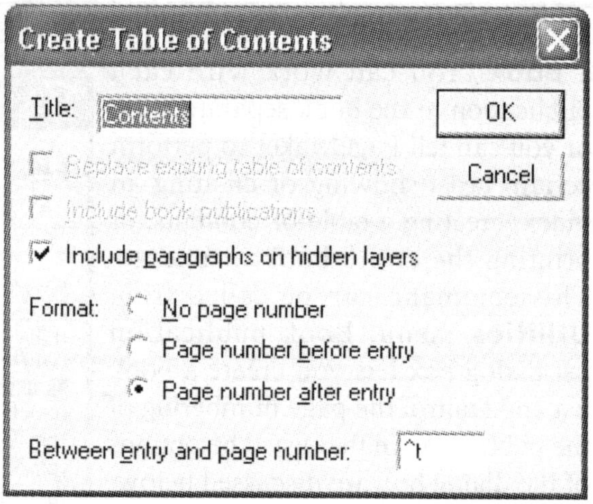

The main 3 steps involved in creating a Table of Contents are as following:

1. Open the style sheet and mark the style which you want to appear in TOC by going through paragraph command and clicking at the bottom where it says whether to be included in TOC or not.
2. Generate the table of contents as defined above by using the TOC command from the Utilities menu.
3. Place the text created in current publication or a new publication for editing/printing.

The Table of Contents dialog box has the following options:

Title

In this box you type the name of TOC which you want to give, PageMaker suggests the name of Contents when you open the box. However, you can change the same by typing a new one.

Replacing existing......

It will be off if there is no table of contents created before. However, in case you have already created one before and are now replacing it with a new one, click it into this. Also you can create a new one to compare with the old one by not clicking this.

Include paragraphs....

When you read about layers you will come to know about the layers which are not visible to you. These can be included for creation of table of contents.

Include book publication

It will be off in case you have not created a book list. Click this to include all the publications of the book.

Format

Various options available under this dialog box are as under:

No page number: Specify if you do not want page numbers to appear in the table of contents.

Page number before entry: Specify if you want page numbers to appear before the entry in the table of contents.

Page number after entry: Specify if you want page number to appear after the entry in the table of contents.

Between entry and page number

This column is used to specify whether you want tab to appear in between the entry and page number. Other options are that you have a carriage return or a number of tabs, etc. The choice is totally yours. You can even have ^tVol-1^t, to make Vol-1 appear alongwith all the page numbers. This can also be defined in the Preference column in the File menu. Another command depending upon the book command is **Index**. Let us see how it works.

Create Index

This command is used to Create index for a single publication or for all the publications in your book list. The index becomes a new story that you can place in an existing publication or in a new publication you create just for the index.

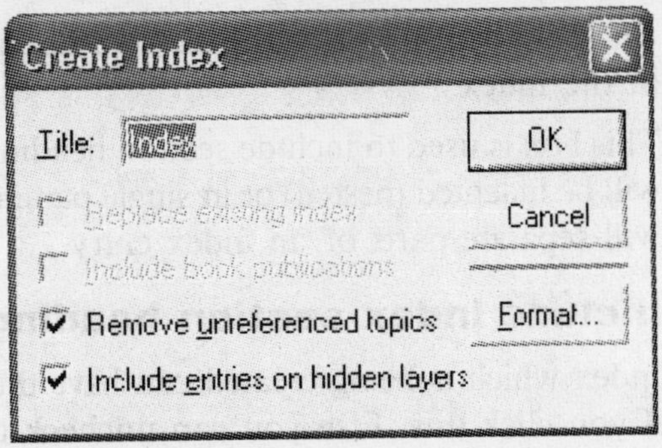

Creating of index is done in 4 steps.

1. Create index entries by using command Create Index entry.

2. Create the index using Create Index command.
3. Review or edit the index entries by using Show Index command.
4. Place the index story on a publication.

Let us start with create index, which can be called from the Utilities menu. Various options here are:

Title

You can give the title to the Index by typing in the box provided for, up to a maximum of 30 characters, PageMaker proposes Index as title for your index, which you can change according to your choice.

Replace existing index

This command is used to replace an existing index which had been created earlier. You can even retain the earlier one and create a new one to compare the two, for this you will have to uncheck this command.

Include book publication

You can generate index for a combined book if the book list is active else you can create the same for a single publication.

Remove unreferenced topics

There maybe few topics which are not cross-referred. You may like to remove them. An unreferenced topic may be a topic which:

- you imported the topic for cross-reference but did not use.
- for which all index entries were deleted.
- left in the topics list after you have removed an index marker in the publication.

Checking this option does not remove the entries in which you selected to Suppress page reference. Uncheck this option if, for example, you are generating a rough index for view and you want to retain the imported topics from a large book list can make your publication file very large, you may want to remove the unreferenced topics when you generate your final index.

Format

Click this option to obtain Index Format dialog box in which you can format certain elements of the index.

This box is used to include section headings in the index, to determine whether index entries will be indented (nested) or in single paragraph (run-in) format and to specify which characters will separate parts of an index entry.

Include index section headings

Index which is being created can have the section headings in the form of A, B, or C, etc., if you click this. Else you can uncheck this.

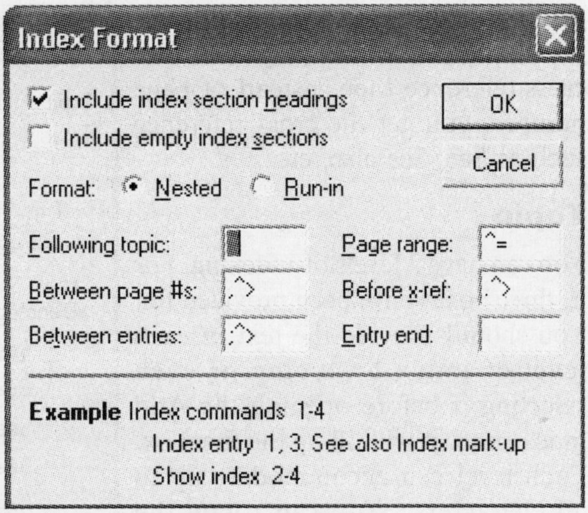

Include empty index sections Supposing a section has no entry may be in section X, then it will create entry for that too with a message no entries.

Format

This is used to select one of the two options available in Page Maker, i.e., Nested and Run-in.

Nested: In this option the text of index appears in an indented format in which each level of an entry is a separate paragraph.

Run-in: In this option the text of index appears in the form of a single paragraph having all levels of each entry.

The following options give you the control over the formatting of the characters which use can be used to form separate parts of the index. These include commas, tabs, semicolons, colons, etc.

Following topic: Specify here the character you want to be inserted between the text and the first entry of page number. The default is two spaces.

Between page #s: Specify here the character you want to get inserted between two page number entries. The default is a comma and en space.

Between entries: Specify here the character you want to be inserted between second and third level entries. The default is semicolon and en space.

Page range: Specify here the character you want to be inserted between first and last number in a range of pages. The default is en dash.

Before x-ref: Specify here the character you want to be inserted before a cross-reference. The default is a period and en space.

Entry end: Specify here the character you want to be inserted between at the end of every referenced entry (in nested format) or to follow the last cross-reference in the topic (in run-in format). The default is no character.

Nest step is to add index entries. This is done by command called **Index Entry** available under the **Utilities** menu.

Index Entry

This command is used to create index in a publication file and to edit the index entries. When you click at Index entry the add index entry dialog box appears, the options of which are discussed below:

Type

It has two options, Page reference or Cross reference. When you click page reference it gives you the page number as the reference. Whereas if you select cross-reference then instead of page numbers you get the cross reference such as See, See also, etc.

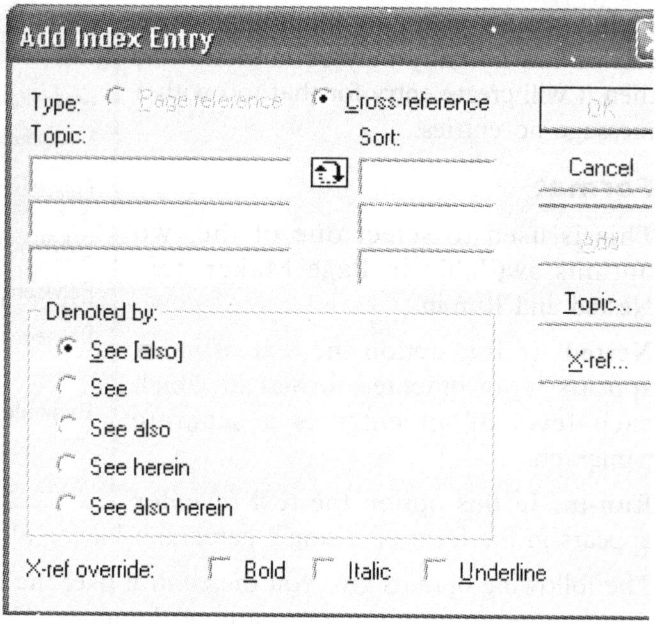

Topic

You can have 3 levels of indexing. For it, three boxes have been provided for. You should provide the text in each level of index by typing or even selecting it before opening the Add index entry, it will fill up the first box. Each level can accommodate up to 50 characters. You can rotate the topic text from one level to another by just clicking in the box.

Sort

The sort boxes corresponding to the topic levels are used to tell PageMaker how to sort each entry in the index. The entries are spelled in the index as they appear in the topics edit boxes but are sorted alphabetically according to the spelling in the sort edit boxes. For example, if the topics references is PM and you want it to be sorted in the index as PageMaker, then type PageMaker in the sort box against the topic box of PM.

Add

Click to add another index entry at the same location after you add an entry, PageMaker puts off this button until you make a change, so that you do not mistakenly add an entry twice. To add another entry, type over existing text in the topics edit boxes and click add or Ok.

Topic

Click this to view the topics already selected and for which the index has already been created. You can also use this option to add topics to the topics listed directly.

Page range

These options are used to define where the discussion of the subject ends, so that PageMaker can supply page number for the references.

Current page: Click if the discussion of the subject is limited to the page on which the marker is located. Use this option when you are certain that the discussion does not continue onto another page/pages.

To next style change: Check this if the discussion on the subject ends at the next style change.

To next use of style: Similar to above check this if the discussion ends at the next instances of a particular paragraph style and then select the style name that marks the beginning of a new subject.

For next paragraphs: Click here if the discussion of the subject continues beyond the current paragraph and then type the number of paragraph in the edit box. If you add or delete text in the discussion be sure to adjust the number of paragraph specification for the page range.

Suppress page range: Click to create an index without a page references. This is useful when you are in the process of revising an index and you want to create entries as placeholder to index later.

Page# override

PageMaker provides 3 options Bold, Italics and Underline for emphasizing index entry page numbers. Selecting any one, two or three option causes the style of the page number to be printed as selected.

PageMaker keeps the setting for page# override—for all new entries until you change it consequently. If you want all cross reference or page reference to be italics, only selected italics the first time you create an index entry.

This way you will be able to create the index entries. Now the next step is to check them. For that we have the command called **Show index**.

Show Index

This is used to see index before it is printed. Here you can edit entries but you cannot add an entry in this. To show the complete index on screen, PageMaker goes through the process of renumbering pages, updating book references and then it shows the complete index. But, this is so when the book list is active, if not it will show the index of the current publication only. In this book list also you can see the index of current publication only by pressing **Ctrl key** while opening **Show Index** command.

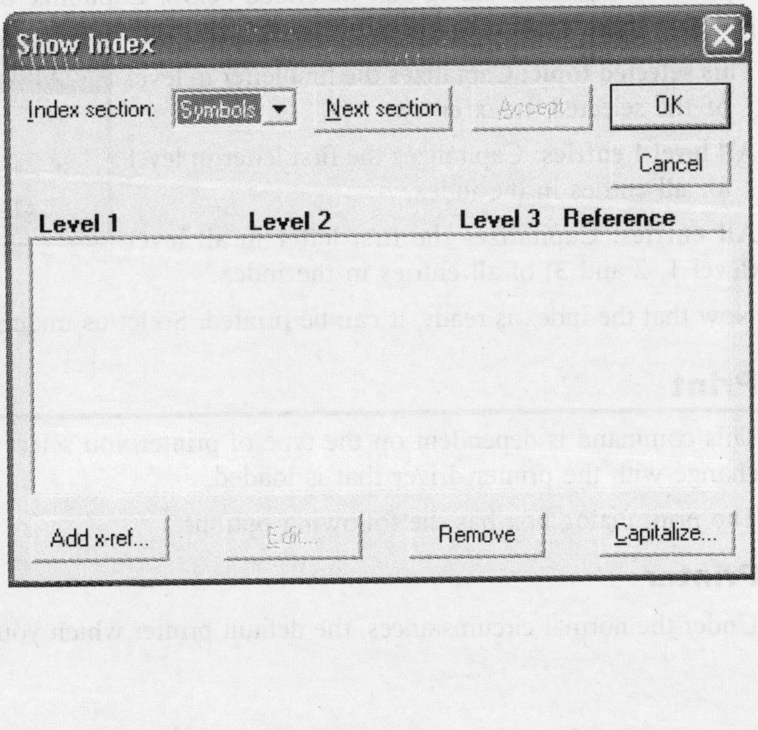

The **Show Index** dialog box lists all index entries in your publication or book stored alphabetically into sections. Topic level are shown as well as all pages of references and cross references.

The dialog box contains:

Index section

PageMaker arranges index entries into sections. Select the section you want to display from the index section list.

Next section

You click this to display the next alphabetical section which is not empty or has at least one entry.

Accept

After you have made the changes to the entries, click this to accept.

Add x ref

Click this to display the add index entry dialog box in which you can add a cross-references to an index entry. If you select an index entry before clicking, add x-ref fills the topic edit boxes.

Edit

This is used to display the edit index entry dialog box in which you can edit any portion of index entry.

Remove

This is used to delete a selected entry from the index. Only the index entry is deleted but the topic reference remains.

Capitalize

Opens the capitalize dialog box described below. Capitalize button is available only if you generate index from a single publication.

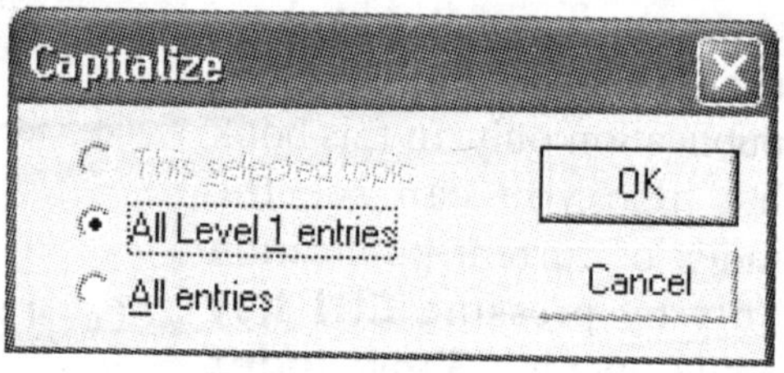

This selected topic: Captalizes the first letter in level 1 of the selected index entry.

All level 1 entries: Capitalizes the first letter in level 1 for all entries in the index.

All entries: Capitalizes the first letter in all level (level 1, 2 and 3) of all entries in the index.

Now that the index is ready, it can be printed. So let us understand the options of printing.

Print

This command is dependent on the type of printer you select to print. The options usually change with the printer driver that is loaded.

The print dialog box has the following options:

Printer

Under the normal circumstances, the default printer which you have selected is shown here.

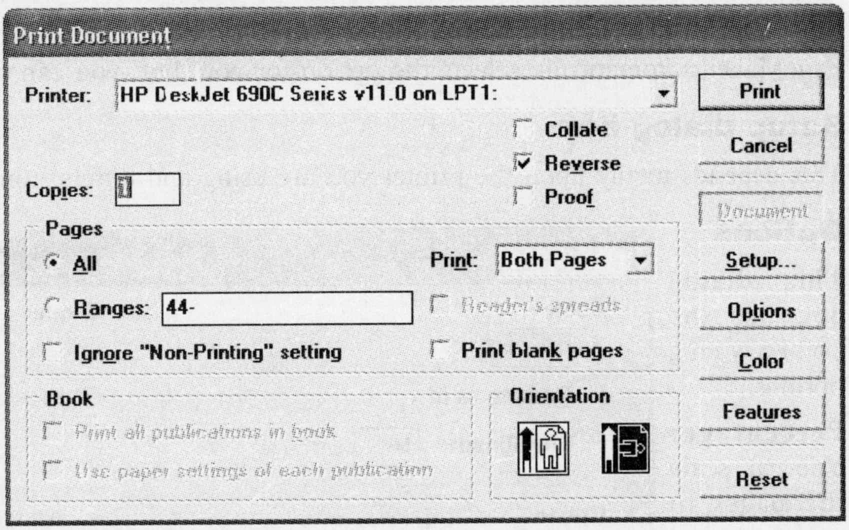

If you have loaded the drivers for more than one printer, you can choose to select any one of them by clicking here.

Collate

This option collates the printed output. This is useful when you are printing multiple copies. Normally when you print pages 1 to 10 with 5 copies, the PageMaker will print 5 copies of pages 1 to 10, starting with 5 copies of page 1 and so on. With this command, it will print page number 1 to 10, 5 times over in a collated form.

Reverse order

By choosing this option, you can print in the reverse order, i.e., while printing 1 to 10 pages, it will print 10 first, then 9 and so on.

Proof

By choosing this option you can print the pages as lower quality proofs.

Copies

Type here the number of copies you want to print.

Pages

Select here the selective pages you want to print, the various options are:

All: Select this to print all pages.

Ranges: Select here the particular pages, you want to print. You can choose to print non-consecutive pages by typing their numbers with a hyphen each and followed by comma (,), e.g., 45-56, 67-78, etc.

Print: You can select to print either Odd pages, Even pages or Both pages

Ignore 'Non-Printing': Click this if you want to print the non-printing characters too.

Reader's spreads: It allows for the evaluation of two-page spreads.

Book

This command is valid if you have the publications lined up in Book. The options here are that you can print all the pages of all the publications in the book or choose otherwise.

Orientation

PageMaker automatically selects the option for you, but, you can choose to be different.

Setup dialog box

This depends totally upon the printer you are using and differs from printer to printer.

Options

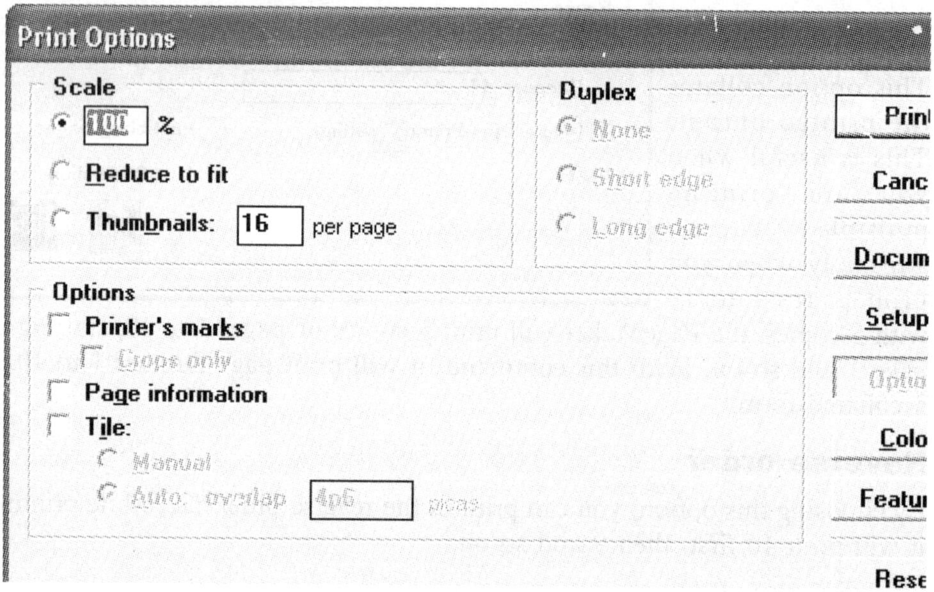

This dialog box has the following options:

Percentage: You can scale the pages to any size before printing.

Reduce to fit: If the page which you have designed is bigger than the paper on which you are printing. With this command you can make it print on the same paper.

Print as Thumbnails: You can print miniature editions of the pages as icons with a maximum number of 16 pages per sheet of paper.

Duplex: The various options here are None, Short edge, and Long edge.

Options: Here are the various options which can be printed on the page itself, i.e., Printer's marks, Page information and if you have used the tiling option, print with a defined overlap option.

Color

This dialog box has the option to print the colour which the printer supports and if not whether to print them as black or else. Also the way the colour separation is to be done.

Features

This again depends on the type of printer you are using.

Now that we have edited the publication and have created Index, Table of Contents of the publication, Spell checked and have made the other formatting of the text. Finally we have printed the publication according to our needs. This finishes the complete process of creation of a book for publication.

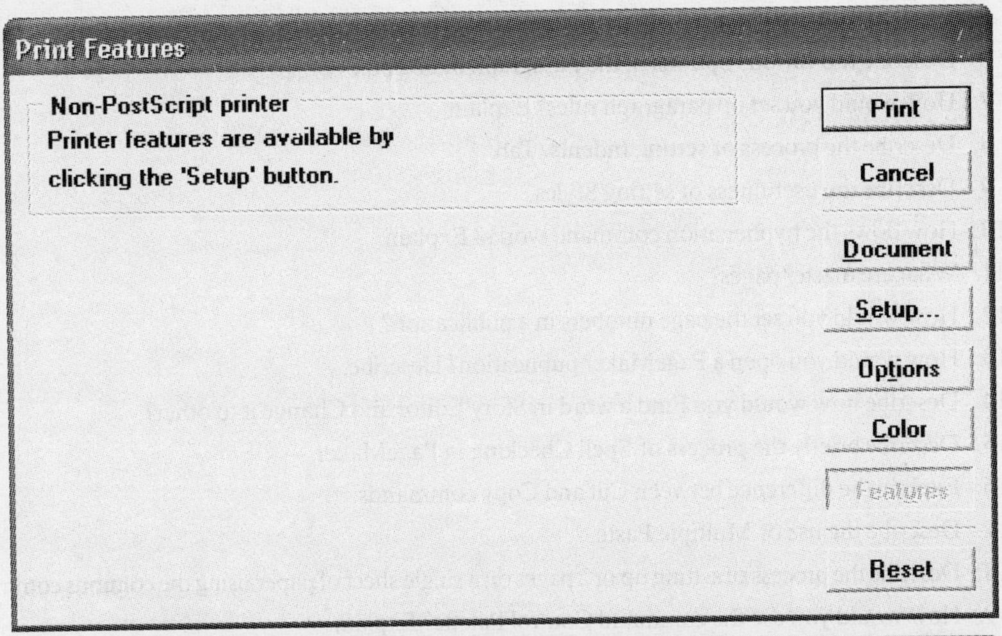

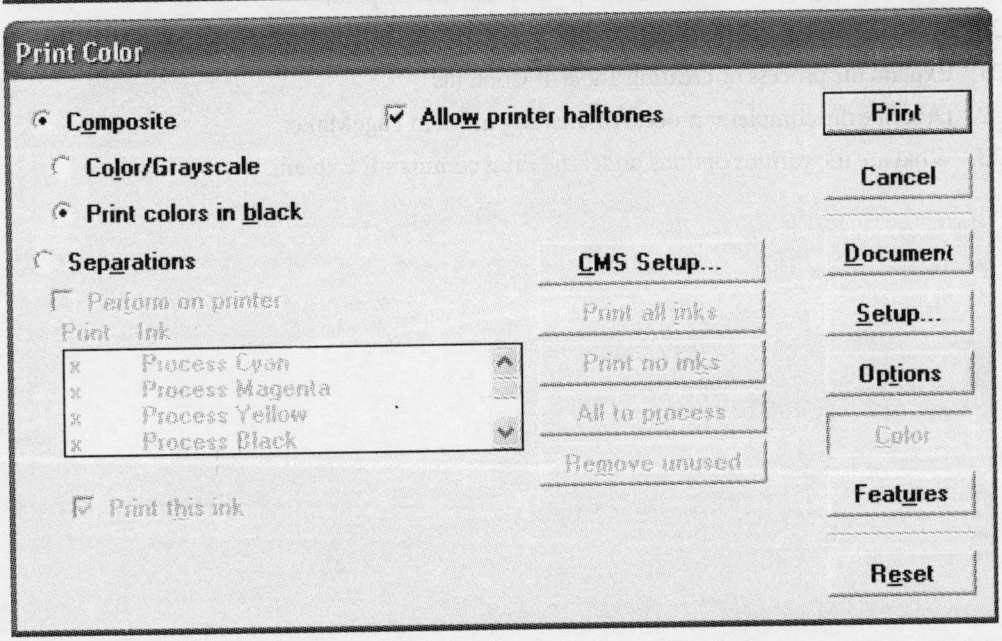

Descriptive Type Questions

1. Describe the various methods of starting PageMaker.
2. Describe how would you setup the dimensions of a new page.
3. How would you check the size of a page? Explain.
4. Explain the steps taken in placing the text in the publication.

5. What all you can change from the character dialog box? Explain.
6. Describe the various options of the Paragraph dialog box.
7. How would you set up paragraph rules? Explain.
8. Describe the process of setting Indents/Tab.
9. Describe the usefulness of setting Styles.
10. How dows the hyphenation command works? Explain.
11. What are master pages?
12. How would you set the page numbers in a publication?
13. How would you open a PageMaker publication? Describe.
14. Describe how would you Find a word in Story Editor and Change it to other?
15. Describe briefly the process of Spell Checking in PageMaker.
16. Explain the difference between Cut and Copy commands.
17. Describe the use of Multiple Paste.
18. Describe the process of setting up of 2 pages on a single sheet of paper using the columns command.
19. How would you use the command Control Palette? Explain.
20. What are the uses of Book command? Explain.
21. Explain the process of creating Table of Contents.
22. Describe the completer process of creating Index in PageMaker.
23. What are the various options under the Print command? Explain.

4 Introduction to CorelDRAW

Using CorelDRAW to Create Drawings

Let us now learn to use CorelDRAW to draw various objects, shapes, line and even use CorelDRAW to create text.

Let us see how it is done.

Working with Lines

To Draw a Line:

1. Select the **Freehand** tool from the toolbox. The mouse pointer will change to a crosshair shaped pointer.
2. Click on anywhere in the Drawing page to draw line.
3. Drag your mouse to the position where you would like to end your line and click again.

To Draw a Straight Line:

To draw a straight horizontal or vertical line, hold the **Ctrl** key on your keyboard while drawing a line. Your line will be drawn in absolute straight line.

Line Spacing and Word Spacing

Adjusting character, line, word or paragraph spacing is very easy in CorelDRAW using the shape-sizing handle. When you drag it up on the bottom shape handle it makes line spacing tighter (less). When you drag it down it increases line spacing (more). When you drag to the right, with the right shape-sizing handle, you can stretch spacing between letters. When you drag to the left, you compress letter spacing.

If you hold down **Ctrl** key while you drag on the shape-sizing handles it changes the effect. Holding down Ctrl key while you drag on the right shape-sizing handle, you increase word spacing. If you hold down Ctrl key while you drag on the down shape-sizing handle, you increase spacing between paragraphs instead of between lines.

To Increase Line Spacing and Letter Spacing :

1. Select the paragraph text frame using the **Pick** tool.
2. Click on the shape tool in the toolbox and note the two shape-sizing handles, one in the lower right corner and one in the lower left corner of the text frame.
3. Drag down on the bottom shape-sizing handle. Note that the line spacing increases.

4. Drag to the right on the right shape sizing handle. This will increase word spacing.

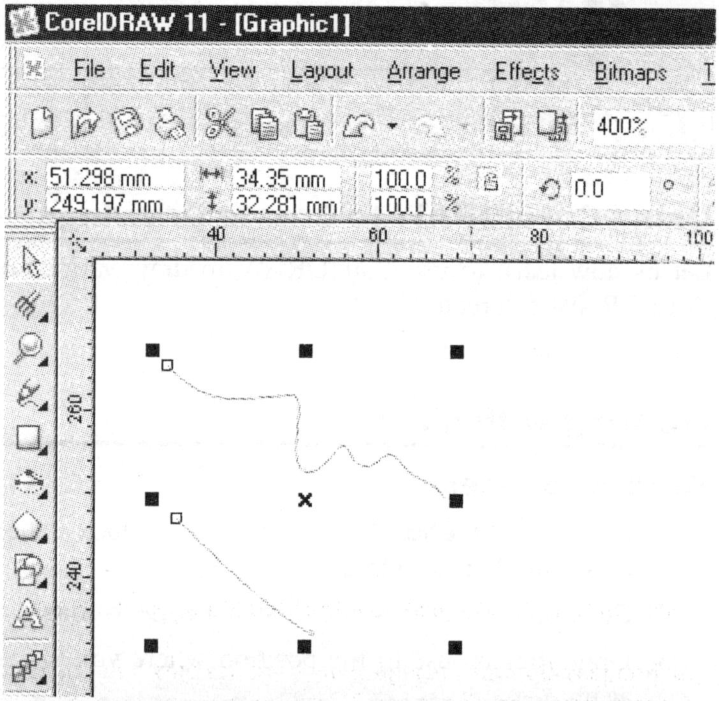

To Increase or Decrease Spacing:

1. Select the paragraph text frame using the **Pick** tool.
2. Click on the Text tool in toolbox and then click & drag the mouse pointer to select the text. The text will be highlighted.
3. Click on the **Text** menu. The Text menu will appear.
4. Click on **Format Text**. The Format Text dialog box will appear, as shown below.
5. Click on the **Paragraph** tab of the Format text dialog box.
6. Type the appropriate spacing width for characters, word or line in the character, word or line text box.
7. Click on Ok to see the changed spacing.

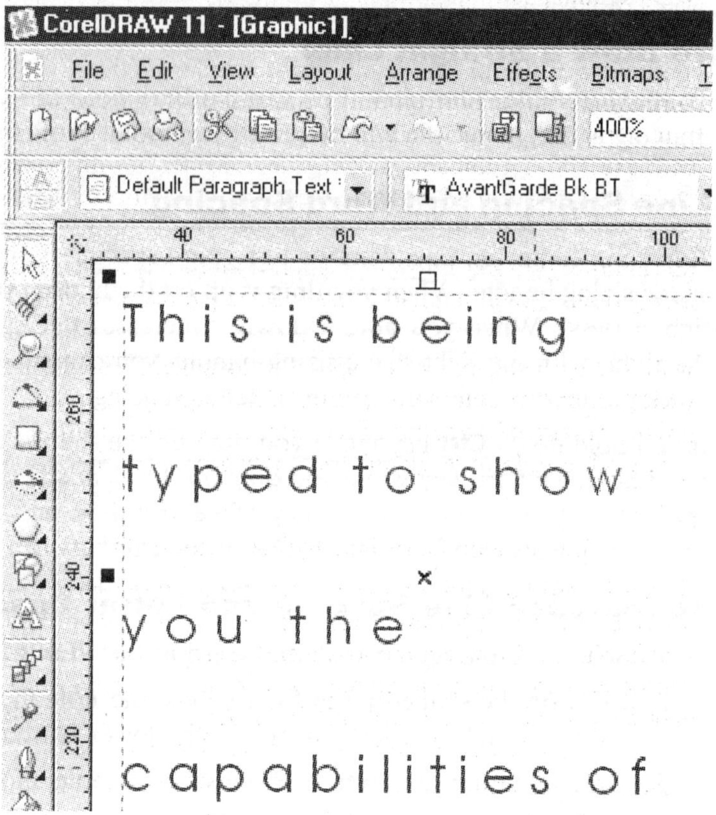

Assign a Drop Cap to Paragraph

You must have seen that sometimes the first character of the paragraph is made of bigger size to highlight it. This is called the Drop Cap.

In CorelDRAW it is done as follows:

1. Draw a paragraph frame and type text in it.
2. In the Text menu, select the Format Text. The format text dialog box will appear.
3. In the Format Text dialog box, click on the **Effect** tab.
4. Here select **Drop cap** from the Effect Type drop-down list. Also choose the number of lines drip you want.
5. Click Ok.
6. Your drop cap will appear on your text, as shown on next page.
7. As seen the drop letter here has taken the 3 lines.

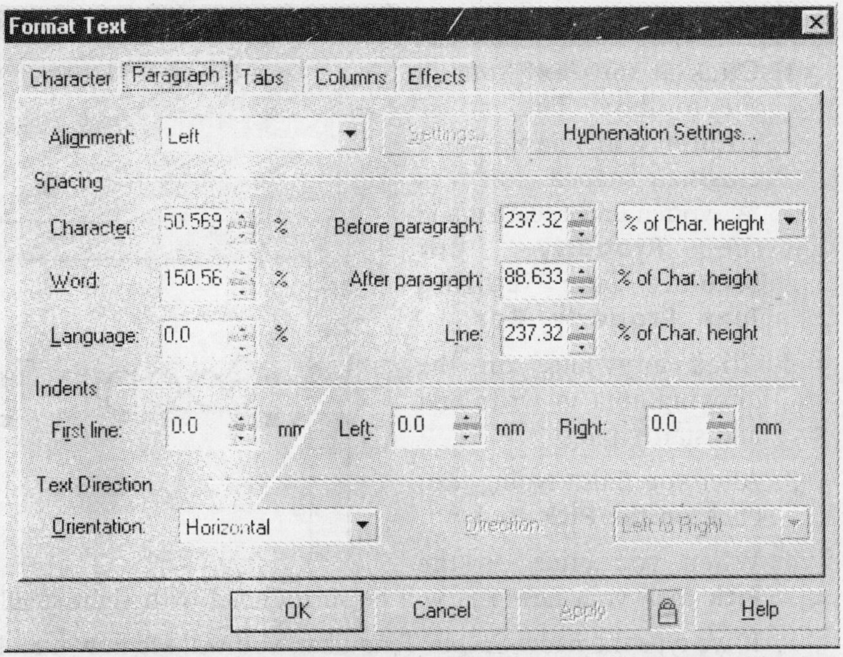

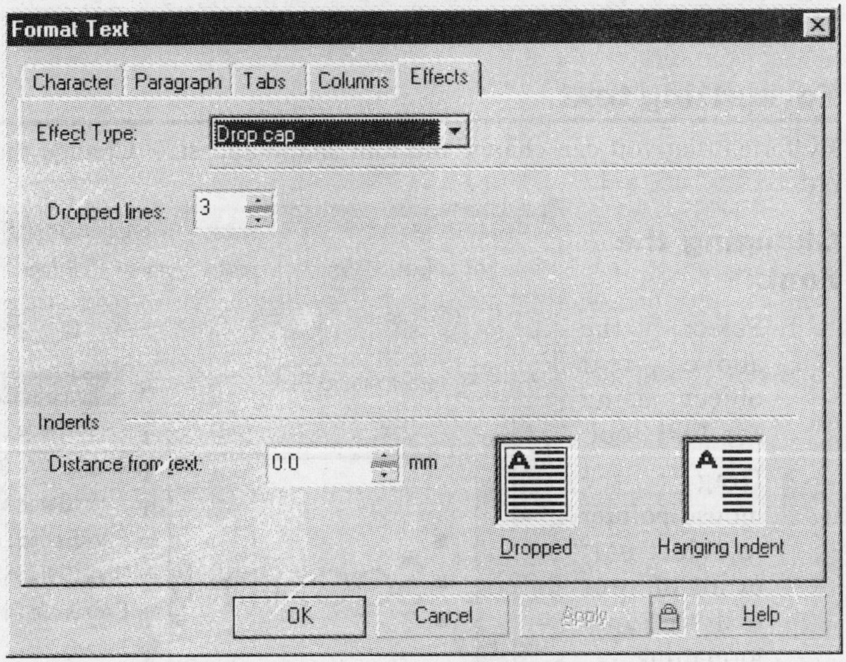

Creating Text

CorelDRAW is quite capable of handling text with ease. You can edit, format, resize, or reshape text as you like. There are two ways in which the text can be defined in CorelDRAW:

Paragraph text and

Artistic text

Artistic text

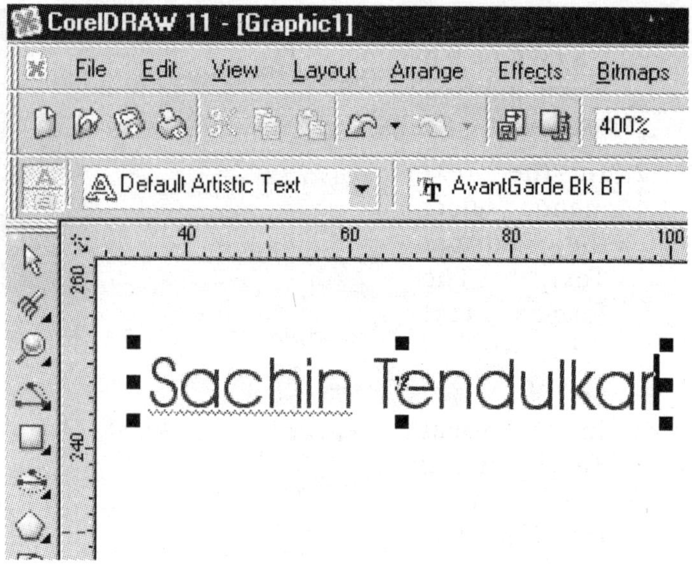

1. Click at the **Text** tool in the toolbox. The mouse pointer will change to a crosshair shaped icon with 'A' written underneath it and the **Property Bar** becomes the **Editing Text Property Bar**.
2. Click anywhere on the drawing area to write text and start typing.
3. After you finish typing text, click on the **Pick** tool.
4. When you click on the **Pick** tool, your new text will be surrounded with eight small square black handles.
5. If we type the name Sachin Tendulkar, you will see how it looks like as shown below.

   After typing it, you may want to format it.

Formatting text

By formatting you can change the font shape and size. Change the style to **Bold**, *Italics*, etc.

Changing the Font:

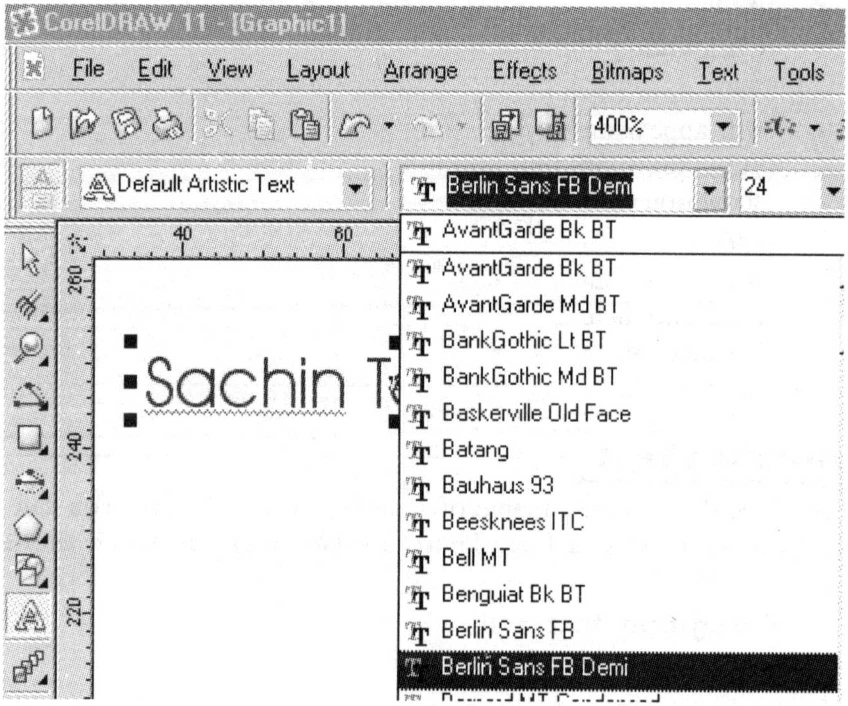

1. Select the above text object using the **Text** tool.
2. Drag the mouse pointer to select part or all of your text to apply formatting.
3. After you have selected the text which you want to format, pull down the

Font List and select a new font of your choice.

4. You can see the preview of the text in the font of you choice appears to the right of the Font name in the **Font List box**.
5. In our case, let us select the font, **Impact** and see how it looks.
6. This can be seen in the figure on the next page.

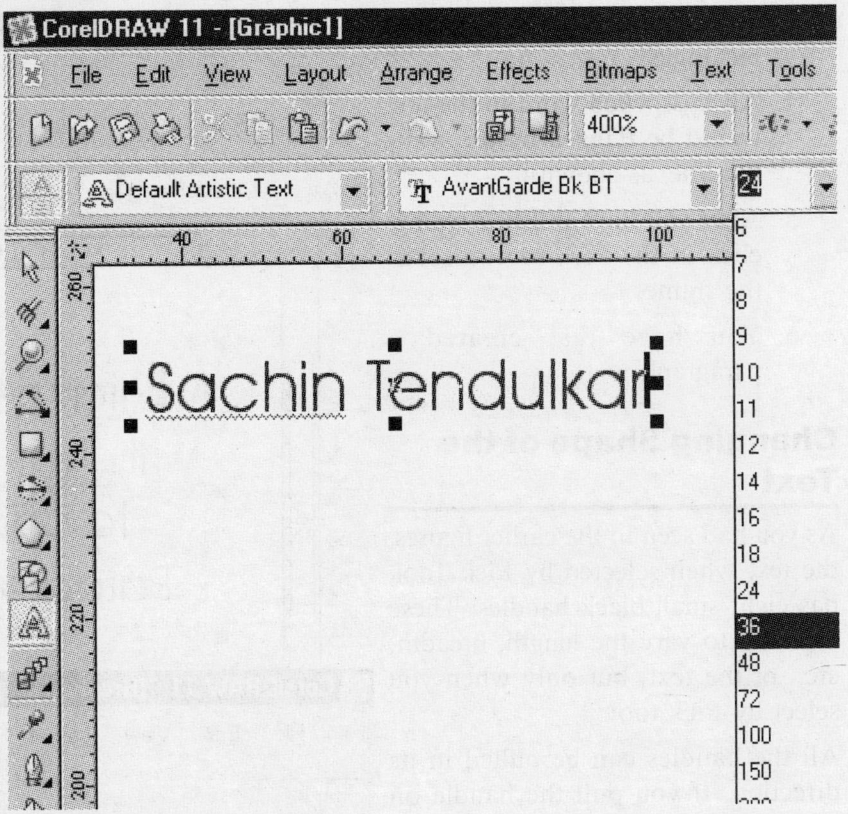

Changing the size

1. Select the text object using the **Pick** tool.
2. Click on the **Text** tool in the toolbox; a cursor will appear.
3. Pull down the **Font Size List** drop-down menu.
4. Click on the **Font Size** which you think is suitable for your text.
5. In our case we would select the size as 36. On the next page you can see how it appars.

   Now that the text is ready, you can reshape it.

Paragraph Text

This is the Corel's answer to the word processing. You name it and it has it; from spell checking to correcting the wrong words as they are typed. The misspelled words are marked with red wavy lines as is done in most of the word processors. Let us see what all can be done with the paragraph text.

Creating Paragraph Text

1. Click on the **Text** tool.
2. Click and drag the mouse to create a rectangle.

3. Type the text in the created rectangle.
4. All misspelled word in the text would be flagged by the wavy red line, as shown.
5. After you have finished typing, click in the Pick tool to select the frame.
6. You have just created a paragraph text.

Changing Shape of the Text

As you had seen in the earlier figures, the text when selected by Pick Tool, has eight small black handles. These are used to vary the length, breadth, etc., of the text, but only when you select by Pick tool.

All the handles can be pulled in its direction. If you pull the handle on the right and drag it to right with the mouse, the whole text is pulled to the right and is right elongated. If you pull to the top, it gets pulled to the top.

But, the best way to do it to drag by pulling the corners so that the whole text is pulled up proportionally. You would see the result of pulling the above text towards the right, pulling it up and then pulling it along the corners so that the text still look proportional.

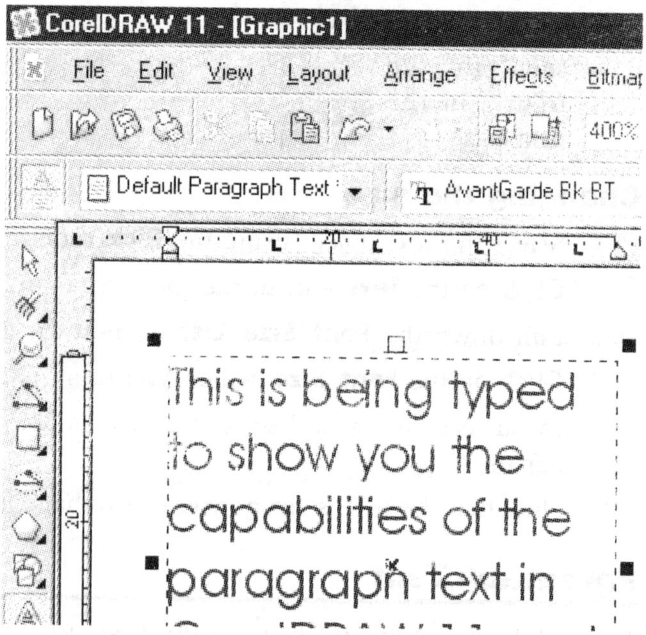

Moving Text

To Move a Text Block:

1. Select the text block using the **Pick** tool.
2. Place the mouse pointer above the X shaped mark which is at the centre of the whole block of text.

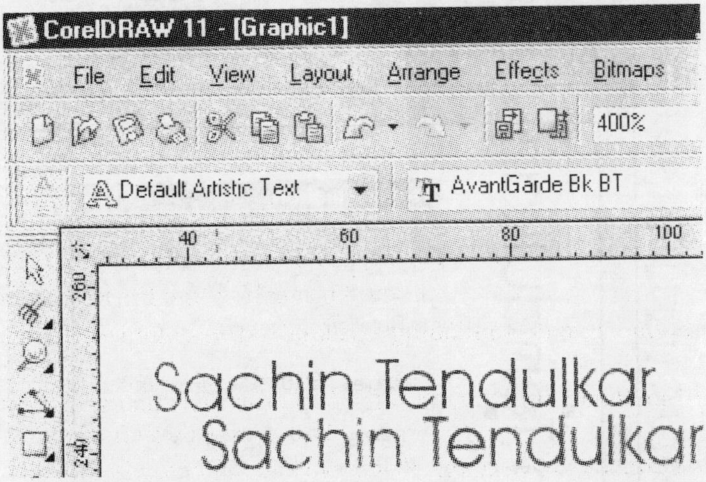

3. Click on it and drag the selected text block.
4. Move the mouse towards the direction where you want to move it to.
5. Release the mouse button once you have reached the new location.

Similarly you can rotate the text too.

Rotating Text

To Rotate a Text Block:

1. Select the text object using the **Pick** tool.
2. Click on the text block again. The small black squares will now turn to curved arrows.
3. Rotate these arrows in clockwise or counterclockwise direction to rotate the selected text.
4. Move it around till you have reached the angle in which you have to rotate the text block.
5. Release the mouse button.

Another way of Rotating the Text:

1. Select the text block by using the Pick tool.
2. Change the rotation angle in the **Rotation Angle** text box, by which you would like to rotate the object.
3. This option is useful if you know exactly how much you want to rotate the selected text block.
4. In the figure below, we have rotated the text to 90^0.

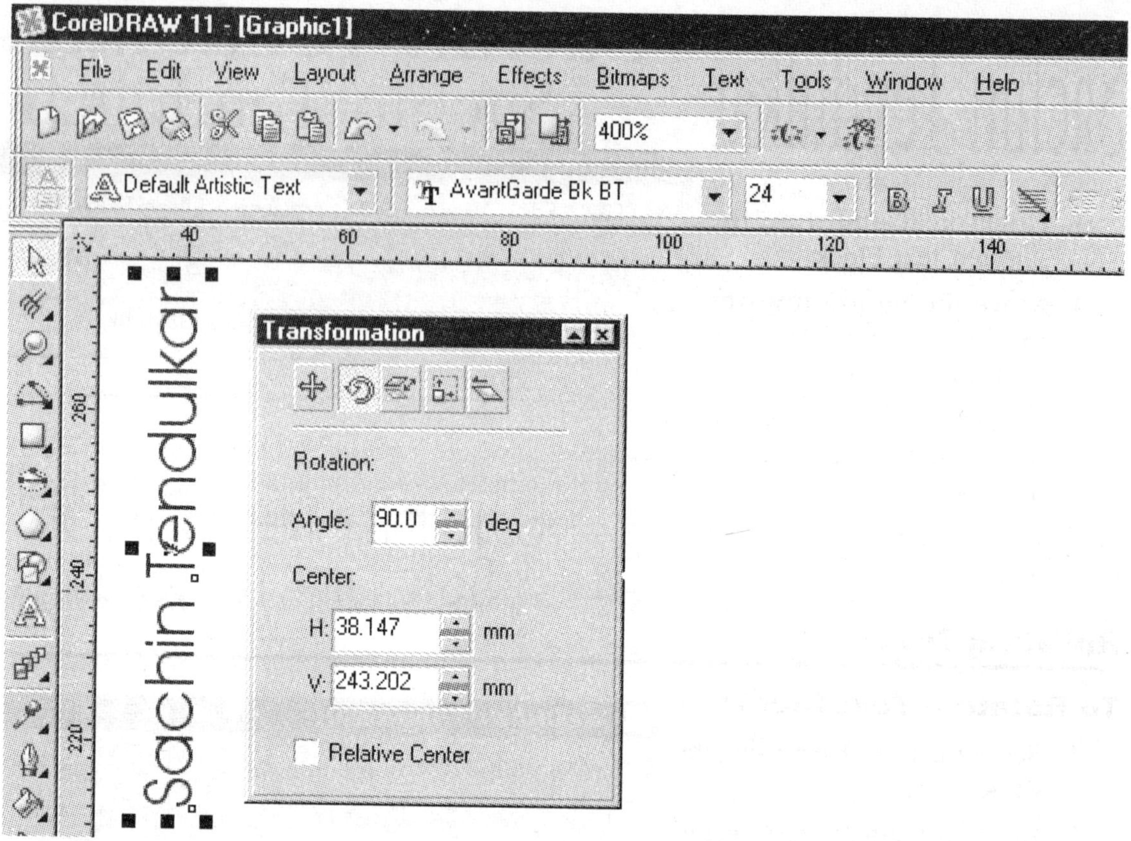

Fill Colour to the Text

To Assign a Fill Colour to a Text:

1. Select the text, as done earlier, using the **Pick** tool.
2. Select the part of the text with the text tool or else let the whole text be selected as it is.
3. Click on any colour in the colour palette on the right side of the screen.
4. In our case we would select the colour, **Magenta**, as shown in the figure here.
5. You may not clearly see this colour since this book is in black and white and colours cannot be shown.

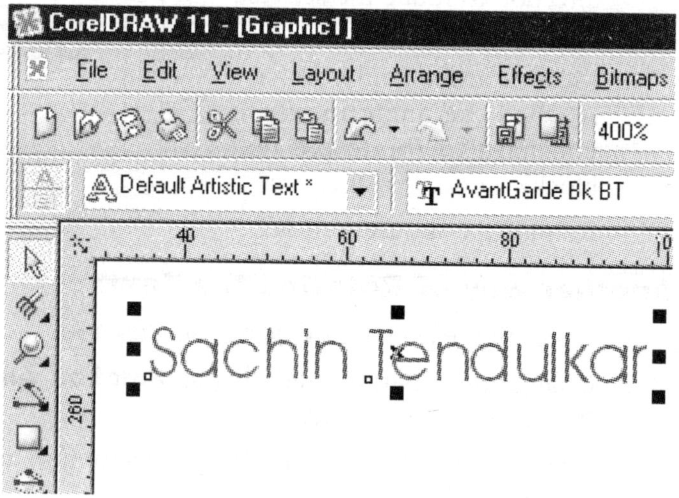

Assigning Outline Colour to the Text:

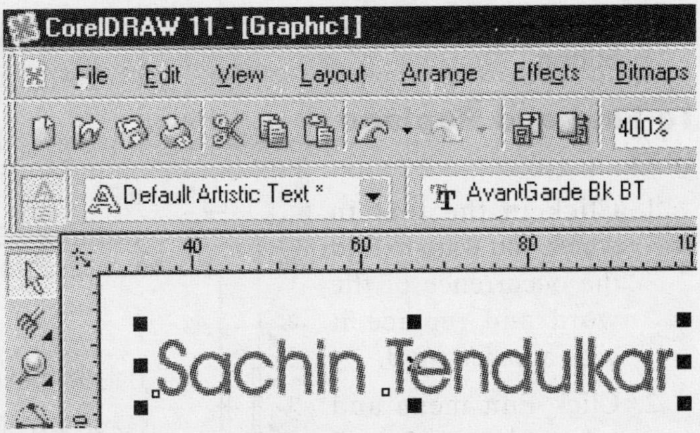

1. Select the text as before.
2. Select the part of the text with the text tool or else let the whole text be selected as it is.
3. Right click on any colour in the colour palette on the right side of the screen.
4. In our case since the text is in Magenta colour, we have selected the outline as **Blue**, as can be seen here.

Fitting Text to a Path

You can position Artistic text along the path of an open object (for example, a line) or closed object (for example, a circle).

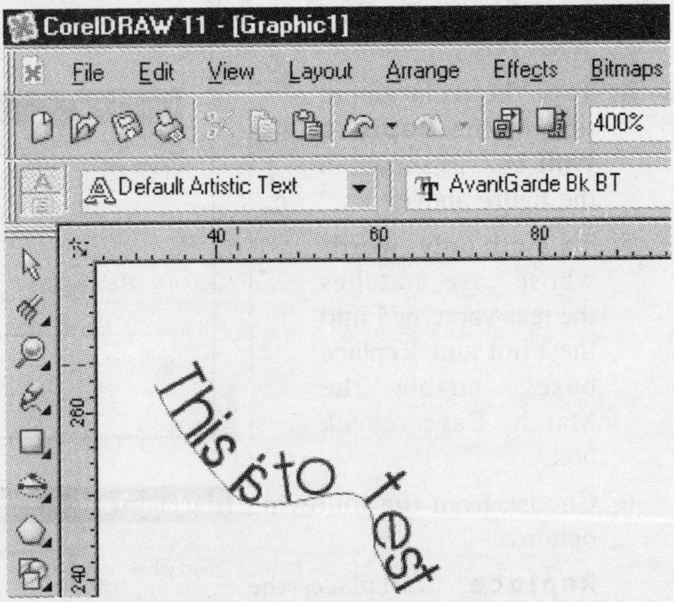

1. Select the path using the Pick tool.
2. Click on Text. The text menu will open.
3. Click to **Fit Text To Path**.
4. Type along the path on your object.
5. You can see the same having been done in the figure shown here.

Finding and Replacing Text

In CorelDraw, you can search for text with specific properties. You can also search and replace specific characters.

To Find Text:

1. Click in the text in which you want to find the occurrence of the word.
2. Click at **Edit** menu and select the command **Find and Replace** and then from the submenu select **Find Text**.
3. Type the text you want to find in the **Find What** box.
4. To find only words whose case matches the text you typed into the Find box, enable the **Match Case** check box.

5. Click the **Find Next** button.

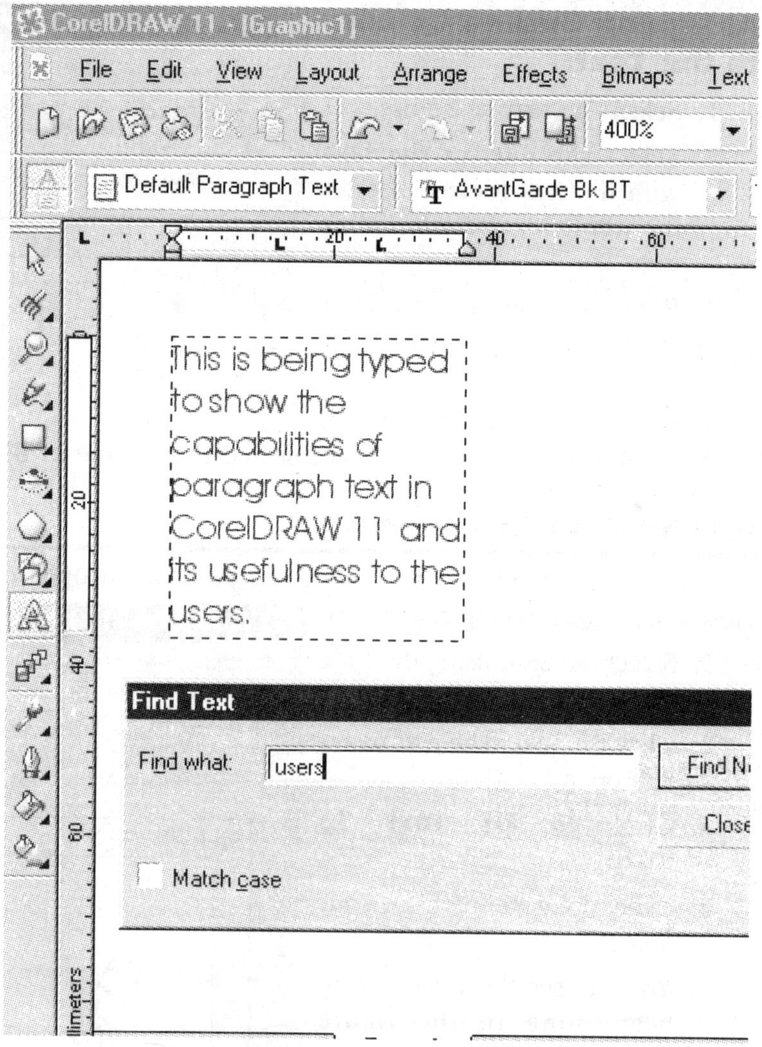

To Find and Replace text

1. Click in the text in which you want to find the occurrence of the word and replace it with another word.
2. Click Edit menu and select the command Find and Replace and **Replace Text** from the submenu.
3. Type the text you want to replace in the Find What box.
4. Type the replacement text in the **Replace With** box, as shown in the figure above.
5. To find only words whose case matches the text you typed into the Find and Replace boxes, enable the Match Case check box.
6. Choose from the following options :

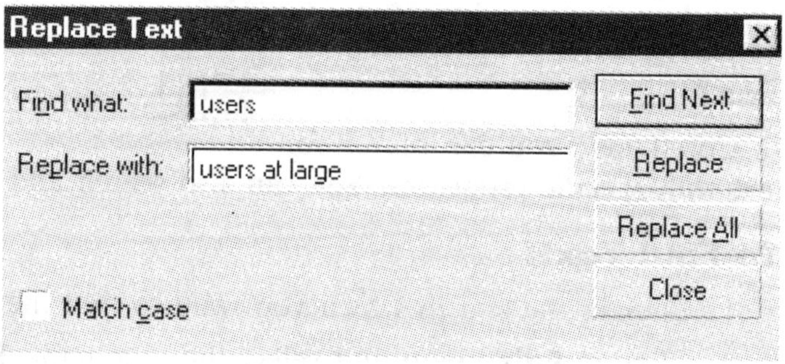

   Replace replaces the first occurrence of the text specified in the Find What box.

   Replace All replaces all occurrences of the text specified in the Find What box.

   Close ends the search

7. Your text has been replaced with the words of your choice.

Working with Shapes and Objects

CorelDRAW has 3 different shape tools that can create **ellipses** (including circles), **rectangles** (including squares), **polygons** and **stars**. You can combine artistic text with these shapes to create impressive and attractive graphics.

Creating Rectangles and Squares

To Draw a Rectangle:

1. To draw a rectangle, select the **Rectangle** tool in the toolbox. The mouse pointer changes to a crosshair with a small rectangle beneath it.
2. Click anywhere in the drawing area and drag the mouse pointer.
3. Release the mouse button where you like the end of the rectangle.

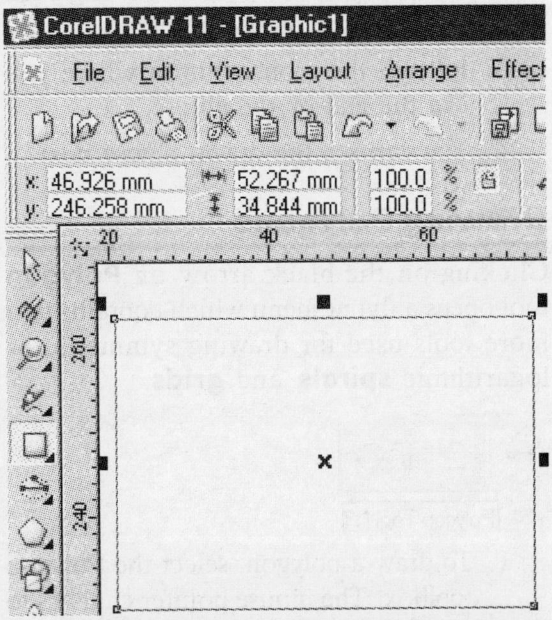

To Draw a Square:

1. To draw a square, select the Rectangle tool in the tool box. The mouse pointer changes to a crosshair with a small rectangle beneath it.
2. Click anywhere in the drawing area and hold down the **Ctl** key while dragging the mouse pointer.
3. Release the mouse button where you like the end of the square.

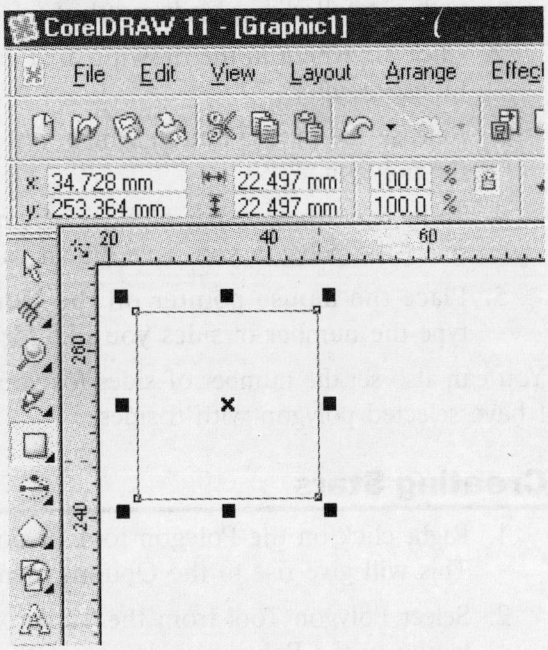

Creating Circles and Ellipses

To Draw a Circle:

1. To draw a circle, select the **Ellipse** tool in the toolbox. The mouse pointer changes to a crosshair with a small ellipse underneath it.
2. Click anywhere in the drawing area and hold down the **Ctrl** key while dragging the mouse pointer.
3. Release the mouse button where you like the end of the circle.

To Draw an Ellipse:

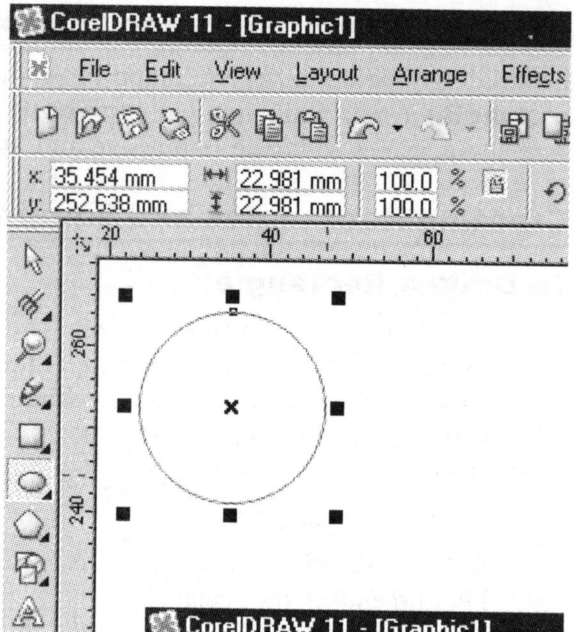

1. To draw an ellipse (also known as an oval), select the **Ellipse** tool in the toolbox. The mouse pointer changes to a crosshair with a small ellipse underneath it.
2. Click anywhere in the drawing area and drag the mouse pointer.
3. Release the mouse button where you like the end of the ellipse.
4. You can see the drawn ellipse next.

Drawing Polygons

Clicking on the black arrow on **Polygon** tool opens a flyout menu which contains two more tools used for drawing symmetric or logarithmic **spirals** and **grids**.

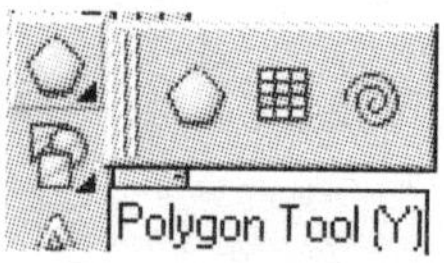

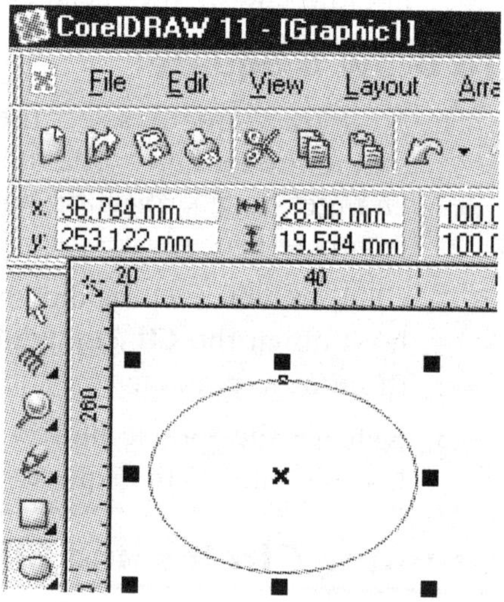

1. To draw a polygon, select the Polygon tool in the toolbox. The mouse pointer changes to a crosshair with a small ellipse underneath it.
2. Click anywhere in the drawing area and drag the mouse pointer.
3. Release the mouse button where you like to end the polygon.
4. To increase the number of sides of your polygon, select the polygon you have drawn using the Pick tool.
5. Place the mouse pointer on the **Number of Points of Polygon** text box and type the number of sides you like for your polygon.

You can also set the number of sides for your polygon and then draw it. In the figure here, I have selected polygon with 6 sides.

Creating Stars

1. Right click on the Polygon tool. A pop-up menu will appear. Click on **Properties**. This will give rise to the Options menu.
2. Select Polygon Tool from the Toolbox. Now, choose the **Polygon as Star** radio button in the Polygon tool area of the Options dialog box.

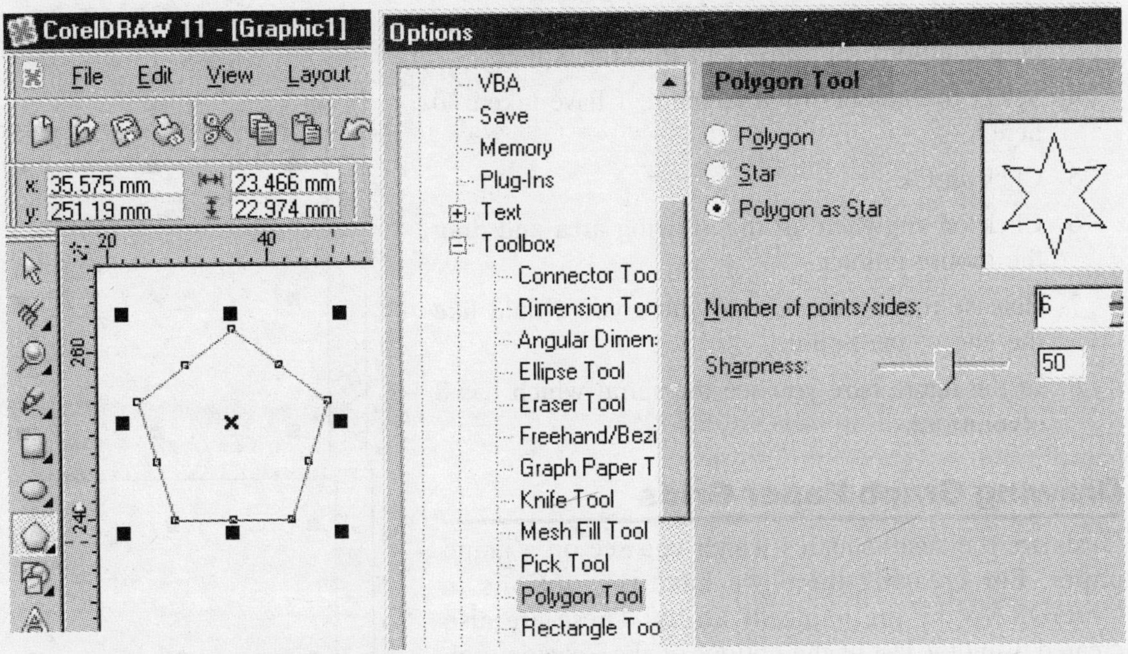

3. Enter the number of sides in the Number of points/sides spin box.
4. Click on Ok.
5. Click anywhere in the drawing area and drag the mouse pointer.
6. Release the mouse button where you would like the end of the Star.

Drawing Spirals

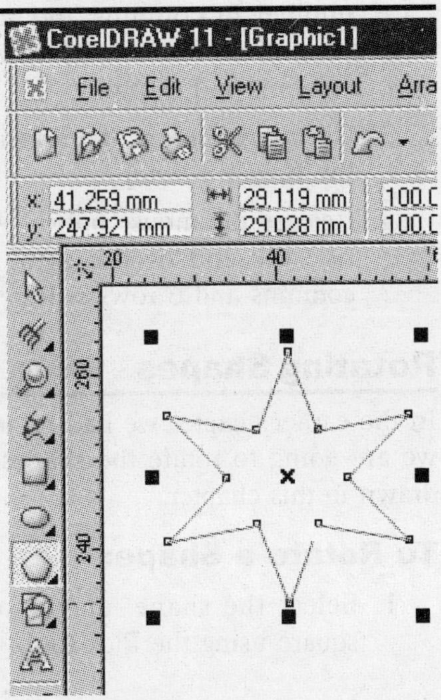

As we had seen earlier the Polygon tool has a number of options. Among them is a spiral tool. This works very similar to the star tool. For creating this we do the following:

1. Click on the **Spiral** tool from the flyout menu of the Polygon tool.
2. Click anywhere in the drawing area and drag the mouse pointer.
3. Release the mouse button where you would like the end of the spiral.

For drawing a Logarithmic spiral you have to do the following: (A logarithmic spiral is the one where the distance between each spiral increases as the spiral outward).

1. When selected see the toolbar.
2. Choose the **Logarithmic** radio button in this toolbar .

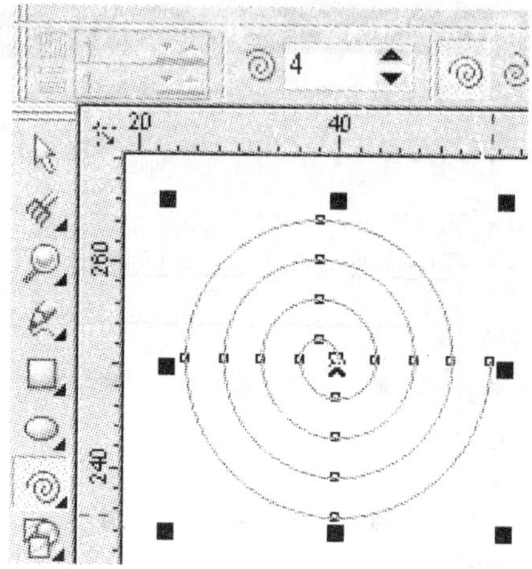

3. Enter the number of revolutions in the Number of revolutions spin box, I have taken 8 here.
4. Select the number of increment, I have taken 40 here.
5. Click in Ok.
6. Click on anywhere in the drawing area and drag the mouse pointer.
7. Release the mouse button where you would like the end of the Spiral.
8. In the figure here you see the spiral which has 8 revolutions.

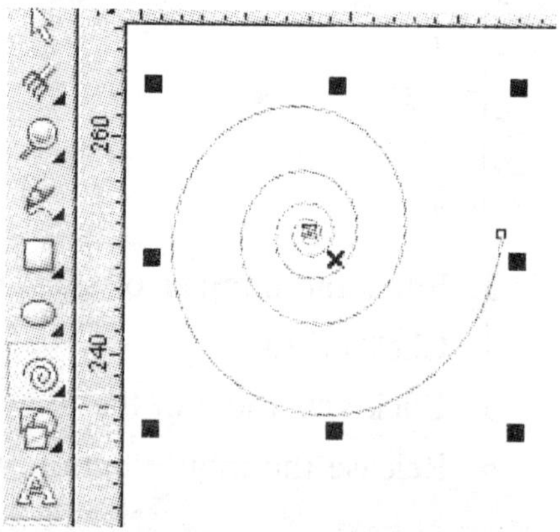

Drawing Graph Paper Grids

Girds are the small squares which you see on a graph paper. For creating them we have the options in CorelDRAW by the name of Grids. These are also created using the last of the options of the Polygon tool.

To Draw Graphic Grids:

1. Select the **Graph Paper** tool from the flyout menu of the Polygon Tool.
2. Place your mouse pointer over the Graph Paper Columns and Rows text box and type the number of columns and rows you like for your grid. For example, we have taken 4 columns and 6 rows.
3. Click anywhere in the drawing area and drag the mouse pointer.
4. Release the mouse button where you would like the end of the grid. Your grid of 4 columns and 6 rows will be created.

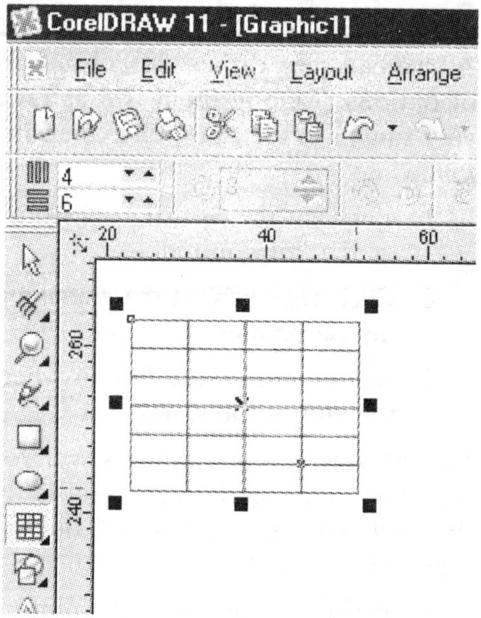

Rotating Shapes

In the earlier chapter we had rotated the text, here we are going to rotate the shapes, which we have drawn in this chapter.

To Rotate a Shape:

1. Select the shape, maybe a rectangle or a square using the Pick tool.

2. Click on the shape again. The handles will change from small black squares to curved arrows.
3. Click and drag the rotation handles in clockwise or counterclockwise direction to rotate the selected object.
4. Release the mouse button and the object will be rotated.

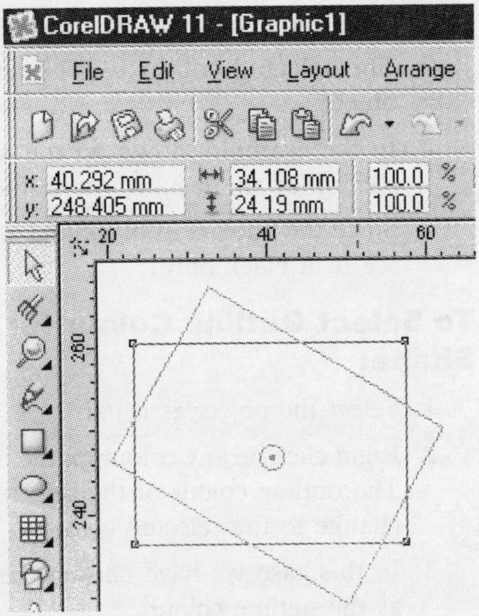

To Rotate a Shape by Fixed Angle:

1. Select the shape as in the above case.
2. Placing your mouse pointer on the Rotation Angle box in the Property Bar and click on it.
3. Enter the rotation angle in the Rotation Angle text box, by which you would like to rotate the object.

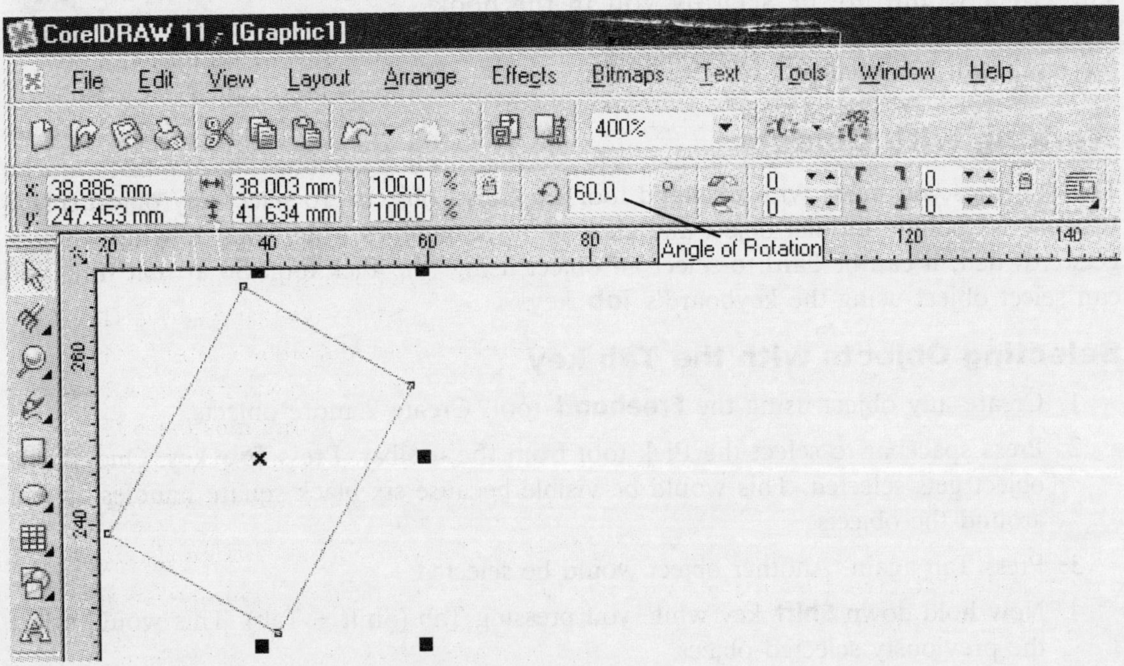

Selecting Fill and Outline Colours

As we had done in the earlier chapter with the text, here we will fill the shapes with the colours.

To Fill Colour to Any Shape:

1. Select the shape in which you want to fill the colours.

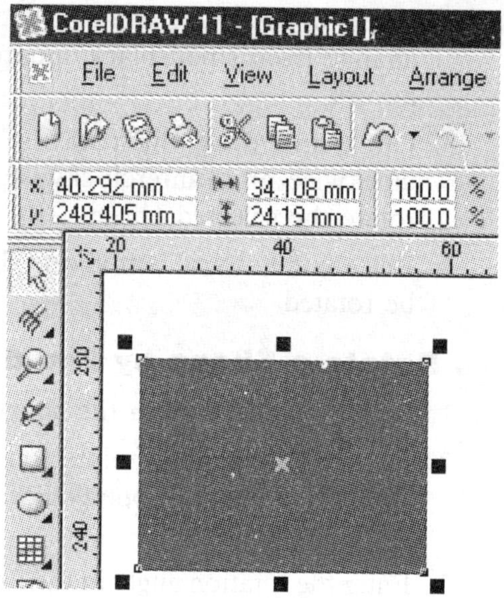

2. Click on any colour on the colour palette.
3. The selected colour will be applied to the object.
4. In the example shown on the next page, we have filled the rectangle with the red colour.

   Since the book is in black and white you will see it in black only.

To Select Outline Colour for any Shape:

1. Select the object as usual.
2. Right click on any colour on the colour palette. The outline colour of the selected object will change to the selected colour.
3. In this case we have chosen tiie blue colour as the outline colour.

The effect would not be seen by you in the book. However, when you do the same on your colour monitor, the result will be excellent.

Working with Objects

The drawings you made with freehand tool are called objects. To select any object, place your mouse pointer on that object and click on it. Sometimes when your drawing window gets crowded, it can be hard to select an object using the Pick tool. So at that time you can select object using the keyboard's **Tab** key.

Selecting Objects with the Tab key

1. Create any object using the **Freehand** tool. Create 2 more objects.
2. Press spacebar to select the Pick tool from the toolbar. Press **Tab** key. One of the object gets selected. This would be visible because six black square handles appear around the objects.
3. Press Tab again. Another object would be selected.
4. Now hold down **Shift** key while you pressing Tab (Shift + Tab). This would select the previously selected object.
5. With Pressing Tab you can select each object in the Drawing desktop.

Selecting Multiple Objects

It is not that you can select only one object at a time. You can select more than one object at a time. Select multiple objects with the Pick tool in following ways:

1. Hold down **Shift** and **Ctrl** key while you click on the Pick tool to select more

objects than one. You can select as many objects as you have on the Drawing window this way.

You can even deselect objects that have been selected by holding down the Shift and Ctrl key and clicking on them.

2. You can also select more than one object at a time by using the Pick tool to draw a marquee (rectangle) around more the objects to be selected.

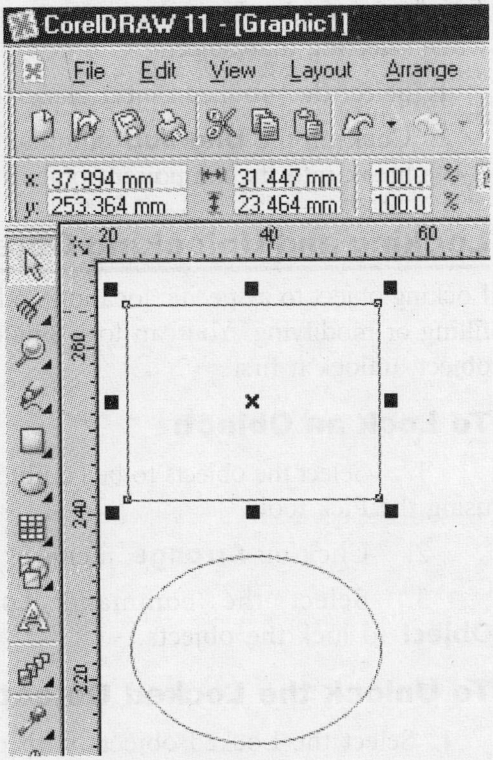

Duplicating Objects

1. To make a duplicate copy of an object, select the object using the Pick tool.
2. Click on **Edit** menu and press **Duplicate**.
3. The duplicate copy of the selected object will be created.

Grouping of the Objects

Once you have created a drawing using various objects, there is always a chance that one of them may move accidentally. So it is always advisable to group them so that the whole set of objects move together and their placing in the group is disturbed.

This marriage is not permanent. You can break them apart too.

You can break a grouped object into it's component objects by ungrouping them. This is useful when you need to make changes to some of the individual objects that comprise a grouped object.

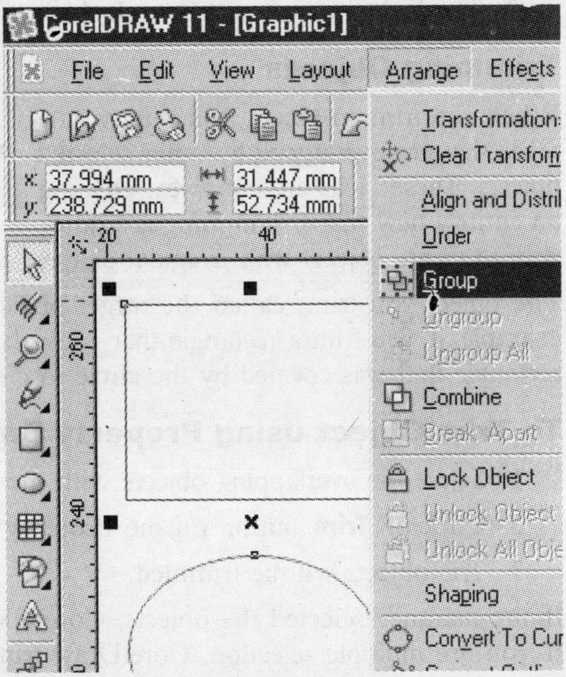

To Group Objects:

1. Select the objects with the Pick tool. To select multiple objects hold down Shift and Ctrl key while selecting them.
2. Click on the **Group** command in the **Arrange** menu. The selected objects will be grouped as a single object.
3. So now if you select and move, the whole grouped item will move together.

To select a single object that is part of a larger grouped object, hold down the Ctrl key while selecting that object.

1. Select the grouped object using the Pick tool.
2. Click on the **Ungroup** command in the **Arrange** menu. The grouped object will break into its component objects.

Locking and Unlocking Objects

Locking object to a specific location and preventing them from accidentally moving, sizing, filling or modifying. You can lock single, multiple or grouped objects. To modify a locked object, unlock it first.

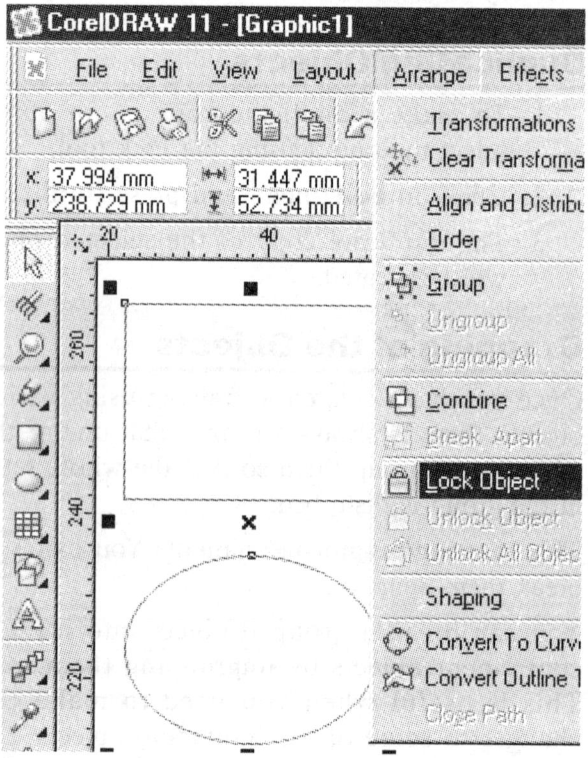

To Lock an Object:

1. Select the objects to be combined using the Pick tool.
2. Click on **Arrange** menu.
3. Select the command **Lock Object** to lock the objects.

To Unlock the Locked Objects:

1. Select the Locked objects with the Pick tool.
2. Click on **Arrange** menu and select **Unlock** Objects.
3. The locked object will be unlocked.

Trimming Objects

When you trim an object, you remove the areas that are overlapped by other selected objects. These areas are cut away, creating an entirely new shape. Trimming is a quick way to create objects with irregular shapes.

The object you trim, called the target object, retains its fill and outline attributes. For example, if you trim a rectangle that is overlapped by a circle, you remove the area of the rectangle that was covered by the circle to create a new, irregular shape.

To Trim Object using Property Bar

1. Select the overlapping objects with the Pick tool by holding the Shift and Ctrl key.
2. Click on **Trim** button on the Property Bar.
3. The objects will be trimmed.

If the marquee selected the objects, CorelDRAW trims the bottom-most selected object. If you use multiple selection, CorelDraw trims the object you selected last.

Aligning Objects

When you are making drawings of highest standard, then precise measurements make lots of difference. In this case the alignment of the objects too give a lot of meaning. CorelDRAW provides you with the facility of aligning the objects in various ways. You can specify whether you want objects to align horizontally or vertically (or both), using their edges or centre points.

To Align a series of Objects Horizontally or Vertically:

1. Select the objects with the Pick tool.
2. Click on **Arrange** menu and select the command **Align and Distribute**.
3. The Align and Distribute dialog box will appear.
4. The choices here are clear. First select the vertical alignments from Left, Center and Right, as shown on the top right of dialog box.
5. Similarly you can select the horizontal alignment.

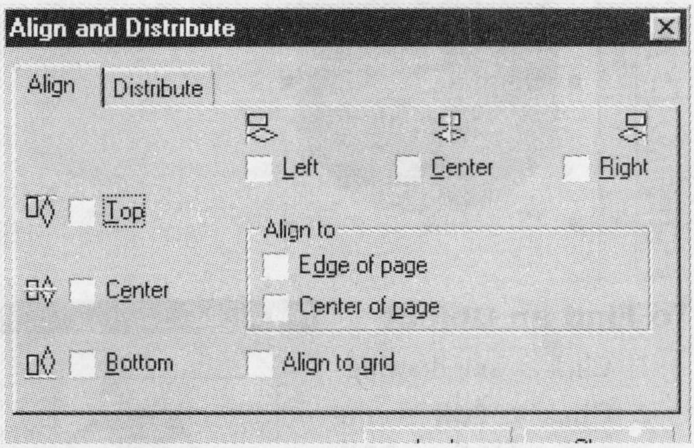

6. Next you can select the other options which are:

Edge of page aligns objects with the edge of the page

Centre of page aligns objects to the centre of the page

Align to grid aligns objects to the nearest grid line

7. Click on Ok.

The selected objects will be aligned as per your specifications.

In the figure below, I have selected the option of aligning the objects centrally and see the result.

Finding and Replacing Objects

The Find wizard takes you step by step through the process of finding objects in your drawings that fit the criteria you specify.

The Replace wizard takes you through the steps of replacing colours, palettes, outline pen properties, text properties (such as font, weight, or size), words, and other properties.

Finding objects

The Find wizard indentifies graphical and text objects that match the search criteria you specify.

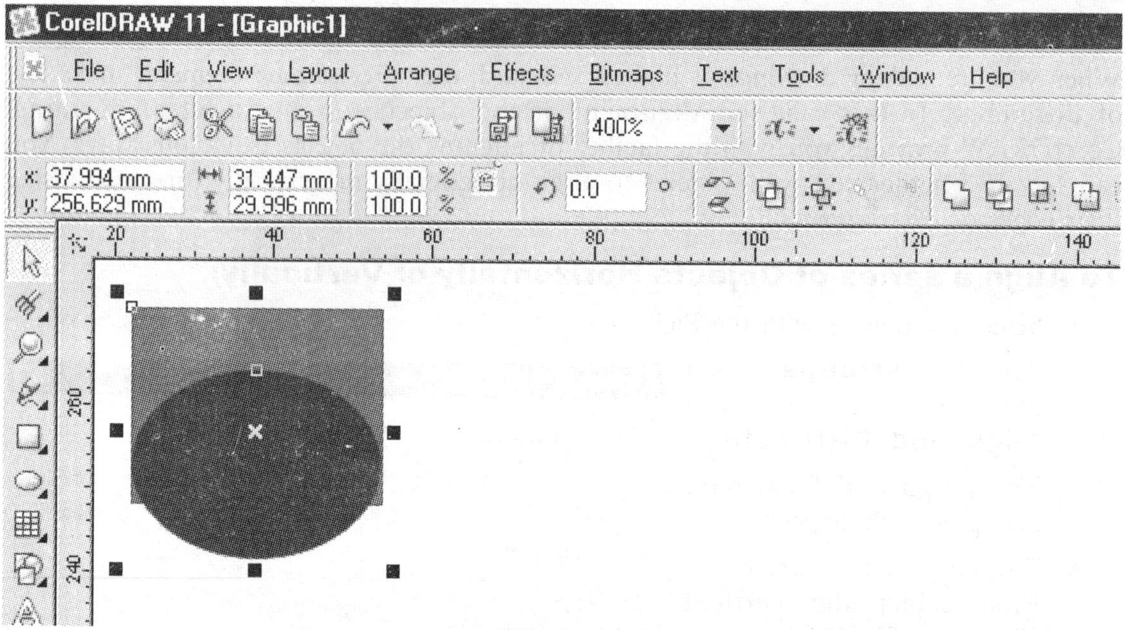

To Find an Object

1. Click at your drawing.
2. Click at **Edit** menu and **Find and Replace** command. Then **Find Objects** from the submenu.
3. In the first dialog box you are given the following options:

   Begin A New Search: Begins a new search.

   Load A Search From Disk: Loads a preset search or the one you've previously saved.

   Find Objects That Match The Currently Selected Object: Finds objects whose properties match those of the currently selected object.

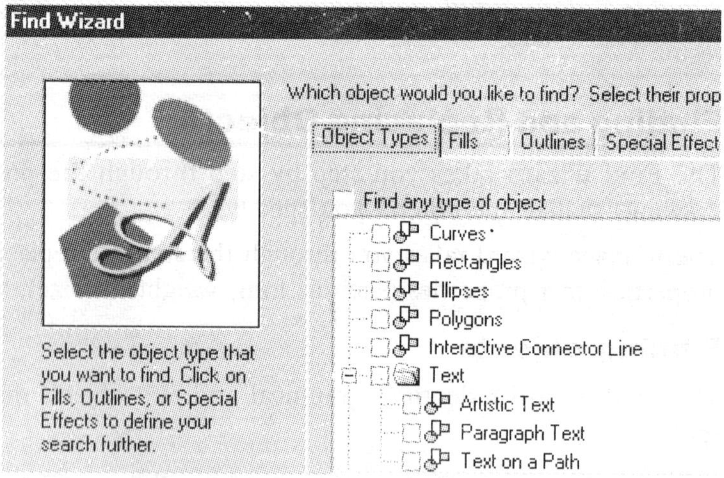

4. Click **Next**.
5. The second dialog box gives you the various options which are there in the drawings.

6. Select one of them and click at **Next**. This way CorelDRAW will take you to various dialog boxes to match the various options which would be there on the object which you want to find.
7. In the end when you click at **Finish**, CorelDRAW will give a toolbar, as shown below, to start the search to find the object.

Replacing Object Properties

The Replace wizard similarly searches for the properties you specify and replaces them with other properties. For example, you can search for specific outline pen properties and replace them with different pen properties.

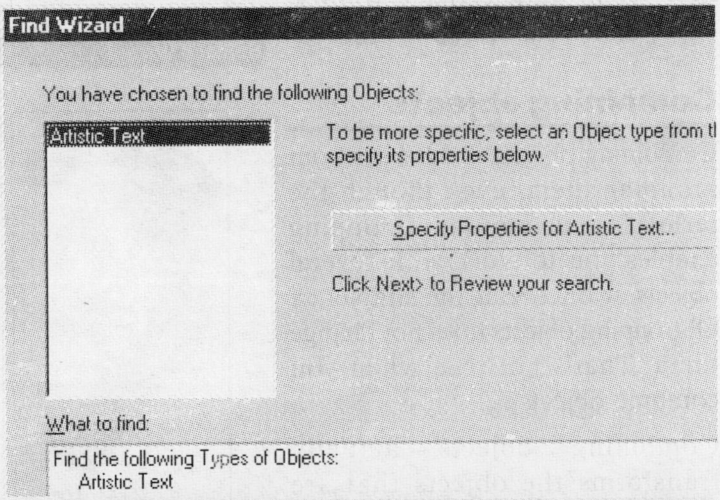

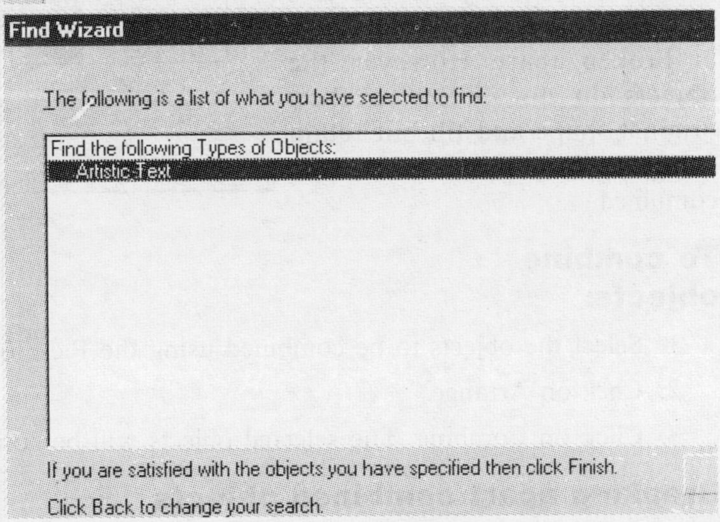

To Replace Object Properties

1. Click at the object whose properties you want to change.
2. Click at **Edit** menu and at the command **Find and Replace**. From the submenu select **Replace Objects**.
3. From the dialog box which you get enable one of the following buttons:

   Replace A Color.

   Replace A Color Model Or Palette.

   Replace Outline Pen Properties.

   Replace Text Properties.
4. Enable the **Apply to Currently Selected Objects Only** check box.

5. Click on the **Next** button.
6. Specify **Find and Replace** properties as required.
7. Click the **Finish** button.

   If the Replace wizard cannot find properties that match your search criteria, it displays a message that no object was found.
8. Click the Find Previous, Find Next, Find All, Replace, or Replace All buttons on the Find and Replace toolbar until your search is finished.

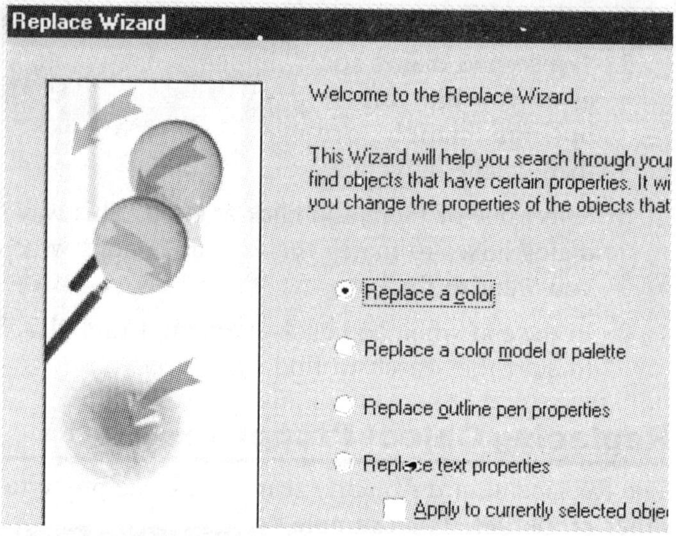

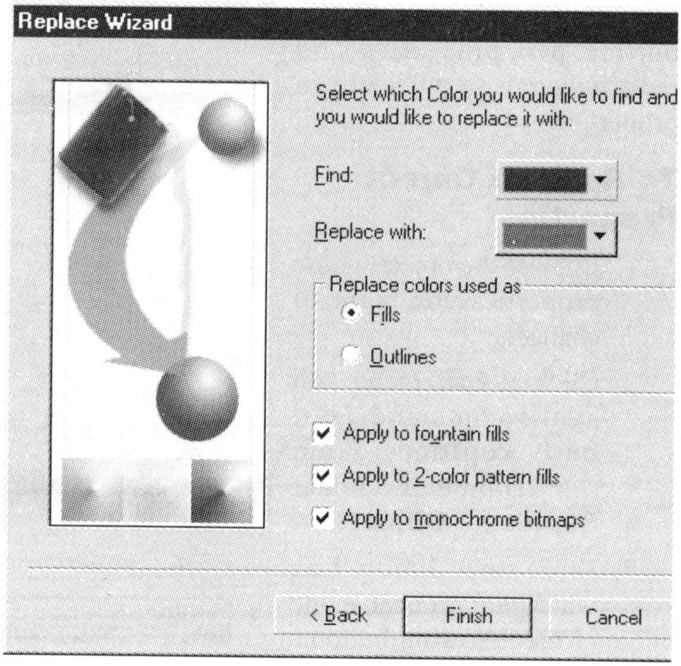

Combining objects

Combining objects is different from grouping them, even though the terms sound familiar. Grouping enables you to work with several objects at once. But the simple act of grouping objects does not change them. That's not true when you combine objects.

Combining objects actually transforms the objects that are combined. Combined objects can be broken apart. However, the objects do not revert to their original shape and fill but retain changes made when they were combined.

To combine objects:

1. Select the objects to be combined using the Pick tool.
2. Click on Arrange.
3. Click on Combine. The selected objects will be combined together.

Breaking apart combined objects

1. Select the combined object with the Pick tool.

2. Click on Arrange. The Arrange menu will appear.
3. Click on Break Apart. The combined object will break apart into component objects.

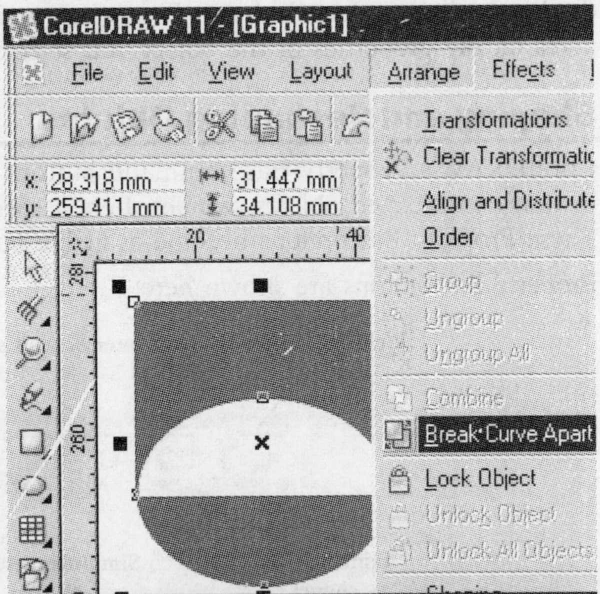

To create a drawing from lines:

1. Select the Freehand tool in the toolbox.
2. Click on the Drawing area.
3. Double click on the next mode in the object.
4. Keep creating new node as needed.
5. Click once (instead of double click) to create your last node.
6. Experiment with a curved line by holding down your mouse key and clicking ad dragging to create a curve.
7. Daw a curve quickly, and then draw it slowiy, Notice how the curve you drew mre slowly reflects your mouse motion in more detail.

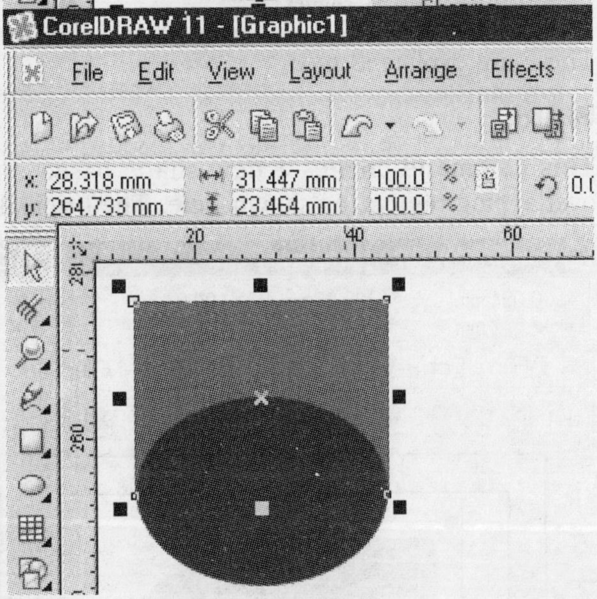

Intersecting objects

Intersecting creates a new object from the area where two or more objects overlap. The shape of this new object can be simple or complex, depending on the shapes you intersect.

The object fill outline attributes depends on the object you define as a target object-the object you intersect with the first selected object(s). The resulting new object uses the fill and outline attributes of this target object.

To intersect object using Property Bar

1. Select the objects with the Pick tool by holding the shift key.
2. Click on Intersect button on the Property Bar.
3. The objects will be intersected.

If the marquee selected the objects, the new intersected object takes on the properties of the bottom-most selected object. If you use multiple selection, the new intersected object takes on the properties of the object you selected last.

Shaping and Reshaping Objects

CorelDRAW's Property Bar command buttons enable you to apply shaping commands instantly to selected objects, which offers a speedy way of applying shaping commands. These Property Bar options become available only while at least two objects are selected. Property Bar buttons are shown here:

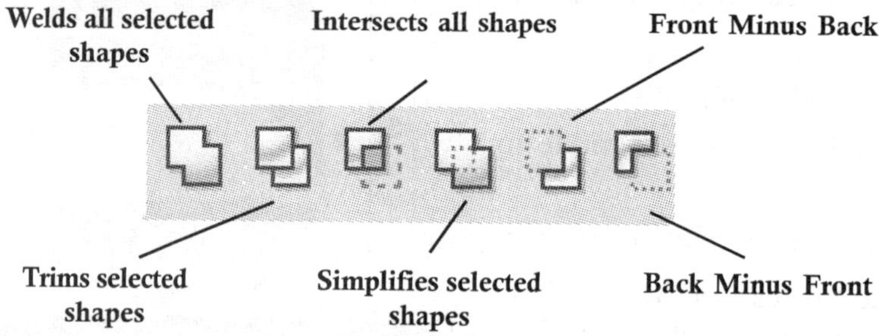

These are explained next.

Weld

This command creates a new shape based on the combined shape of two (or more) overlapping objects, as shown here. The original objects are automatically deleted.

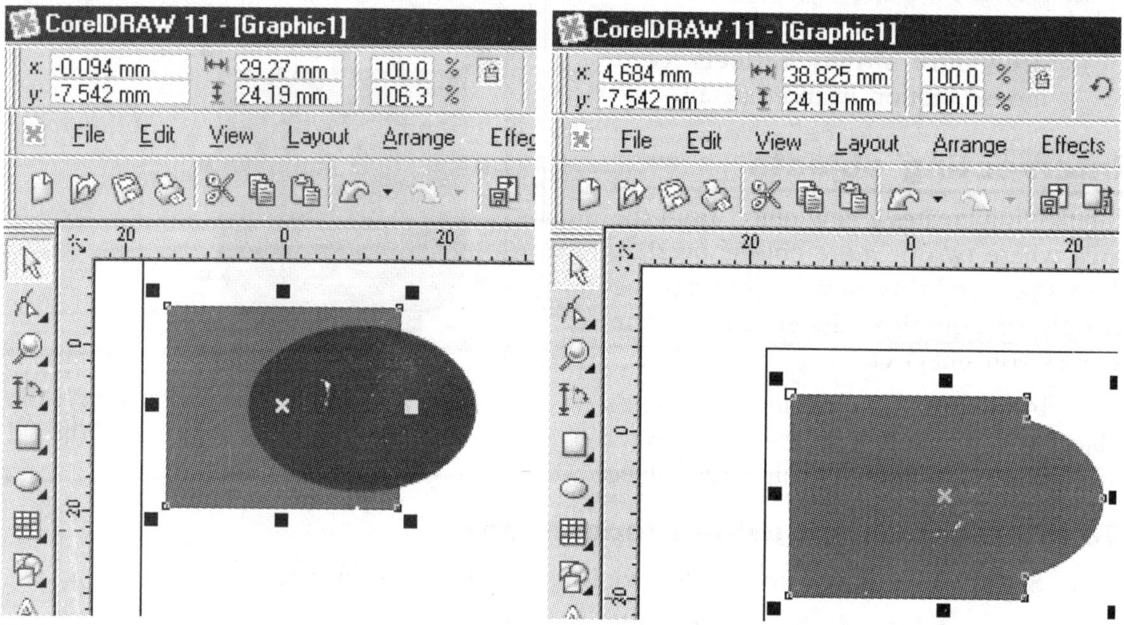

Trim

This command has the effect of removing a portion where the objects overlap each other, as shown next. There original are automatically deleted.

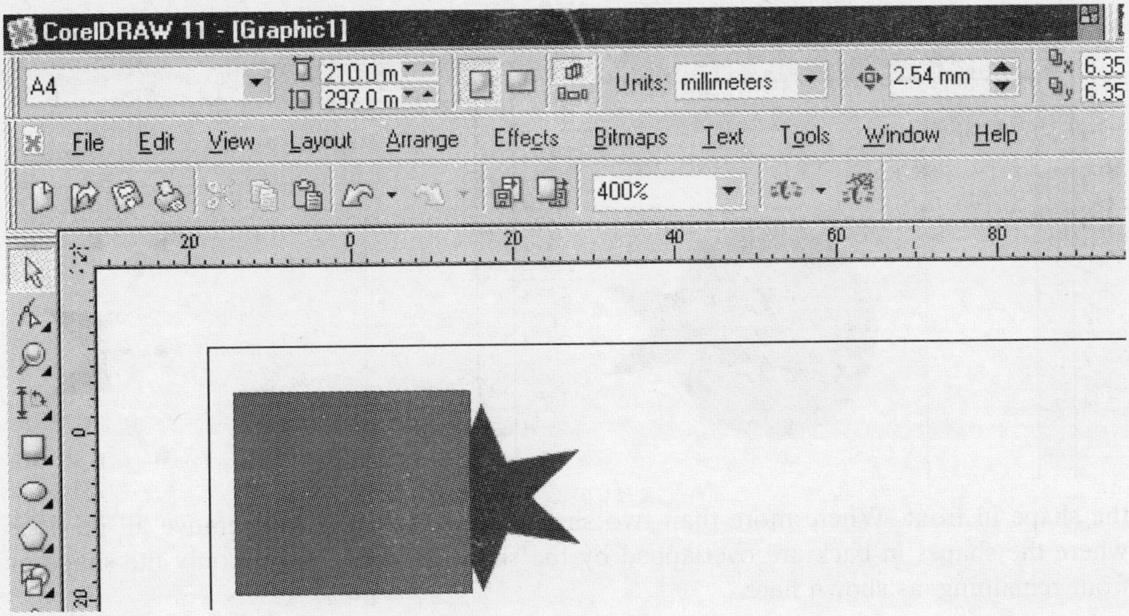

Intersect

This command creates a new object based on the actual overlapping portion of two or more objects, as shown next. The original objects remain intact.

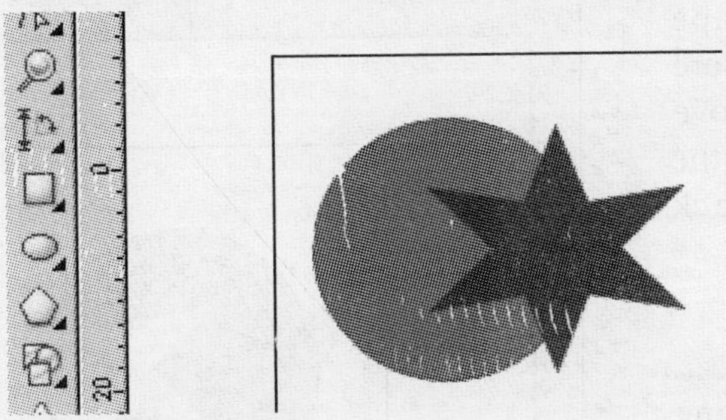

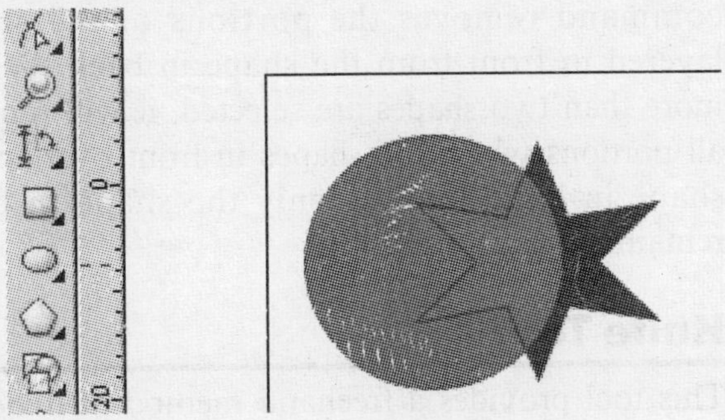

Simplify

This command enables you to remove all nonvisible and hidden portions of objects layered behind objects in front, as shown next. This command is useful for making an intricated arrangement of drawing shapes far less complicated by removing any hidden portions and/or separating linked objects—all in a single command.

Front Minus Back

The key to understanding the results of this shaping command lies in its name. While at least two shapres are selected, applying the Front Minus Back command removes the hidden portion of the shape layered in back from

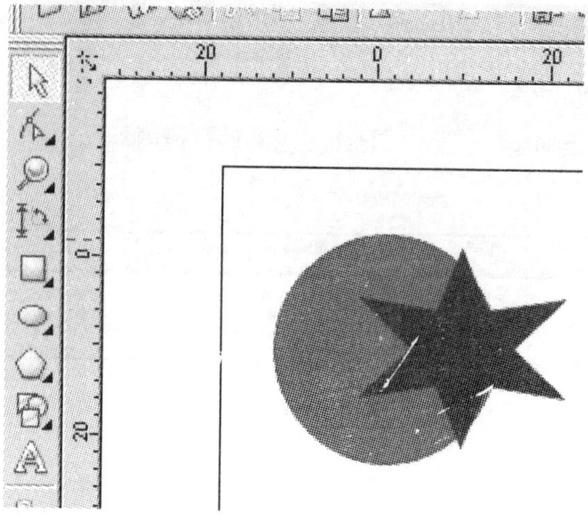

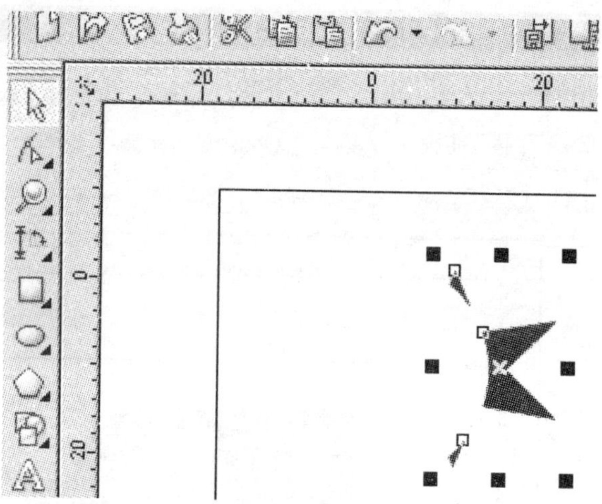

the shape in front. Where more than two shapes are selected, it will remove all portions where the shapes in back are overlapped by the shape in front, leaving only the shape in front remaining, as shown here.

Back Minus Front

This shaping command works in reverse of Front Minus Back. While at least two shapes are selected, applying the Back Minus Front command removes the portions of the shape layered in front from the shape in back. Where more than two shapes are selected, it will remove all portions where the shapes in front overlap the shape in back, leaving only the shape in back remaining, as shown here.

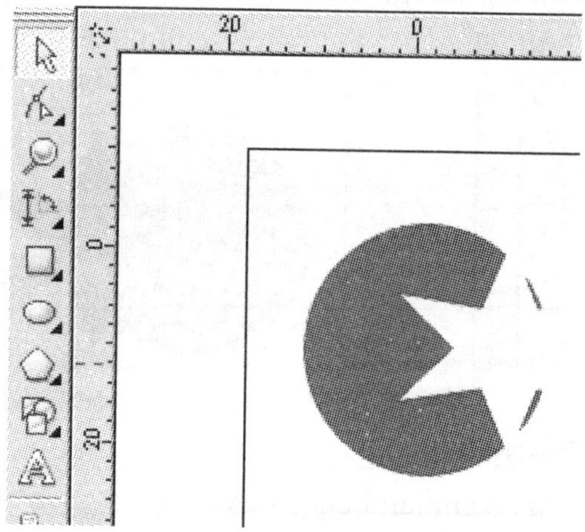

Knife Tool

This tool provides a freehand method of dividing objects into portions. It provides you with a click and drag method of cutting path. To perform a cutting operation using knife tool, you must click the edges of the shape, you want to cut.

To perform a straight cut using the knife too.

1. Create a object you want to cut and choose the knife tool from the toolbox. While the knife tool is selected, your cursor changes to resemble the point of a cutting tool.
2. Begin your cut by holding the knife tool cursor over one edge of your object. Notice the cursor changes angle slightly and perpendicular to the object's edge. Click the object edge once to define the starting point of the cut.
3. Define the end point of the cut by clicking any other point on the object's edge. Your straight cut is complete and the object is now divided into separate edges.

To perform a freehand cut using the knife tool.

1. Create a object you want to cut and choose the knife tool from the main toolbox.
2. Define the starting point of your cut, and hold the knife tool cursor over the edge of your object.
3. At this precise point, click and hold while dragging along the path you want to cut toward the inside of the object's shape. Continue holding-and-dragging through the object interior toward a different point on the dge of the object. Notice that as you hold-and-drag the cursor inside the object's shape, the knife tool cursor changes angle again and a preview of the cutting path appears.
4. When you reach the end of your cutting path at a different point on the object's outer edge, the cursor changes once again to its perpendicular state. At this point release your mouse button. Your cutting operation is complete.
5. Once you knife cut is complete, notice that the object has been divided into at least two portions. To verify this, choose the Pick Tool from the main toolbox, click each of the cut portions once, and notice that each includes its own slection handles, indicating they are separate objects.

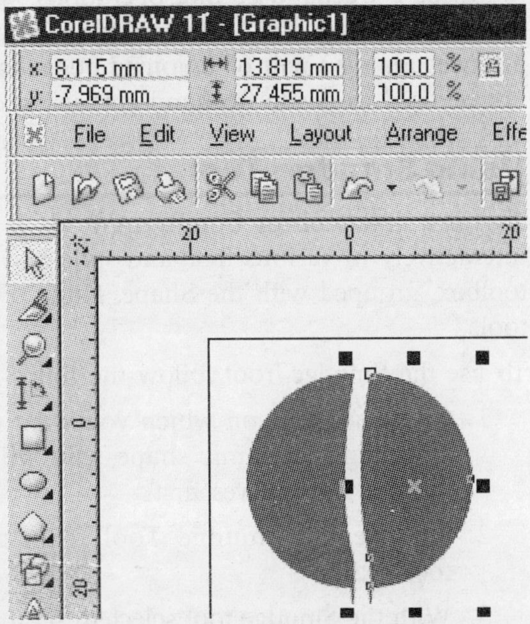

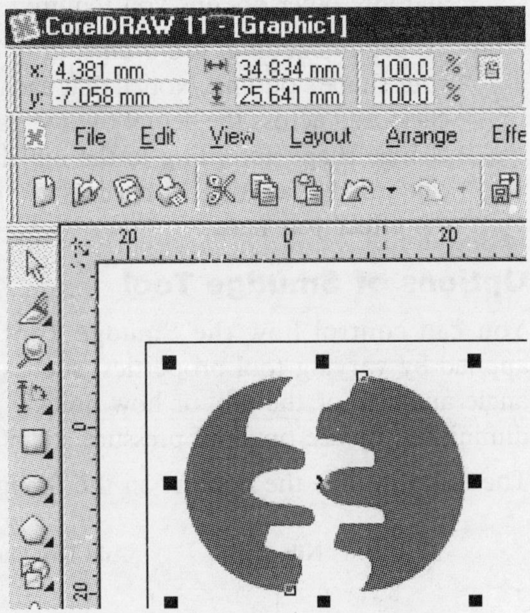

Knife Tool options

Various options of the knife tool are given below:

Leave as One Object   Auto-Close On Cut Mode

Leave As One Object

While this option is not selected, the knife tool cuts objects and breaks apart the two divided portions into individual objects. While this option is selected, the cutting operation results in compound paths that are not separated, even though a straight or freehand cut has been performed.

Auto-Close On Cut

This option is the drfault state and sets the knife tool behaviour to create closed path objects following a freehand cutting operations, which is just what you had expected. While this option is seleted, the knife tool may be used only in break paths at specific points—in essence, adding a pair of unjoined nodes to the path. While in this state, the knife tool may not be used to create freehand cuts using click dragging actions.

Using Smudge Tool

This is a new tool for CorelDRAW 11. It offers the ability to alter the outlines of shapes interactively in various freehand style ways. You will find the Smudge Tool, in the main toolbox, grouped with the Shape, Knife, Eraser, Roughen Brush and Freehand Transform tools.

To use the Smudge Tool follow the following steps:

1. Create a shape on which you want to use the Smudge Tool. If you are creating or selecting a dynamic shape, you will need to convert it to curves first.
2. Choose the Smudge Tool from the main toolbox.
3. With the Smudge tool selected, set the nib size and any other options you require.
4. To begin smuding, use a click-drag action on your shape's outline. Notice that each time you click-drag across the actual outline path, it will change shape according to the nib shape. You can smudge as long as neccessary to achieve the effect you need.

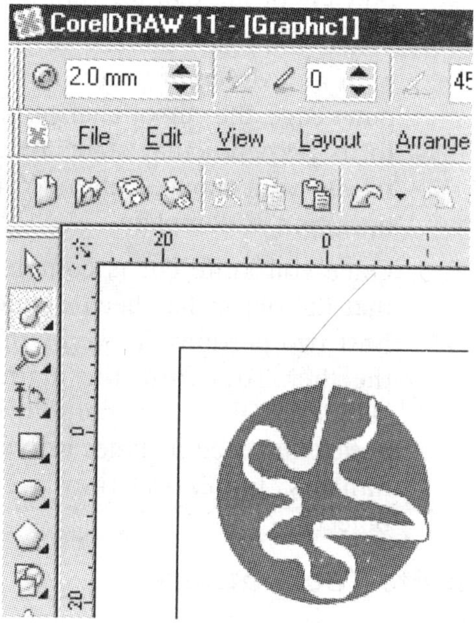

Options of Smudge Tool

You can control how the Smudge Tool effect is applied by varying tool properties, such as the tilt, angle and size of the nib, or how quickly the effect diminishes, or use optional pressure stylus settings.

The following are the options on the Smuge tool Property Bar.

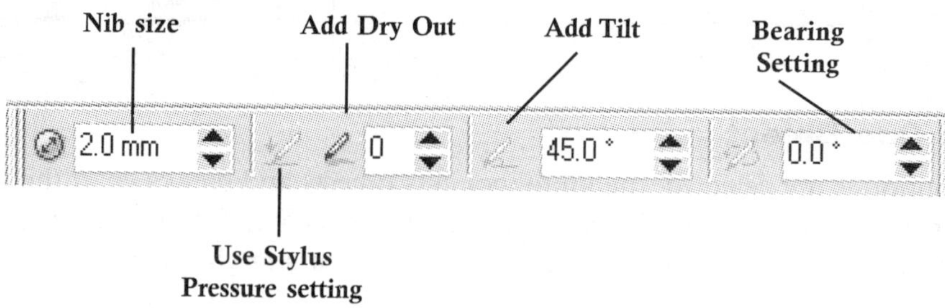

Nib size

The Smudge Tool nib size may be set within a range between 0.03 and 2.0 inches, the default of which is 0.1 inch.

Use Stylus Pressure

If you crrrently have a pressure stylus installed on your stystem, you may choose this option to have the Smudge Tool interpret your stylus pressure values. The more pressure applied, the wider the smudge.

Dry Out

This option sets a rate for the effect of gradually reducing the width of your smudge accordint to the speed of your click-drag action and may be set within a range between 0 and 10. Higher values cause your smudge to be reduced in width more quickly while a setting of 0 deactivates the Dry Out effect.

Tilt

The tilt value enables you to control the elliptical shape of the Smudge Tool nib. Tilt is measured in degrees and may be set within a range between 15, a flat shaped nib, and 90, a circular shaped nib. Tilt and bearing values work in combination with each other to control the smudge nib shape.

Bearing

The Bearing setting enables you to set the angle of the Smudge Tool cursor measured in circular degrees, 0 to 360. The effects of changing the Bearing setting are most noticeable at lower Tilt values—such as a Tilt value of 15 degrees.

Copying the Objects

CorelDRAW 11 provides several ways to create copies of selected objects. Each has its own advantages and is quick to use.

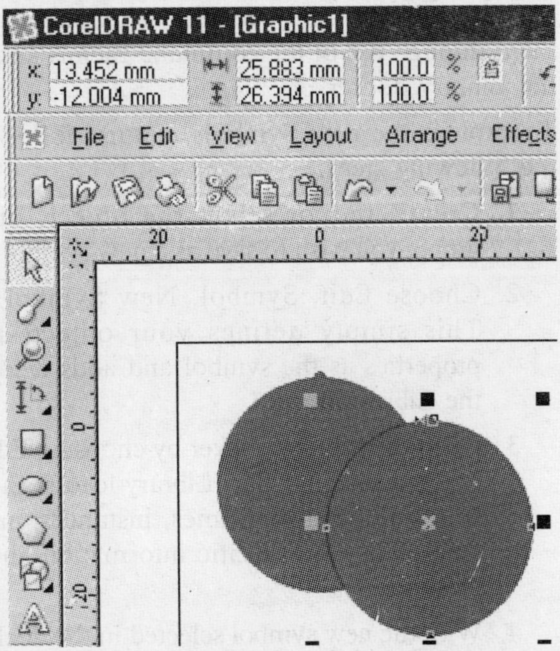

Right Mouse Click Method

Clicking the right mouse button while tranforming, rotating, or moving an object with the Pick tool creates a copy. The object currently being dragged becomes the copy, leaving the original object unchanged.

The small + symbol beside the cursor indicates that a copy has been created, as shown here.

Spacebar Method

Pressing the spacebar while transforming,

rotating, or moving an object with the Pick Tool creates a copy. Doing this causes a copy to be created in situ, meaning a copy is dropped each time the spacebar is pressed.

Pressing and holding the spacebar causes you key repeat action to create multiple copies so as long as the spacebar is held.

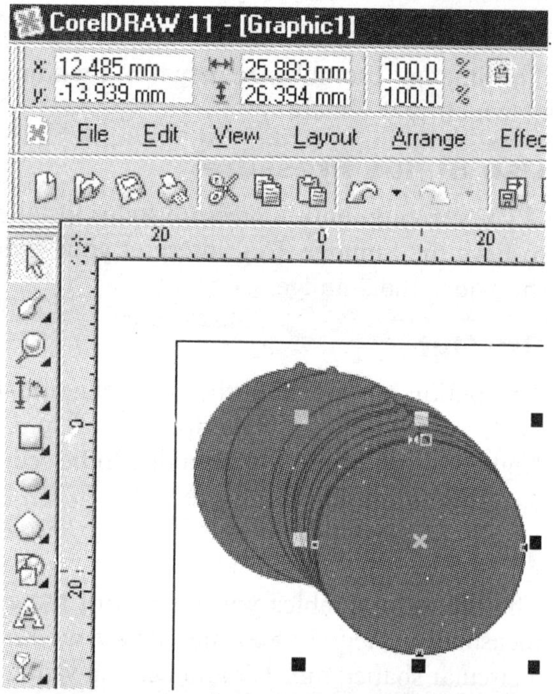

Pressing Numeric + key

Pressing the + key on your numeric keypad creates a copy of the selected object in exactly the same position and arranged in front of the original. After pressing the + key, the copy becomes the selected object.

You may create as many copies as you want using this method, but be aware that each additional copy hides the original behind it.

Creating Symbols

The ability to define objects as symbols is a brand new feature for CorelDRAW 11. Using Symbols, you can create just one object and make it a symbols can be duplicated without significantly altering the file size of your document. The new Symbols feature involves defining objects as symbols and managing them through use of the command menus and the Library docker.

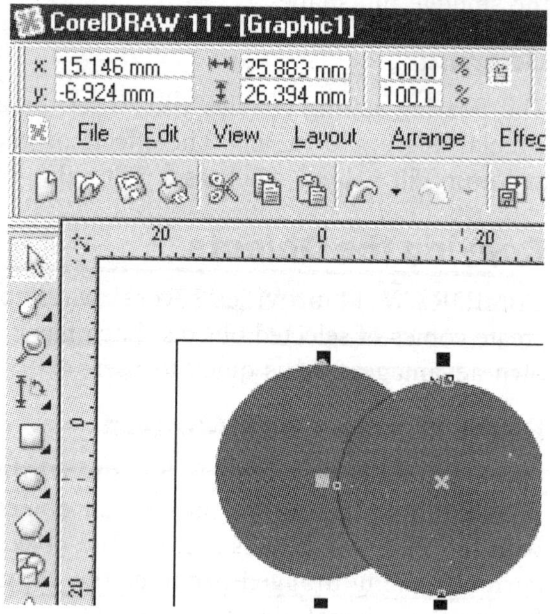

To explore the new Symbols feature, follow the following steps:

1. Create and/or select the object, or group, you wish to save as a new symbol.
2. Choose Edit, Symbol, New Symbol. This simply defines your object(s) properties as the symbol and adds it to the Library docker.
3. Open the Library docker by choosing Edit, Symbol, Library. Your new symbol is listed in the docker list. The Library features a preview of the shape(s) with a brief summary of the number of frames, instances, and behaviours listed. The list portion of the docker displays specific information about the symbol such as its Name, Type, and Descriptions.
4. With the new symbol selected in the docker list, click the Insert button. A new instance

of the symbol is added to your document page, in the original page position when defined as a symbol, and the Symbol Preview summary now indicates that two instances exist. Notice also that the Status Bar indicates that a symbol is selected in your document instead of the native shape name.

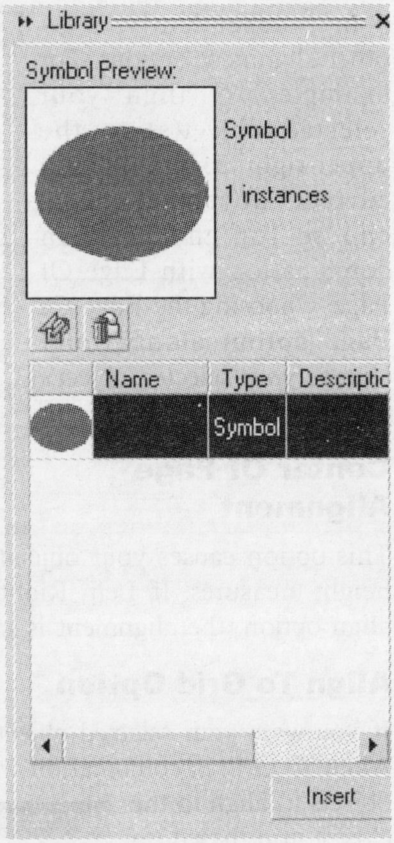

5. To edit a symbol, locate and select any of its instances, and click the Edit button in the docker, or click the Edit Symbol button in the Property Bar, after which the instance is ready for editing. Perform any editing changes and click at the Finish Editing. This level button a the lower-left corner of your document window. The original symbol and all its instances will reflect the editing changes in the Library docker list and throughout your document.

Aligning Objects

CorelDRAW allows you to align various objects according to your needs. Various options which can be used are shown in the dialog box, shown here. Once the option is selected, click the Preview button to confirm your choice, click the Apply button to apply your choice, and then click the Close button to confirm the alignment and close the dialog box.

Let us see the various options of the aligning of objects.

Vertical Alignment

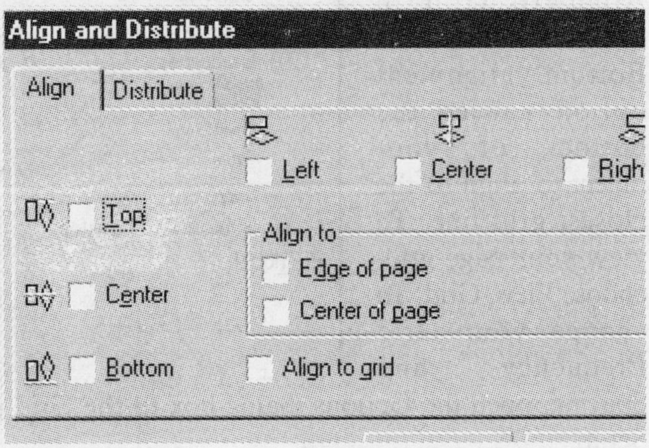

Choose Left, Center, or Right to align your objects accodingly. The following illustration shows all the three alignments, i.e., Left, Centre and Right.

Horizontal Alignment

While aligning objects horizontally, you have the option of using the Top, Centre or Bottom portions of your selected objects. Only one of these 3 options may be selected at any given time. While using either the Top or Bottom alignment option, the furthest object from the center of your selection determines the point at which the objects align.

Edge of Page Alignment

Three options exist for aligning objects in relation to your page borders in combination with

—or independently of — other alignment options. For example, to align your selected object(s) to the upper-right corner of your current document page, choose Top and Right in combination with Edge Of Page. Choosing the Edge Of Page option alone won't change your selected object's alignment.

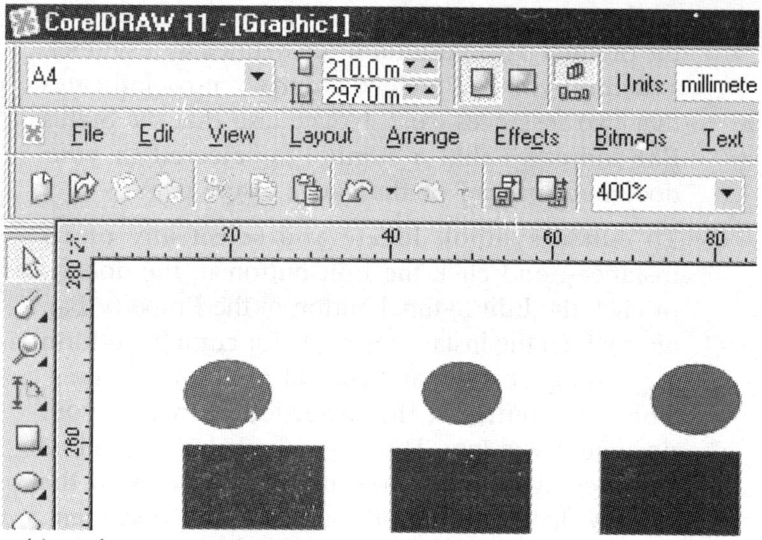

Center Of Page Alignment

This option causes your object(s) to be centered on your page based on their width and height measures. If Left, Right, Top, or Bottom is selected as the vertical or horizontal align option, the alignment is immediately changed to Center.

Align To Grid Option

If you want your selected object(s) to align with the closest grid line on your page, choose Align To Grid in combination with other options. Choosing this option causes your selected objects to align to the closest grid, based on your selection. For example, choosing Align To Grid in combination with the Bottom alignment option causes the bottom of your object to align to the closest grid line. To view your page grid, choose View, Grid. To change your Grid Frequency and Spacing, open the Options dialog box to the Grid page by choosing View, Grid And Ruler Setup.

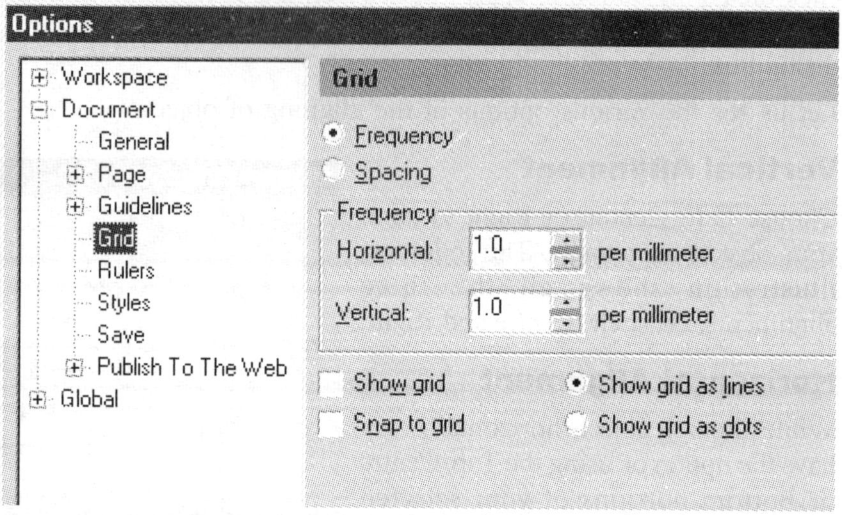

Choosing Center of Page as the align option automatically selects both vertical Center and horizontal Center options in the Align tab. To select both vertical and horizontal center options quickly at the same time, without centering your objects in relation to the page, double click the Center of Page option upon first opening the dialog box.

Object Manager

All layer functions are performed using the Object Manager docker. This docker enables you to navigate document pages; create and name layers, select and move objects between layers; and set layers as editable, printable, and/or visible.

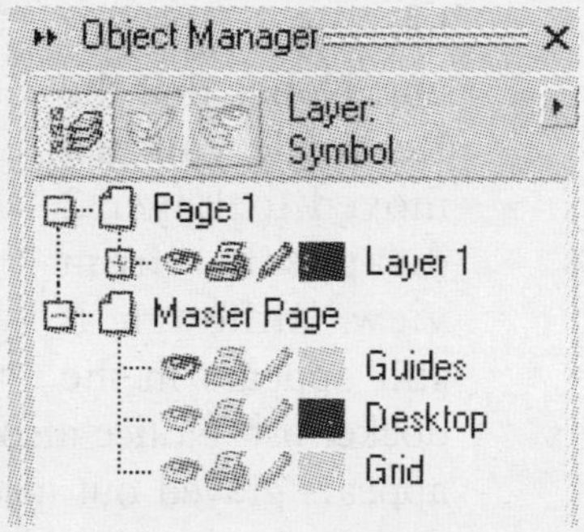

To open the Object Manager docker, choose Tools, Object Manager. The Object Manager shows a listing of the layers, each accompanied by options and a flyout menu. A Master Page also appears and includes default layers for controlling Guides, the Desktop and Grid objects.

1. Open a new document and open the Object Manager docker by choosing Tools, Object Manager. Notice that the docker lists each page of your document. Each page features a default layer named Layer 1, accompanied by three symbols and a black colour indicator.

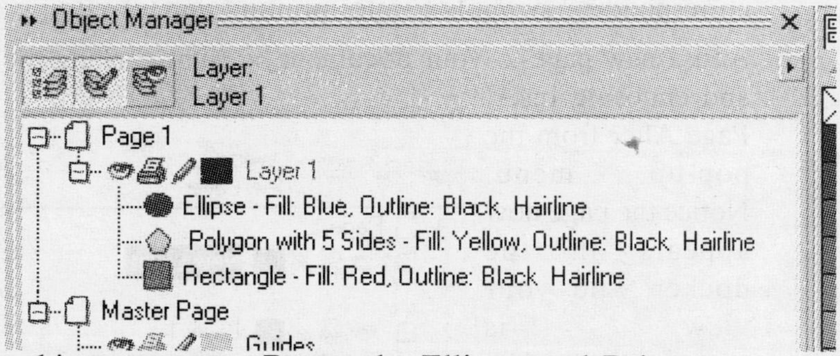

2. If your document is new and contains no objects, create a Rectangle, Ellipse, and Polygon on your document page and colour them differently. As you create your objects, they appear as objects belonging to Layer 1 on Page 1, and they are accompanied by symbols and brief descriptions. This is because the active layer is Layer 1.

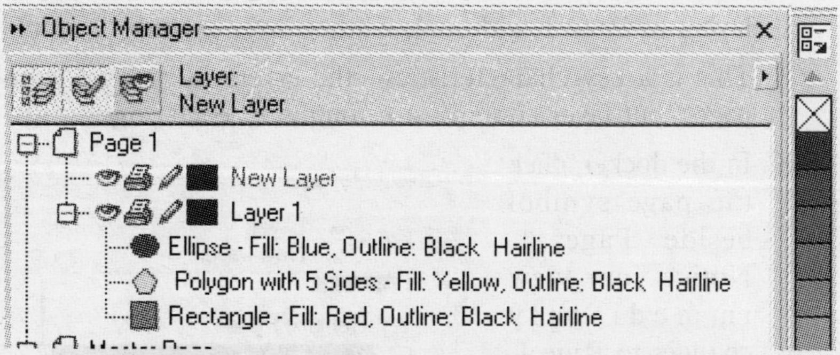

3. Click at the New Layer button. A new layer named Layer 2 appears above your active Layer 1. Name the new layer by typing while it is still selected and press Enter. Notice that Layer 2 is now your active layer and highlighted in red in the docker list.
4. In the Object Manager docker list, click to select the Rectangle. Notice that the Rectangle also becomes selected in your document. Using a click-drag action, click-and-drag the Rectangle within the Object Manager docker onto the new Layer 2 and release the mouse button. Notice that the Rectangle in your document has not changed position, but in the docker, it now appears under Layer 2. You have just moved the Rectangle object from one layer to another.

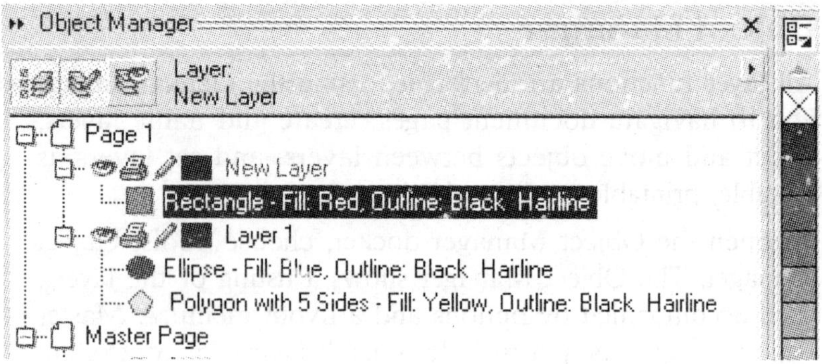

5. Single click the Eye symbol beside Layer 2, so it becomes grayed out. Notice that the Rectangle you just moved to Layer 2 disappears from view, although it still appears in the docker list. Notice also that the information describing the Rectangle on Layer 2 now appears grayed out also.

   This action toggles the display of all objects on a specific layer. Clicking the other corresponding symbols toggles printing and/or editing of a specific layer.

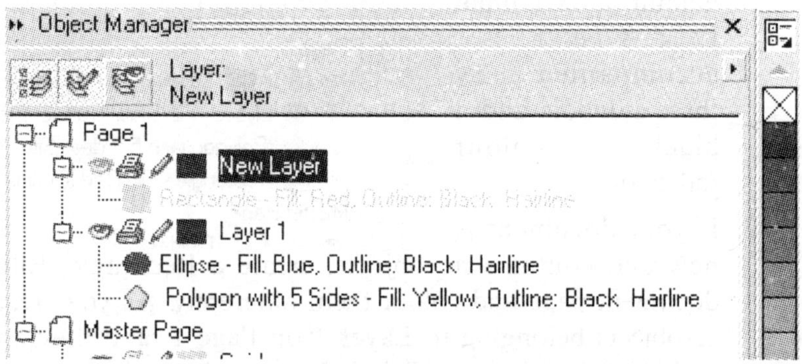

6. Add a new page to your document by right-clicking the page symbol next to Page 1 and choosing Insert Page After from the pop-up menu. Notice the page now appears in the docker, and your view is automatically changed to Page 2.
7. Click to expand the Page 2 structure to view its contents. Notice that Page 2 also includes the same two layers as Page 1, although neither layer includes any objects.

   This is a key characteristics—the layers for your document remain constant across pages, but layer contents are unique to each page.

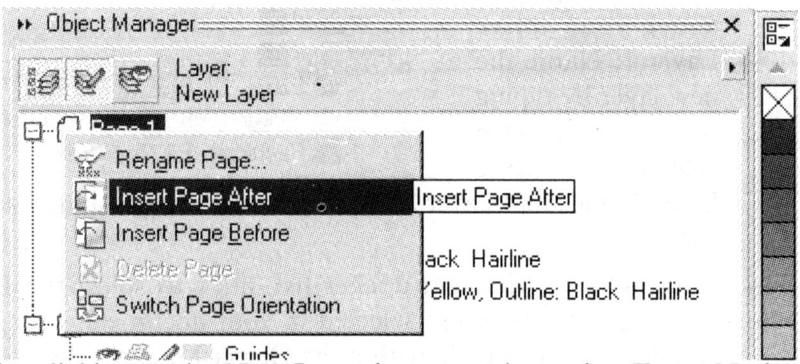

8. In the docker, click the page symbol beside Page 1. Notice your view immediately changes to Page 1, demonstrating the page navigation function.
9. Create a third layer for your document by clicking at the New Layer button and pressing Enter. Notice that the layer is added to all document pages.

   Click the new layer once to ensure that is is selected, and create a new object on

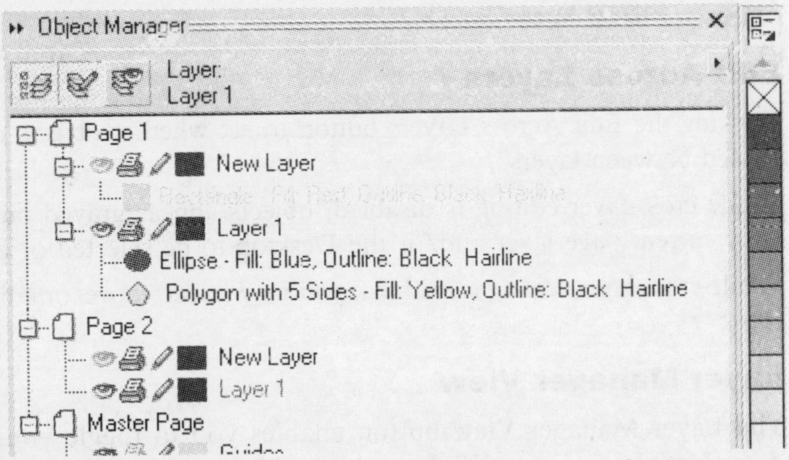

your document page. Notice that the new object is automatically created on the new layer. This demonstrates that new objects are created on the selected layer on your current page.

10. Click the Eye symbol beside Layer 2 to make it visible again. All 3 objects should now be visible on Page 1. Using the Pick Tool, drag the Rectangle, Ellipse, and Polygon objects on your document page to overlap each other, while leaving them on their current layers.

    Notice that the Ellipse and Polygon objects on Layer 1 appear behind the Rectangle on Layer 2. This is because Layer 2 is ordered above Layer 1.

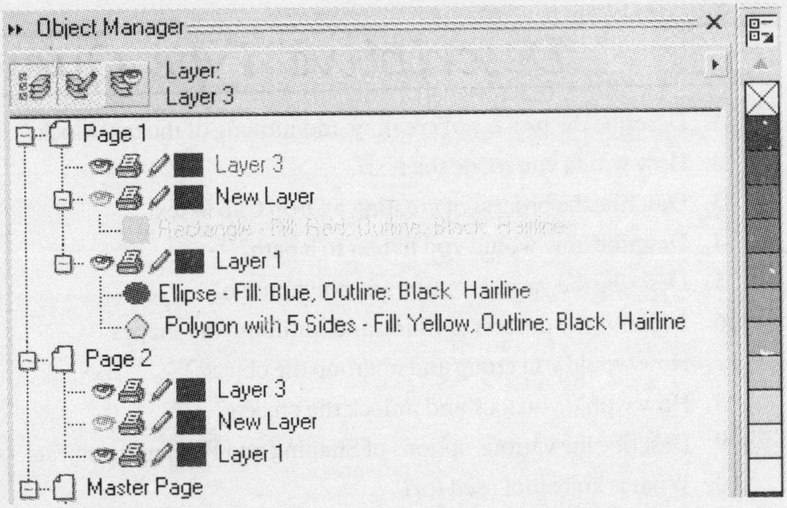

11. Using a click drag action in the Object Manager docker, click the text label of Layer 1 on Page 1, drag it vertically upward and just above the position of Layer 2, and then release the mouse button.

    Notice that the Ellipse and Polygon objects now appear in front of the Rectangle. This action changes the order of your layers. As you drag, the cursor changes to indicate the new insertion point before the mouse button is released.

Editing from Object Manager

Three view state buttons at the top of the Object Manager docker enable you to set the information display and editing behaviour. Clicking each button toggles its state on or off, each of which has the following effects:

Show Object Properties

Click the Show Object Properties button to set whether properties associated with each object are listed in the docker.

Edit Across Layers

Clicking the Edit Across Layers button to set whether objects may be selected, moved, or copied between layers.

While cross-layer editing is disabled, objects appear grayed out, enabling only objects on your current page layer and/or the Desktop to be selected or edited.

While cross-layer editing is enabled, you may select, move, or edit any object on an unlocked layer.

Layer Manager View

The Layer Manager View button enables you to toggle your view to show only your document's layers listed. When working with complex documents that feature multiple pages, layers, and objects, using this view can make managing Layer properties significantly easier. In this case, all page and object information is omitted.

Descriptive Type Questions

1. Describe the process of creating and moving of the text block.
2. How would you rotate the text?
3. Describe the process of creating a Drop Cap in text.
4. Describe how would you fit text to a path?
5. Describe the various options of polygon tool.
6. Describe the process of filling and outlining the shapes.
7. How would you group and ungroup the objects?
8. How would you lock and unlock the objects?
9. Describe the various options of Shaping and Reshaping objects.
10. What is knife tool used for?
11. How is Smudge tool used?
12. Describe the various methods of copying objects.
13. Describe the various types of alignments in CorelDRAW 11.
14. How would you create symbols?
15. How would you edit layers?
16. How would you copy objects?
17. How would you create symbols?
18. How would you align objects?
19. What is the use of Object Manager?
20. How would you create a polygon?

5 Introduction to Adobe Illustrator

Introduction

Adobe Corporation, which has software like Photoshop and PageMaker has Illustrator too. It is interesting to note that it is in its version number 10 living upto the challenge of the market, which is flooded with various graphics software. Its biggest competitor is CorelDRAW.

Illustrator Screen

I have told you now about the various commands of Illustrator, let me now tell you what the Illustrator screen, actually has. You can see the various contents of the screen on the next page. Various items of the screen are described below.

Menu Bar

The menu bar provides access to Illustrator's 10 menus. Click a menu name to display a list of commands that perform various operations. To choose a command, drag your cursor on top of it so it becomes highlighted, then release. Keyboard shortcuts appear to the right of commands. If a command is dimmed, it is not available at the current situation and

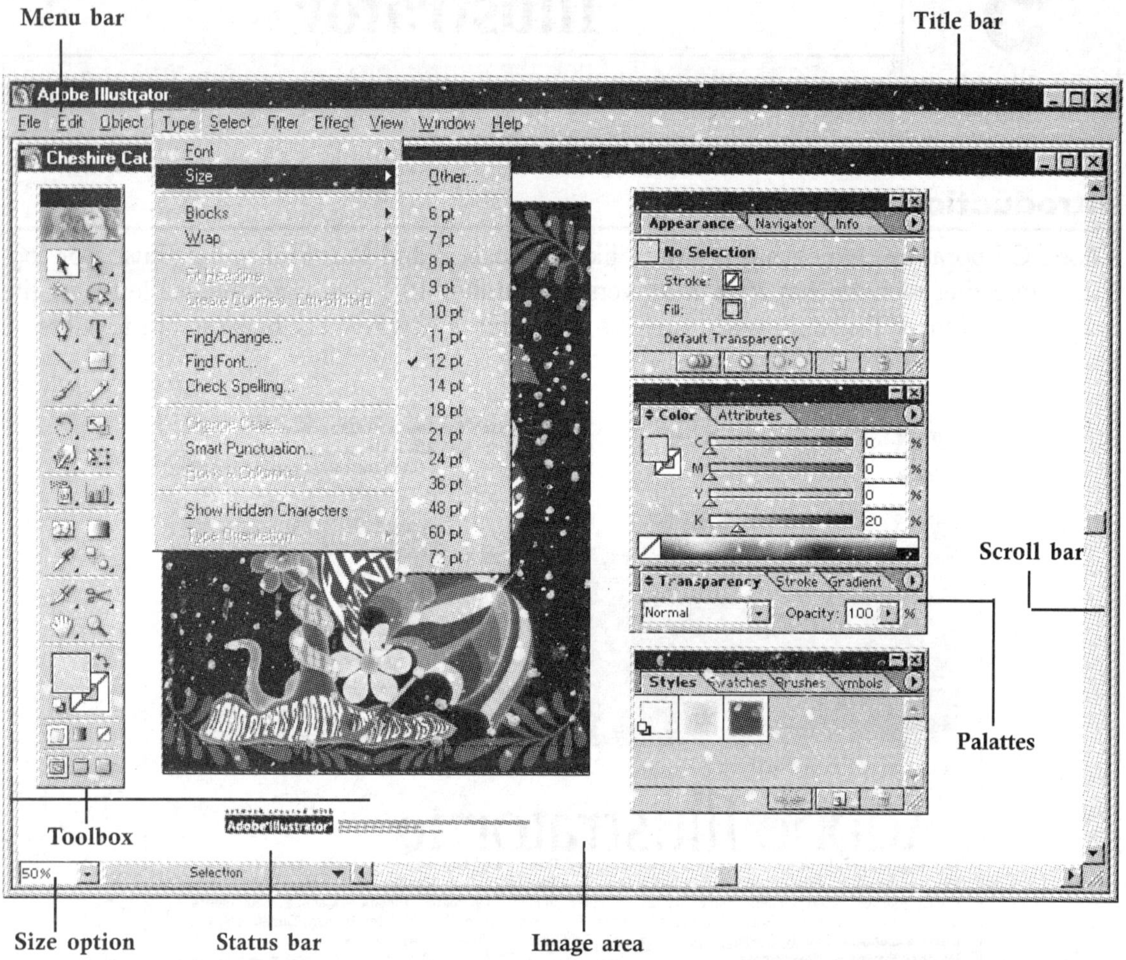
Menu bar
Title bar
Adobe Illustrator
File Edit Object Type Select Filter Effect View Window Help
Cheshire Cat
Font
Size
Blocks
Wrap
Find/Change...
Find Font...
Check Spelling...
Smart Punctuation...
Show Hidden Characters
Other...
6 pt
7 pt
8 pt
9 pt
10 pt
11 pt
12 pt
14 pt
18 pt
21 pt
24 pt
36 pt
48 pt
60 pt
72 pt
Appearance Navigator Info
No Selection
Stroke
Fill
Default Transparency
Color Attributes
Transparency Stroke Gradient
Normal
Opacity: 100 %
Styles Swatches Brushes Symbols
Scroll bar
Palattes
Toolbox
50%
Selection
Size option
Status bar
Image area

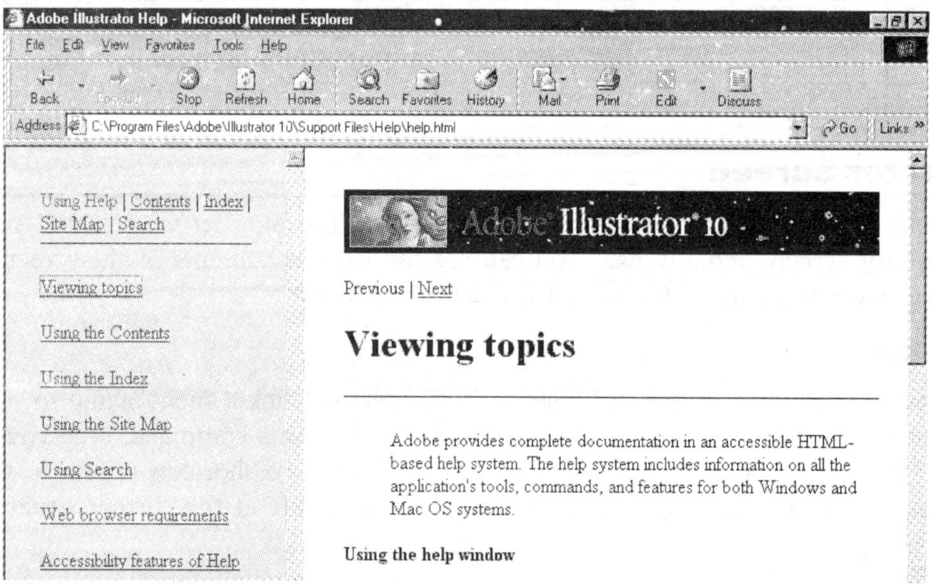
Adobe Illustrator Help - Microsoft Internet Explorer
File Edit View Favorites Tools Help
Back Forward Stop Refresh Home Search Favorites History Mail Print Edit Discuss
Address C:\Program Files\Adobe\Illustrator 10\Support Files\Help\help.html
Go Links
Using Help | Contents | Index | Site Map | Search
Viewing topics
Using the Contents
Using the Index
Using the Site Map
Using Search
Web browser requirements
Accessibility features of Help
Adobe Illustrator 10
Previous | Next
Viewing topics
Adobe provides complete documentation in an accessible HTML-based help system. The help system includes information on all the application's tools, commands, and features for both Windows and Mac OS systems.
Using the help window

you can't choose it. If a right-pointing arrowhead follows a command name, choosing the command displays a submenu of additional commands. To choose Object>>Command Paths>>Release, for example, you would click the word Object in the Menu bar to open the Object menu. You would then move down to the Compound Paths command, then over to the submenu and then click the Release command. This closes the menu and applies the command.

Toolbox

The toolbox includes 24 default tools and 36 alternate tools. To select a tool, click its icon. Later in the chapter you will be introduced to these tools one by one. The bottom portion of the toolbox offers three sets of controls. The color controls let you change the colors of an object's stroke and fill as well as interchange colors. The paint styles controls let you select a solid color, a gradient or none (that is, see-through) for your fill or stroke. And in the final row, the image window controls give you control over the display of the foreground window. The toolbox is known generically as a palette. In addition to the tool box, Illustrator provides a number of other palettes all of which are detailed later in the chapter.

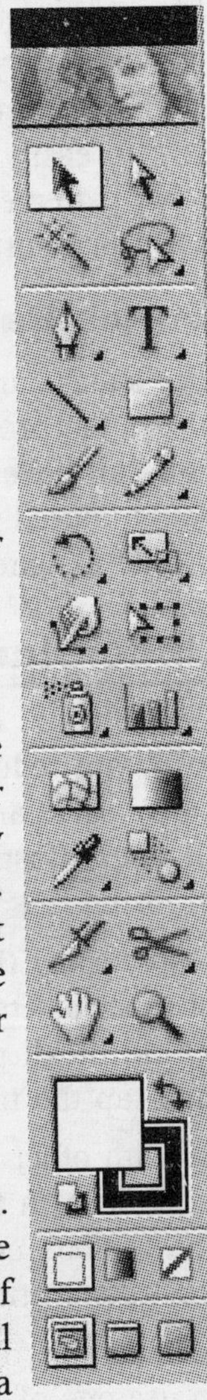

Illustration Window

The illustration window is the large window in the middle of the desktop. A window appears for every open illustration. The title bar lists the name of the document, the relative viewing size, the document color mode and the type of preview currently chosen. If the illustration has not been given a name, the name appears as "Untitled art," followed by a number.

You can move the illustration window by dragging the title bar. Close the illustration by clicking in the close box in the upper left corner (or in the upper right corner of the window to enlarge or reduce the size of the window manually. Click the zoom box again to reduce the window to its previous size. In Windows users, this corresponds to the maximize/restore box that sits just to the left of the close box. To the left of that, Windows provides the minimize box, which reduces Illustrator to a button on the Windows taskbar without quitting the program.

Artboard

The page with the drop shadow in the middle of the window is the art board. This represents the size of the drawing you want to create. Surrounding the artboard is the pasteboard. You can move objects out into the pasteboard if you like and these objects will be saved with your illustration, but they will not print. Experienced artists typically use the pasteboard as a storage area for objects they can't quite bear to delete. The dotted line around the image able area shows the portion of the artboard your printer can actually print. Most printers can't print to the extreme edges of a page. Together, the artboard and pasteboard are generically known as the drawing area.

Scroll Bars

The scroll bars appear along the right and bottom edges of the illustration window, as they do in most Windows applications. They allow you to move your drawing with respect to the window to better see various portions of your illustration. Click one of the arrows at the end of a scroll bar to nudge the drawing a small distance' click in the gray area of a scroll bar to move the drawing a greater distance. Drag the tab in either scroll bar to move the drawing manually.

Size Option Box

The size option box in the lower left corner of the illustration window lets you change the view size of your artwork. Simply click the size option box, enter any permitted value and hit Enter. You can reduce the view to as little as 3.13 percent of the actual size, allowing you to easily see the largest possible artboard size that Illustrator permits. Going to the other extreme, you can expand a square inch to a respectable 6-1/3 square feet by choosing 6400 percent.

Status Bar

The status bar just to the right of the size bar lists all kinds of moderately useful information about the program. Click the status bar to display a pop-up menu of status bar options, you can have the status bar list the active tool, the date and time, the amount of RAM going unused inside Illustrator, the number of available undos and redos or the type of color profile assigned to the document.

Understanding Tools

The toolbox, like any other palette, is entirely independent of all other desktop elements, so if you reduce the size of a drawing window the toolbox remains unchanged, with 24 tools visible and easily accessible. The toolbox serves and is positioned in front of any and all open illustrations. You can move the toolbox by dragging its tittle bar and hide it by choosing the Windows>>Hide Tools command.

To redisplay the toolbox, choose Window >> Show Tools. You can hide the toolbox and all other palettes by pressing the Tab key. Press Tab again to bring all the palettes back. To get rid of all palettes except the toolbox, press Shift+Tab (that is, hold the Shift key and then tap the tab key).

As with other graphics and publishing programs, you select a tool in Illustrator by clicking on its icon in the toolbox. Illustrator highlights the active tool so it stands out prominently. The toolbox contains 24 tool slots. In addition to the default tools occupying these slots, Illustrators offers 36 alternate tools that are initially hidden.

For example, Illustrator hides the polygon, star and spiral tools under the ellipse tool slot. To use one of these hidden tools, you have to click the and hold the ellipse icon to display a pop-up menu of alternates. Select the desired tool as you would a command – that is, by highlighting the tool and releasing the mouse button. Slots that offer alternate tools have tiny right-facing arrowheads in their lower right corners.

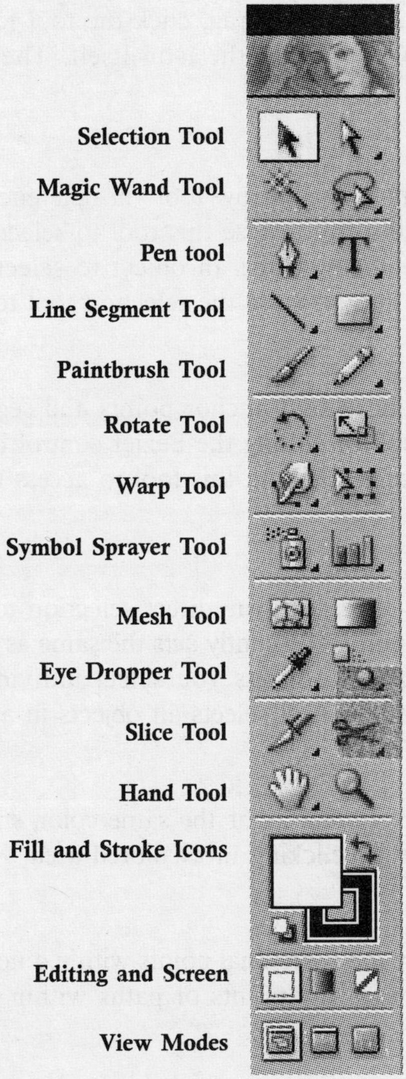

Tear off

Slots have an added benefit of letting you tear off the tools so they appear in their own little row. Just drag your cursor over to the tearoff icon (indicated by the small arrowhead) at the end of the slot. Release the mouse. That slot appears in its own little toolbar. You can then position the slot anywhere on your window. You can even have multiple slots for the same tools.

Illustrator 10 adds two lasso tools. If you've ever spent too much time selecting and deselecting elements to get exactly the items you want, you're going to love these lassos. The lasso tool (black arrowhead) selects complete objects, similarly to the regular selection tool directly above it. The direct selection lasso (white arrow head) selects points and parts of grouped objects like the direction selection tool above it.

The following paragraphs explain how to use each of Illustrator's 53 tools in the illustration window. For example, if an item instructs you to drag, click the tool icon to select it and then drag inside the drawing area; don't drag on the icon itself. These are intended as introductory descriptions only.

Selection Tool

The selection tool – which is usually called the "arrow tool" in deference to its appearance – is active when you first start illustrator. Use this tool to select object that you've created so you can manipulate them. Click an object to select the entire object. Drag an object to move it. You can also use the selection tool to select text blocks.

Direct Selection Tool

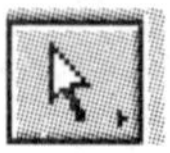

Click with this hollow arrow to select individual anchor points and segments in a line or shape. This is also the perfect tool for editing the Bezier control handles that govern the curvature of segments. Alt-click while in this tool to access the group selection tool.

Group selection

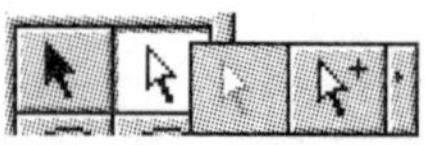

Click with this tool or just Option/Alt-click with the direct selection tool to select whole objects at a time. Though it frequently acts the same as the standard arrow tool, the group selection tool lets you select individual objects inside groups, whereas the arrow tool selects all objects in a group.

Magic Wand Tool

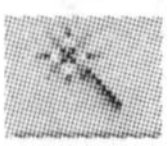

The magic wand tool lets you select objects of the same color, stroke weight, stroke color, opacity, or blending mode by clicking in a colored area.

Direct Select Lasso Tool

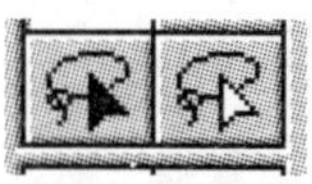

Drag with this tool to select the individual points within a non-rectangular area. When you release the mouse, any points or paths within the lasso area will be selected.

Pen Tool

This is Illustrator's most powerful drawing tool. Use the pen tool to draw a line as a series of individual points. Click to add the corners to a line, drag to add arcs. You can also Option/Alt-drag on an arc to change it to a cusp. Illustrator automatically connects your points with straight or curved segments. Option/alt-click while in this tool to access the convert direction tool.

Add point

Click a segment with the add point tool to insert a new point into a line. Option/Art-click to access the delete anchor point tool.

Delete point

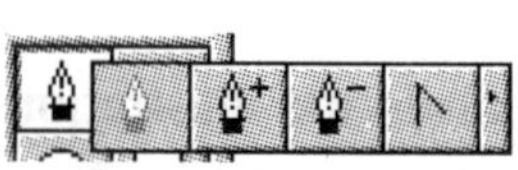

Click a point with this tool to remove the point while leaving the line intact. That's why we'd rather call this the remove point tool –

"deleting" a point would create a hole. Option/Alt-click to access the add anchor point tool.

Convert point

Use this tool to change a corner in a line to an arc or vice versa. Click an arc to make it a corner, drag on a corner to make it an arc.

Type Tool

Click with this tool and then enter text from the keyboard to create a line of type in the standard left-to-right format. To create a text block with type that automatically wraps from one line downs to the next, drag with the type tool and then start from one line downs to the next, drag with the type tool and then start banging away at the keyboard. You can also use this tool or one of the other five type tools to highlight characters in a text block – allowing you to edit or format them. Shift-click while in this tool to access the vertical type tool.

Area type

Click a line or shape to create text that wrap inside an irregular boundary. Option/Art-click to access the path type tool. Shift-click to access the vertical area type tool.

Path type

Click a line or shape to create text that follow the contours to the object, better known as text on a curve. Option/Alt-click to access the area type tool. Shift-click to access the vertical path type tool.

Vertical type

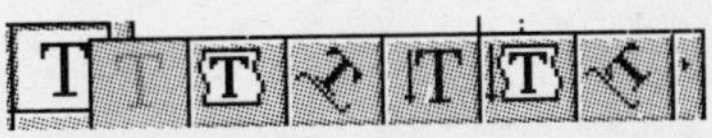

Very similar to the type tool, this tool arranges text vertically, the way Japanese script appears. Click with this tool and then enter text from the keyboard to create an ascending column of type. To create a text block with type that automatically wraps from one column to the next (from right to left), drag with the vertical type tool and then start them magic fingers fluttering. Option/Alt-click to access the vertical path type tool. Shift-click to access the type tool.

Vertical area type

Click a line or shape to create text that fills an irregular boundary column. Option/Alt-click to access the vertical path type tool. Shift-click to access the area type tool.

Vertical path type

Click a line or shape to create text that follows the contours of the object. As you probably guessed, one letter will stack upon the next to form a column that follows the curve. Option/alt-click to access the vertical area type tool. Shift-click to access the path type tool.

Line Segment Tool

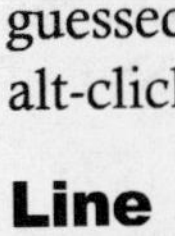

Use the line and arc segment tools to quickly and easily create individual lines and arcs by dragging. The Line and Arc Segment dialog boxes display the values of the last segment created.

Arc Tool

The Arc tool allows you to create an arc.

Spiral Tool

The spiral tool creates a spiral-shaped object of a given radius and number of winds; that is, the number of turns that the spiral completes from start to finish.

Rectangular Grid Tool

Use the grid tools to quickly draw rectangular or polar grids. Specify the grid size and the number of dividers, and then drag to create the grid anywhere on the artboard. The rectangular grid tool creates rectangular grids of a specified size with a specified number of dividers.

Polar Grid Tool

Use the grid tools to quickly draw rectangular or polar grids. Specify the grid size and the number of dividers, and then drag to create the grid anywhere on the artboard. The polar grid tool creates concentric circles of a specified size and a specified number of dividers.

Rectangle Tool

This tool works just like the ellipse tool, except that it makes rectangles and squares. Shift-drag to draw a square or Alt-drag to create a rectangle from center outward.

Rounded rectangle

If you want your rectangles to have rounded corners, use this tool. To adjust the roundness of the corners of future shapes, click with the tool in the drawing area. Shift-drag to draw a rounded square. As you may have guessed, you can Option/Alt-drag to create a rounded rectangle from the center outward.

Ellipse Tool

Drag with this tool, previously called the oval tool to draw an ellipse. You can also Shift-drag to draw a circle or Alt-drag to draw an ellipse from the center outward. Click with the tool to enter numerical dimensions for your ellipse.

Polygon

When you drag with this too, you draw a regular polygon, like a triangle or pentagon. Click with the tool to change the number of sides.

Star

Drag with this tool to draw a star with symmetrical points. Option-drag to constrain the star so opposite arms are perfectly aligned, as for a five-pointed American star or a Star of David. Click with the tool to change the number of points.

Flare

The flare tool creates flare objects with a bright center, a halo, and rays and rings. Use this tool to create an effect similar to a lens flare in a photograph.

Paintbrush Tool

This tool creates an open path that is automatically styled with one of the calligraphy, artistic,

scatter or pattern brushes. Double-click the icon to set the sensitivity of the paintbrush. Like the pencil tool, the paintbrush can also be used to modify a previously drawn brushstroke.

Pencil Tool

Formally known as the freehand tool, the pencil tool makes a freeform line when you drag

with it, much as if you were drawing with a pencil. If you are not satisfied with the final result, simply drag over the part of your path you wish to correct and the offending snippet toes the line.

Smooth

Use the smooth tool to reposition points and reshape paths quickly. After you drag with this tool, Illustrator will add or remove points (or even more points) in an attempt to streamline the path and smooth it out.

Erase

With the erase tool, you drag over a segment of an entire path to remove it. This allows you to open closed paths and delete unnecessary paths easily.

Rotate Tool

This tool lets you rotate selected objects. Click with the tool to determine the center of

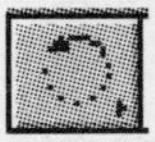

the rotation and then drag to rotate the objects around this center. Or just drag right off the bat to position the center of the rotation smack dab in the center of the selected objects. You can also Alt-click with the tool or double click the rotate tool icon in the toolbox to specify a rotation numerically.

Reflect

Reflecting an object flips the object across an invisible axis that you specify. Copy while reflecting to create a mirror image of an object.

Twist

The Twist command and the twist tool rotate a selection more sharply in the center than at the edges.

Scale Tool

This tool and the two other transformation tools, reflect and shear, work just like the rotate tool. The only difference is that the scale tool enlarges and reduces selected objects.

Shear

Drag with the oddly named shear tool to slant or skew selected objects. The effects of Shift-dragging are generally easier to predict; when the Shift key is down, the shear tool slants objects horizontally or vertically.

Reshape

Click and drag with this tool on an open path to deform the path in a freeform manner. The result of the deformation is entirely dependent on which points of the object were selected.

WarpTool

Stretches objects as if they were made of clay. When you drag or pull portions of an object using this tool, the pulled areas attenuate.

The twirl tool

Creates swirling distortions of an object.

The pucker tool

Deflates an object by moving control points toward the cursor.

The bloat tool

Inflates an object by moving control points away from the cursor.

The scallop tool

Adds random, smooth, arc-shaped details to the outline of an object.

The crystallize tool

Adds random spike, arc-shaped details to the outline of an object.

The wrinkle tool

Adds random arc and spike-shaped details to the outline of an object.

Free Transform Tool

The free transform tool allows you to scale, rotate, reflect and shear as well as properly

four-point distort selected paths, all right on screen. A lame version of this tool that uses a dialog box is found under Filter >> Distort >> Free Distort. A live version of the Free Distort filter is found under Effect >> Distortion and Transform >> Free Distort. This allows you to transform an object without permanently changing its shape.

Symbol Spray Tool

Use the symbol sprayer tool to create a set of symbol instances or add more instances to an existing set.

Symbol Shifter tool

The symbol shifter tool moves symbol instances around. It can also change the relative paint order of symbol instances in a set.

Symbol Scruncher tool

The symbol scruncher tool pulls symbol instances together or apart. Use this tool to shape the density distribution of a symbol set

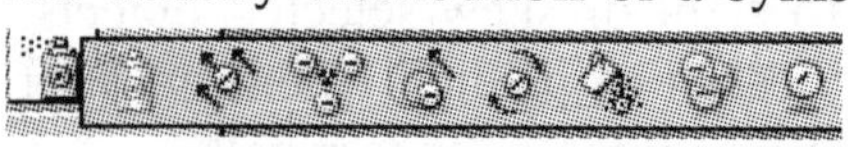

Symbol Sizer tool

Use the symbol sizer tool to increase or decrease the size of symbol instances in an existing symbol set

Symbol Spinning tool

Use the symbol spinner tool to orient the symbol instances in a set. Symbol instances located near the cursor orient in the direction you move the cursor. As you drag the mouse, an arrow appears above the cursor to show the current orientation of symbol instances

Symbol Stainer tool

Use the symbol stainer tool to colorize symbol instances. Colorizing a symbol instance changes the hue toward the tint color, while preserving the original luminosity.

Symbol Styler tool

The symbol styler tool applies the selected style to the symbol instance

Symbol Screener tool

Use the symbol screener tool to increase or decrease the transparency of the symbol instances in a set.

Column Graph Tool

Drag with this tool to specify the rectangular boundaries of a standard column graph. Shift-dragging constraints the boundary to a square and Option/Alt-dragging forms rectangular boundaries from the center out. Illustrator then presents you with a spreadsheet in which you can enter your data. Double-click the graph tool icon in the toolbox to specify the options for the graphs you want to create.

Stacked column

This tool and the seven other graph tools that follow work just like the column graph tool, except that dragging with this tool specifies the boundaries of a stacked column graph.

Bar

Drag with this tool to specify the boundaries of a stacked horizontal bar graph in which each entity appears farther to the right.

Line

Drag with this tool to specify the boundaries of a line graph – you know, your basic dot-to-dot with a few labels to make it look official.

Area

Drag with this tool to specify the boundaries of an area graph. It's the color-within-the-lines evolution of the line graph.

Scatter

Drag with this tool to specify the boundaries of a pie graph. Enough said.

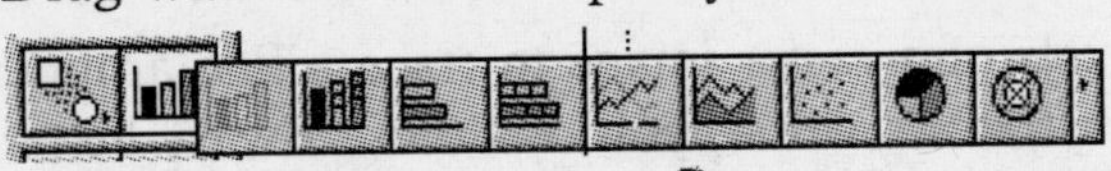

Radar

Drag with this tool to specify the boundaries of a radar graph. This is the ideal graph for confusing anyone attending your presentation.

Mesh Tool

The mesh tool, the Create Mesh command, and the Expand command can all be used to transform an object into a mesh object. A mesh object is a single, multicolored object on which colors can flow in different directions, and transition smoothly from one point to another. By creating a fine mesh on an object and manipulating the color characteristics at each point in the mesh, you can precisely manipulate the coloring of the mesh object. You can also apply color to four mesh points at the same time by clicking the patch between them, to create broad color changes on part of the object.

Gradient Tool

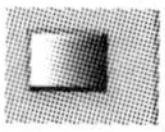

Drag inside a selected object that's filled with a gradation to change the angle of the gradations, as well as the location of the first and last colors. Shift-drag to constrain your drag to 45-degree increments.

Eyedropper Tool

Click or drag across text to copy the text attributes. These attributes can then be applied to other text using the paint bucket. Click an object to copy its fill and stroke attributes to the toolbox. You can also double-click an object to copy the colors from that object to all selected objects. Set the eyedropper options by double-clicking the icon in the toolbox.

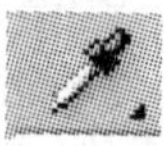

Paint bucket

Click or drag across text to apply the attributes copied by the eyedropper. Click an object with the paint bucket tool to apply the fill and stroke from the toolbox to the object. Set the paint bucket options by double-clicking the icon in the toolbox.

Measure

Drag with this tool to measure the distance between tow points. Alternatively, you can click in one spot and then click in another. Illustrator displays the measurements in the Info palette.

Blend Tool

The blend tool allows you to create custom gradations. After selecting two or more objects with one of the arrow tools, use the blend tool to click a point in one object, then click a point in the others. Illustrator creates a collection of intermediate shapes between the two objects and fills these with intermediate colors. Blends can also be created using the blend command.

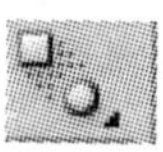

Autotrace

Click or drag within 6 screen pixels of a raster image to trace a line around the image. This tool is easily Illustrator's worst; you're almost always better off tracing images with the pen or pencil.

Slice Tool

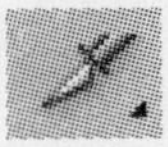

This tool allows you to divide your drawing into slices.

Scissors Tool

Click a line to cut it into two. Illustrator inserts two points at the spot where you click, one for each line.

Knife

Drag with the knife tool to slice shapes into new shapes, just as if you had dragged through them with a real knife. The knife tool is a little too sharp though; it cuts though any objects in its path, whether they're selected or not.

Hand Tool

Drag with the hand tool to scroll the drawing inside the illustration window. It is much more convenient than the scroll bars. You can also double-click the hand tool icon in the toolbox to fit the entire artboard into the illustration window.

Page

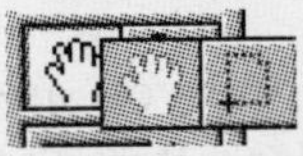

Drag with the page tool to move the imageable area within the artboard. Unless the artboard is larger than the printed page size, you don't have to worry about this tool. Double-click the icon in the toolbox to automatically reposition the imageable area to the lower left corner of the artboard.

Zoom Tool

Click with this tool to magnify the size of the illustration. This doesn't affect the printed size of the drawing, just how it looks on screen. Alt-click to zoom out. You can also draw with the tool to surround the exact portion of the illustration you want to magnify. Double-click the zoom tool icon to view your drawing at the very same size it will print.

Working in Illustrator

Now that you know what Illustrator has, let us start working with it. Well, as you would do with any other software, create a New document or file, as you may say.

For this just press, Ctrl-N or click at New from the File menu.

When you choose File>>New you are given the New Document dialog box, as shown next. Fortunately the decisions you make here can be changed easily later on. You can however, press Ctrl+Alt+N to bypass the New Document dialog box and use the settings from the previous document. This new document dialog box has the following options.

Name: This one is easy; what name would you like the document to have? Because the default – "Untitled" followed by a number – is a rather bland name for a document, you should think of something snappy.

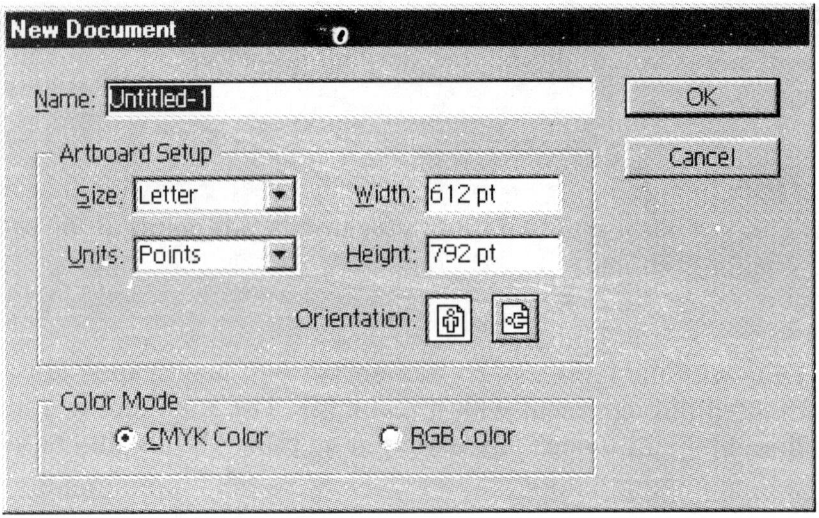

Artboard Size: Sometimes you may care about the size of the artboard; sometimes you may not. It depends on what kind of document you want to create. If you're creating a drawing, logo or other graphic that you intend to place into a layout program such as InDesign or QuarkXPress, then you aren't interested in how the big the artboard is in Illustrator. When you import an Illustrator drawing into page layout programs, all empty portions of the artboard are cropped away, leaving just the graphic itself. Therefore, the size of the graphic is all that matters.

But issues such as page size, orientation and placement are important any time you are going to print directly from Illustrator or make a PDF file. These issues can also affect the size of Web graphics. For instance, if your page size is huge, you could end up with huge Web graphics as well.

Color Mode: There are only two options, so you've got a fifty-fifty chance of being right. First, you need to decide whether Illustrator will limit your colors to either CMYK colors, which are usually used for print jobs or RGB colors, which are used for Web graphics. So if your job is going to be separated by a commercial printing process, you should choose CMYK. If it's going to the Web, choose RGB. Unlike what happens in Photoshop, in Illustrator choosing RGB doesn't make your file and smaller. There are no extra channels in Illustrator that make a CMYK file bigger than an RGB one.

Once you've made your selections in the New Document dialog box, click OK and your document window appears. Now you're ready to hunker down and to work.

On the other hand if you want to be very precise about the width and height of the page, then go to Document Setup from the File menu and change the options in the dialog box, as shown next.

Various options of the dialog box are:

Size: This pop-up menu lets you choose from a bunch of predefined artboard sizes.

Units: Select an option from this pop-up menu to change the measurement system for the current drawing only.

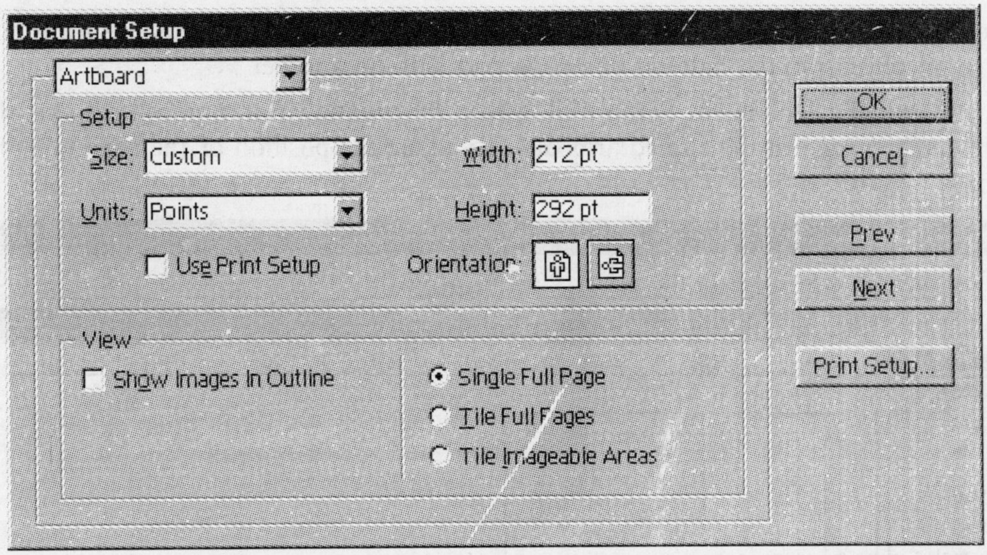

Use Page Setup: If you want to match the artboard to the printed page size, select this check box.

Width and Height: If you don't want to use one of the predefined settings, specify the width and height of the artboard by entering values into these options boxes. It doesn't matter which value you enter first and which second – by default, the smallest value is treated as the width and the largest as the height. To change this, you have to select a different Orientation icon.

Orientation: Here you specify whether your artboard is taller than it is wide or vice versa. Be sure to select an option. Regardless of how you enter values in the Dimensions option boxes, Illustrator conforms to the selected orientation.

Show Images in Outline: When this preference setting is turned off, a placed image does not display properly in the outline mode. Instead, it appears as a rectangle, bisected by two diagonal lines. When the check box is selected, Illustrator shows a monochrome version of the image in the artwork mode. Placed imaged of all varieties always show up in the preview mode and of course they always print – regardless of the Show Images in Outline check box.

Single Full Page: The three radio buttons next to the Show Images in Outlines check box determines how Illustrator prints oversized artboard. Single full page is the default setting. It instructs Illustrator to display just one set of dotted lines and print just one page, regardless of the size of the artboard. Some artists like to use this option with a slightly oversized artboard so they can adjust the way the illustration fits on the page using the page tool.

Tile Full Pages: Select this option to display as many whole pages as will fit in the drawing area. No partial pages are allowed. This is the option to select when creating a multipage document such as a newsletter. Illustrator numbers the page boundaries inside the artboard so you know the order in which the pages will print.

Tile Imageable Areas: By selecting the Tile Imageable Areas radio button, you tell Illustrator to chop up the artboard into as many imageable areas as will fit, thus ensuring no gap between an object printed half on one page and half on another.

Once you exit the Document Setup dialog box, by pressing Enter, you'll see the altered page boundaries against the altered artboard. To adjust the position of the page boundaries, read on.

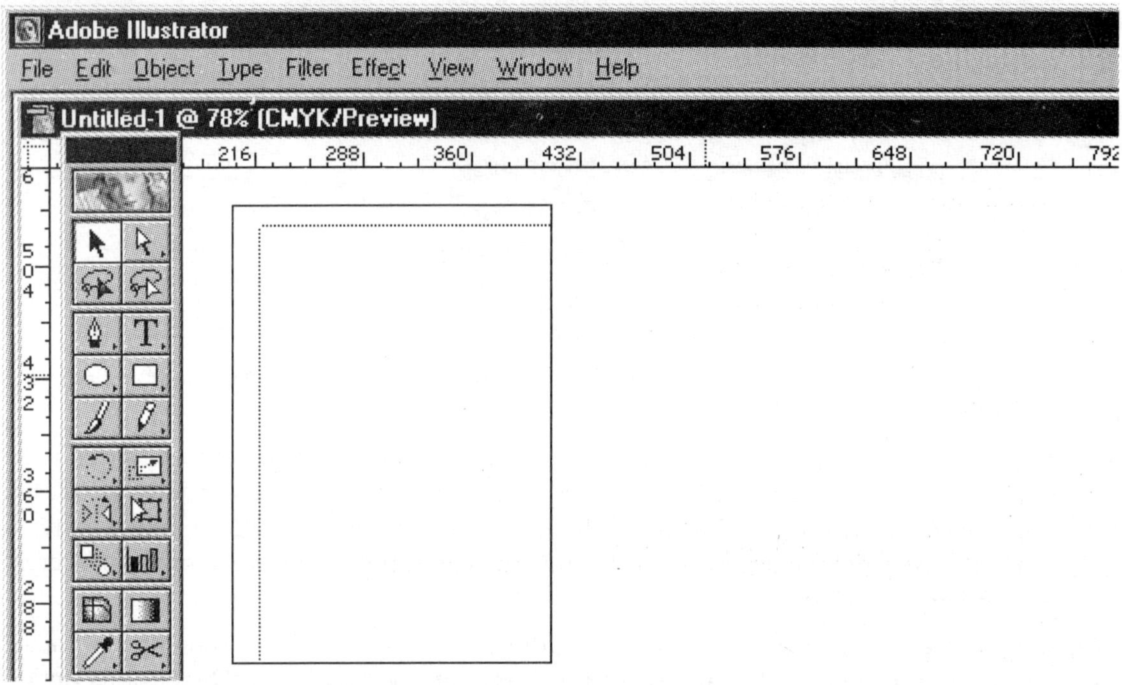

Positioning the Pages on the Artboard

You can't move the artboard. The artboard is always positioned smack dab in the center of the pasteboard. However, you can move the page boundaries with respect to the artboard using the page tool. The page tool is the first alternate tool in the hand tool slot. Select this tool and then click or drag inside the artboard to set the location of the lower left corner of the imageable area of a printed page. To automatically lineup the page boundaries with the lower left corner of the artboard, double-click the page tool in the toolbox.

Opening an Existing File

Illustrator lets you have multiple illustration windows open at a time. You can open an illustration saved to disk by choosing File>>Open or pressing Ctrl+O (the letter O), all without closing any open windows.

You can open four kinds of files in Illustrator.

- Drawings previously created in Illustrator.
- Drawing created in FreeHand or some other drawing program and saved in either the Illustrator file format or the format native to the other drawing program.
- Documents created in InDesign, QuarkXPress or FreeHand and exported in EPS format or documents converted to the PDF format.

- ❑ Images saved as TIFF, JPEG or some other compatible format.

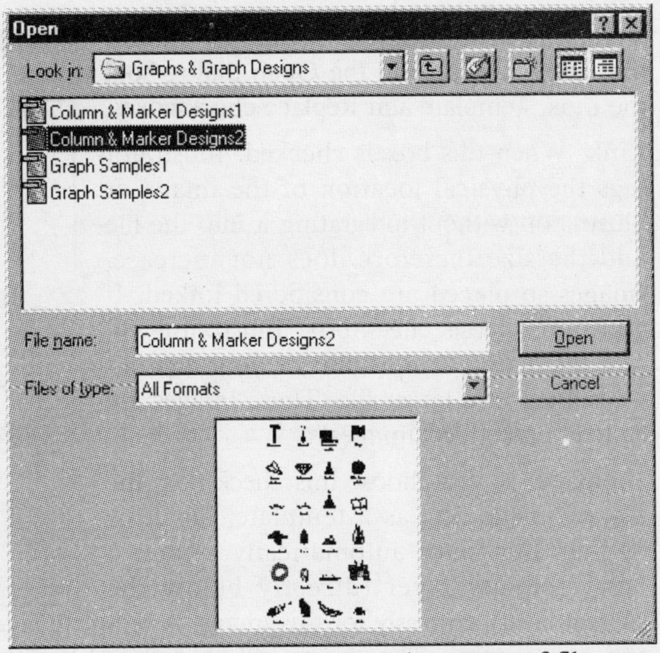

The Open dialog box includes a thumbnail preview of the selected illustration or image. The beauty of the preview is that you don't have to open the graphic in order to remember what it looks like. Click the Show Preview button to open the preview area in the dialog box. Illustrator can also display the PICT previews included with some EPS files. If you turn the option off, the preview disappears and Open dialog box collapses to save screen space.

Showing Files

The Open dialog box also has a pop-up menu where you an choose what types of files you want to see. The choices are:

All Readable Files: This lets you see all files that Illustrator knows it can open. This option is the default and helps you focus on the files you want to work with.

All Files: Choose this option to see all files in the current folder, whether Illustrator can open them or not. Every once in a while you may be lucky and you can force Illustrator to open a graphic that it doesn't think it can open.

File Types: You an also choose to display only a specific type of file that Illustrator knows it can open. For instance, you may only want to open CorelDraw files. You can choose that file type and only open those files. This list also helps you understand which the file types Illustrator does recognize.

Placing an Image

If you want to add an illustration or an image to the illustration you're working on, choose File>>Place. Rather than creating a separate illustration window, selected so you can begin working on it immediately. You can move or transform Illustrator. You can also apply Photoshop filters to placed images. When you choose File>>Place, Illustrator displays the Place dialog box, as shown below. These boxes are identical in form and function except for their names of course and the Place dialog box contains an additional option box, discussed below.

Both Open and Place request that you locate and select the drawing that you want to work with. The dialog box lets you search through the folders on all available hard drives, CD-ROMs and floppy disks. Sometimes you can even preview what the file looks like before you open or place it.

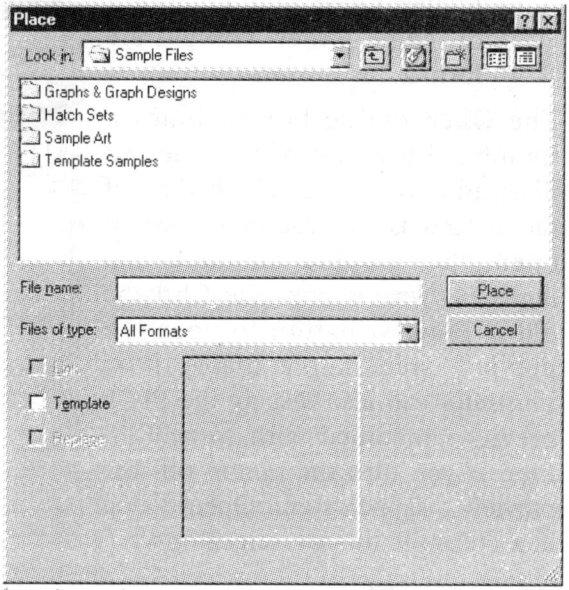

The Place dialog box has additional options that aren't available in the Open dialog box: the Link, Template and Replace check boxes.

Link: When this box is checked, Illustrator tags the physical location of the image or illustration without integrating it into the file and the size therefore does not increase. Images so placed are considered linked. If you turn off this check box, Illustrator will save the placed item as part of your artwork – resulting in a larger file. These images are called "embedded images".

Template: If you choose this check box, the placed image acts as a template, ideal for tracing. Illustrator automatically creates a new template layer (directly below the current layer) expressly for this image. A template layer is automatically set as visible, locked and non-printing. The image will be dimmed by 50 percent.

Replace: Instead of simply placing an image, you can replace a previously placed image with a new one. First select the image that you want to replace in your artwork. Then choose File>> Place, select the new image from the scrolling field, check the Replace check box and press the Return/Enter key.

The Links Palette

Illustrator offers a palette devoted to the organization and keeping of all your placed images, linked and embedded. For each image you place in a document, Illustrator creates a link in the Links palette – this term is used for both linked and embedded images. The link may also include one of three small informational icons.

Embedded icon: This means all the information about the image is incorporated in the Illustrator file. You can create an embedded image by deselecting the Link check box when you place the file, choosing Embed Image from the Links palette menu or by applying any of the commands that rasterizes an image within the file.

Modified icon: If you change a linked image outside of Illustrator. Illustrator displays the modified icon. This is a gentle reminder that you need to update the linked image.

Missing icon: This icon never shows up when you first place an image. It appears when you open a file that contains a linked image that Illustrator can no longer locate. Perhaps you've moved the file to a new location or you've thrown the file away. Whatever the case, this icon alerts you that the original is no longer available. You can either relink the image or replace it with another image.

No icon whatsoever: This lack of an icon tells you that you have a linked image in proper working order.

The Link Palette's pop-up menu contains options that you view and modify the images associated with the different links. The first six options require that either an image is selected in your document or that a link is selected in the Link palette. These options are:

Go to Link: With a link selected, choose this option (or click the second icon from the left along the bottom of the palette) and Illustrator will select the image associated with the link and center it in the document window.

Update Link: If you've modified the original file of a linked image currently open in Illustrator, this command lets you update the image. Select the image's link and choose this option (or click the second icon from the right along the bottom of the palette).

Edit Original: Choose this option to open the original image in the application in which it was created. If the original image wasn't created on your computer, the image will open in the most appropriate application (as dictated by your operating system and the image's format). This option affects only linked images because embedded images, as integrated parts of your document, no longer have originals.

Replace: If you decide that an image is wrong for your document, select its link from the Link palette and choose this option. This standard Place dialog box will display. Select the image that you'd prefer in the place of the original. As was the case when you placed the original image, you'll have the option of linking or embedding the new image via the Link check box.

Embed Image: Choose this option to encode a inked image's information into your document. This embeds the image, just as though you had deactivated the Place dialog box's Link check box when first placing the image.

Information: With a link selected, choose this option (or double-click the link) to display the Link Information dialog box. Here you'll find information about the image including its name, location on disk, size in bytes, kind (that is, its file format), creation and modification dates and any changes you that made to its scaling or angular orientation.

Show: You can opt to show all links in the Links palette or just those in which you are interested.

Sort: Choose the appropriate option to sort the links by name, kind or status. Sorting links by status groups the links into those that are missing, modified or up-to-date.

Accepted File Formats

File formats are different ways to save or export a file to disk. Just as Betamax and VHS are different videotape formats, TIFF and PCX are different image formats. By supporting a wider variety of formats, Illustrator can accept graphics from all kinds of Macintosh and Windows applications. Now I define here the various formats supported by Illustrator 10, starting with the various Illustrator format and continuing through the others in alphabetical order.

Now we come to various formats.

Acrobat PDF: In reality, a native Illustrator 10 file is actually an Acrobat 1.4 file hiding under an Illustrator icon. This means that Illustrator files are already in the Acrobat PDF (Portable Document Format) and can be made part of a PDF pre-press workflow. You can trade PDF files with other Windows users and regardless of which program you used to create the original file or which fonts you used to format the text, all anyone needs to view the file is the Acrobat reader. Illustrator goes one better, letting you edit and graphic objects within the Acrobat document itself.

Amiga IFF: The Amiga was an experiment in desktop computers pioneered by Commodore in the 80s. Adobe recognizes that there still may be many files originally saved in this format. To this end, Illustrator lets you open and save IFF (Interchange File Format) files. IFF is the Amiga's all-around graphic format.

AutoCAD Drawing (DWG) and AutoCAD Interchange (DXF): AutoCAD is program used by engineers and architects. DWG is the standard file format created by AutoCAD.DXF is the tagged data format of those files.

BMP (BMP): BMP is the native format for the cheesy little Paint utility that ships with Windows. BMP is the equal of PCX, supporting 16 million colors and high resolutions. If there is any way that you can avoid working with BMP files, do so. However, if you get a BMP image, rest assured that you can place it into your illustration.

Computer Graphics Metafile (CGM): CGM is a vector-based file format that is used by a wide variety of programs. Think of CGM as the common language between different vector programs.

CorelDRAW 5, 6, 7, 8 (CDR): Although it can't export in the CorelDRAW format. Illustrator does let you open files created in CorelDRAW versions 5, 6, 7 and 8. Of course, not all effects and attributes will translate correctly when opened in Illustrator.

Encapsulated PostScript (EPS): The EPS format combines a pure PostScript description of an illustration with a preview so you can see what the image looks like on screen. Years ago EPS files were the only way to get Illustrator artwork into page layout programs. However, programs such as InDesign and PageMaker can now import native Illustrator files. If you are working with those programs, you should consider using the native Illustrator format. For other layout programs, such as QuarkXPress, use EPS files.

FilmStrip (FLM): FilmStrip is the format used by Adobe Premiere and Adobe Photoshop FilmStrip organizes frames into a long vertical strip. A gray bar separates each frame. Though Photoshop is a far more useful program for editing FilmStrip file you can open and add to these files in Illustrator.

FreeHand 4, 5, 6, 7 (FH4, FH5, FH6, FH7, FH8): Yes it is possible to open FreeHand files in Illustrator.

Graphics Interchange Format (GIF89a): Originally designed for transferring compressed graphics with a modem, GIF is the most extensively used graphics format on the Web. It supports upto 256 colors and LZW compression, as does TIFF (mentioned later).

JPEG: It is very widely used Web graphics format and is best used for compressing photographs and other continuous-tone images, in which the distinction between immediately neighboring pixels is slight. Any image that include gradual color transition qualifies for JPEG compression. JPEG is not well suited to screen shots, line drawings and other high-contrast images.

Kodak Photo CD: Photo CD is the affordable photographic scanning technology that leaves some flatbed scanners behind. You can take a roll of undeveloped film, color negatives or slides in to your local Photo CD dealer and have the photos scanned onto a CD-ROM. Each CD holds 100 images, allowing you to acquire a library of images without taking up a lot of room in your home or office.

Metafiles (WMF, EMF): These files are actually the broad description of any files that contain commands that are used to draw graphics. Strictly speaking, Illustrator files are a type of metafile. WMF stands for Windows Metafile, the 16-bit files used by the Windows operating system to display pictures. EMF stands for Enhanced Metafile, a more advanced from the Windows metafile, which contains 32-bit information.

PC Paintbrush (PCX): PCX doesn't stand for anything. Rather, it's the extension that PC Paintbrush assigns to images saved in its native file format. PCX is one of the most popular image for formats in use today, largely because PC Paintbrush is the oldest painting program for DOS. PCX images can include up to 16 million colors.

Photoshop 5 (PSD): Illustrator can open and place images stored in Photoshop's native format. This means you do not have to save a copy of a Photocopy file as a TIFF or EPS in order to add it to Illustrator documents. Even better, you can open Photoshop files and any Photoshop layers can be converted into distinct images in Illustrator – complete with transparency and with masks applied.

PICT (PIC, PCT): The PICT (Macintosh Picture) format is a graphics exchange format Apple designed more than ten years ago and has updated irregularly over time. You can save both object-oriented illustrations and photographic images in the PICT format, but the format isn't ideally suited to either. Frankly, TIFF is better for images and EPS is better for illustrations.

Pixar (PXR): Pixar created a few 3-D graphics applications for the Mac, including MacRenderMan, ShowPlace and Typestry. The company working own 3-D magic using mondo-expensive Pixar workstations. Illustrator can open a still image created on a Pixar machine.

Portable Network Graphics (PNG): Designed to outperform and eventually replace GIF, PNG compression doesn't sacrifice quality supports both 24-bit and 48-bit images. Thus, PNG files are larger than GIF, JPEG or TIFF files (unless you are exporting a grayscale image and are generally best suited for smaller images).

Scalable Vector Graphics (SVG) and Scalable Vector Graphics Compressed (SVGZ): Welcome to the world of the future. Scalable Vector Graphics is a vector file to mat that can be coded directly into XML documents. SVG files offer many benefits over other formats: They are smaller than GIF or JPEG files, can be scaled up or down, can be made part of searches and can handle animation.

Shockwave Flash (SWF): Until very recently it was hard to get anyone from Adobe to even use the term SWF – Macromedia's proprietary format for Web animations. Now there are two Adobe products – Illustrator and LiveMotion that create SWF animations. Adobe animations let you create very intricate animation extremely small file size. So Illustrator lets you export as SWF animations.

Targa: TrueVision's Targa and NuVista vide boards let you overlay computer graphics and animation onto live video. The effect is called chroma keying being typically a key color is set aside to let the live video show through. TrueVision designed the Targa format to support 32-bit images that include so-called alpha channels capable of displaying the live video. Illustrator doesn't know a video from a redeo, but it can place a still Targa image.

Tag Image File Format (TIFF): Developed by Aldus (which is now part of Adobe) to standardize electronic images so you could easily import them into PageMaker, TIFF (Tag Image File Format) is one of the most widely supported formats across Windows platforms. Unlike PICT, it can't handle object-oriented artwork, but it is otherwise unrestricted, supporting 16 million colors and virtually infinite resolutions.

Saving Your Work

Well, we all know the importance of saving the files, specially in country like ours where power cuts are many and uninformed. So you do not know when your system is going to go blank. It is better to save your file at different intervals regularly, specially if you are working on important files. Illustrator gives you 4 different save options.

Save: This is the command that writes the current information about the named file on the disk. If there is no file on the disk, then Illustrator treats the Save command as a Save As.

Save As...: The Save As command is where you can name the file, make decisions about its format and then write the file to disk. You can also use the Save As command to make different versions of your document. When you Save, Save As or Save A Copy, you are creating a file that is in the Illustrator family: either an Illustrator file, an EPS file or a PDF file. All three types of files can be opened and modified by Illustrator; not so with the Save for Web and Export commands. Remember, even if you named the file when you first opened the document, you must perform a Save As command to actually name the file on a disk.

Save a Copy...: When you choose Save A Copy, you send a copy of the newly named file off to sit on the disk. But you're still working on the original file. The best way to think of Save a Copy is to imagine you're about to do something really strange to your document. Before you make that drastic move, use Save A Copy to make a copy of your work at that point. Then you can do whatever you want to the file.

Save for Web...: This command really isn't a save, but is an export. However, unlike the Export command, the Save For Web opens up a large dialog box, as shown on the next page – actually a mini-program inside Illustrator – where you an play around with different Web format sizes and optimization settings for Web files.

Export: The Export command gives you a list of different file format that Illustrator can convert your file into. Most of these convert your elegant line drawings to pixilated facsimiles.

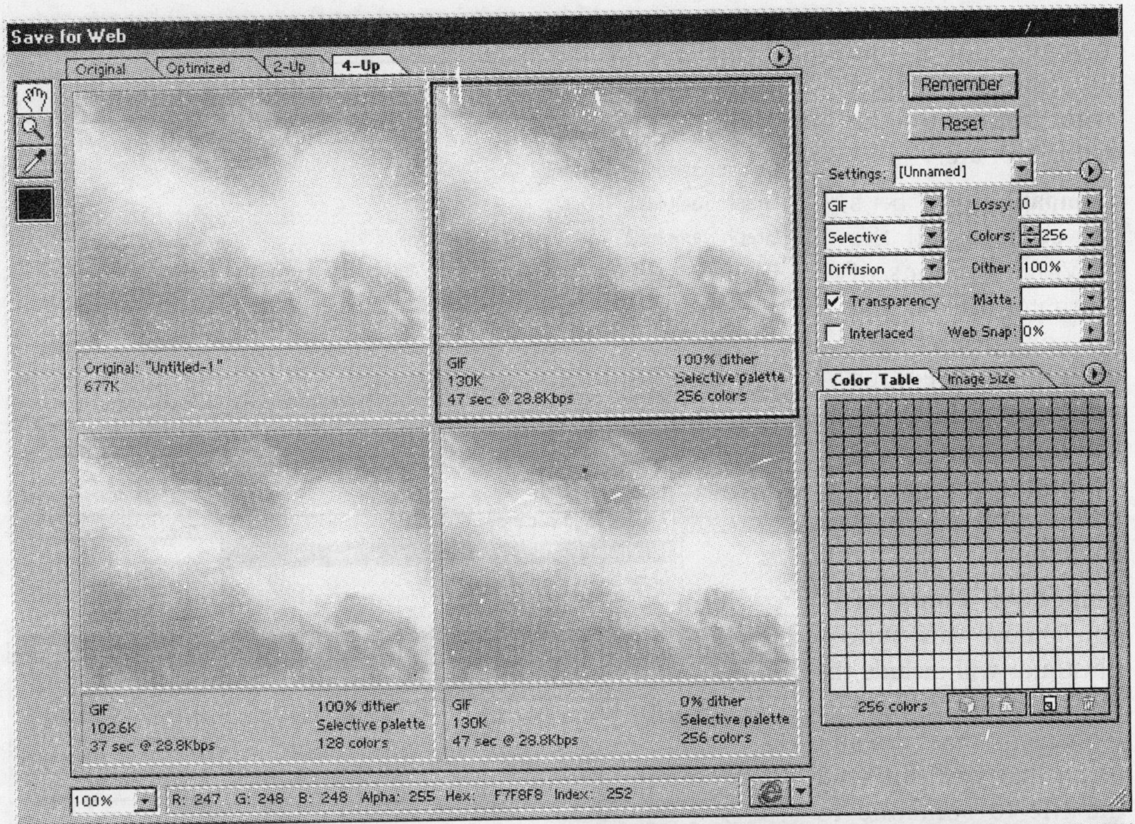

Selecting a File Format

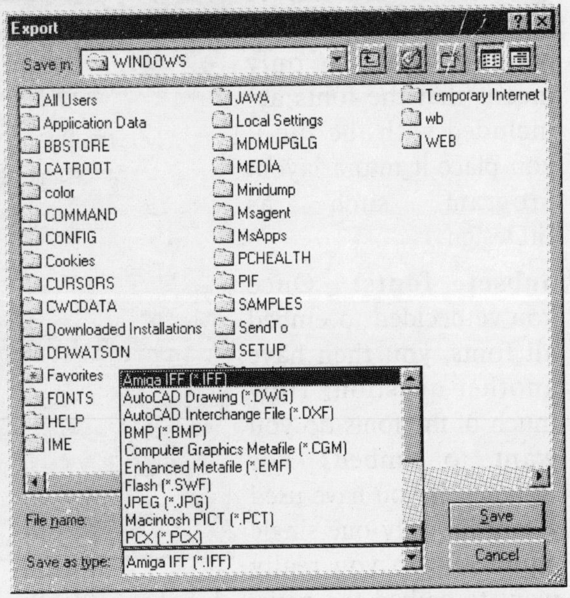

The most complex option in the Save dialog box is the Format menu that lets you specify the file format you want to use to preserve your illustration. Your choices are Illustrator, Illustrator EPS or Acrobat PDF. If you choose Illustrator, you are then faced with another dialog box where you need to set which version of Illustrator you would like to make your file compatible with, as shown below. The only time you need to change the version compatibility is if you need to send your file to somebody who hasn't upgraded to Illustrator 10.

If you save an illustration in any format other than Illustrator 10 or Illustrator 10 EPS, make sure you have created a backup version of the illustration first in the Illustrator 10 format! Otherwise, you are needlessly and deliberately throwing away some amount of your hard work.

When you click at Save with Illustrator as file type, you get another dialog box, as shown

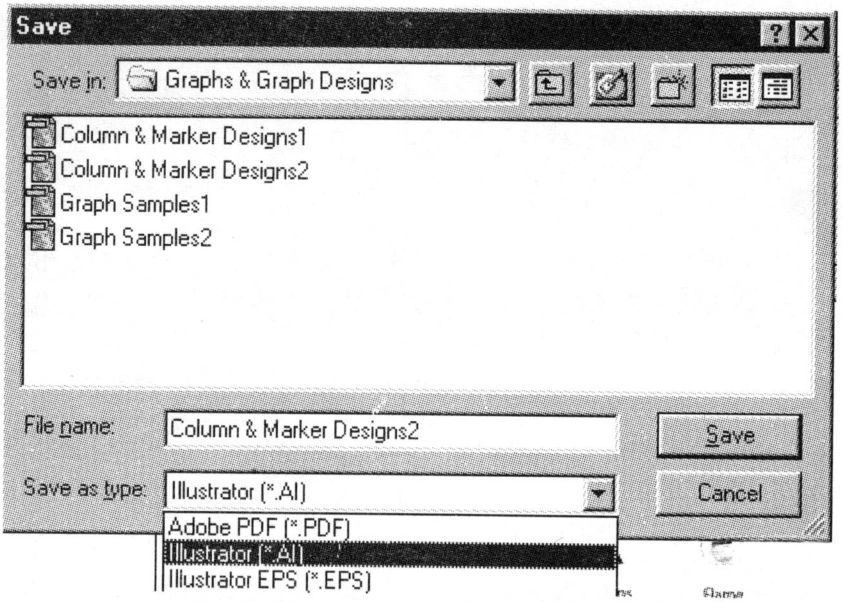

next, to choose the format of the Illustrator. Various other options of the dialog box are:

Compatibility: This list contains all the previous versions of Illustrator back to 3.0. If you don't care about previous versions of Illustrator, leave the most recent version selected so you don't lose anything.

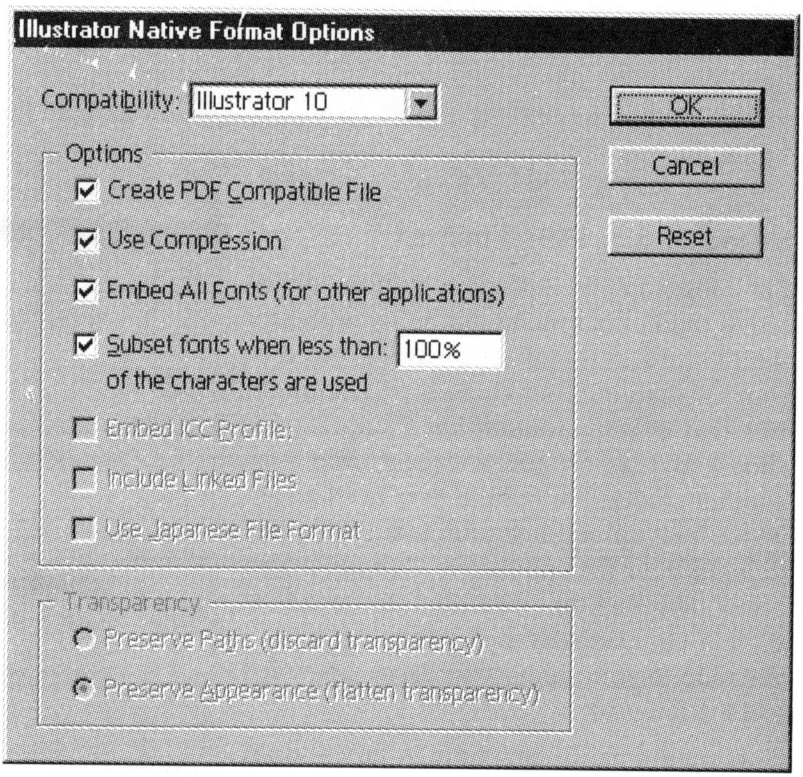

Embed All Fonts: If you choose this option, Illustrator will include the fonts used with the file. However, that doesn't mean that you can send the file to someone to work on it who doesn't own the fonts. It only means that the fonts are included with the file if you place it into a layout program such as InDesign.

Subset fonts: Once you've decided to embed all fonts, you then have another question: How much of the fonts do you want to embed? For instance, if you have used a font for only one single character, do you really want to embed the entire alphabet and other characters in the font? This option lets you choose only those characters used. However, if you want to make sure the entire character set is included, set this to 100 percent.

Include ICC profile: Check this if you want to keep the color management system attached to the file. Deselect this if you would like another application to handle the color management.

Include Linked Files: Like the option to include fonts, this doesn't mean you can throw away the linked file if you are going to work on the file. It means if you place it into a layout program, there's enough information to print the file.

Use Japanese File Format: If you save in a version of Illustrator before version 6, you need to choose this if you want the Japanese file format. This is not the case for present day Illustrator, because now the Illustrator format is universal.

Transparency: This option only shows up if you save in a version prior to Illustrator 10. You need to decide what to do with any objects that have a transparency, drop shadow or other special effect assigned to them. Preserve Paths throws away the effect but keeps the path shapes. Preserve Appearance rasterizes the image.

Saving an EPS Illustration

This is the second option which you can use. To use an illustration in InDesign or QuarkXPress, select Illustrator EPS from the Format pop-up menu. After you click the Save button or press Enter, Illustrator displays the EPS Format dialog box, as shown below. You can probably figure out the majority of these options on your own, but we may as well run through them, if only to eliminate all possible confusion.

Compatibility: This menu is the same as the one for the native Illustrator format.

Preview: These options control the screen preview that Illustrator attaches to an EPS file. If you're sending the file to a Windows machine, choose TIFF (8-bit Color). You can also set the preview to transparency or opaque if you choose the TIFF preview. Remember, the preview doesn't change the actual information in the file. However, some non-PostScript printers do use the information in the preview to print the file.

Include Linked Files: This is the same as the one for the native Illustrator format. Checks this option if you would like to send just one EPs file.

Include Document Thumbnail: Always select this check box. It creates a thumbnail of the illustration so you can preview it form the Open dialog box inside Illustrator, Photoshop and an increasing number of other programs.

Use Japanese File Format: Same story as in the native Illustrator dialog box.

Include Document Fonts: If you use a font in your illustration that you're not sure is as popular with your audience as it is with you check this option. The file will be a bit larger, depending on the size of the font file, but you ensure that your document will appear with the font you intended. Just remember, someone who doesn't own the fonts still won't be able to edit the file.

CMYK PostScript: With this option selected, Illustrator will automatically convert RGB colors to their CMYK equivalents as needed.

PostScript Level: When you send your artwork to a PostScript printer, there are different levels of PostScript that are used to print the file. Level 3 is the most sophisticated and can handle any effect or feature in Illustrator. Level 2 is less complex. Some features, such as the gradient mesh, are converted into raster images if the printer uses level 2. Level 1 is the most primitive. If you know your printer can handle level 3 information, choose it. If not, use level 2. Don't pick level 1 unless you've been specifically told to do so.

Transparency: This is the same as the options in the native Illustrator dialog box.

Illustrator is pretty clever. In most cases you can just press the Return/Enter key quickly get you out of the EPS Format dialog box. The default settings ensure there's no loss of information even if you weren't paying a lick of attention to what you were doing. That's the kind of service any decent program is all too happy perform.

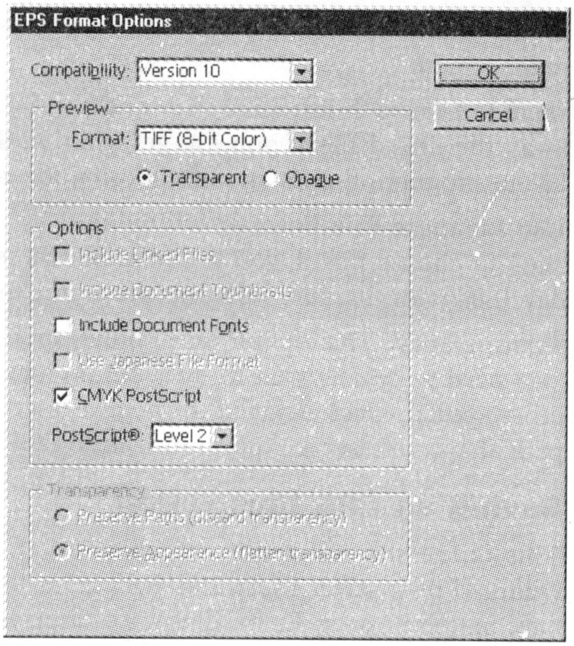

Using Drawing Tools

Now we come to the serious business of using the drawing tools to draw the various items on the screen. In fact, drawing in Illustrator is actually a three-part process. You draw lines and shapes, you manipulate these objects and apply special effects and you stack the objects one in front of another like pieces of paper in a collage.

But before we go any further and start drawing, we must understand few points.

Points and Segments

Points are those which are required to create a line. The bits of line between points are called segments. A segment can be straight, as if it were drawn against the edge of a ruler. A straight segment flows directly from one point to another in any direction. A segment may also curve, like the outline of an ellipse. Curved segments connect two points in an indirect manner, ending inward or outward along the way.

Strokes and Fills

If you draw a line on the paper with 2 different pencils, one with thick lead and another with thin lead, the lines would look different. But, you can achieve the same by using the same pencil too. Although a line drawn with a dull pencil is heavier than a line drawn with a sharpened one, the thickness of any line fluctuates depending on how hard you press the pencil tip to the page.

In Illustrator, the thickness (or weight) of an outline is absolutely consistent throughout the course of a path. In other words, different paths can have different weights, but the weights of each path is constant.

The thickness of an outline is called the stroke. In addition to change weight of the stroke, you can change its color. Strokes can be black, white, gay or any of several million colorful variations.

You can also color the interior of a path by assigning it a fill. Like a stroke, a fill may be black, white or any color.

Now we can start with the drawings.

Drawing a Rectangle

To draw a rectangle, select the rectangle tool and then click and drag inside the drawing area. The point at which you start dragging sets one corner of the rectangle; the point at which you release sets the opposite corner as shown in the figure on the next page. The two remaining corners line up vertically or horizontally with their neighbors. You can also use the rectangle tool as follows:

1. If you press the Alt key while drawing with the rectangle tool, the start point of your drag marks the center of the rectangle. As before, the release point becomes a corner point.
2. Shift-drag with the rectangle tool to draw a perfect rectangle – also called a square. You can press and release the Shift key in mid-drag to switch between drawing a rectangle or a square.
3. Alt+Shift+drag with the rectangle tool to create a square from center to corner.
4. Press the tilde (~) key while dragging with the rectangle tool to create a series of rectangles, all of which border on a common point. Press Alt+~ while you drag to create a series of concentric rectangles.

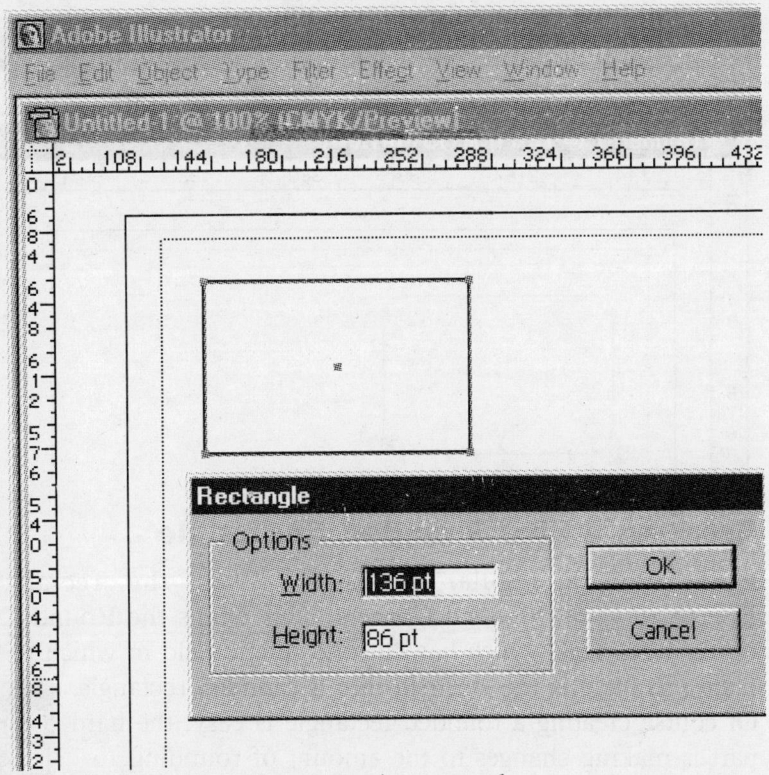

5. Press the spacebar while dragging to move the rectangle rather than change its size. When you get it positioned properly, release the spacebar and continue dragging or release.

Using Numbers

You can also enter the dimensions of a rectangle numerically. Click with the rectangle tool

– that's right, just click inside the drawing area – to display the dialog box as shown in the figure above. Here you can enter values for the Width and Height options.

After you press Enter or click OK, Illustrator creates a rectangle to your exact specifications. Well, for square you will give the same width and height. Here the numbers are given in terms of points where a point is 1/72 of an inch.

Rounding off a Rectangle's Corners

To draw a rectangle with rounded corners, select the rounded rectangle tool from the rectangle tool slot and drag away. Illustrator creates a shape with eight points – two along each side with a curved segment around each corner – as shown below. You control the roundness of the corners by changing the Corner Radius value in the General Preferences dialog box.

You can also click with the rounded rectangle tool and enter a value into the Corner Radius option box. Once you draw with the rounded rectangle tool, there is no way to change the roundness of the corners. Illustrator 10 now lets you add live rounded corner's to rectangles.

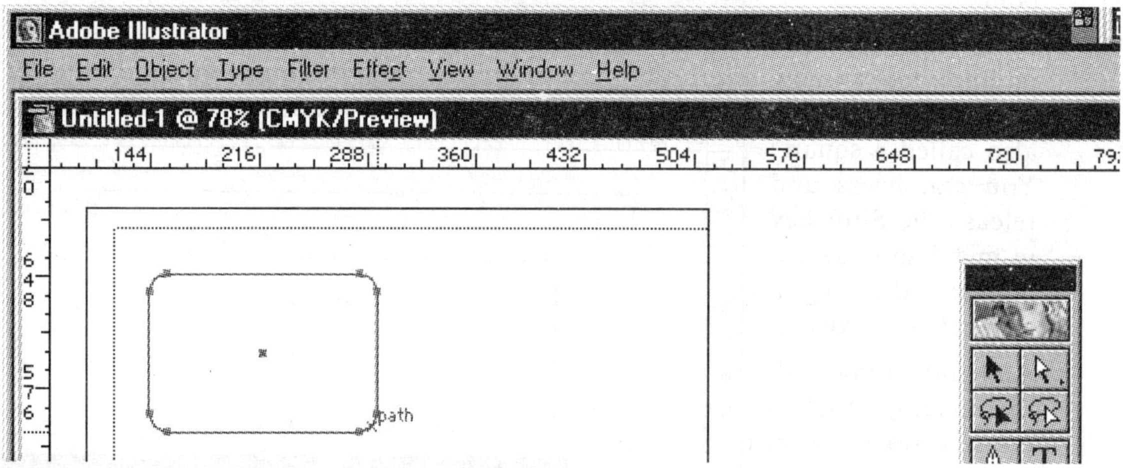

Creating a Live Rounded Rectangle

First draw a regular rectangle. With the rectangle still selected, choose Effect>>Stylize>>Round Corners. This opens the Round Corners dialog box, as shown on the next page, which has but one simple field in which to enter the radius amount. The plain rectangle is transformed into a rounded rectangle. Of course creating a rounded rectangle is easy; the hard part is making changes to the amount of rounding.

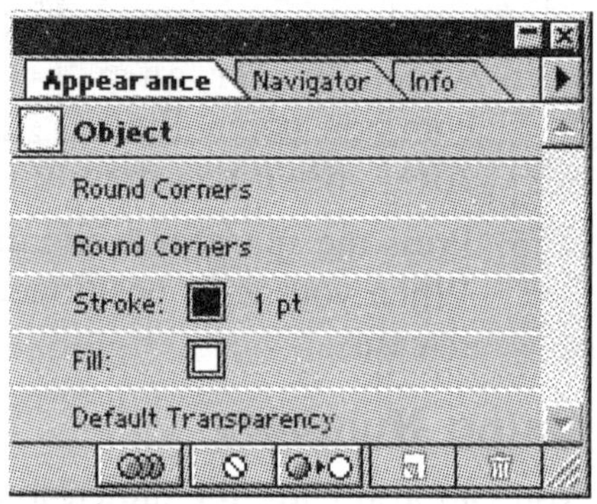

To change the size of the corner radius, you need to open the Appearance palette.

With the object selected, you will see a listing for Round Corners. Double-click the entry and the Round corners dialog box appears again.

Make whatever changes you want to the corner radius.

If you get totally tired of the rounded corners, drag the Round Corners listing into the Appearance palette's trash – instantly you've got your regular rectangle again.

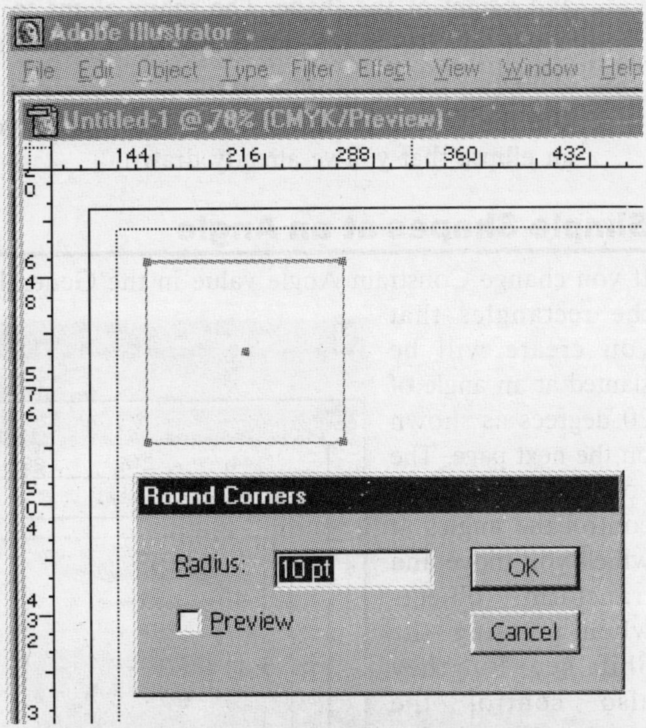

Drawing an Ellipse

Ellipse and circle belong to the circle family. When it comes to drawing ellipse and circles, the ellipse tool is the one for the job. Simply click and drag along a diagonal line to form your ellipse. It fills the imaginary rectangle you create as you drag.

In most other respects, the ellipse tool works much like the rectangle tool:

1. Alt+drag with the ellipse tool to create an ellipse outward from the center. As always, the release point becomes the middle of an arc, determining the size and shape of the ellipse.
2. Shift+drag to draw a perfect ellipse (also called a circle). Alt+Shift+drag to draw a circle from the center point outward.
3. Press the tilde (~) key while dragging with the ellipse tool to create a series of ellipses. Press Opt/Alt-while you drag to create a series of concentric ellipses.
4. Press the spacebar while dragging to move the ellipse rather than change its size. When you get it positioned properly, release the spacebar and continue dragging or release.
5. Click in the drawing area to bring up the Ellipse dialog box. It contains Width and Height options for specifying the width

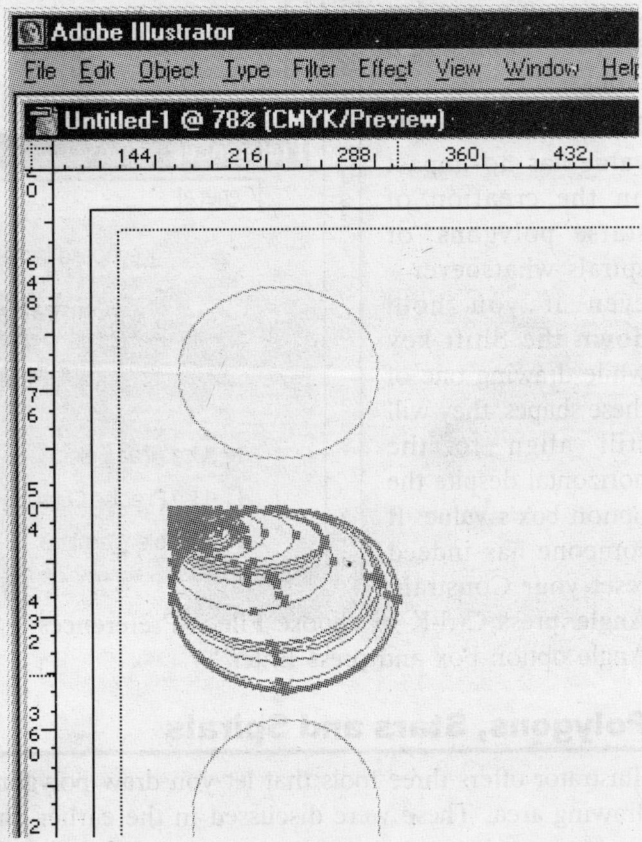

and height of the shape. The shape aligns to your click point by the middle of the upper left arc. If you press Alt+click with the ellipse tool, the ellipse align by its center.

6. Use the W and H values in the Transform palette to change the width and height of an ellipse that you've already drawn.

Simple Shapes at an Angle

If you change Constrain Angle value in the General Preferences dialog box to say 20, all the rectangles that you create will be slanted at an angle of 20 degrees as shown on the next page. The constraint axes control the angles at which you move and transform objects when pressing the Shift key. But they also control the creation of rectangles, ellipses and text blocks.

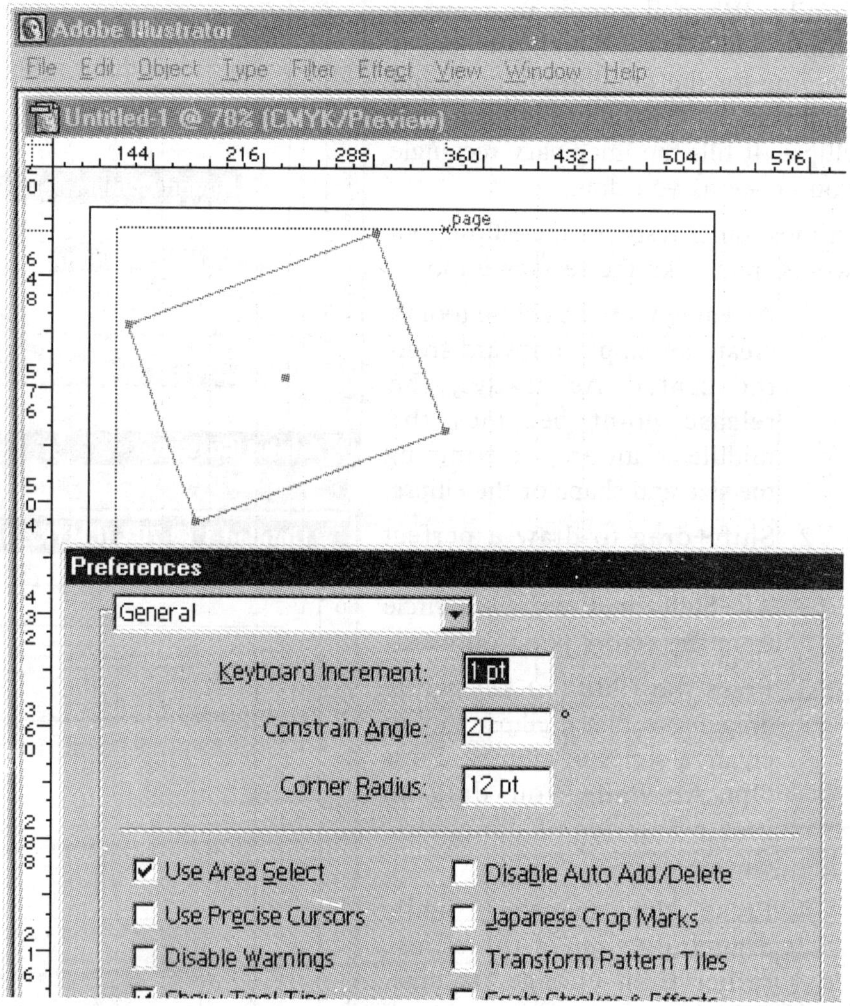

The Constrain Angle value has no impact on the creation of stars, polygons or spirals whatsoever – even if you hold down the Shift key while drawing one of these shapes, they will still align to the horizontal despite the option box's value. If someone has indeed reset your Constrain Angle, press Ctrl-K or choose File>>Preferences >>General. Enter 0 into the Constrain Angle option box and press Enter.

Polygons, Stars and Spirals

Illustrator offers three tools that let you draw polygons, stars and spirals by dragging in the drawing area. These were discussed in the earlier chapter. The new functions still leave a thing or two to be desired, particularly when it comes time to edit the paths, for example, you can't automatically change the number of points in a star after you create it.

Drawing a Regular Polygon

A regular polygon is a shape with multiple straight sides – each side is identical in length and meets its neighbors at the same angle. An equilateral triangle is a regular polygon, as a square. Other examples include pentagons, hexagons, octagons and just about any other shape with a gon in its name, as shown in the figure below.

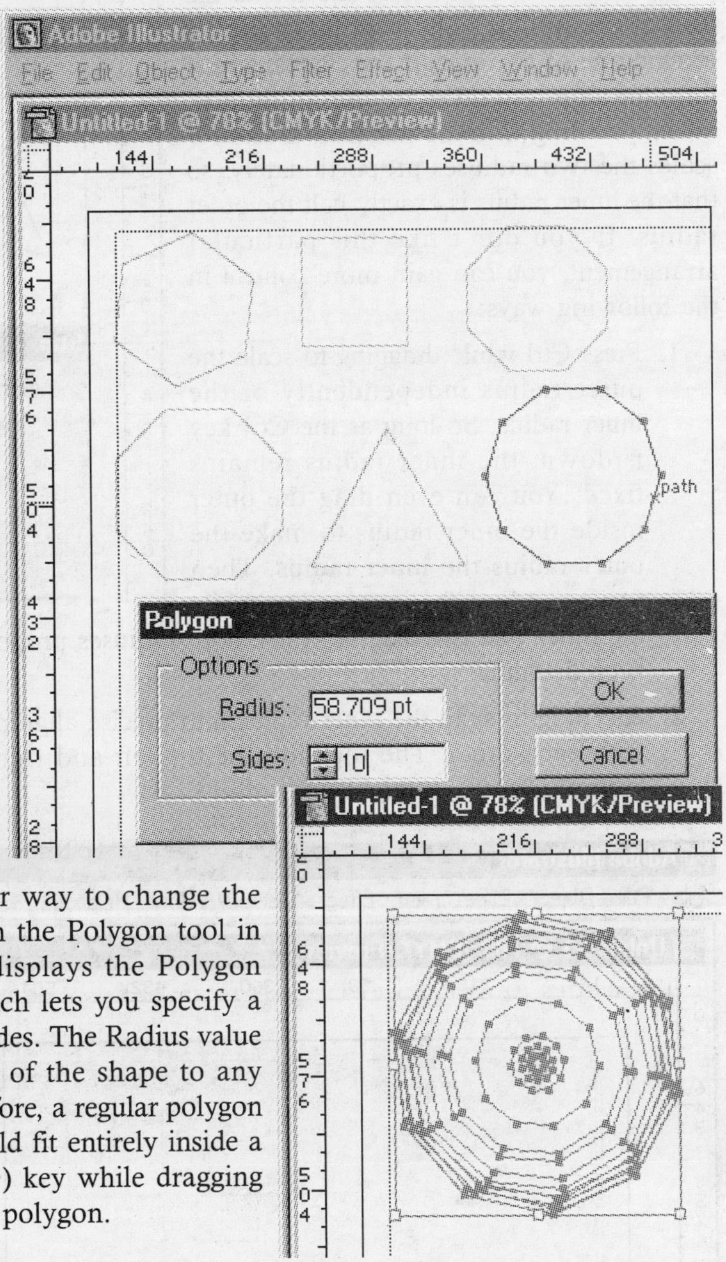

To draw a polygon, select the polygon tool and drag in the drawing in the drawing area. You always draw a polygon from the middle outward, whether you press the Alt key or not. The direction of your drag determines the orientation of the shape. By default, Illustrator draws hexagons (six-sided shapes) with the polygon tool. You can change the number of sides while dragging with the polygon tool by pressing the up and down arrow keys. The up arrow key adds a side: the down arrow key deletes one. Another way to change the number of sides is to click with the Polygon tool in the drawing area. Illustrator displays the Polygon dialog box, as shown here, which lets you specify a Radius value and a number of sides. The Radius value is the distance from the center of the shape to any corner point in the shape. Therefore, a regular polygon with a radius of 100 points would fit entirely inside a circle with a radius the tilde (~) key while dragging to create a series of concentric polygon.

Drawing a Star

Illustrator lets you draw regular stars, in which each spike looks just like its neighbors. To draw a star, drag with the star tool, which is the second alternative tool in the ellipse tool slot. Illustrator of the star tool by pressing the Ctrl and Alt keys as you drag. A star is made up of two sets of points, one at the points where the spikes meet and one at the tips of the spikes. These points revolve around one of two imaginary circles, which form the inner and outer radiuses of the star. When you drag with the star tool, Illustrator scales the two radiuses proportionately, so that the inner radius is exactly half the outer radius. If you don't like this particular arrangement, you can gain more control in the following ways:

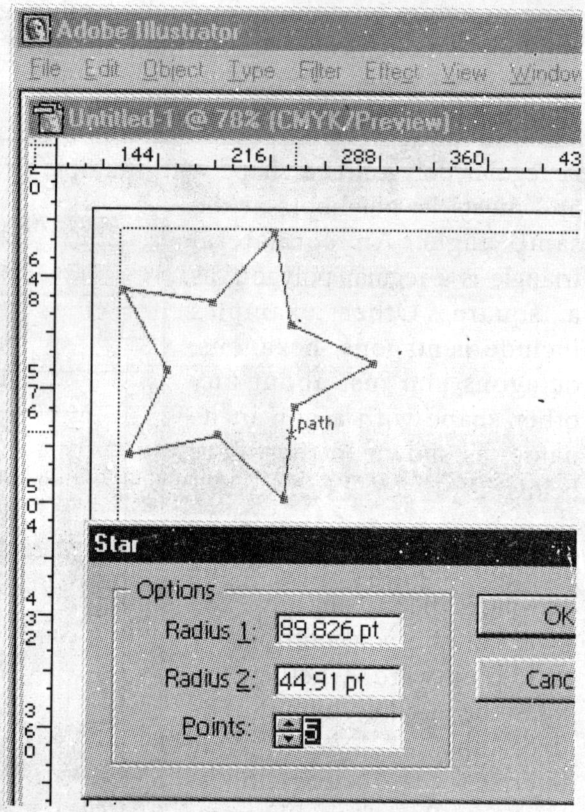

1. Press Ctrl while dragging to scale the outer radius independently of the inner radius. So long as the Ctrl key is down, the inner radius remains fixed. You can even drag the outer inside the inner radius to make the outer radius the inner radius. Then you can adjust the inner radius while the outer one is fixed. To resize both radiuses proportionally again, release Ctrl and keep dragging.
2. Alt+drag to snap the inner radius into precise alignment so that opposite spikes align with each other. The top sides of the left and right sides of a five-sided star, for example, from a straight line.

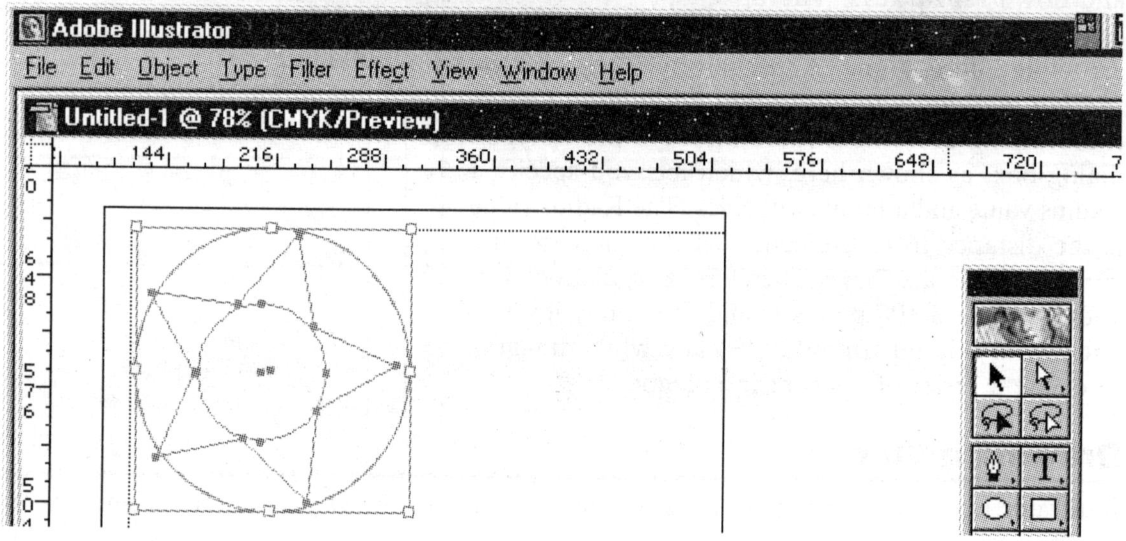

3. Because Ctrl and Alt keys have mutually exclusive effects on a star, they cannot be in effect at the same time. If you do hold down both the Ctrl and Alt keys, Alt takes precedent.

Creating Double Star

The star tool also lets you draw a double star. That's the type of star where the lines are visible across each other – not that there's a huge demand for such a shape, but it is an interesting variation on the traditional star.

To draw a double star, here's what you need to do:

1. Drag with the star tool and hold down the mouse button throughout these steps.
2. Press the down arrow key until you have a three-sided star, the least number of sides permitted.
3. Tap both the Ctrl and Alt keys.
4. Press the up arrow key until you've reached the desired number of sides. Once you're at four sides, you'll see the double star configuration.
5. Adjust the double star's size, placement and orientation as you would a regular star's – with the Ctrl key, Shift key and spacebar, respectively.

Creating a Spiral

Spirals don't exactly lend themselves to a wide range of drawing situations, but they are great to look at. Spirals are one of the most difficult things to create in Illustrator. To draw, just drag with the spiral and the spiral grows outward from its center. The Spiral dialog box, as shown on the next page has the following options.

Radius: Enter a Radius value to specify the size of the spiral. This represents the distance from the center of the shape to the last point on the spiral.

Decay: The decay value determines how quickly the spiral loops in on itself. Small values result in short loops. Larger values – up to 99.99 percent – result in more tightly packed spirals.

Segments: Enter the number of curved segments between points into the Segments option box. Each segment represents a quarter coil in the spiral.

Style: Select a radio button to coil the spiral counterclockwise or clockwise. (This assumes a Decay value of less than 100 percent. If the Decay is higher than 100, the spiral coils in the opposite direction.)

By itself, an increased Segments value may not result in more coils. You have to raise both the Decay and Segments values to wind the coils more tightly. This is because Illustrator drops segments when Decay is too low to accommodate them. Once you're set the spiral dialog box, you can drag new spirals directly on the page. However, you might want to make your spiral experience more interactive. Fortunately Illustrator lets you control spirals as you drag.

Controlling Spirals

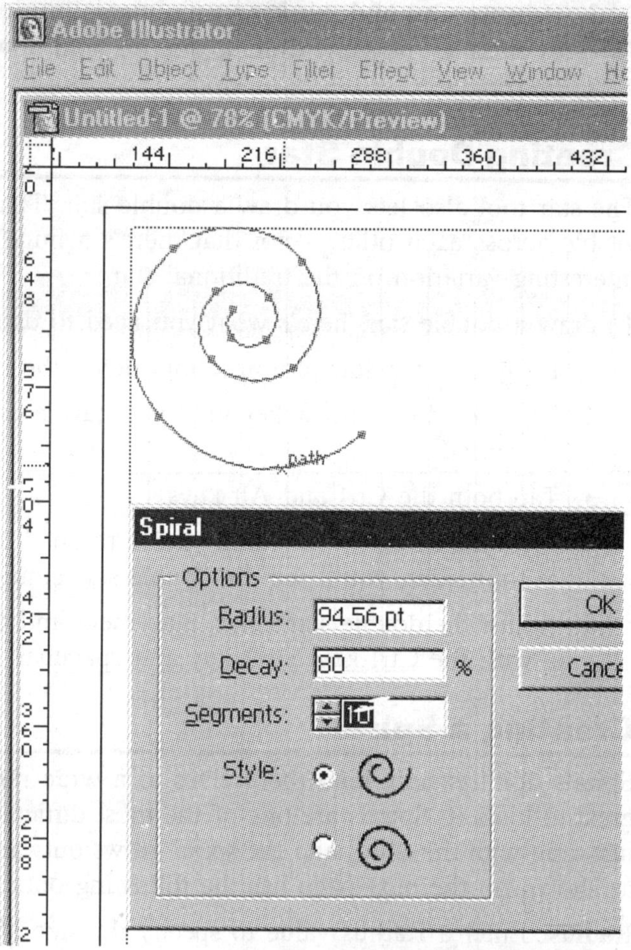

You an modify coils without resorting to the Spiral dialog box. It takes a little getting used to, but it works. Here's how:

1. When you drag with the spiral tool, you're changing the radius and rotating the spiral around. We just want to get that straight before we go for any farther.
2. Press the Ctrl key while dragging to modify the decay. Drag outward to lower the decay; drag inward to raise it. If you drag inward past one of the coils, the spiral flips on itself, indicating a decay of more than 100 percent.
3. Don't press the Ctrl key the moment you start dragging or you'll pop the Decay value to some ridiculously low number such as 7 percent. Start dragging and then press Ctrl in mid-drag. Release the key to modify the radius again.
4. Press the up and down arrow keys while dragging with the spiral tool to raise and lower the number of segments in a spiral.
5. You can also change the number of segments by pressing the Alt key. Alt-drag toward the center of the spiral to delete segments and reduce the radius. Drag outward to both add segments and increase the radius, thus better accommodating the new coils.
6. If you press both Ctrl and Alt simultaneously, Ctrl takes precedence.
7. You can also press the spacebar while dragging with the spiral tool to reposition the path. Shift-drag to constrain the spiral to some 45-degree angle.

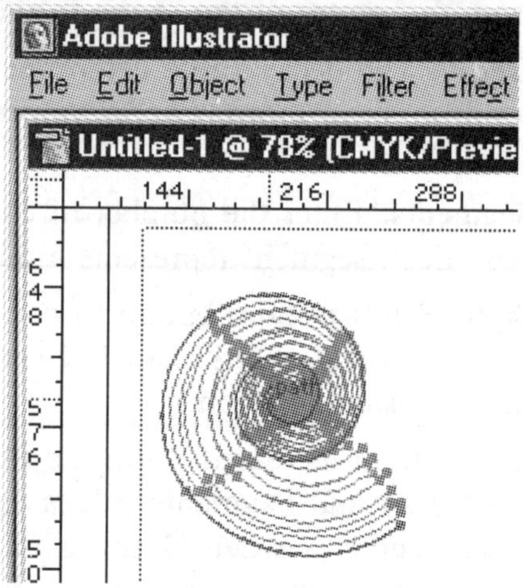

8. You can create a series of spirals by pressing the tilde (~) key as you drag.

Selection and Curves

Whether you use Illustrator's pencil, paintbrush or autotrace tool, you still get the same thing – paths divided by anchor points. A drawing tablet helps, but only to communicate smoother lines to Illustrator; it doesn't helps Illustrator better interpret your beautiful work.

Arrows and Lassos

The arrows, also known as the selection, direct selection and group selection tools, are the most powerful of selection tools. Not only can they select objects and points, but if you drag with them they move things around. Lassos (also known as the lasso and direct selection lasso) aren't as powerful the arrow tools. They can only select things; if you want to move the selection around, you have to switch to an arrow.

The Plain Black Arrow Tool

The selection tool – which we call the arrow tool to distinguish it from its selection friends – is the most straightforward of them. When the arrow tool is active, you can click anywhere along the outline of a path to select the path in its entirety. If the Use Area Select check box to turned on inside the General Preferences dialog box, you can also click inside the path to select it, provided the path has a fill. After selecting a path with the arrow tool, you can move it, apply a transformation or perform any other manipulation that affects the path as a whole. You cannot move points or bend segments. If the path has been grouped with other paths, the arrow tool selects the entire group, prohibiting you from altering the grouped path independently of another.

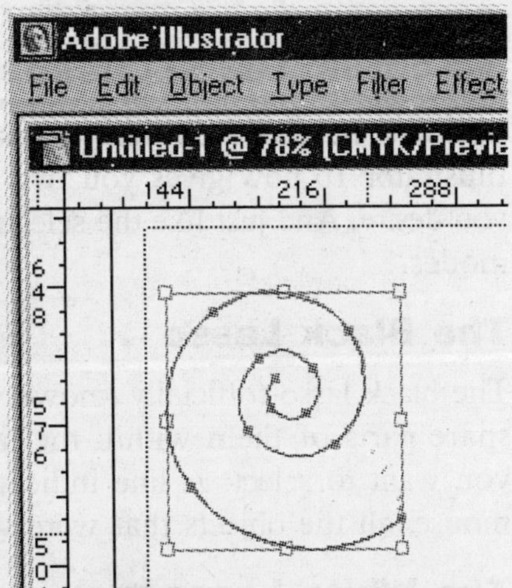

Here are few other ways to select paths with the arrow tool:

- ❑ When you click a path, you not only select the path you click, you also deselect any previously-selected path. To select multiple paths, click the first path and then hold the Shift key as you click each additional path you want to select (this is called a Shift-click). The Shift key prevents Illustrator from deselecting paths as you click new ones.
- ❑ Another way to select multiple paths is to marquee them. Drag from an empty portion of your drawing area to create a dotted rectangular outline, called a marquee. You select all paths that even slightly inside this outline when you release the mouse button.
- ❑ You can combine marqueeing with Shift-clicking to select multiple paths. You can also drag a marquee while pressing Shift, which adds the surrounded objects to the present selection.
- ❑ If you Shift-click an object that is already selected, Illustrator declares it.

Direct Selection Tool

The direct selection tool is the hollow (white) arrow in the upper right corner of the toolbox. Click with the direct selection tool to select an individual point or segment in a path. If you click a point, you select the point; if you click a segment, you select the segment. This works even if the path that contains the point or segment is part of a group.

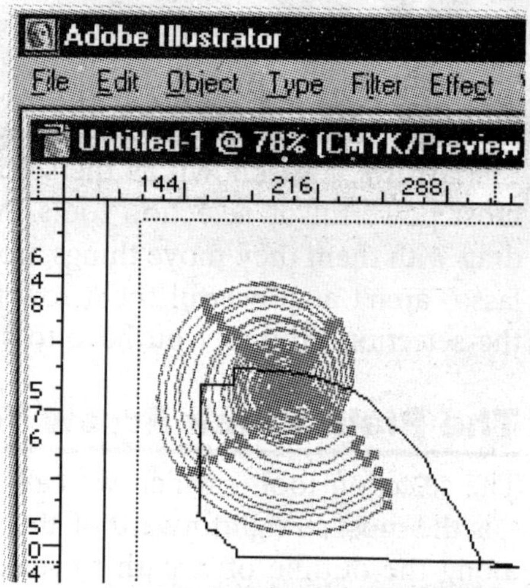

The following list summarizes these and other ways to select elements with the direct selection tool:

- ❑ If the Use Area Select check box in the General Preferences dialog box is turned on (as it is by default), you can click inside a filled shape to select the entire path. This assumes that the shape has a fill.
- ❑ Shift-click a point or segment to add it to the current selection. You can also Shift-marquee around elements. If you Shift-click a point or segment that's already selected, it becomes deselected. The same goes for Shift-marqueeing.
- ❑ Alt-click a point or segment to select an entire path. This is a great way to select paths inside groups.
- ❑ Alt-marquee or Alt-Shift-click paths to select multiple paths at a time.

Selecting Using Lassos

You may have noticed that the marquees created by the arrow tools are always rectangular. Illustrator 10 now gives you two lasso tools that let you round up selections in any shape you desire. And just like the selection tools, the lassos are divided into two different selection modes.

The Black Lasso

The black lasso (officially known as the lasso tool) selects entire objects – even if you only snare parts of them within the lasso marquee. Simply drag the lasso around the objects you want to select. A line indicates the area that is being selected. When you release the mouse, all the objects that were within the lasso marquee will be selected as shown next.

The White Lasso

The White lasso (officially known as the direct selection lasso tool) selects parts of objects. Drag around the points or segments you want to select. When you release the mouse, only those points or segments that were within the lasso marquee will be selected, as shown in the figure on the next page, the direct selection lasso allows you to select points that would require many different passes dragging with the arrow tools.

Adding More Lasso Selections

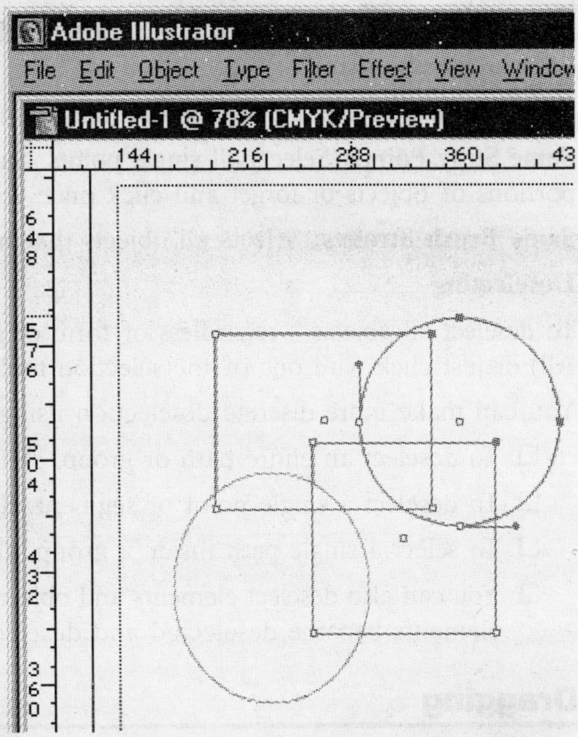

The lasso tools work slightly differently than the other selection tools. If you hold the shift key, you will see a small plus sign next to the lasso cursor. This indicates that the next loop of the lasso will add to the selection. But the lasso do not deselect selected items when you use the Shift key. They only add to the selection. To deselect as you lasso you have to press and hold down the Alt key.

Selecting Everything

If you want to select all paths in your drawing, choose Edit >> Select All or press Ctrl-A. Illustrator selects every last point segment and other element throughout the illustration, even if it's on the pasteboard.

Inversing the Selection

To select everything that's not selected and deselect what is selected, choose Edit>>Select>>Inverse. It's Illustrator's way of letting you reverse a selection. Both the Select All and Inverse commands make it easier to select most of the objects in a complicated drawing. You can choose Select All and then Shift-click the objects you don't want to select. Or start off by clicking and Shift-clicking the stuff your don't want to select and choose Edit>>Select >> Inverse. Either way works fine; it's entirely a matter of personal preference.

Other Selection techniques

There are actually several other techniques for selecting things. For instance, you can select all the objects on layers, by using the Layers palette. You can also select objects by attributes using the Selection commands. These commands are all found under the submenu after Edit>>Select. Various other methods of selections are:

Same Fill and Stroke: Selects all objects that have the same fill and stroke attributes.

Same Fill Color: Selects all objects that have the same fill color. The stroke colors may vary.

Same Stroke Color: Selects all objects that have the same stroke color. The stroke weight may vary as well as the fill colors.

Same Stroke Weight: Selects all objects that have the same stroke weight. The stroke color may vary as well as the fill attributes.

Same Blending Mode: Selects all objects that the same type of blending mode as found in the Transparency palette. All other attributes may vary.

Same Opacity: Selects all objects that have the same percentage of opacity applied. All other attributes may vary.

Same Masks: Selects all objects that are acting as masks to hide areas of other objects.

Same Stray Points: Selects all single points. Single points can get left over when you delete portions of objects or forget and click once with the pen and then don't click again.

Same Brush Strokes: Selects all objects that have brush strokes applied.

Deselecting

To deselect all objects – regardless of form or gender – press Ctrl-Shift-A (Edit >>Deselect All) or just click with one of the selection tools on an empty portion of the drawing area.

You can make more discrete deselection using the Shift key:

- ❑ To deselect an entire path or group, shift-click the object with the arrow tool.
- ❑ To deselect a single point or segment, Shift-click it with the direct selection tool.
- ❑ To select a single path inside a group, alt-shift click it with the direct selection tool.
- ❑ You can also deselect elements and objects by Shift-marqueeing around them. Selected elements become deselected and deselected elements become selected.

Dragging

Once you're selected a point or segment, you can move it around, changing its location and stretching its path. In fact, dragging with the direct selection tool is the single most common method for reshaping a path inside Illustrator. You can move selected points independently of deselected points. And you can stretch segments or move Bezier control handles to alter the curvature of a path. The next few pages explain all aspects of dragging.

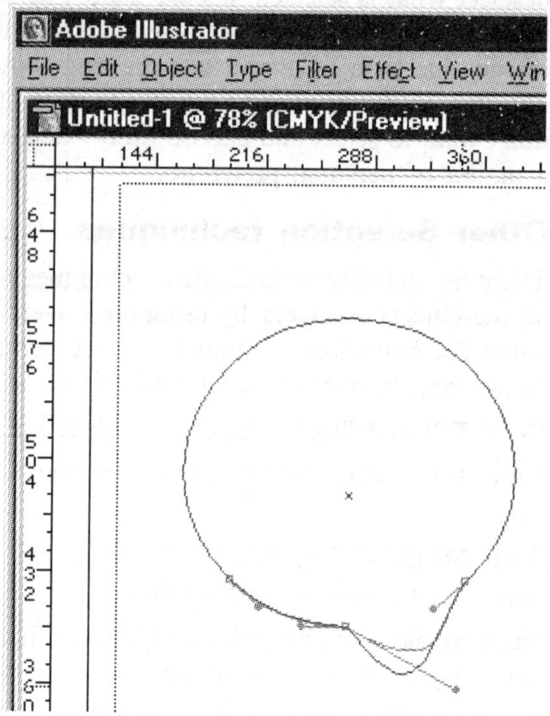

Dragging Points

To move one or more points in a path:

1. Select the points you want to move with the direct selection tool.
2. Drag any one of them.
3. Squeal with delight.

When you drag a selected point, all over selected points move the same distance and direction. When you move a point while a neighboring point remains stationary; the segment between the two points shrinks or stretches in length to accommodate the change in distance, as shown in the above figure.

Pen Tool

The pen tool is capable of creating anything from schematic newspaper charts to detailed scenes of heightened reality. For nearly a decade, Illustrator's pen tool was the reigning champ and no other program offered anything that came close. Now Adobe has taken Illustrator's pen tool and with a few microscopic exceptions, added it to InDesign. You can also find a more primitive version of the pen tool in Adobe Photoshop. It's a testament to the elegance of the original.

Pen Tool Basics

When drawing with the pen tool, you build a path by creating individual points. Illustrator automatically connects the points with segments. The following list summarizes how you can use the pen tool to build paths in Illustrator.

Path building: To build a path, create one pointer after another inside the drawing area until the path is the desired length and shape. You create and position a point by either clicking or dragging with the pen tool. Clicking creates a corner, dragging creates a smooth point. Illustrator draws a segment between each new point and its predecessor.

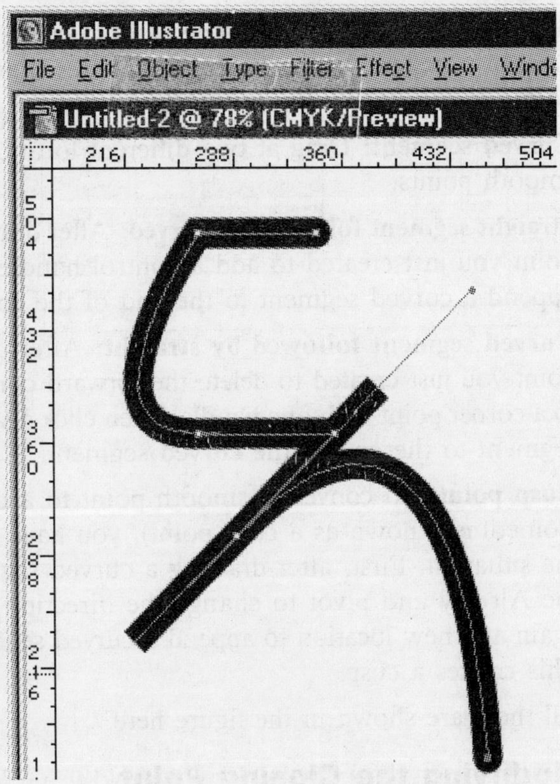

Adjusting a point: Midway into creating a path, you can reposition points or change the curvature of segments that you've already drawn. To move a point while you are still creating it, press and hold the spacebar. You can then reposition the point on the fly. Release the spacebar and continue creating points. If you've already created a point but wish to modify it before moving on to the next point, just press the Ctrl key to access the direct-selection tool, press Ctrl+Tab if the arrow tool comes up instead, and drag the points, segments and control handles as desired. When you've finished, release Ctrl and continue adding points.

Closing the path: To create a closed shape, click or drag on the first point in the path. Every point will then have one segment coming into it and another segment exiting it.

Leaving the path open: To leave a path open, so it has a specific beginning and ending, deactivate the path by pressing Ctrl+Shift+A (Edit>> Deselect All). Or you can press Ctrl to get the arrow or direct selection tool and click an empty portion of the drawing area. Either way, you deactivate the path so you can move on and create a new one.

Extending an open path: To reactivate an open path, click of drag one of its endpoints.

Illustrator is then ready to draw a segment between the endpoint and the next point you create.

Joining two open paths: To join one open with another open path, click or drag an endpoint in the first path, then click or drag an endpoint in the second. Illustrator draws a segment between the two, bringing them together in everlasting peace and brotherhood.

Defining Points and Segments

Points in a path act a little road signs. Each points steers the path by specifying how a segment enters it and how another segment exists it. You specify the identify of each little road sign by clicking or dragging, sometimes with the Alt key gently but firmly pressed.

The following items expiain the specific kinds of points and segments you can create in Illustrator.

Corner point: Click with the pen tool to create a corner point, which represents the corner between two segments in a path.

Straight segment: Click at two different locations to create a straight segment between two corner points.

Smooth point: Drag with the pen tool to create a smooth point with two symmetrical Bezier control handles. A smooth point ensures that one segment fuses into another to form a continuous arc.

Curved segment: Drag at two different locations to create a curved segment between two smooth points.

Straight segment followed by curved: After drawing a straight segment drag from the corner point you just created to add a control handle. Then drag again at a different location to append a curved segment to the end of the straight segment.

Curved segment followed by straight: After drawing a curved segment click the smooth point you just created to delete the forward control handle. This converts the smooth point to a corner point with one handle. Then click again at a different location to append a straight segment to the end of the curved segment.

Cusp point: To convert a smooth point to a corner point with two independent handles (sometimes known as a cusp point), you have a couple of different options depending on the situation. First, after drawing a curved segment, don't release the mouse button. Add the Alt key and pivot to change the direction of the forward control handle. Then drag again at a new location to append a curved segment that sprouts off in a different direction. This creates a cusp.

All these are shown in the figure here.

Modifying the Closing Point

When you close a shape, you click, drag and alt-drag, just as you do when creating other points. But because you modify and close in one gesture, it seems a good idea to revisit these techniques within this slightly different context:

- ❑ Click the first point in a path to clip off any control handle that may have been threatening to effect the closing segment and you'll close the path with a corner point.
- ❑ If the first point in the path is a smooth point, drag it to make sure it remains smooth, thus closing the path with an arc.
- ❑ If the first point is a corner point, drag to add a control handle that curves the closing segment.
- ❑ To convert a smooth point to a cusp on closing. Alt-drag the first point in the path. In this case, you must press the Alt key before you start the drag. Pressing the alt key after you're into the drag has no effect.

Working with the Pen

In the next three sections, I will explain to you the way Pen tool works. First I will show you how to use corner points, then smooth points and finally cusps. Clicking with the pen tool is a wonderful way to create straight-sided polygon. Unlike the shapes you draw with the regular polygon tool, pen tool polygons may be any shape or size.

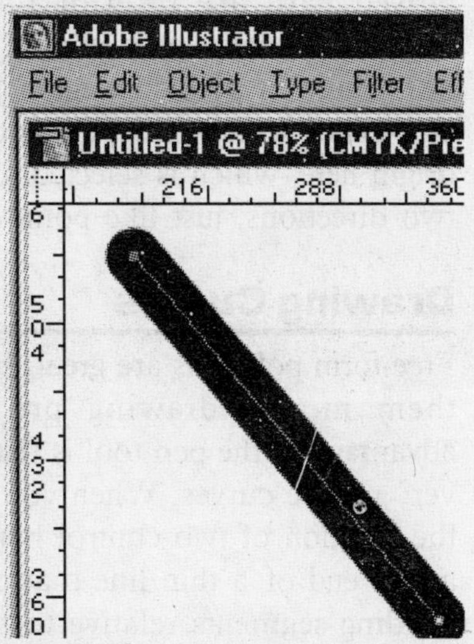

Click to create a corner point: Select the pen tool and click in the drawing area to create a corner point. The little x next to the pen cursor disappears to show you that a path is now in progress. The new corner point appears as a filled square to show that it's selected. It is also open-ended, meaning that it doesn't have both a segment coming into it and a segment going out from it. In fact, this new corner point – point A – is not associated with any segment whatsoever.

Click to add another corner point: Click at a new location in the illustration to create a new corner point-we'll call it point B. Illustrator automatically draws a straight segment from Point A to point B, as shown here. Notice that point a now appears hollow rather than filled, showing that point A is the member of a selected path, but is itself deselected. Point B is selected and open-ended. Illustrator automatically selects a point immediately after you create it and deselects all other points.

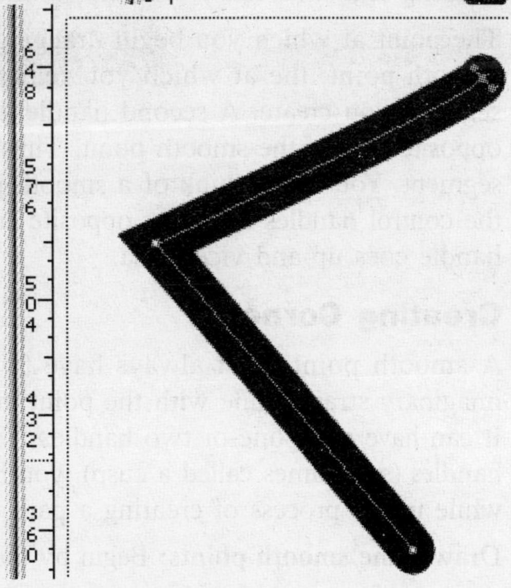

Click to add yet another corner point: Click a third time with the pen tool to create a third corner point – point C. Since a point may be associated with no more than two segments, point B is no longer open-ended, as shown in the figure here. Such a point is called an interior point.

Click the first point in the path: You can keep adding points to a path one at a time for as long as you like. When you're finished, you can close the path by again clicking on point A, as shown here. Illustrator displays the close cursor to show you that it's ready to draw the last segment. If you don't see the close cursor (the pen cursor augmented with a little 0 in the bottom right), you don't have it positioned properly. Since point A is open-ended, it willingly accepts the segment drawn between it and the previous point in the path.

Click to start a new path: All points in a closed path are interior points. Illustrator displays the new path cursor, as shown in the next figure. If you click again, with the pen tool you create a new independent point, shown as origin here, which is selected and open ended in two directions, just like point A.

Drawing Curves

Free-form polygons are great, but you can create them in any drawing program. The real advantage to the pen tool is that it lets you draw very precise curves. When you drag with the pen tool to create a smooth point, you specify the location of two control handles. Each of these handles appears as a tiny circle perched at the end of a thin line that connects the handle to its point. These handles act as levers, bending segments relative to the smooth point itself.

The point at which you begin dragging with the pen tool determines the location of the smooth point; the at which you release becomes a control handle that affects the next segment you create. A second handle appears symmetrically from the first handle, on the opposite side of the smooth point. This handle determines the curvature of the most recent segment. You might think of a smooth point a if it were the center of a small seesaw, with the control handles acting as opposite ends. If you push down on one handle, the opposite handle goes up and vice versa.

Creating Corners

A smooth point must always have two Bezier control handles, each positioned in an imaginary straight line with the point itself. A corner point, however much more versatile. It can have zero, one or two handles. To create a corner point that has one or two control handles (sometimes called a cusp), you must manipulate an existing corner or smooth point while in the process of creating a path.

Draw some smooth points: Begin by the drawing the path as shown in the figure here. You

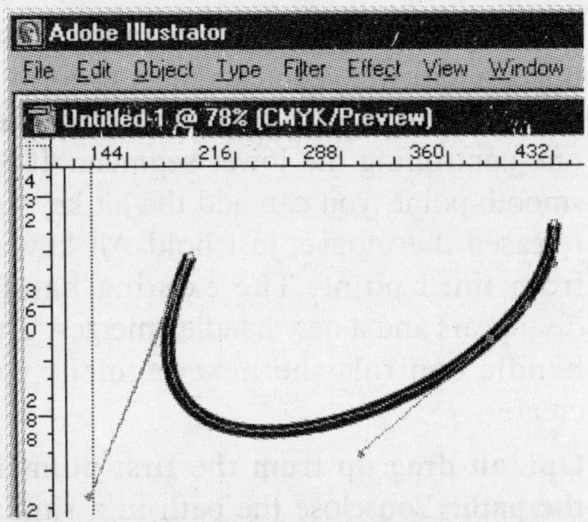

do this by dragging three times with the pen tool: First drag downward from first point, then drag leftward from second point and finally drag up from third point. The result is an active path composed of three smooth points.

Click the last point created: Illustrator lets you alter the most recent point while in the process of creating a path. Suppose that you want to flatten off the top of the path to create a sort of tilted bowl. Because you can associate smooth points only with curved segments, you must convert the top two smooth points to corner points. To convert the most recent point – the one on the left – position the pen tool over last point so the pen changes to the cusp (the normal pen cursor with an additional little carat in the lower right corner). Then click to amputate the forward handle, which does not yet control a segment.

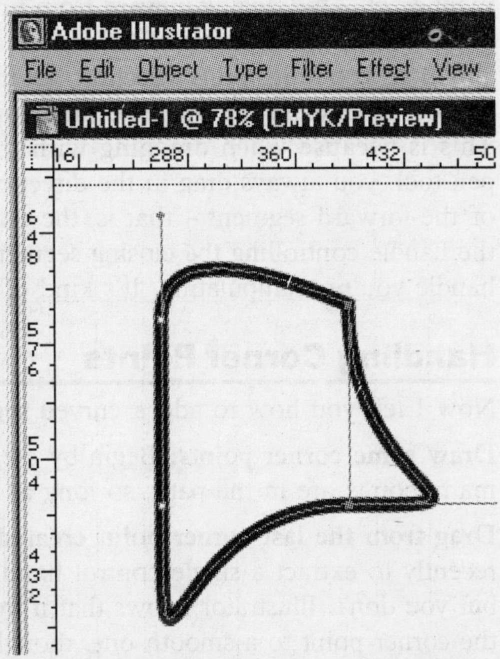

Click the first point in the path: You now have an open path composed of two smooth points and a cusp. You still need to close the path and amputate a handle belonging to first point. A single operation–clicking on the first smooth point–accomplishes both maneuvers. It's that simple. With one click, you close the path and amputate the control handle that would otherwise have curved the closing segment. Hence, the new segment is straight, bordered on both sides by corner points with one handle each. If you don't release the mouse button, you can delete the forward handle from third point by another method. You construct the path as explained in step 1, except that you don't release the mouse button after dragging with the pen to form the forward control handle belonging to last point. Continue to hold down the mouse button and press the alt key. You can now drag the forward handle independently of the backward handle. Drag the forward handle back into last point until it disappears. The advantage is you modify the path as you drag. Just make sure the forward handle is completely gone.

Converting Smooth Points to Cusps

These steps show you how to close the path from with a concave top, resulting in a crescent shape:

Draw some smooth points: Begin again by drawing the path described in the first step of the previous section.

Alt-drag down from the last point created: The segments in a crescent are curved, but the upper and lower segments meet to form two cusps. You need to change the two top smooth points to cusps with two control handles apiece – one controlling the upper segment and one controlling the lower segment. If you still have the mouse pressed as you create the smooth point, you can add the alt key and pivot the control handle down. If you've already released the mouse, just hold Alt key and position the cursor over the point. Then drag from third point. The existing handle disappears and a new handle emerges. This handle controls the next segment you create.

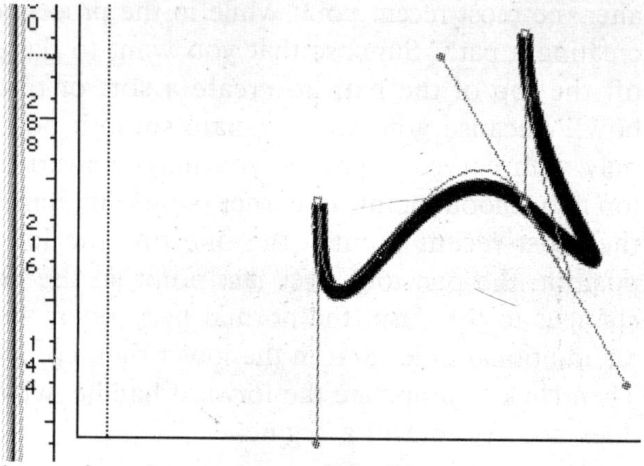

Opt/alt-drag up from the first point in the path: You close the path in a similar manner, by Alt-dragging upward from first point. Notice the location of the cursor as you drag. You drag in one direction, but the handle emerges in the opposite direction. This is because when dragging with the pen tool, you always drag in the direction of the forward segment – that is, the one that exists the current point. Illustrator positions the handle controlling the closing segment symmetrically to your drag, even if it is the only handle you're manipulating. It's kind of weird, but it's Illustrator's way.

Handling Corner Points

Now I tell you how to add a curved segment to a path composed of straight ones:

Draw some corner points: Begin by creating the straight-sided path. It doesn't matter how many points are in the path, so long as they're all corner points.

Drag from the last corner point created: Drag from the corner point you've created most recently to extract a single control handle. You may think you need to hold Alt key here, but you don't. Illustrator knows that if you drag you want to create curves. It won't convert the corner point to a smooth one, though. It simply adds a Bezier handle to create a curve for the segment you're about to create.

Drag from the first point in the path: To close the path, drag from the first corner point in the path. Once again, you drag in the direction opposite the emerging Bezier control handle. Illustrator won't curve the first segment, only the one you're currently working on.

Adding Points to a Path

It is not that you are restricted to the number of points which are already there on the path, you can always add more points as per your needs.

Appending a point to the end of an open path: If an existing path is open, you can add points to either end of it. First activate one of its end points by clicking or dragging it with the pen tool. When you position the pen tool over an inactive endpoint, you get the activate cursor, which looks like a pen with a little slash next to it. Drag from the point if you want to retain or add a control handle; click if you want to trim off a control handle or avoid adding one and Alt-drag if you want to change the direction of a handle. Then click and drag to add more points to the path. You can also lengthen an open path by dragging from one of its end points with the pencil tool. In the unlikely event the path touches a portion of a tracing template, you can even use the autotrace tool.

Closing an open path: Once the path is active, you can close it. Just click, drag or Alt-drag the opposite endpoint with the pen tool. You can also close a path with the pencil tool by dragging from one endpoint to the other.

Insert a point into a segment: To insert a new interior point into a path, select the add point tool and click anywhere along a segment (except on an existing point). Illustrator inserts the point and divides the segment in two. Illustrator automatically inserts a corner or smooth point depending on its reading of your path. You don't have to actually switch to the add point tool. If you've got the pen chose, simply position the cursor over an empty spot on any segment. The regular pen cursor gains a little plus sign (so it looks just like the add point cursor).

Removing Points from a Path

To delete an entire path, you just select it with the arrow tool and press the Backspace/ Delete key. You can do it from menus too, just choose Edit>>Clear. To delete a point or segment, try out one of the following techniques.

Delete a point and break the path: To delete a point, select it with the direct selection tool and press the Delete key. When you delete an interior point, you delete both segments associated with that point, resulting in a break in the path. If you delete an endpoint from an open path, you delete the single segment associated with the point.

Delete a segment: You can delete a single interior segment from a path without removing a point. To do so, click the segment you want to delete with the direct selection tool and press Delete. Deleting a segment always creates a break in a path.

Delete the rest of the path: After you delete a point or segment, Illustrator selects the remainder of the path. If the path is broken into two parts, both parts will be selected. To delete the whole path, just press Delete a second time. This can be a handy technique if you don't want to switch to the arrow tool. Just click some portion of the path and press Delete twice in a row to delete he whole path.

Remove a point without breaking the path: If you want to get rid of a point but don't want to create a break in the path, select the delete point tool and click the point you want to disappear. Illustrator draws a new segment between the two points neighboring the deleted point.

Converting Points between Corner and Smooth

The convert point tool lets you change a point in the middle of a path from corner to smooth or smooth to corner. When a path is shaped wrong, this tool is absolutely essential. You can change the identity of an interior point in any of the following ways:

- **Smooth to corner:** Using the convert point tool, click a smooth point. This converts it to a corner point with no control handles.
- **Smooth to cusp:** Drag a control handle belonging to a smooth point to move it independently of the other control handle, thus converting the smooth point to a cusp.
- **Corner or cusp to smooth:** Drag from a corner point or cusp to convert it to a smooth point with two symmetrical control handles. Once you have the smooth point, you can use the convert point tool on either handle to change the point into a cusp.

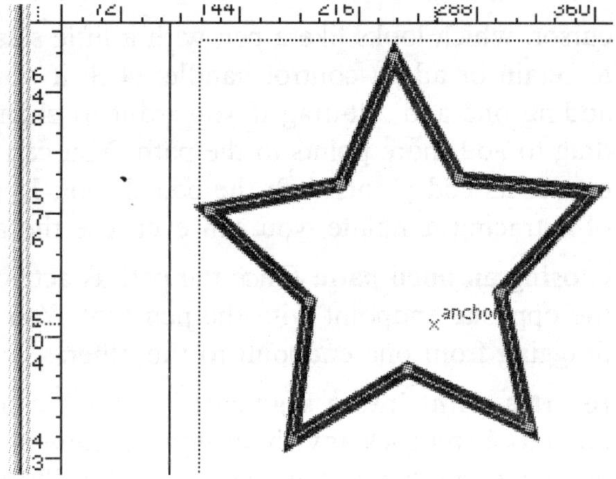

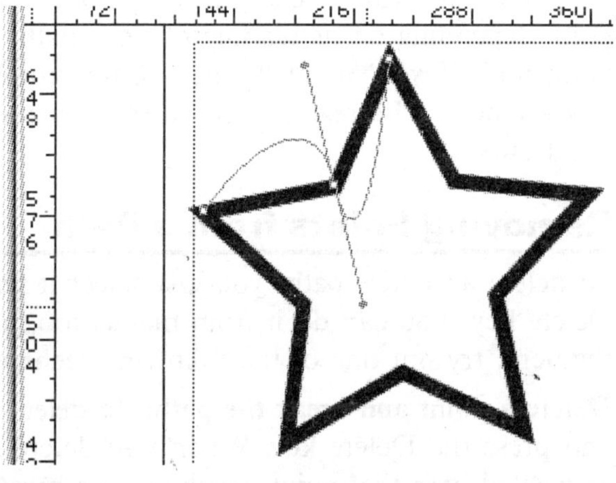

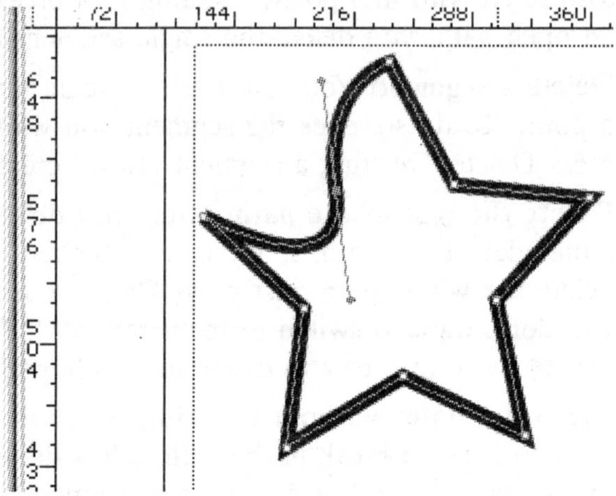

The figure on the next page shows a path created with the star tool. Like any star, it's made up entirely of corner points and straight segments. But with the help of the convert point tool, you can put some curve, as the following steps show.

Drag from one of the points along the inner radius: Select the convert point tool and drag from one of the inner radius points as shown on the next page. The corner point changes to a smooth point with symmetrical control handles, bending both neighboring segments.

Drag the inside control handle outside the star: Drag the control handle that moved inside the star to a position outside the star, so that the two spikes form mirror images of each other, as shown in the figure below. This converts the smooth point to a cusp, permitting the control handles to move independently.

Repeat Steps 1 and 2 on all the inner radius points: By dragging control handles from all the points and converting them to cusp points, you can create the flower shape shown in the figure next.

Continue to adjust the handles until they're just right: With the convert point tool, click and drag on any handle that does not suit your fancy.

Redo Undo Operations

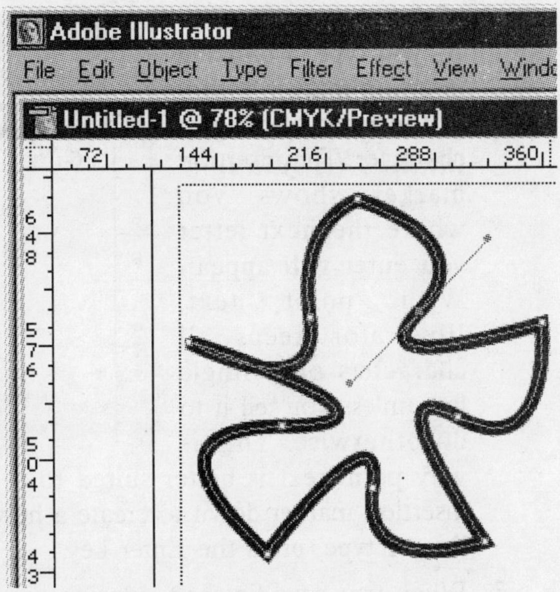

Just as you can undo as many as 200 consecutive actions, you can redo up to 200 consecutive undos by choosing Edit>>Redo or pressing Ctrl+Shift+Z. You can choose Redo only if the Undo command was the most recent operation performed otherwise, Redo is dimmed. Also if you undo a series of actions, perform a new series of actions, and then undo the new series of actions to the point where you had stopped undoing previously, you can't go back and redo the first series of undos. Instead, you can either continue to undo from where you let off or redo the later set of actions.

Handling Text in Illustrator

Illustrator's text capabilities are very vast as would see in the course of this chapter. First we will understand how to create text and apply attributes like fonts, paragraph settings, spacings, etc. Later we look at more effective ways of handling text, like, converting text to a curve, setting text inside free-form text blocks, applying effects to Adobe's specialized Multiple Master fonts, converting letter outlines to fully editable paths and even present text in the Japanese vertical style.

First, we create text objects.

Creating Text Objects

Illustrator provides 6 tools for creating text, as was told to you in the first chapter. But, first let us concentrate on the type tool (the one that looks like a T). With the type tool, you can create a text object – which is any object that contains type – in one of two ways:

- ❑ Click with the type tool within the drawing area and a few words of type for a logo or headline. This kind of text block is called point text, because Illustrator aligns the text to the point at which you click.
- ❑ Drag with the type tool to draw a rectangular text block. Then enter your text from the keyboard. Illustrator fits the text to the rectangular text block, automatically shifting text that doesn't fit on one line down to the next. Create a text block when you want to enter a full sentence or more.

1. Select the type tool and click in some empty portion of the drawing area with the new block cursor. The new block cursor shows that you are about to create a new text object. After you click with the type tool, Illustrator creates an alignment point, which appears as an x in the outline mode. Illustrator aligns the text to this point.
2. Enter the desired text from your keyboard. By default, the text appears to the right

of the alignment point. As you type, a blinking insertion marker flashes to the right of the last character. The insertion marker shows you where the next letter you enter will appear. With point text, Illustrator keeps all characters on a single line unless you tell it to do otherwise. This is why point text is better suited to a few words or less. If you want to move the insertion marker down to create a new line of type, press the Enter key.

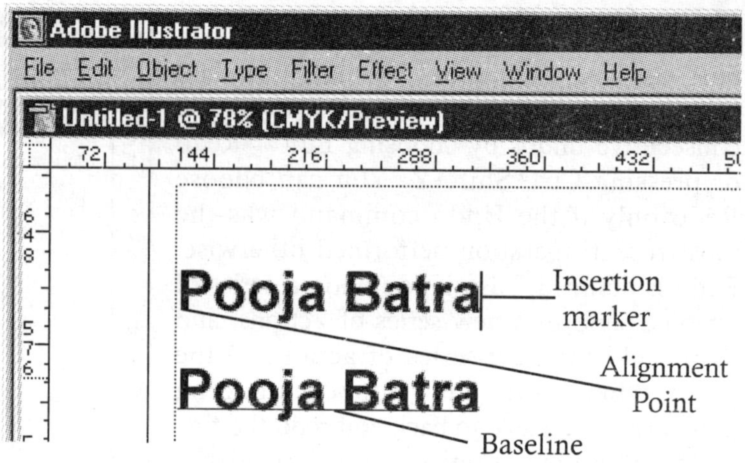

3. When you have finished entering your text, hold the Ctrl key and click the text. Then release the Ctrl key. The text block appears selected as shown in the figure on the next page. The alignment point now looks like a filled square, just like a selected anchor point.

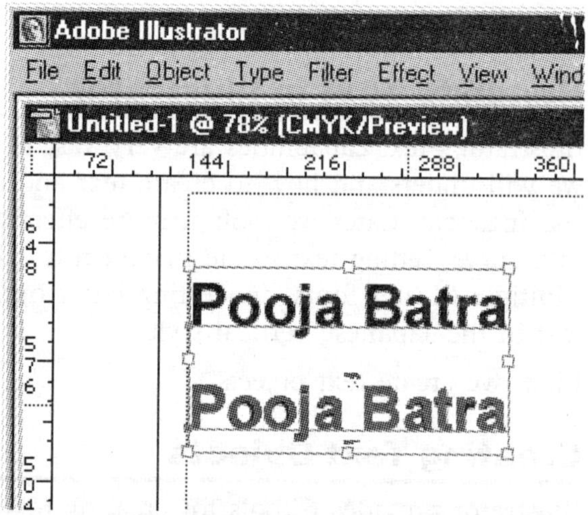

You can drag the alignment point with any of the three selection tools to reposition the text in the drawing area. You can also drag point text by its baseline, which is the line that runs under each line of type. The baseline is the imaginary line on which letter sit. Some lowercase characters – g, j, p, q and y – descend below the baseline. Lastly, you can move point text by dragging on the text itself. The exception to this last technique is when the Type Area Select option of the Type and Auto Tracing Preference dialog box is turned off.

Text in Blocks

Point text is easy to create, but because Illustrator forces all text onto a single line unless told to do otherwise, point text is not well suited to whole paragraph and longer text. To accommodate lengthy text, you need to create a text block:

1. Drag with the type tool. This creates a rectangle, as shown in the example on the next page, just at if you were dragging with the rectangle tool. This rectangle represents the height and width of the new text block. When you release the mouse, Illustrator shows you a box with a blinking insertion marker. You will also see a center point, just as in a standard rectangle.

2. Enter type from the keyboard. If a letter would extend beyond the right edge of the text block, Illustrator sends the word down to start a new line of type. Known as automatic wrapping, this is precisely the capability that point text lacks.
3. After you stop entering text, hold the Ctrl key and click the text. Then release the Ctrl key. The text block appears selected, showing off four corner points connected by straight segments and a center point hovering in the middle. Baseline underscore the type to indicate that the letters themselves are selected.

Resizing and Reshaping Text Blocks

You can reposition a text block by dragging either the rectangular boundary or one of the baseline with the arrow tool. Or you can drag directly on the text itself. You can also change the size and shape of a text block with the direct selection tool. For example, let's say that the next you entered from the keyboard doesn't entirely fit inside the text block. Or the text block isn't wide enough to accommodate a particularly long word.

The little square with a minus sign in it shows that Illustrator had to break the word everybody onto two lines. The square with a plus sign shows that there is more text than can fit inside the text block and is temporarily hidden. This text is called overflow text. By resizing a text block, you can fit long words on a single line, reveal overflow text or simply change how words wrap from one line to the next. To resize a text block, you have to use the direct selection tool to select and modify the rectangular boundary independently of the text inside it.

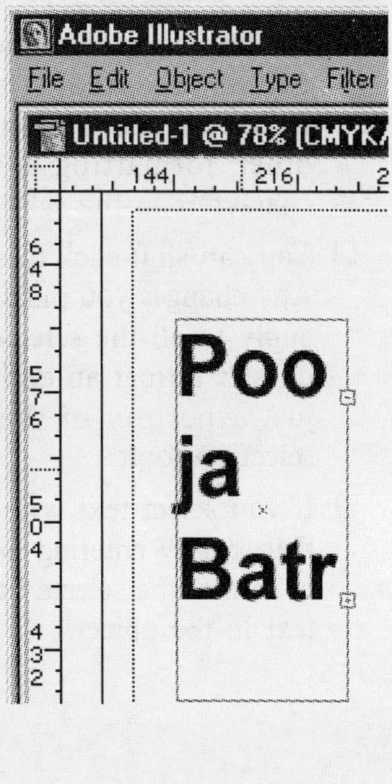

Create your text block: After creating the text block, select the direct selection tool.

Deselect the text block: If your first impulse is to resize the block by dragging a corner point, resist the feeling. You'll turn the block into a kite-shaped object. To reshape the block and keep it a rectangle, you have to select one of the segments and drag it, just as if you were resizing a standard rectangle. And – just to make things as painful as possible – you can't select a segment until you deselect path. So choose Edit>>Deselect All or press Ctrl+Shift+A to deselect the text block.

Select the right or bottom edge of the text block: If you're working in the preview mode, the text block outline disappears. This makes selecting an edge of the text block rather difficult.

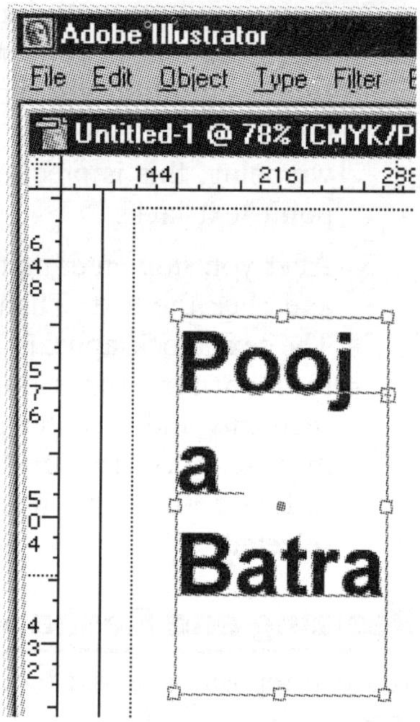

That's why you need to drag a tiny marquee around the portion of the outline you want to move. If you want to make the text block wider, drag a marquee around the right side. If you want to make the text block taller, marquee the bottom side. In either case, you select the desired edge.

Shift-drag the edge: To maintain the rectangular shape of the text block, shift-drag the right segment to the right or Shift-drag the bottom segment downward.

When you release the mouse button, Illustrator rewraps the text and displays as much overflow text as will fit. If there is still more overflow text, the little plus icon remains in the lower right corner of the text block. In addition to dragging points and segments, you can:

- Change the corner points to smooth points with the convert point tool.
- Drag the control handles to bend the segments.
- Insert or remove points with the add point and delete point tools.
- Select a segment and press Delete to open the path.
- Extend the open path using the pen or pencil tools.

Selecting and Editing Text

Before you can change a single character of type or change how text looks on the page, you have to select the type using the arrow or the type tool.

- Clicking along the baseline of a line of type with any selection tool selects all type in the object. If you change the font, type size, style or some other formatting attribute, you change all characters in the selected text object.
- You can shift-click to select multiple text objects. Any changes you make to the text formatting will apply to all the selected text objects. Illustrator doesn't format an entire text block if you select just a portion of the outline with the direct selection tool.
- If you select text with a type tool, you can edit that text by entering new text from the keyboard or format the selected text independently of other text in the object.

Selecting with the Type Tool

The type tool is the most common instrument for editing type in Illustrator because it affords the most control. The following items explain how to select type with the type tool:

- Drag over the characters that you want to select. Drag to the left or to the right to select characters on a single line; drag upward or downward to select characters on multiple lines. The selected text becomes highlighted as shown on next page. Selected text has to be continuous. You cannot select alternate words for example or for that matter select the first line, skip the second line and then select the third line.
- Double-click a word to select it. Hold down the mouse button on the second click and drag. Your selection will be whole worlds.
- Triple-click to select an entire paragraph, from one return character to the next. Hold down the mouse button on the third click and drag to select additional paragraphs.
- Click to set the insertion marker at one end of the text that you want to select and then Shift+click at the opposite end of the desired selection. Illustrator highlights all characters between the first click and the Shift+click.
- Click anywhere in a text block and press Ctrl-A or choose Edit >>Select All, to select all text in the object. After you click with the type tool to set the insertion marker inside a text object, you can use the arrow keys to move the insertion marker around or select text.
- Press the left or right arrow key to move the insertion marker to the left or right one character.
- Press the up or down arrow key to move the insertion marker up or down one line.
- Press Ctrl+right arrow move the insertion marker one whole word to the right. Press Ctrl+left arrow to move back a word.
- Press Ctrl+up arrow to move the insertion marker to the beginning of the paragraph. Press Ctl+down arrow to move it to the end of the paragraph.
- Press Shift along with any of these keystrokes to select text as you move the insertion marker. For example, press Shift+right arrow to select the character after the insertion marker. Press Ctrl+Shift+up arrow to select everything from the insertion marker to the beginning of the paragraph.

Adding Text

After you highlight some text, you can format it or replace it by entering new text from the keyboard.

- To delete selected text, press the Backspace/Delete key.
- You can remove the selected text and send it to the Clipboard by choosing Edit>>Cut or Ctrl-X).
- To leave the selected text intact and send a copy to the Clipboard choose Edit>>Copy or Ctrl-C.

- ❑ You can even replace the selected text with text that you cut or copied earlier by choosing Edit>>Paste or Ctrl-V. The pasted text retains its original formatting.

Formatting Text

Formatting means nothing more than changing the way characters and lines of text look. Illustrator provides an exhaustive supply of formatting functions that let you modify far more than you'll ever want to. You can divide formatting attributes into two categories – those that apply to individual characters of type and those that apply to entire paragraphs.

- ❑ **Character-level formatting** includes option such as typeface, size, leading, kerning and tracking, baseline shift and horizontal scaling. To change the formatting of one or more characters, you select the characters with the type tool and apply the desired options. Illustrator changes the highlighted characters and leaves surrounding characters unaltered.
- ❑ **Paragraph-level formatting** includes indents, alignment, paragraph spacing, letter spacing and word spacing. To change the formatting of a single paragraph, you need only position the blinking insertion marker inside that paragraph. Illustrator changes the entire paragraph to matter how little of it you select. To change the formatting of multiple paragraphs, select at least one character in each of the paragraphs you want to modify.

Character-Level Formatting

To format characters, you can either choose commands from Type menu or use the options in the Character palette. The letter is the more convenient. To display the Character palette, choose Type>> Character or press Ctrl-T. By default, the Character palette shows only six options, as shown below. But if you choose the Show Options command from the pop-up menu, you expand the palette to display several more options, as shown below.

Let us discuss the various options which you can change from this dialog box.

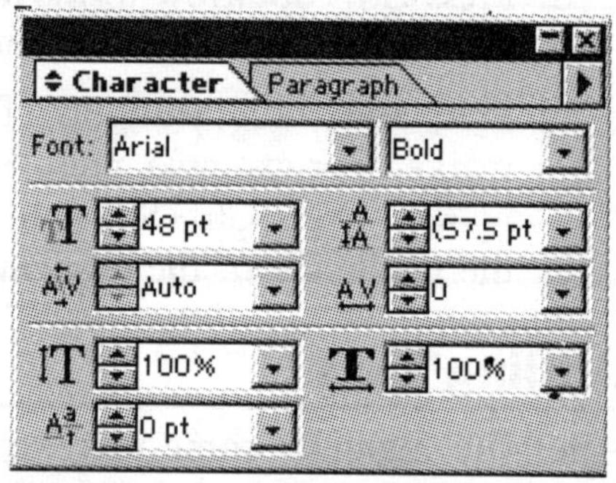

Selecting a Typeface

You can select a font from the Type>>Font submenu or from the Font pop-up menu in the Character palette. For example, to assign Arial Bold, you would choose Type>>Font>>Arial>>Bold. If you know the name of the font you want to apply, just enter the first few letters of its name into the Font option box in the Character palette. Each time you enter a character, Illustrator tries to guess which font you want.

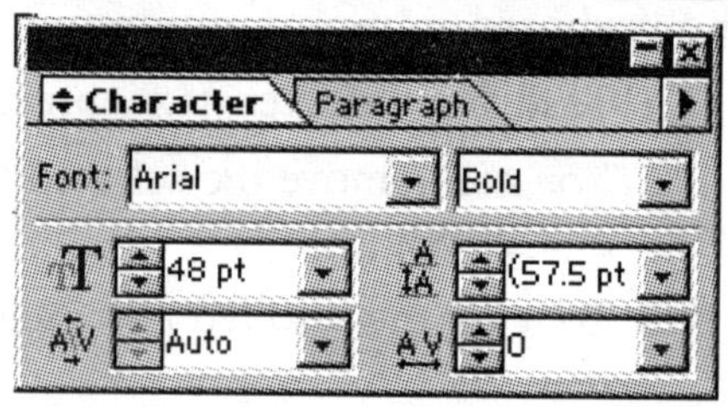

To change the style, press the Tab key and enter the first few letters of the style, such as B for Bold or I for italic. You can also right-click and choose a font from the Fonts submenu in the context-menu.

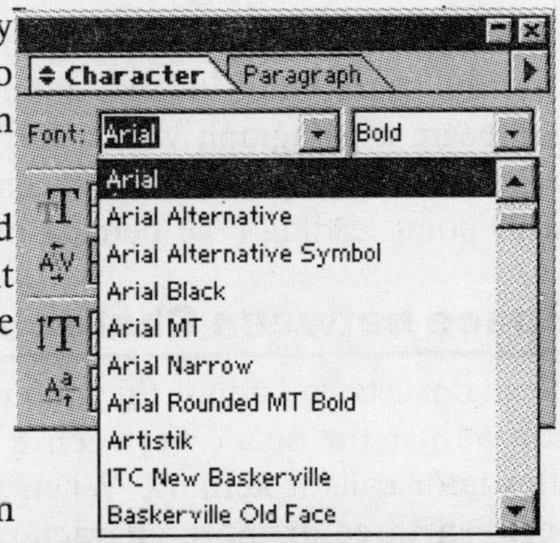

You may notice that Illustrator doesn't let you apply electronic styles such as underline. Illustrators inability to assign electronic styles inhibits its compatibility with TrueType fonts.

If a TrueType font doesn't have a submenu of stylized fonts next to its name in the Type>>Font submenu, it means that the fonts on your machine don't include the stylized versions of that font.

Reducing/Enlarging Type

To change the size of any selected type, choose a size from the Type>>Size submenu. If you choose Others, you'll be sent to the size option in the Character palette.

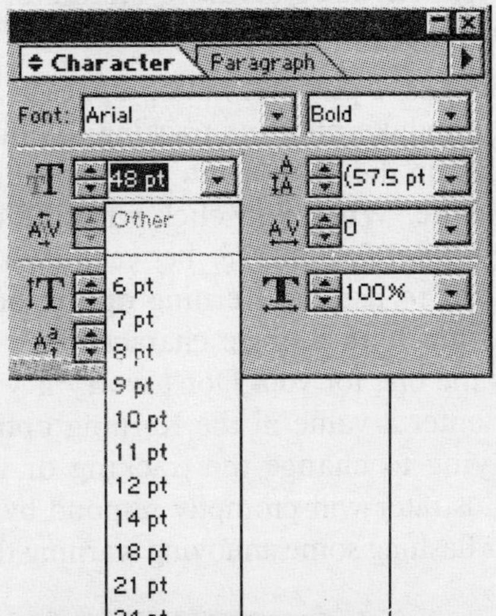

Type size, as it is called, is measured in points from the top of an ascender (such as a d or an f) to the bottom of a descender (such as g or p). You can enter any value between 0.1 (1/10 the size of the smallest character) and 1296 (four times the size of the largest character) in 0.01–points increments.

If you dramatically reduce the size of a line of type, it appears as a gray bar. Illustrator figures it's too small to be readable on screen, so why waste the time trying to draw it accurately? If you want to see text at smaller sizes, change the greeking amount in the Type and Auto Tracing Preferences.

To change the type size of the selected text by five times the Size/Loading value, do the following:

Press Ctrl-Alt-Shift-> or Ctrl-Alt-Shift-<

Distance between Lines

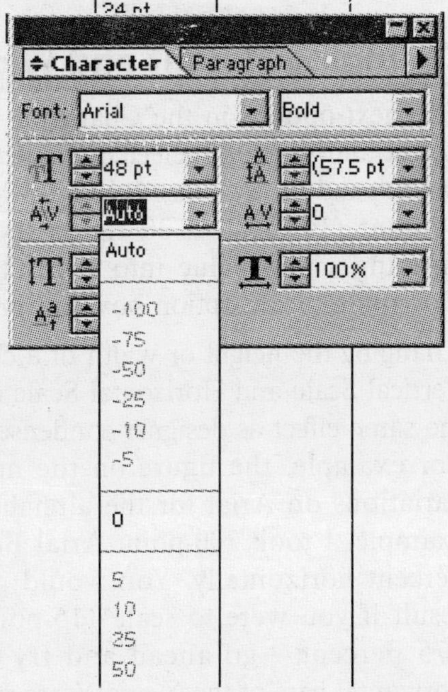

Leading specifies the distance between a selected line of type an the line below it, as measured in points form one baseline to the next. Therefore, 14-point leading leaves a couple of points of extra room between two lines of 12-point type. You can change the leading by entering a value into the Leading option box in the Character palette.

To speed things up, select some text and press Alt-down arrow to increase the leading or Alt-up arrow to decrease it.

Select Auto from the Leading pop-up menu in the Character palette to make the leading equal to 120 percent of the current type size (rounded off to the nearest half-point). If a line of text contains characters with two different leading specifications, the larger leading prevails. If you begin a paragraph with a large capital letter, for example, you might combine a 24-point character and the 12-point character use auto leading, then the entire line will be set at 29-point leading (120 percent of the 24-point type size).

Space between Characters

Illustrator lets you adjust the amount of horizontal space between characters of text. When you adjust the space between a pair of characters, Illustrator calls it kerning. When you adjust the space between three or more characters, Illustrator calls it tracking.

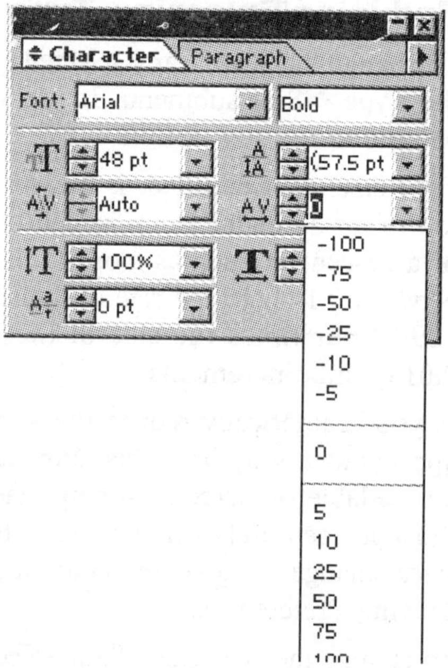

Illustrator provides option boxes in the Character palette for both kerning and tracking – commands for these don't exist in the Type menu and appear only in the Character palette. When you click with the type tool to position the insertion marker between two characters, you will want to use the Kerning option box. When you select so much as a single character, the Tracking option box is the one for you. Don't worry if you get them confused – enter a value in the Kerning option box when you're trying to change the tracking or vice versa – because Illustrator will promptly respond by either doing nothing or flashing some annoying warning that you're mistreating it.

Changing Height and Width of Characters

The next options in the Character palette, Vertical Scale and Horizontal Scale modify the height and width of selected characters, respectively. You can expand or condense type anywhere from 1 to 10,000 percent (1/100 to 100 times its normal width) by entering a new value into either the Vertical Scale or Horizontal Scale option box and pressing Return/Enter.

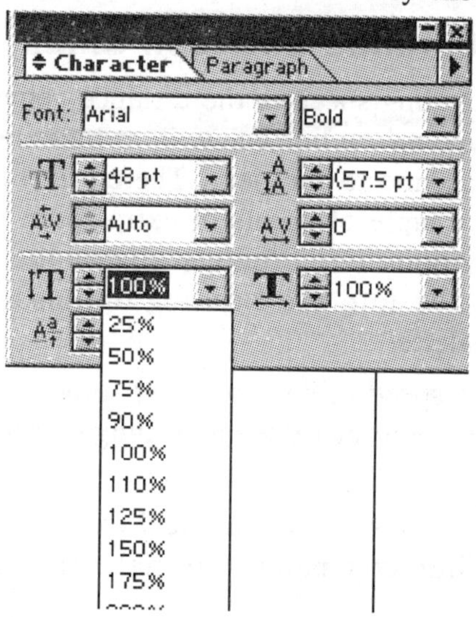

Changing the height or width of a character distorts. The Vertical Scale and Horizontal Scale options do not create the same effect as designer-condensed or expanded fonts. For example, the figure on the next page shows two variations on Arial for the alphabet XYZ. In the first example, I took 200-point Arial Bold and scaled it 50 percent horizontally. You would get almost the same result if you were to scale 115-point type vertically to 175 percent – go ahead and try it. Notice how the horizontal bars of the X and Y are much thicker than the vertical stems. This is because Horizontal Scale affects vertical proportions and leaves horizontal proportions untouched.

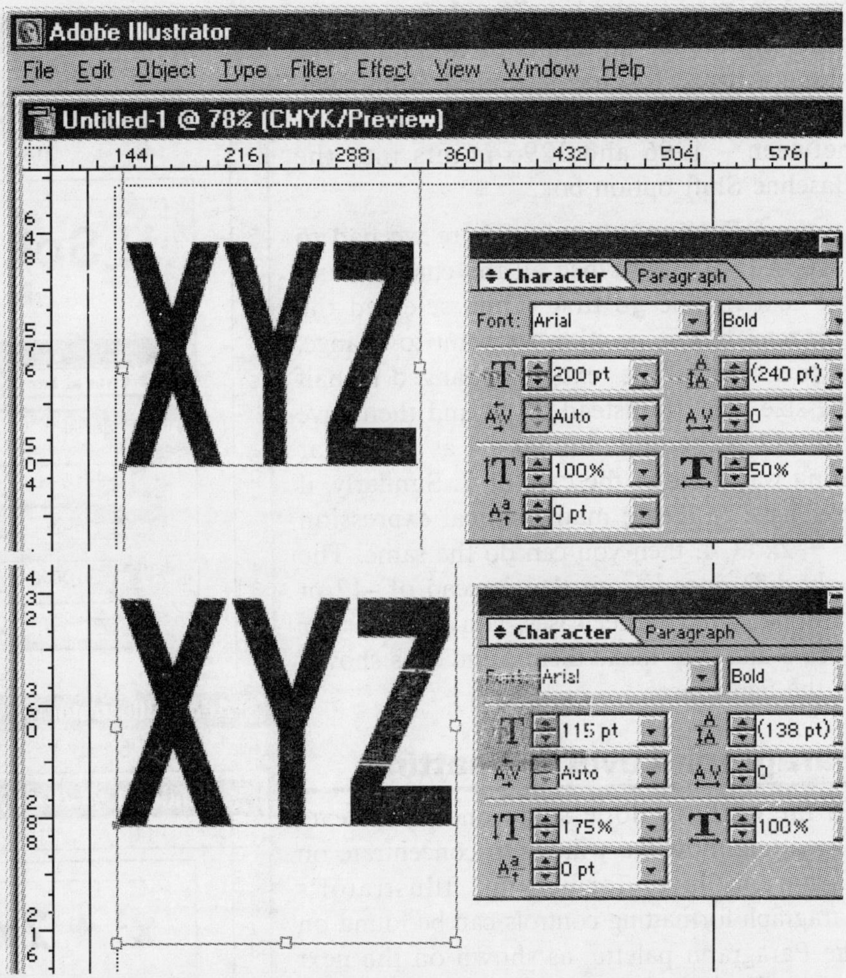

With this in mind, you should remember a few things when using the Vertical Scale or Horizontal Scale option:

- ❑ If you want the type to appear distorted, go for broke. There are no hard and fast rules in page design; type that specifically calls attention to itself can be just as effective as type that doesn't, if you have a bold design and an open-minded audience.
- ❑ If slightly widening or narrowing a few lines of type will make them fit better on the page, you can get away with Horizontal Scale values between 95 and 105 percent; no one will notice.
- ❑ Changing both the vertical and horizontal factors by the same amount is the same as changing the size. So if you enter 50 percent into both the Vertical Scale and Horizontal Scale option boxes, the result is the same as if you had change the value in the Size option box to half of its original value.

Superscript and Subscript

The Baseline Shift option in the lower half of the Character palette determines the distance between the selected type and its baseline. A positive value, or called Superscript, raises the characters above the normal text; a negative value, also called Subscript, lowers characters below the normal text. The default value of 0 leaves them sitting on the baseline, where they typically belong.

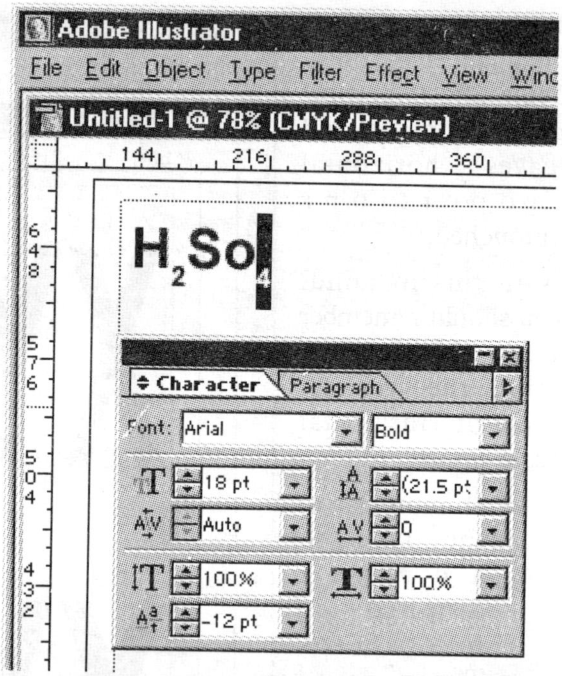

You can modify the baseline shift to create superscripts and subscripts or to adjust type along a path. To change the baseline shift, select some type and then enter any value between – 1296 and 1296 points into the Baseline Shift option box.

In the following example, where we had to type in H_2So_4, we typed all the characters of the text in one go first. Then selected the character whose position we want to change, in this case 4. The text was changed to half the size, i.e., 18 instead of 36 and then gave it a –12 point shift, to make 4 as $_4$. Similar thing was done in the case of 2. Similarly, if you have to create mathematical expression $x^3 + 2x^2 + 4$, then you can do the same. The only difference here is that instead of –12 pt as done in the earlier cases, you do 12 pt for both 3 and 2 to make them ^{3} and ^{2}, as shown in the figure here.

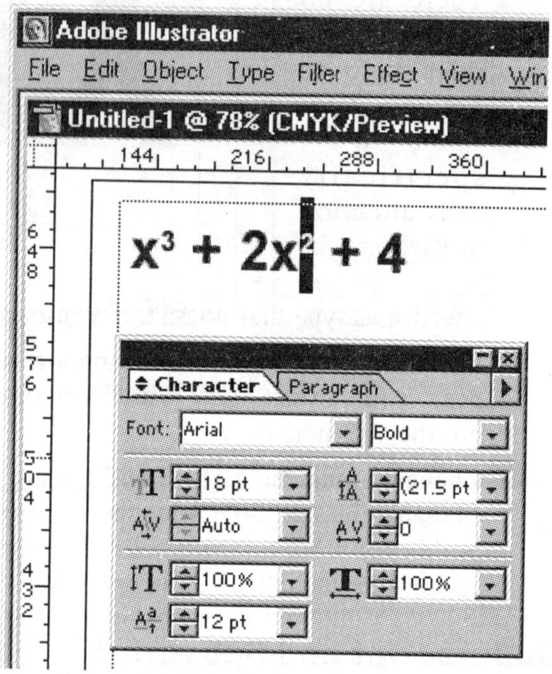

Paragraph-Level Formatting

So far we have done some character level formatting, now we will try to concentrate on paragraph level formatting. Illustrator's paragraph formatting controls can be found on the Paragraph palette, as shown on the next page. To display the palette, choose Type>>Paragraph or press Ctrl-M. By default the Paragraph palette is collapsed.

Choose the Show Options command from the Paragraph palette submenu to expand the palette and display the options. Various options of the dialog box are shown on the next page. You can show/hide the Paragraph palette by pressing Ctrl+M again.

Let us now see the various options of the paragraph dialog box.

Alignment

It is your choice to have the text aligned in a particular manner. Those of you who are familiar with Word Processing must be knowing more about text alignment than others. By alignment you can do the following:

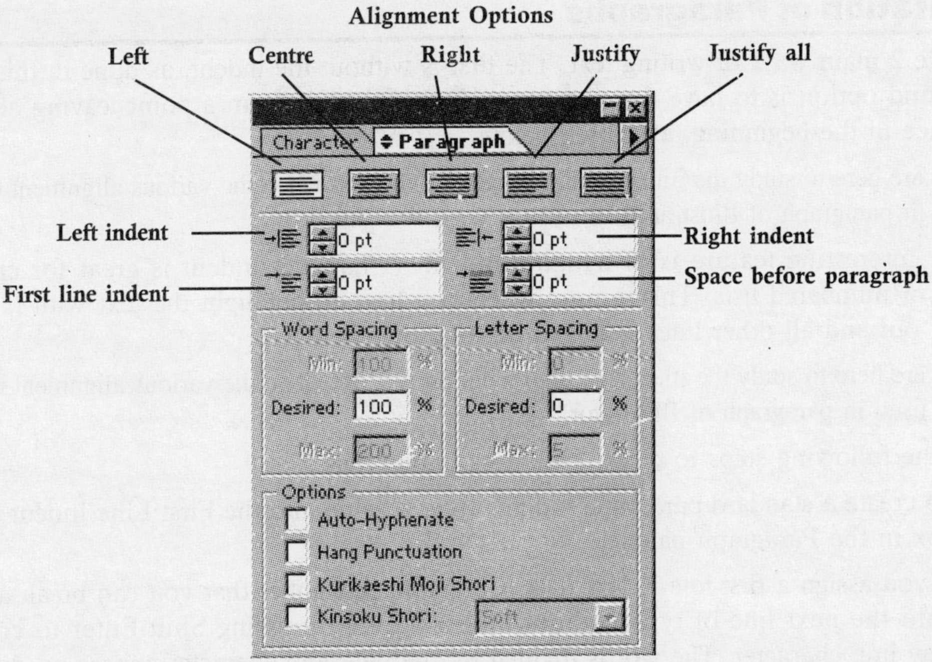

- To align a paragraph so that all the left edges line up (flush left, ragged right), press Ctrl-Shift-L or select the first alignment icon in the Paragraph palette. For example,

We are here to study the impact of alignment on the text when the various alignment options are used in paragraph of Illustrator.

- To center all lines in a paragraph, press Ctrl-Shift-C or select the second Alignment icon in the Paragraph palette. For example,

We are here to study the impact of alignment on the text when the various alignment options are used in paragraph of Illustrator.

- To make the right edges of a paragraph line up (flush right, ragged left), press Ctrl-Shift-R or select the third Alignment icon. For example,

We are here to study the impact of alignment on the text when the various alignment options are used in paragraph of Illustrator.

- You can also justify a paragraph, which stretches all lines except the last line of a paragraph so they entirely fill the width of the next block. To justify a paragraph, press Ctrl-shift-J or select the fourth Alignment icon. For example,

We are here to study the impact of alignment on the text when the various alignment options are used in paragraph of Illustrator.

- If you want to force justify the last line in a paragraph, press Ctrl-Shift-F or click the last Alignment icon in the Paragraph palette. This forces the last line to finish at the end of the line.

We are here to study the impact of alignment on the text when the various alignment options are used in paragraph of Illustrator.

Indentation of Paragraphs

There are 2 main ways of writing text. The first is without the indent, as done in this book. The second option is to have the first line indented to start from a point leaving about ½ inch space in the beginning, as shown below.

We are here to study the impact of alignment on the text when the various alignment options are used in paragraph of Illustrator.

Another interesting feature is of hanging indent. A hanging indent is great for creating bulleted or numbered lists. This is used when you have to highlight the text with first line standing out and all other lines indented in, as shown below.

- We are here to study the impact of alignment on the text when the various alignment options are used in paragraph of Illustrator.

Follow the following steps to create indenting paragraphs.

- To create a standard paragraph indent, enter a value into the First Line Indent option box in the Paragraph palette.
- If you assign a first-line indent to a paragraph, remember that you can break a word onto the next line of type without indenting it by pressing Shift-Enter to create a new line character. The words divided by the new line character appear on different lines, but are part of the same paragraph.
- To create a hanging indent, enter a positive value into the Left Indent option box and the inverse of that value in the First Line Indent option box.
- You can have to set the tab so the first lines up with the others. You can press the Tab key to get the bullet to insert a tab character. Then choose the Type>>Tab Rulers command to display the Tabs palette and created a left tab.

Paragraph Spacing

You can have some space after and before the paragraph. For this you have to use Spacing Before Paragraph option box to insert some extra space before a selected paragraph. This so-called paragraph leading helps separate one paragraph from another, much like a first-line indent. Most designers use first-line indents or paragraph leading to distinguish paragraphs, but not both. The two together are generally considered design overkill. In this particular book, a paragraph spacing of 9 points have been used.

Letters and Words Spacing

The middle options in the Paragraph palette let you control the amount of space that Illustrator places between words and characters in a text block. As you might imagine, word spacing controls the amount of space between words; letter spacing controls the amount of space between the letters.

There are two primary reasons for manipulating spacing:

- To give a paragraph a generally tighter or looser appearance. You control this general spacing using the Desired options.

- ❑ To determine the range of spacing manipulations Illustrators can use when justifying a paragraph. Illustrator tightens up some lines and loosens others to make them fit the exact width of your text block. You specify limits using the Min. and Max. options.

When spacing flush left, right or centered paragraphs, Illustrator relies entirely on the two Desired values. In fact, the other options are dimmed. All values are measured as a percentage of a standard space, as the information contained in the current font determines. For example, a Desire Word Spacing value of 100 percent inserts the width of one space character between each pair of words in a paragraph.

Reducing of enlarging this percentage makes the space between words bigger or smaller. A Desired Letter Spacing of 10 percent inserts 10 inserts of the width of a space character between each pair of letters. Negative percentages squeeze letters together and a value of 0 percent spaces letters normally.

If you select one or more justified paragraphs, the Min and Max. options become available. These values give Illustrator some wiggle room when tightened and spreading lines of type. Word Spacing and Letter Spacing values must be within these ranges:

- ❑ The Min. Word Spacing value must be at least 0 percent; the Min. Letter Spacing must be at least 50 percent. Both must be less than their respective Desired values.
- ❑ The Max. Word spacing value can be no higher than 1,000 percent; Max. Letter Spacing can be no more than 500 percent. Neither can be less than its respective Desired value.
- ❑ Each desired value can be no less than its corresponding Min. value and no higher than the corresponding Max. value.

Following examples show the various options.

Activating Automatic Hyphenation

There are three ways to hyphenate text in Illustrator:

- ❑ Enter a standard hyphen character (-) between two words you want to hyphenate. This is usually found in hyphenated words like 3-inch mark or hyphenated names such as Biddle-Barrows. Don't use the standard hyphen between the letters of a word, though. If you edit the text later on, you may end up with stray hyphens breaking a word in the middle of a line.
- ❑ A much better idea is to insert a discretionary hyphen, which disappears any time it is not needed. You can enter a discretionary hyphen by pressing Ctrl-Shift-hyphen(-). If no hyphen appears when you enter this character, it simply means that the addition of the hyphen does not help Illustrator break the word. You can try inserting the character at a different location or expanding the width of the text block to permit the word to break.
- ❑ The third option is to let Illustrator do the hyphenating for you by selecting the Auto Hyphenate check box in the Paragraph palette.

If you do decide to us automatic hyphenation then this is how you will proceed.

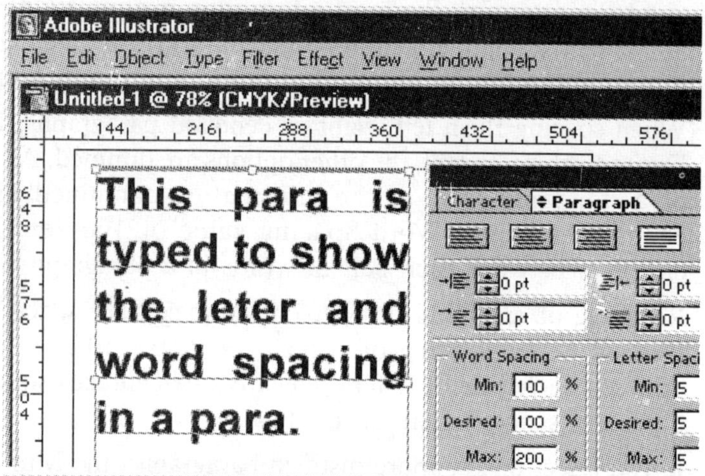

Turn on auto hyphenate: With the arrow tool, select the text block you want to hyphenate turn on the Auto Hyphenate check box in the Paragraph palette. Illustrator adds hyphens where it deems necessary.

Choose the hyphenation options: If you want to limit where and how hyphenation occurs, choose the Hyphenation command from the Paragraph palette pop-up menu. The Hyphenation Options dialog box, as shown above will appear.

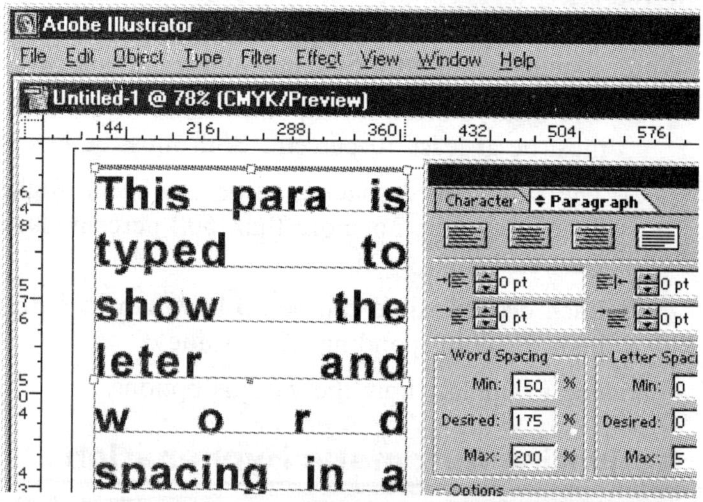

Specify how many letters must appear before and after a hyphen: In the Hyphenation Options dialog box, enter a value into the first Hyphenate option box to specify the minimum number of letters that can come between a hyphen and the beginning of a word. Enter a value into the next option box to determine the minimum number or letters between a hyphen and the end of a word. For example, with both values set to 2, Illustrator could split the word apple as ap-ple, because both the first and last syllables are at least two letters long.

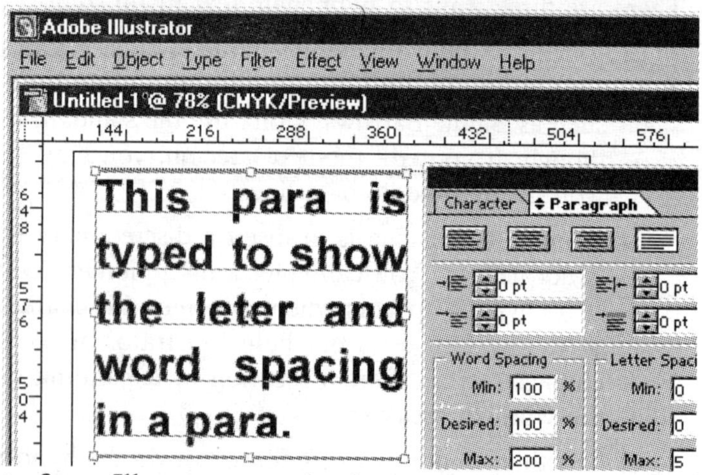

Specify the possible number of consecutive hyphens: If you want to limit the number of consecutive lines of Illustrator can hyphenate, select the Limit check box and enter the maximum limit in the option box. By default, the value is set to 3, so Illustrator can hyphenate no more than three consecutive lines before it has to permit one line to go without hyphenation. But as far as we're concerned, any more than two hyphenated lines in a row looks amateurish and interferes with legibility.

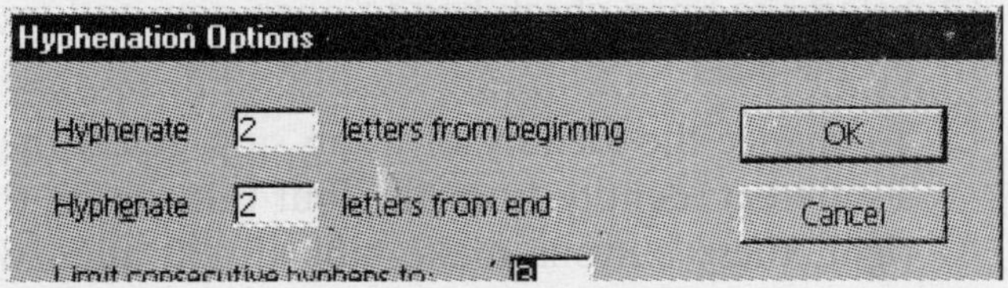

Prepare to groove as Illustrator implements all your secret hyphen-related desired: Click the OK button or press Enter.

Working with Tabs

Tabs have been there since the days of typewriter. But, unfortunately, there the tabs were restricted to only one, i.e., left one. Here we have the option of having 4 different type of tabs, i.e., Left, Right, Centre and Decimal. You use tabs to align character precisely.

There are really only two rules to using tabs:

1. Never press Tab twice in a row (thus creating two tab characters).
2. To specify the width of a tab character, adjust the tab stop settings in the Tabs palette.

Tabs Palette

Choose Type>>Tab Ruler or press Ctrl-Shift-t to display the Tabs palette, as shown here. This palette lets you position tab stops and align tabbed text.

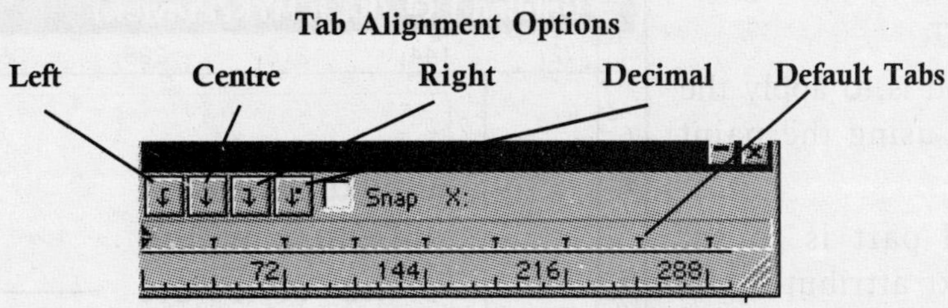

Like the Paragraph palette, the tab ruler affects entire paragraphs, whether they're entirely or only partially selected. The following items explain how the tab ruler works and offer a few guidelines for using it.

- When you first bring up the Tabs palette, Illustrator automatically aligns it to the selected paragraph. To align the palette to a different paragraph, select the paragraph and click in the size box on the far right side of the title bar (or just to the left of the Windows close box).
- To create a tab stop, click in the ruler along the bottom of the palette or click inside the tab strip just above the ruler. If you drag the tab stop, Illustrator projects a vertical alignment guide from the Tab palette. The line moves with the tab stop, permitting you to predict more accurately the results of your adjustment. The Tabs palette also tracks the numerical position of the tab stop – with respect to the left edge of the text block – just below title bar.
- When you create a new tab stop, all default tab stops (those little Ts) to the left of the new stop disappear. The default stops merely tell Illustrator to space tabbed text every half inch.
- A question mark in the tab ruler means that at least one line of selected text does not align to that tab stop. Just click the tab stop to make all selected lines align.

- ❑ Select the Snap check box to align new and moved tab stops to the nearest increment on the ruler.
- ❑ To change the identity of a tab stop, select the tab stop by clicking on it, then select a different identity from the four buttons on the left side of the palette. From left to right, these buttons make tabbed text align with the left side, center, right side or decimal point.
- ❑ To delete a tab stop, drag it upward, off the tab strip and out of the palette. The X: item reads *delete*. To delete all tab stops, Shift-drag upward on the leftmost tab stop in the ruler.
- ❑ You can also cycle through the units of measurement by pressing Ctrl-Shift-U.

The Text Eyedropper and Paint Bucket

Illustrator gives you a easy way to sample the text attributes from one set of text and then apply it to another. You do it by using the eyedropper and paint bucket tools. There are three parts to using these tools.

- The first part is to sample the text attributes using the eyedropper.
- The second is to apply the attributes using the paint bucket.
- The final part is to set which text attributes the tools should copy and apply.

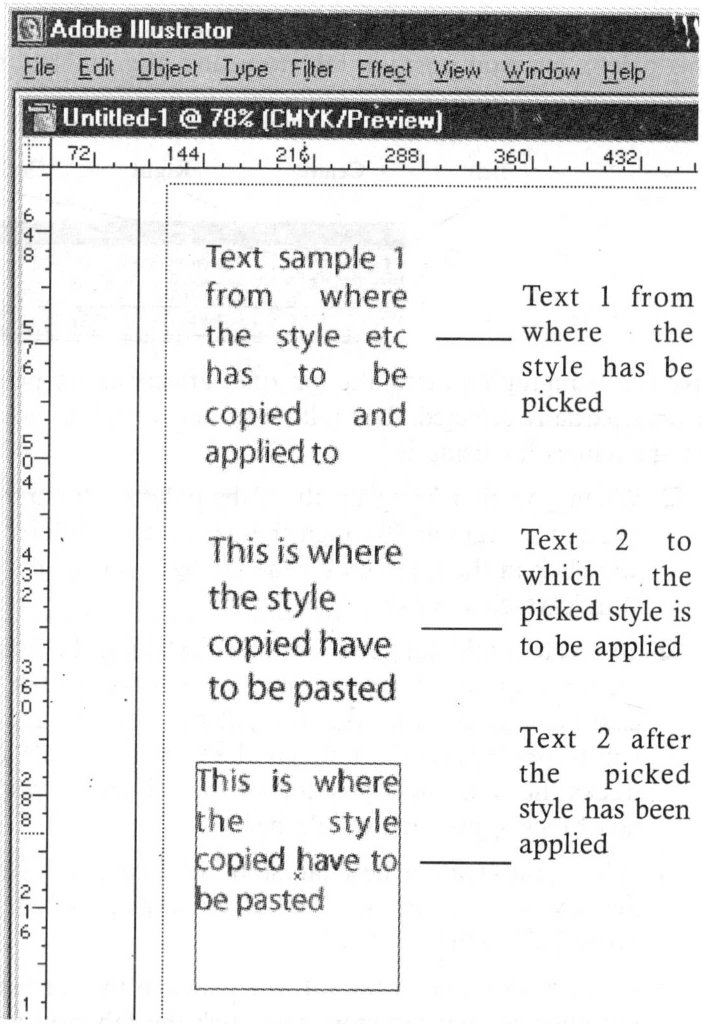

Sucking up Attributes with the Eyedropper

To sample text attributes with the eyedropper tool, choose the eyedropper tool. Position the tool over the text that you want to sample. When a small T appears next to the eyedropper cursor, you know that the eyedropper is in the text mode.

Click or drag the eyedropper over the text that you want to sample. A click sucks up the text attributes exactly under the cursor. A drag samples the attributes from the text where the mouse button is released at the end of the drag. If you drag with the eyedropper, the tip of the eyedropper cursor turns black to show that the attributes are being sampled.

Next page shows the text after and before using the eyedropper key.

Pouring out Attributes with Paint Bucket

To apply text attributes, you can choose the paint bucket tool from the alternate eyedropper slot in toolbox. However, because, you most likely already have the eyedropper tool selected, simply hold the Alt key. This toggles between the eyedropper and paint bucket. Position the paint bucket over the text that you want to change. Look for the small T next to the cursor; this tells you that the paint bucket is in the text mode. Unlike the eyedropper, there is a real difference between clicking and dragging with the paint bucket. If you simply click with the paint bucket, you apply the text attributes to all the text in the text object.

However, you may want to apply text attributes to specific areas of a text object. To do that, you need to drag with the paint bucket tool across the text. As you drag, a box appears around the characters that are chosen. When you release the mouse button, those characters will be changed. If you don't see the T next to the paint bucket cursor, then the paint bucket will apply only the fill and stroke attributes of the text that has been sampled.

Configuring Eyedropper and Paint Bucket

By default, the eyedropper and paint bucket will sample and apply all the character and paragraph attributes of the text. However, you can configure the tools so that they sample and only certain attributes. For instance, you can set the tools so they sample and apply only character attributes, but not the paragraph ones.

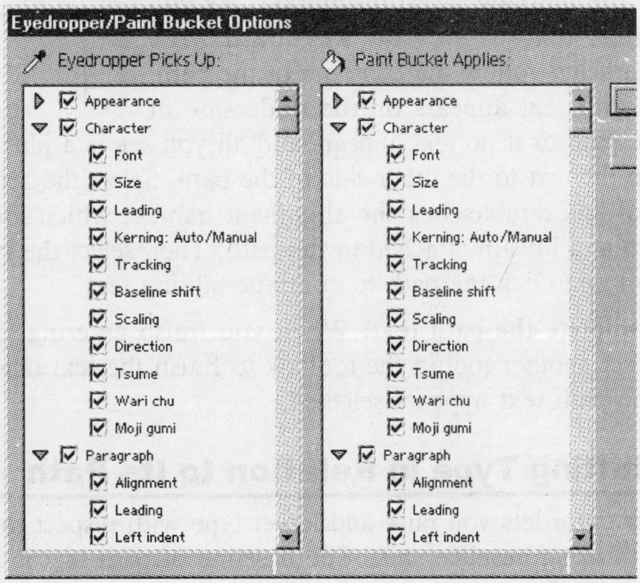

To configure the tools, double-click either the eyedropper or the paint bucket in the toolbox. The Eyedropper/Paint Bucket Options dialog box appears as shown below. Use the check boxes to choose which attributes you want each tool to recognize. The settings for the eyedropper and point bucket remain in effect for new documents and new sessions of Illustrator.

Creating Various Text Effects

Now we come to other part of the text, i.e., where you can attach text to a curve, wrap text inside an irregular outline, flow text from one text block to another and wrap text around graphics. If you plan to use Illustrator to create documents that contain a fair amount of text, you can import text from a word processor and then check the spelling, perform complex search and replace operations and even export the text back out to disk.

Merging Text with Curve

Illustrator lets you bind a line of text to a free-form path. To create type along the outline of a path, follow these simple steps:

Draw a path: Curved paths work better than those with sharp corners, so you'll probably want to avoid corner points and cusps and stick with smooth points. Ellipses, spirals, and softly sloping paths work best. Grab the smooth tool if you need to smooth out a path.

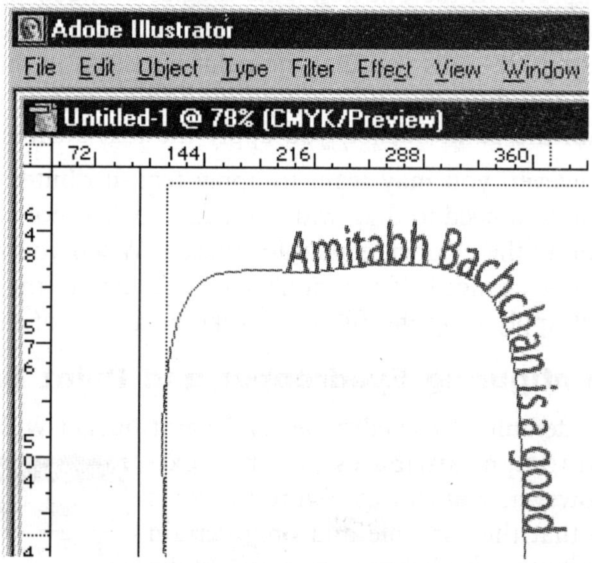

Select the path type tool: To get the path type tool, drag from the type tool in he toolbox to display a pop-up menu. The path type tool looks like a T on a slanted line.

Click the path and start typing: The point at which you click determines the position of the blinking insertion marker. As you enter text from the keyboard, the characters follow the contours of the path. If your text appears on the underside of the path or if no text appears and all you see is a plus sing inside a little box, your need to flip the text to the other side of the path. Select the arrow tool and double-click the alignment handle, which looks like and I-beam attached to the path. Then select the type tool and click the path to continue adding text.

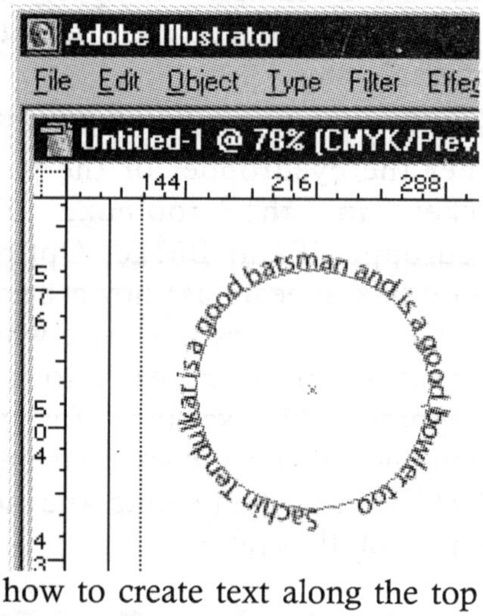

Complete the path text: When you finish entering text, select another tool in the toolbox to finish the text object. The path text appears selected.

Shifting Type in Relation to Its Path

Illustrator lets you raise and lower type with respect to its path using baseline shift. The baseline of path text is the path itself so moving type away from the baseline likewise moves it away from the path. The following steps demonstrate why baseline shift is useful. They show you how to create text along the top and bottom halves of a circle – a job for baseline shift if there ever was one.

Draw a circle: You know how to do it, shift-drag with the ellipse tool.

Alt-click with the type tool at the top of the circle: Illustrator snaps the alignment handle to the top center of the shape.

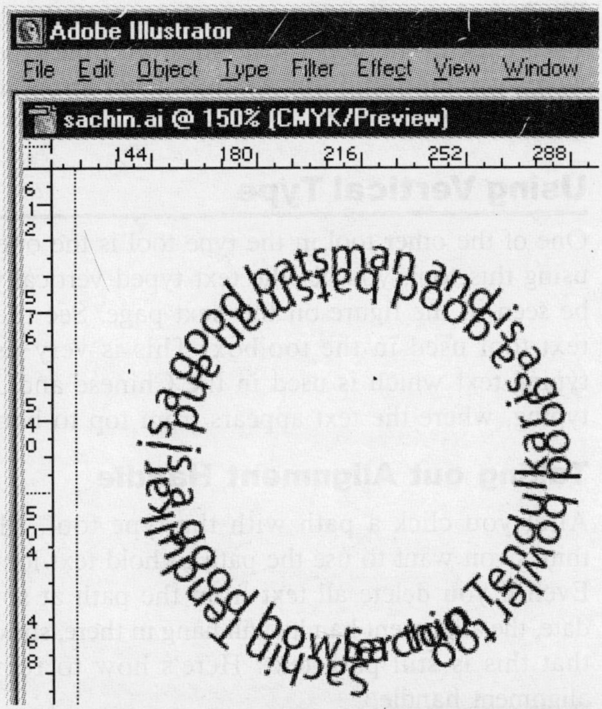

Enter the text you want to appear along the top of the path: Just enter the text which you want to, it can be just any text.

Center the text: Press Ctrl-Shift-C or click the second icon in the Paragraph palette. As long as the alignment handle is positioned at the top of the shape, you can use Illustrator's alignment formatting functions to position text around the handle. It comes in handy when you want to get things exactly right.

Format the text as desired: Press Ctrl-A to highlight the text. Then format at will. You may use any font or size, but on circle text looks good as Caps.

Clone your text: This is the most important step and one of the trickiest to pull off. First select the path text with the arrow tool. Then drag the alignment handle around the path to the bottom of the circle. Without releasing – don't release till we say so – drag upward so the type flips to the other side of the path. Then drag down ever so carefully until your cursor snaps onto the bottom point in the circle. Finally, press the Alt key and release the mouse button. You can now release the alt key. A clone of the type moves and flips to the interior of a cloned circle.

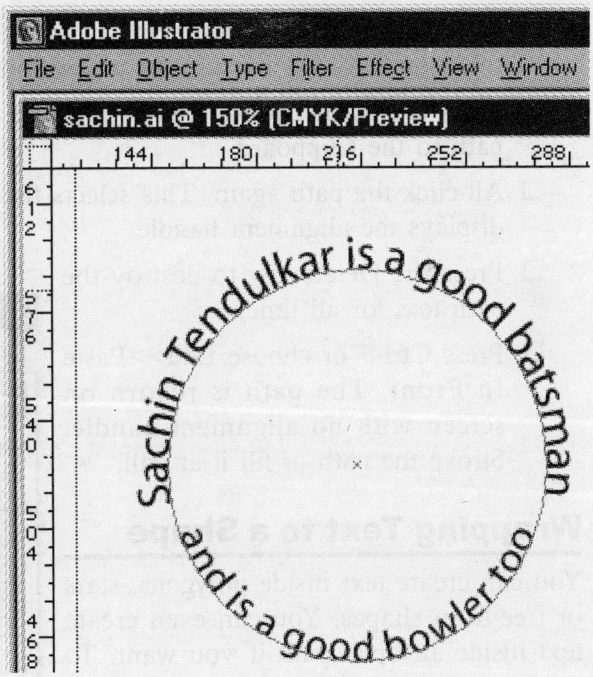

Edit the bottom type as desired: Click inside the cloned text with the type tool and press Ctrl-A to select it. Then enter the words that you want to appear along the bottom of the circle.

Shift the bottom text downward: You've noticed that the upper and lower text blocks don't align properly. You need to move the lower text outward without flipping it. While the text is still active, press Ctrl-A to highlight the lower text block. Because you want to lower the type with respect to its path, press Alt-Shift-down arrow to move the type downward 2 points.

Similarly lower the text along the top of the circle: Press Ctrl-Shift-A to deselect the text. Then click in the upper text block with the type tool and press Ctrl-A to highlight the first words you created. Press Alt-shift down arrow several times to lower the top text so it aligns with the bottom text.

Using Vertical Type

One of the other tool in the type tool is the one with vertical direction. When text is typed using this tool, you get the text typed vertically, as can be seen in the figure on the next page. See the type of text tool used in the toolbox. This is very useful for typing text which is used in the Chinese and Japanese typing, where the text appears from top to bottom.

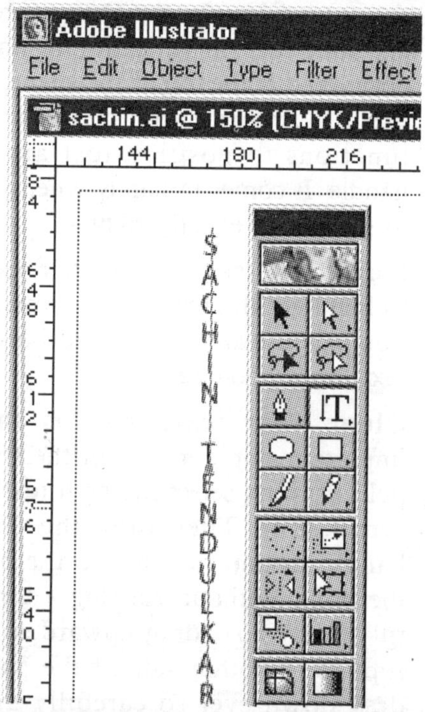

Taking out Alignment Handle

After you click a path with the type tool, Illustrator thinks you want to use the path to hold text for all time. Even if you delete all text from the path at some later date, the alignment handle will hang in there, showing you that this is still path text. Here's how to remove the alignment handle.

- Select the path by Alt-clicking it with the direct selection tool. Do not use the arrow tool.
- Press Ctrl-C or choose Edit>>Copy to copy the path to the Clipboard.
- Alt-click the path again. This selects the text and displays the alignment handle.
- Press the Delete key to destroy the path text for all time.
- Press Ctrl-F or choose Edit>>Paste In Front. The path is reborn on screen with no alignment handle. Stroke the path or fill it at will.

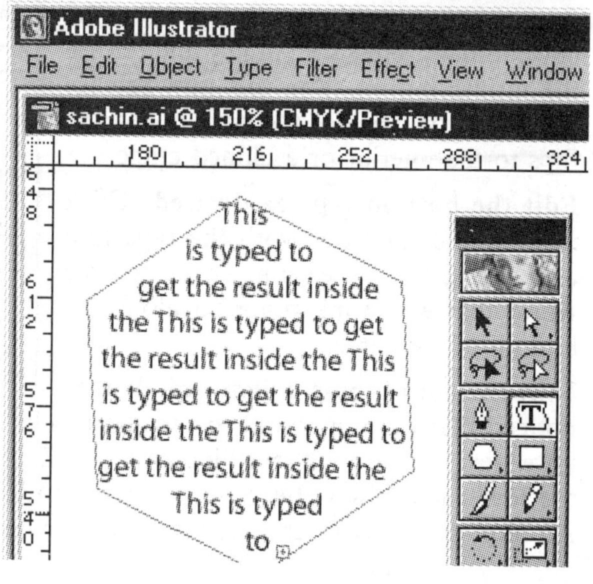

Wrapping Text to a Shape

You can create text inside polygons, stars or free-from shapes. You can even create text inside an open path if you want. To create type inside a path, do the following:

Draw a path: Unlike path text, area text works just as well with corner points as with smooth points. But keep the corners obtuse – wide rather than sharp. It's very difficult and in many cases impossible, to fill sharp corners with text.

Select the area type tool: Select the area type tool from the type tool pop-up menu in the tool box. The area type tool looks like a T trapped in Jell-O.

Click along the outline of the path and enter some text: You must click the outline of the path; you can't click inside the path to add text. A blinking insertion marker appears at the top of the path. As you enter text, it fills the path. Words that would otherwise exceed the edge of the shape wrap to next line.

Complete the path text: Select the type tool or some other tool to finish off the text block. You'll get something like the area text shown on the last page.

Wrapping Type Around Graphics

Illustrator was the first drawing program that allowed wrapping of text around graphics. This feature instructs Illustrator to wrap type automatically around the boundaries of one or more graphic objects.

Wrapping text around a graphic is a four-step process.

Select the paths that you want to wrap the text around: After selecting the paths with the arrow tool, choose Object>>Groupto keep the paths together.

Position the paths with respect to the text: Drag the group into position and then choose Object>>Arrange>> Bring To Front. The paths must be in front of the text block to wrap properly.

Select the text block that you want to wrap: Shift-click the text block with the arrow tool to add it to the selection. Illustrator can wrap text blocks and area text around graphics, but it cannot wrap point text or path text.

Wrap the text: Choose Type>>Wrap >>Make and Illustrator wraps the text around the graphics and fuses text and paths into a single wrapped object.

Importing and Exporting Text

Despite Illustrator's text capabilities, you should find it easier to use a word processing program to edit text and apply formatting attributes. You can also export text from Illustrator into these same word processing file formats. Doing so allows you to recover and work with text that has been laid out in an Illustrator document and even lets you transfer text that has been laid out in an Illustrator document and even lets you transfer it to a mightier layout program such as QuarkXPress.

When importing a text file, Illustrator reads the file from disk and copies it to the illustration window. As this copy is being made, the text file passes through a filter that converts the file's formatting commands into formatting commands recognised by Illustrator. Illustrator lets you import text in the following formats.

- Microsoft Word 6, 95, 97, 98, 2000
- RTF (Rich Text Format), Microsoft's coded file format.
- Plain text with no formatting Whatsoever, also known as with no formatting whatsoever, also known as ASCII.

The following list describes how Illustrator handles a few prevailing formatting attributes an offers a few suggestions for preparing each:

- **Typeface:** If Illustrator can't fine the typeface in your system – if the document was created on another machine, for example – it substitutes the default font, Myriad.
- **Type style:** Illustrator does not apply electronic styles the way word processors do. As a result, bold and italics styles convert successfully, but most others do not. If Illustrator comes across a style for which a stylized font does not exist – underline, outline, strikethrough, small caps and so on – the program simply ignores the style. The exceptions are superscript and subscript styles, which transfer intact thanks to Illustrator's baseline shift function.
- **Type size and leading:** All text retains the same size and leading specified in the word processor. If you assign automatic leading or single spacing inside the word processor, Illustrator substitutes its own automatic leading, which is 120 percent of the type size.
- **Alignment:** Illustrator recognizes paragraphs that are aligned left, center and right, as well as justified text.
- **Paragraph returns:** Illustrator successfully reads paragraph return character (which you create by pressing the Enter key).
- **Indents:** All paragraph indents, including first-line, left and right indents remain intact. (Hanging indents won't look quite right, because Illustrator doesn't import tab stops.) Adjusting the margins in your word processor may also affect indentation in Illustrator. To clear the indents, just click the individual Indent option names in Illustration Paragraph palette.
- **Paragraph spacing:** Some word processors divide paragraph spacing into two categories: "before spacing," which precedes the paragraph, and "after spacing," which follows the paragraph. Illustrator combines them into the Leading before —value in the Paragraph palette, essentially retaining the same effect.
- **Tabs, tab stops and tab leaders:** Illustrator imports tab characters successfully. But it ignores the placement of tab stops and tab leaders (such as dots

and dashes) are a complete mystery to the program. Use the Tabs palette to reset the tab stops as desired.

- ❑ **Special characters:** Many word processors provide access to special characters that are not part of the standard character set. These include em spaces, nonbreaking hyphens, automatic page numbers, date and time stamps and so on. Of these, only the discretionary hyphen character transfers successfully.
- ❑ **Page markings:** Illustrator ignores page breaks in imported text as well as headers, footers and footnotes.

If you can't find a formatting option in this list, chances are Illustrator simply ignores it.

Spell Checking

Spell checkers are a must for most of the programs, in fact, that even Illustrator offers one. So can check the spelling of your text in the following manner.

Choose File>>Check Spelling: Because Illustrator automatically checks the spelling of all text, hidden or visible, in your drawing, you don't have to select any text. Illustrator sets about revealing your mistakes. If Illustrator doesn't locate any words missing from its dictionary, it displays an egostroking message about your excellent spelling. If the program finds mistakes, it lists all mistakes throughout the entire document in the Misspelled Words list at the top of the Check Spelling dialog box, as shown on the next page.

Select all words that are spelling properly: Scroll through the Misspelled Words list to see which words are truly misspelled and which words Illustrator is simply too inexperienced in the ways of the world to know. If a word is spelled to your satisfaction, you can either add it to Illustrator's dictionary or simply skip the word for the time being.

Click the Add to List button: This adds the selected words to Illustrator's auxiliary dictionary, so that the program will never again bug you about the spelling. If you'd rather ignore the words for the time being, click the Skip button. Click Skip all to tell Illustrator to ignore all occurrences of these particular words.

Select a word that's misspelled: To correct a word that is indeed misspelled, select it from the Misspelled Words list. Illustrator highlights the first occurrence of the word in the story and displays a few alternative spellings in the Suggested Corrections list.

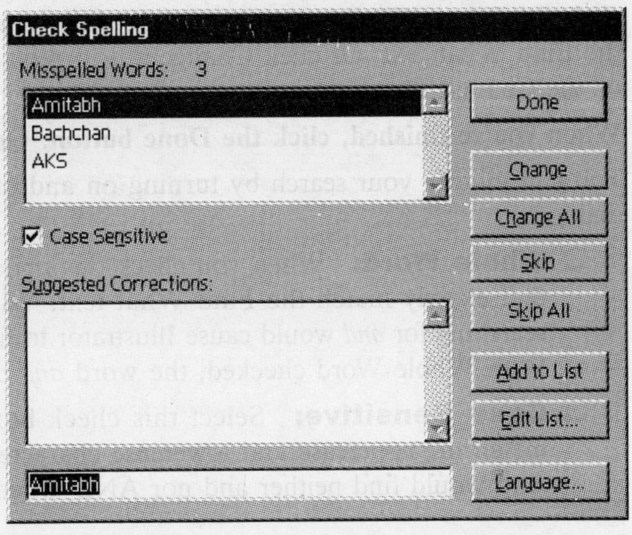

Select the proper spelling: If one of the alternative spellings in the Suggested Corrections list is correct, click it. If none of the spellings is correct, enter the new spellings in the option box below the list.

Click the Change button: Or you can press the Enter key or double-click the proper spelling in the Suggested Corrections list. If you know that many words are misspelled in the same say, click the Change All button to correct all misspellings at once. Illustrator corrects the spelling of the words in the illustration window and moves on to the next misspelled word.

End the spell checking: After you tell Illustrator to either add, skip or change every word in the Misspelled Words list, an alert box tells you it's finished. If you want to cut things off early, click the Done button, press the Escape key, or press Ctrl-(Period).

Search and Replace

Another of word processing strong point is search and replace. It is available in Illustrator too. As you know it is used to find a particular word in the text and if required, replaced with another word. This is how it is done.

Click with the type tool on the location where you want to begin the search: If you have selected the arrow tool, for example, Illustrator searches all stores throughout the entire drawing, from beginning to end. But if you want to limit your search to a specific area of a story, click in the story with the type tool. By default, Illustrator searches forward from the insertion marker' it does not search the text before the insertion marker. You can reserve the direction of the search by selecting the Search Backward check box.

Choose Type>>Find/Change: Illustrator brings up the Find/change dialog box, as shown on the next page.

Enter the text you want to find and the text you want to replace it with: Enter the search text in the Find What option box, press Tab and then enter the replacement text in the Change to option box. If you don't want to replace the text – you're just trying to find it – don't enter anything in the Change To option box.

Click the Find Next button: Or press Enter. Illustrator highlights the first occurrence of the word in the illustration window.

Replace the word and move on: Click the Change button to replace the selected text. Or click the Change/Find button to replace the text and then look for the next occurrence of the Find What text. Or click Change All to replace all Find What text with the contents of the Change To option box.

When you're finished, click the Done button: Or press Ctrl-(period) or Esc.

You can modify your search by turning on and off the check boxes in the middle of the dialog box:

- ❑ **Whole Word:** When you check this option, you limit the search to whole words that exactly match the Find What text. With this option unchecked, for example, searching for *and* would cause Illustrator to find the characters inside *grand* and *bland*. With Whole Word checked, the word *and* must appear by itself.
- ❑ **Case Sensitive:** Select this check box to search for characters that exactly match the uppercase and lowercase characters in the Find What text. Searching for And would find neither and nor AND when this option is selected.

- **Search Backward:** This option begins the search at the insertion marker and proceeds backward toward the beginning of the story.
- **Wrap Around:** To search the entire illustration, no matter where the insertion marker is currently located, select Wrap Around. This option begins the search at the insertion marker and proceeds to the end of the story, starts over at the next story, starts again at the beginning of the first story and winds up back at the insertion marker.

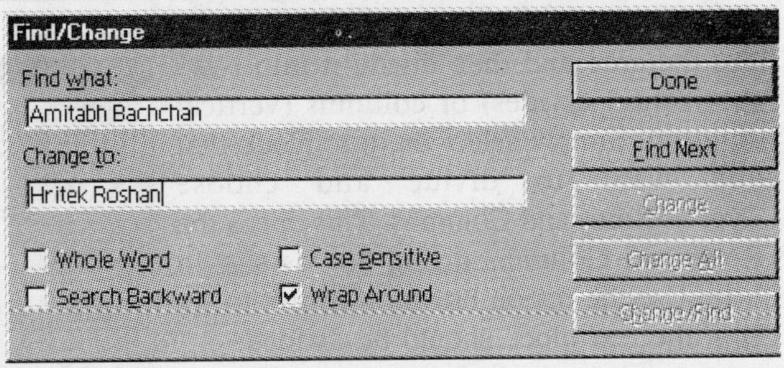

Replacing Fonts

You can press the Type>>Find Font key combination to launch another of Illustrator's amazing search functions. This time, instead of replacing words, Illustrator lets you search for one font and replace it with another. For this do the following:

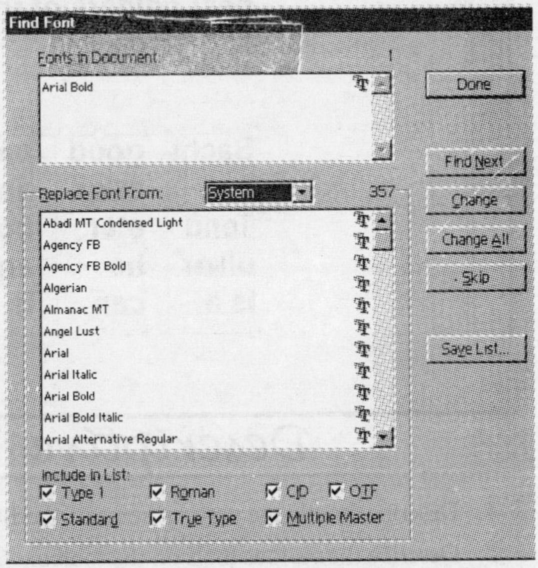

Choose Type>>Find Font: In response, the Find Font dialog box comes on screen, as shown here.

Select the font that you want to remove from the Fonts in Document list: Illustrator highlights each occurrence of the font in the illustration window.

Select the substitute font from the Replace Font From list: Initially, this list contains only the names of those fonts that are used in the current illustration. If you want to choose from a wider variety of fonts, select the System command from the Replace Font From pop-up menu, which instructs Illustrator to list every font loaded on your system. You can pause the font listing by clicking anywhere on an empty portion of the dialog box. To start the listing again, turn on and off one of the check boxes at the bottom of the dialog box.

Click Change or one of the other buttons: The Change button replaces the first occurrence of the bad font and searches for the next. To change all occurrences of the font simultaneously, click the Change All button. If you're feeling a little more selective, you can opt not to change the found font and click the Find Next button to ignore that occurrence of a font and move on to the next. The Skip button performs the exact same function as the Find Next button.

Click the Done button when you're finished: Or press Return, Escape or Ctrl-. (period).

Using Rows and Columns

The Rows and Columns of Illustrator command lets you create a single text block that fills the area and then divide it into rows (horizontal divides) or columns (vertical dividers). Simply select the text block that you want to divide and choose Type>>Rows and Columns. This opens the Rows and Columns dialog box as shown here. Use the option boxes or arrows to set how the text block should be divided.

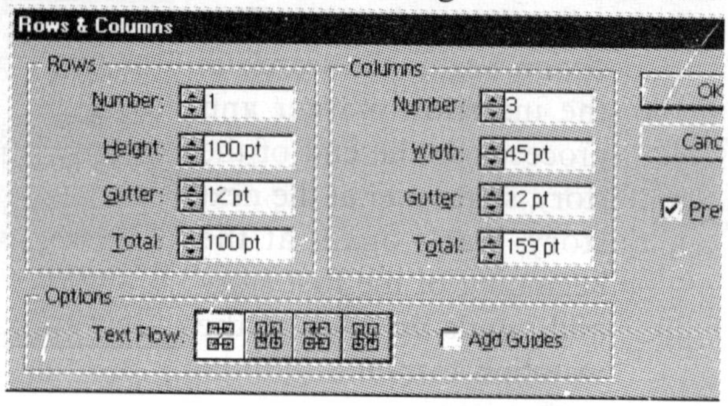

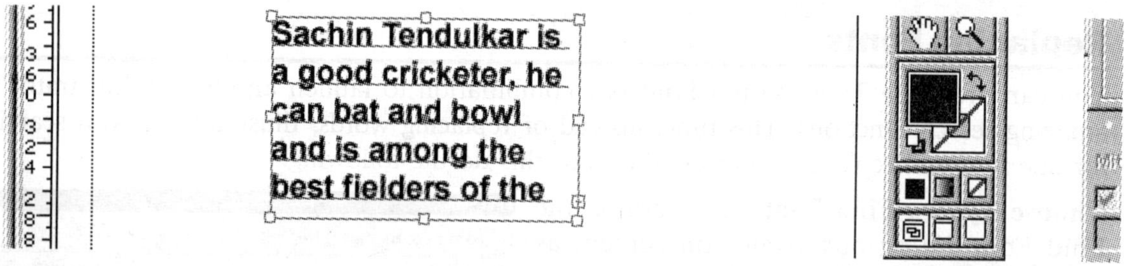

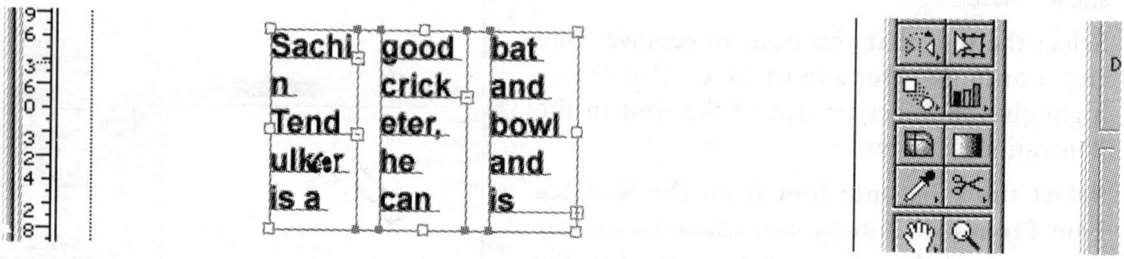

Descriptive Type Questions

1. Describe, briefly the various items of the Illustrator screen.
2. Describe the various tools on the toolbox.
3. Describe the contents of the following Preferences.

   Type and Auto — Units and Undo

   Guides and Grid — Smart Guides

   Hyphenation Options — Plug-ins and Scratch Disk

   Files and Clipboard
4. How would you customize a Palette's Appearance
5. How would you do the colour settings?

6. How would you position the pages on the artboard?
7. Describe the process of opening an existing file.
8. Describe the process of placing an image on artboard.
9. Describe the options of Links Palette.
10. Which are the various file formats accepted by Illustrator.
11. Describe the process of saving a file in Illustrator.
12. Describe the process of saving a file in EPS format.
13. What do you understand by Points and Segments?
14. What are Strokes and Fills?
15. Describe the various methods of drawing a rectangle.
16. How is an Ellipse drawn in Illustrator?
17. How would you draw different shapes at an angle?
18. Describe the process of creating the followings:
    (a) Stars (b) Spirals
    (c) Polygons (d) Double Star
19. Describe the working of Arrows and Lassos.
20. What can you do with the Plain Black Arrow Tool?
21. What is Direct Selection Tool? How is it used?
22. How would you select an object using Black Lasso?
23. How would you select with White Lasso?
24. How would you select everything on the artboard?
25. How would inverse all the selection?
26. What do you understand by Dragging?
27. What is the function of Pen tool?
28. Describe the working with the Pen tool.
29. How would you draw curves?
30. How would you convert smooth points to cusp?
31. How would you add points to a path?
32. How would you remove points from a path?
33. Describe the various Redo and Undo Operations.
34. How do you create text objects?
35. How is text created in blocks?
36. How would you resize and reshape the text blocks?
37. How would you select and edit the text?
38. Describe the process of selecting the text with Type tool.
39. How would you add more text to the text block?
40. Describe the process of formatting text.

41. What all you can change at Character level formatting?
42. How can you change the space between characters?
43. Describe the process of changing Height and Width of the characters.
44. How would you create Superscript and Subscript?
45. What sort of alignments are used in Paragraph level formatting?
46. How would you change the letter and word spacing?
47. How would you hyphenate the text?
48. How would you set the tabs in the text?
49. Describe the complete process of sucking attributes from the text and pouring them on another text.
50. What are the type of type effects that you can perform in Illustrator?
51. How can you merge text with the curve?
52. How would you shift the text in relation to its path?
53. Describe the process of typing the text in vertical format.

6 Keyboard Shortcuts

Microsoft Windows

General keyboard shortcuts

Press	*To*
Ctrl+C	Copy.
Ctrl+X	Cut.
Ctrl+V	Paste.
Ctrl+Z	Undo.
Delete	Delete.
Shift+Delete	Delete selected item permanently without placing the item in the Recycle Bin.
Ctrl while dragging an item	Copy selected item.
Ctrl+Shift while dragging an item	Create shortcut to selected item.
F2	Rename selected item.
Ctrl+Right Arrow	Move the insertion point to the beginning of the next word.
Ctrl+Left Arrow	Move the insertion point to the beginning of the previous word.
Ctrl+Down Arrow	Move the insertion point to the beginning of the next paragraph.
Ctrl+Up Arrow	Move the insertion point to the beginning of the previous paragraph.
Ctrl+Shift with any of the arrow keys	Highlight a block of text.
Shift with any of the arrow keys	Select more than one item in a window or on the desktop, or select text within a document.
Ctrl+A	Select all.
F3	Search for a file or folder.
Alt+Enter	View properties for the selected item.
Alt+F4	Close the active item, or quit the active program.
Alt+Enter	Displays the properties of the selected object.
Alt+Spacebar	Opens the shortcut menu for the active window.
Ctrl+F4	Close the active document in programs that allow you to have multiple documents open simultaneously.
Alt+Tab	Switch between open items.
Alt+Esc	Cycle through items in the order they were opened.
F6	Cycle through screen elements in a window or on the desktop.

F4	Display the Address bar list in My Computer or Windows Explorer.
Shift+F10	Display the shortcut menu for the selected item.
Alt+Spacebar	Display the System menu for the active window.
Ctrl+Esc	Display the **Start** menu.
Alt+Underlined letter in a menu name	Display the corresponding menu.
Underlined letter in a command name on an open menu	Carry out the corresponding command.
F10	Activate the menu bar in the active program.
Right Arrow	Open the next menu to the right, or open a submenu.
Left Arrow	Open the next menu to the left, or close a submenu.
F5	Refresh the active window.
Backspace	View the folder one level up in My Computer or Windows Explorer.
Esc	Cancel the current task.
Shift when you insert a CD into the CD-ROM drive	Prevent the CD from automatically playing.

Dialog box keyboard shortcuts

Press	*To*
Ctrl+Tab	Move forward through tabs.
Ctrl+Shift+Tab	Move backward through tabs.
Tab	Move forward through options.
Shift+Tab	Move backward through options.
Alt+Underlined letter	Carry out the corresponding command or select the corresponding option.
Enter	Carry out the command for the active option or button.
Spacebar	Select or clear the check box if the active option is a check box.
Arrow keys	Select a button if the active option is a group of option buttons.
F1	Display Help.
F4	Display the items in the active list.
Backspace	Open a folder one level up if a folder is selected in the **Save As** or **Open** dialog box.

Natural keyboard shortcuts

You can use the following keyboard shortcuts with a Microsoft Natural Keyboard or any other compatible keyboard that includes the Windows logo key () and the Application key ()..

Press	*To*
	Display or hide the **Start** menu.
+Break	Display the **System Properties** dialog box.
+D	Show the desktop.
+M	Minimize all windows.

+Shift+M	Restores minimized windows.
+E	Open My Computer.
+F	Search for a file or folder.
Ctrl+ +F	Search for computers.
+F1	Display Windows Help.
+ L	Lock your computer if you are connected to a network domain, or switch users if you are not connected to a network domain.
+R	Open the **Run** dialog box.
	Display the shortcut menu for the selected item.
+U	Open Utility Manager.

Accessibility keyboard shortcuts

Press	*To*
Right Shift for eight seconds	Switch FilterKeys on and off.
Left Alt +left Shift +Print Screen	Switch High Contrast on and off.
Left Alt +left Shift +Num Lock	Switch MouseKeys on and off.
Shift five times	Switch StickyKeys on and off.
Num Lock for five seconds	Switch ToggleKeys on and off.
+U	Open Utility Manager.

Windows Explorer keyboard shortcuts

Press	To
End	Display the bottom of the active window.
Home	Display the top of the active window.
Num Lock+Asterisk on numeric keypad (*)	Display all subfolders under the selected folder.
Num Lock+Plus Sign on numeric keypad (+)	Display the contents of the selected folder.
Num Lock+Minus Sign on numeric keypad (-)	Collapse the selected folder.
Left Arrow	Collapse current selection if it's expanded, or select parent folder.
Right Arrow	Display current selection if it's collapsed, or select first subfolder.

Adobe Photoshop

Viewing

Action	*Result*
Double-click hand tool, or Ctrl + Ø (zero)	Fits image in window
Double-click zoom tool, or Alt + Ctrl + Ø (zero)	100% magnification
Ctrl + key or - key	Zooms in or out
Ctrl + spacebar, or Alt + spacebar	Zoom in pointer or Zoom out pointer

Shift + Enter in Navigator palette percentage box active	Applies zoom percentage, and keeps zoom
Ctrl + drag over preview in Navigator palette	Zooms in on specified area of an image
Spacebar + drag, or drag view area box in Navigator palette	Scrolls image with hand tool
Page Up or Page Down	Scrolls up or down 1 screen
Shift + Page Up or Page Down	Scrolls up or down 10 units
Home or End	Moves view to upper left corner or lower right corner
\	Toggles layer mask on/off as rubylith

Selecting and Moving Objects

Any marquee tool (except single column and single row) + drag	Repositions marquee while selecting
Any selection tool + Shift or Alt + drag	Adds to or subtracts from selection
Any selection tool + Shift + Alt + drag	Intersects a selection
Shift + drag	Constrains marquee to square or circle (if no other selections are active)
Alt + drag	Draws marquee from center (if no other selections are active)
Shift + Alt + drag	Constrains shape and draws marquee from center
Ctrl (except when hand tool or any pen tool, path, shape tool, slice, rectangle image map, circle image map, or polygon image map tool is selected)	Move tool
Alt + drag	Switches from Magnetic lasoo tool to Lasoo tool
Alt + click	Switches from Magnetic lasoo tool to Polygon lasoo tool
Move tool + Alt + drag selection	Moves copy of selection
Any selection + arrow keys	Moves selection area 1 pixel
Move tool + arrow keys	Moves selection 1 pixel
Ctrl + arrow keys	Moves layer 1 pixel when nothing selected on layer
Magnetic lasoo tool + [or]	Increases/decreases detection width
Crop tool + Enter or Esc	Accepts cropping or exits cropping
Measure tool + Alt + drag end point	Makes protractor
Shift key + drag guide	Snaps guide to ruler ticks
Alt + drag guide	Toggles guide orientation

Painting

Any painting tool + Alt (also any shape tool + Alt)	eyedropper tool

eyedropper tool + Alt + click	Selects background color
eyedropper tool + Shift key	eyedropper tool
eyedropper tool + Alt + click	Deletes eyedropper tool
Any painting or editing tool + number keys (e.g., 0 = 100%, 1 = 10%, 4 then 5 in quick succession = 45%) (For Airbrush, use Shift key + number keys)	Sets opacity, tolerance, strength, or exposure for painting mode
Any painting or editing tool + Shift key + number keys (e.g., 0 = 100%, 1 = 10%, 4 then 5 in quick succession = 45%) (For Airbrush, omit Shift key)	Sets flow for painting mode
Shift key + Plus key Minus key	Cycles through blending modes
Alt + Backspace, or Ctrl + Backspace	Fills selection/layer with foreground or background color
Alt + Ctrl + Backspace	Fills from history
Shift + Backspace	Displays Fill dialog box
/	Lock transparent pixels on/off
Any painting tool + Shift key + click	Connects points with a straight line

Editing

Ctrl + drag type when Type layer is selected	Moves type in image
Horizontal type tool + Shift key + Ctrl + L, C, or R	Aligns left, center, or right
Vertical type tool + Shift key + Ctrl + L, C, or R	Aligns top, center, or bottom
Shift key + arrow keys , or Shift key + Ctrl + arrow keys	Selects 1 character left/right or 1 line down/up, or 1 word left/right
Shift key + click	Selects characters from insertion point to mouse click point
Arrow keys, or Ctrl + Arrow keys	Moves 1 character left/right, 1 line down/up, or 1 word left/right
Shift key + click or click + drag	Designates new origin over existing type
Double-click, triple-click, quadruple-click, or quintuple-click	Selects word, line, paragraph, or story
Ctrl + H	Shows/Hides selection on selected type
Shift key + Ctrl + U	Toggles Underlining on/off
Shift key + Ctrl + /	Toggles Strikethrough on/off
Shift key + Ctrl + K	Toggles All Uppercase on/off
Shift key + Ctrl + H	Toggles Small Caps on/off
Shift key + Ctrl + +	Toggles Superscript on/off

Shift key + Alt + Ctrl + +	Toggles Subscript on/off
Shift key + Ctrl + X	Chooses 100% horizontal scale
Shift key + Alt + Ctrl + X	Chooses 100% vertical scale
Shift key + Alt + Ctrl + A	Chooses Auto leading
Shift key + Ctrl + Q	Chooses 0 for tracking
Shift key + Ctrl + J	Justifies paragraph, left aligns last line
Shift key + Ctrl + F	Justifies paragraph, forces last line
Shift key + Alt + Ctrl + H	Toggles paragraph hyphenation on/off
Shift key + Alt + Ctrl + T	Toggles single/every-line composer on/off
Shift key + Ctrl + < >	Decreases/increases type size of selected text 2 pts/px
Alt + Down Arrow Up Arrow	Decreases/increases leading 2 pts/px
Shift key + Alt + Down Arrow Up Arrow	Decreases/increases baseline shift 2 pts/px
Alt + Left Arrow Key Right Arrow Key	Decreases/increases kerning/tracking 20/1000 ems

Path Editing

Direct selection tool + Shift key + click	Selects multiple anchor points
Direct selection tool + Alt + click	Selects entire path
Pen tool + Alt + Ctrl + drag	Duplicates a path (works with any pen tool)
Ctrl	Switches from path selection tool, pen tool, add anchor point, delete anchor point, or anchor point tool to direct selection tool
Alt	Switches from Direct selection pointer to Add to selection pointer when over path
Alt + Ctrl	Switches from Direct selection tool to Anchor point tool when pointer is over anchor point or direction point
Alt	Switches from Pen tool or Freeform pen tool to Anchor point tool when pointer is over anchor or direction point
Magnetic pen tool + double-click	Closes path
Magnetic pen tool + Alt + double-click	Closes path with straight-line segment

Slicing and Optimizing

Shift key + Ctrl + Y	Toggles browser dither for selected image pane in Optimized view
Alt + Ctrl + Y	Toggles through gamma previews in selected image

	pane
Ctrl + Y	Toggles through Optimized/2up/4up/Original window
Ctrl	Toggles between slice tool and slice selection tool
Shift key + drag	Draws square slice
Alt + drag	Draws from center outward
Alt + Shift key + drag	Draws square slice from center outward
Spacebar + drag	Repositions slice while creating slice
Right mouse button on slice	Opens context-sensitive menu

Adobe PageMaker

100%/Fit in window	**Ctrl + Alt + Click**
200% size	**Ctrl + 2**
200%/100% toggle	**Ctrl + Alt + Shift + Click**
400% size	**Ctrl + 4**
50% size	**Ctrl + 5**
75% size	**Ctrl + 7**
Acquire	**Alt + F + Q**
Activate control palette	**Ctrl + ‘**
Actual Size	**Alt + V + A or Ctrl + 1**
Add pages	**Ctrl + Alt + Shift + G**
Align center	**Ctrl + Shift + C**
Align left	**Ctrl + Shift + L**
Align Objects	**Alt + E + A or Ctrl + Shift + E**
Align right	**Ctrl + Shift + R**
Alignment	**Alt + T + A**
All caps	**Ctrl + Shift + K**
Apply change and return to layout in control palette	**Shift + Enter**
Apply change and stay at same option in control palette	**Enter**
Arrange Icons	**Alt + W + A**
Attach/detach content and frame	**Ctrl + F**
Auto leading	**Ctrl + Alt + Shift + A**
Autoflow	**Alt + L + F**

Bold	**Ctrl + Shift + B or F6**
Book	**Alt + U + B**
Bring Forward	**Ctrl + Shift +]**
Bring to Front	**Ctrl +]**
Bullet	**Alt + 8**
Carat	**Shift + 6**
Cascade all open stories	**Shift + [Cascade]**
Cascade	**Alt + W + D**
Change character	**Ctrl + H**
Change page to fit in window	**Shift + click page icon**
Change to frame	**Ctrl + Shift + Alt + F**
Change in Story Editor	**Alt + U + H**
Character specifications dialog box	**Ctrl + T or Alt + T + T**
Clear Ruler Guides	**Alt + V + C**
Clear	**Alt + E + L**
Click select paragraph	**Triple click with text tool**
Click select word	**Double click with text tool**
Close all open documents	**Shift + Close on the File menu**
Close all stories	**Shift + [close story]**
Close current story window	**Ctrl + W or Alt + F + C**
Colour palette	**Ctrl + J**
Column Guides	**Alt + L + C**
Constrain move vertical/horizontal	**Shift + drag item (first move sets constrained direction)**
Constrained line tool	**Alt + Shift + F3**
Control palette	**Ctrl + '**
Copy book list to all book publications	**Ctrl + [book]**
Copy existing topics for new entry	**Ctrl + Ok in topic dialog box**
Copy Master Guides	**Alt + L + M**
Copy	**Alt + E + C or Ctrl + C or Ctrl + Insert key**
Copyright symbol	**Alt + G**
Create fast index entry in story editor	**Ctrl + Shift + Y**
Create index entry	**Ctrl + Y**

Create Index	**Alt + U + I**
Create proper name entry	**Ctrl + Alt + Y**
Create TOC	**Alt + U + T**
Cropping tool	**Alt + Shift + F2**
Cut	**Alt + E + T or Ctrl + X or Ctrl + Delete key**
Decrease one point size	**Ctrl + Shift + <**
Decrease to next standard size	**Ctrl + Alt + <**
Define Colors	**Alt + U + C**
Define new Color in Colors Palette	**Double or Ctrl + click**
Define new master page in Master Pages Palette	**Ctrl + click**
Define new style in styles palette	**Ctrl + click**
Define Styles	**Alt + T + D or Ctrl + 3**
Deselect All	**Alt + E + D**
Discretionary hyphen	**Ctrl + Shift + hyphen**
Display all except tools	**Shift + Tab**
Display list valid value for option in control palette	**Esc**
Display Master Items	**Alt + V + D**
Display Non-printing items	**Alt + V + N**
Display/hide all palettes	**Tab**
Display/hide Color palette in Colors Palette	**Ctrl + J**
Display/hide control palette	**Ctrl + (lower case tilde)**
Display/hide Hyperlinks in Hyperlinks Palette	**F10**
Display/hide Hyperlinks palette in Hyperlinks Palette	**Ctrl + 9**
Display/hide Master Pages palette in Master Pages Palette	**Ctrl + Shift + 8**
Display/hide nonprinting	**Ctrl + Alt + N**
Display/hide Styles palette in styles palette	**Ctrl + B**
Document Setup	**Alt + F + M or Ctrl + Shift + P**
Down one line	**Down arrow or keypad 2**
Down one paragraph	**Ctrl + down arrow or Ctrl + keypad 2**
Down one screen	**Page Down or Keypad 3**
Drag left indent marker only	**Shift + drag indent**
Edit Color in Colors Palette	**Double click or Ctrl + click**
Edit Hyperlinks in Hyperlinks Palette	**Double click item**

Edit item in Palette list	**Double click or Ctrl + Click**
Edit Master Page in Master Pages Palette	**Double click or Ctrl + click**
Edit original (OLE)	**Double click object**
Edit original	**Alt + Double Click Object or Alt + E + O**
Edit Story	**Alt + E + E**
Edit story in Layout View	**Triple click text block with pointer tool**
Edit style in styles palette	**Double click or Ctrl + click**
Ellipis	**Alt + 0133**
Ellipse (Oval) tool	**Shift + F5**
Em dash	**Alt + Shift + hyphen**
Em space	**Ctrl + Shift + M**
En dash	**Alt + hyphen**
En space	**Ctrl + Shift + N**
End of paragraph	**Enter**
Entire Pasteboard	**Alt + V + P or Ctrl + Shift + 0**
Exit	**Alt + F + X**
Expert Kerning	**Alt + T + K**
Expert Tracking	**Alt + T + R**
Export	**Alt + F + E**
Fill and Stroke	**Alt + E + A or Ctrl + U**
Fill	**Alt + E + L**
Find character in story editor	**Ctrl + F or Alt + U + F**
Find next character	**Ctrl + G or Alt + U + X**
Fit in Window	**Alt + V + W or Ctrl + 0**
Font	**Alt + T + F**
Force Justify	**Ctrl + Shift + F**
Forced line break	**Shift + Enter**
Frame dialog box	**Alt + E + F**
General Preferences dialog box	**Ctrl + K**
Go Back	**Alt + L + B**
Go Forward	**Alt + L + W**
Go to next frame	**Ctrl + Alt +]**
Go to next option in control palette	**Tab or arrow key**

Go to Page	**Alt + L + G or Ctrl + Alt + G**
Go to previous frame	**Ctrl + Alt + [**
Go to previous option in control palette	**Shift + Tab or arrow keys**
Grabber constrained	**Alt + Shift + drag or Shift + F7**
Grabber hand	**Alt + Drag or Shift + F7**
Grabber hand, constrained	**Option + Shift + drag pan**
Grabber hand, pan the view	**Option + drag**
Group	**Alt + E + G or Ctrl + G**
Guides (toggle)	**Ctrl + ;**
Hide Guides	**Alt + V + G**
Hide Rulers	**Alt + V + R**
Hide Scroll Bars	**Alt + V + B**
Hide Tools	**Alt + W + T**
Horizontal Scale	**Alt + T + S**
Hyphenation	**Alt + T + H**
Image	**Alt + E + I**
Increase one point size	**Ctrl + Shift + >**
Increase to next standard size	**Ctrl + Alt + >**
Indents/Tabs	**Alt + T + I or Ctrl + I**
Index Entry	**Alt + U + E**
Insert Object	**Alt + E + I**
Insert Pages	**Alt + L + I**
Installed filter list	**Ctrl + About PageMaker on toolbar**
Italic	**Ctrl + Shift + I or F7**
Justify	**Ctrl + Shift + J**
Kern apart .01 em	**Alt + Right arrow**
Kern apart .04 em	**Ctrl + Alt + Right arrow**
Kern together .01 em	**Alt + Left arrow**
Kern together .04 em	**Ctrl + Alt + Left arrow**
Layers palette	**Ctrl + 8**
Layout/Story Editor (toggle) in Layout View	**Ctrl + E**
Leading	**Alt + T + L**
Left one character	**Left arrow or keypad 4**

Left one word	**Ctrl + Left arrow or Ctrl + keypad 6**
Line tool	**Shift + F3**
Link Info	**Alt + E + N**
Link Options	**Alt + E + O**
Links Manager	**Alt + F + K or Ctrl + Shift + D**
Lock Guides	**Alt + V + L**
Lock Position	**Alt + E + L or Ctrl + L**
Magic Stretch proportional	**Ctrl + Shift + drag handle of bitmap**
Magic Stretch regular	**Ctrl + drag handle of bitmap**
Magnifying tool	**Alt + Shift + F7**
Magnifying tool—bigger in Layout View	**Ctrl + spacebar + click or drag**
Magnifying tool—smaller in Layout View	**Ctrl + spacebar + Alt + click**
Mask and Group	**Ctrl + 6**
Mask	**Alt + E + M**
Master page palette	**Shift + Ctrl + 8**
Measurement system in control palette	**Ctrl + Alt + M**
Minimize Palette size	**Double click palette tab**
New document	**Ctrl + N or Alt + F + N**
No track	**Ctrl + Shift + Q**
Non breaking hyphen	**Ctrl + Alt + hyphen**
Non breaking slash	**Ctrl + Alt + /**
Non breaking space	**Ctrl + Alt + spacebar**
Non-Printing	**Alt + E + R**
Normal	**Ctrl + Shift + spacebar or F5**
Nudge object	**Use arrow keys or Ctrl + palette nudge buttons**
Nudge regular in control palette	**nudge buttons**
Nudge, power move in control palette	**Ctrl + [nudge]**
Ok/Cancel all open dialog boxes	**Shift + Ok/Cancel**
On/Off selected button in control palette	**Spacebar**
Open document	**Ctrl + O or Alt + F + O**
Oval Frame tool	**Alt + Shift + F5**
Page number marker	**Ctrl + Alt + P**

Page turn (next)	**Page Up**
Page turn (previous)	**Page Down**
Paragraph symbol	**Alt + 7**
Paragraph dialog box	**Alt + T + P or Ctrl + M**
Paragraph/character view	**Ctrl + Shift + (lower case tilde)**
Paste Multiple	**Alt + E + M**
Paste Special	**Alt + E + S**
Paste	**Alt + E + P or Ctrl + V**
Place	**Alt + F + L or Ctrl + D**
Plug-in Palettes	**Alt + W + L**
Plug-ins	**Alt + U + P**
Pointer tool	**F9 or Ctrl + spacebar**
Polygon Frame tool	**Alt + Shift + F6**
Polygon Settings	**Alt + E + P**
Power nudge	**Shift + arrow or Shift + nudge buttons**
Power paste	**Ctrl + Alt + V**
Preferences	**Alt + F + F**
Print	**Alt + F + P or Ctrl + P**
Printer Styles	**Alt + F + Y**
Proportional stretch	**Shift + drag corner handle**
Proportions, restore	**Shift + drag corner handle**
Proxy control point in control palette	**Arrow keys**
Question mark	**Shift + /**
Quit/Exit	**Ctrl + Q**
Quotation mark single close	**Alt +]**
Quotation mark single open	**Alt + [**
Quotation marks close	**Alt + Shift +]**
Quotation marks open	**Alt + Shift + [**
Recent Publications	**Alt + F + R**
Rectangle Frame tool	**Alt + Shift + F4**
Rectangle tool	**Shift + F4**
Redraw, high resolution	**Ctrl + Shift + view**
Registration trademark	**Alt + R**

Remove all cross-references	**Ctrl + Shift + [remove]**
Remove all entries	**Ctrl + Alt + Shift + [remove]**
Remove all master objects in Master Pages Palette	**Ctrl + none**
Remove all page references	**Ctrl + Alt + [remove]**
Remove objects and all guides in Master Pages Palette	**Shift + click**
Remove objects and column guides in Master Pages Palette	**Alt + Shift + click + [none]**
Remove objects only in Master Pages Palette	**Alt + Click**
Remove Pages	**Alt + L + R**
Remove Transformation	**Alt + E + T**
Return to previous page	**Ctrl + Page Up or Ctrl + Page Down**
Reverse	**Ctrl + Shift + V**
Revert to last mini-save	**Shift + Revert on the File menu or Alt + F + V**
Right one character	**Ctrl + right arrow or Ctrl + keypad 6 or Right arrow or keypad 6**
Rotate 45 degree increments	**Shift + Rotate tool**
Rotate around center of object	**Ctrl + Rotate tool**
Rotating tool	**Shift + F2**
Rounded Corners	**Alt + E + C**
Rules (toggle)	**Ctrl + R**
Save all documents	**Shift + Save from File menu**
Save As	**Alt + F + A or Ctrl + Shift + S**
Save	**Alt + F + S or Ctrl + S**
Scaling/cropping in control palette	**Arrow key toggle**
Section symbol	**Alt + 6**
Select All	**Alt + E + A or Ctrl + A**
Select multiple elements	**Shift + Click**
Select multiple subordinates	**Ctrl + Shift + Click**
Select subordinate item	**Ctrl + click**
Selection mode	**Hold down Shift key while using a navigation shortcut**
Send Backward	**Ctrl + Shift + [**
Send Guides to Back	**Alt + V + U**
Send mail	**Alt + F + D**

Send to Back	**Ctrl + [**
Set all page to same view	**Alt + desired view**
Show Colours	**Alt + W + C**
Show Control Palette	**Alt + W + P**
Show Hyperlinks	**Alt + W + H**
Show index	**Ctrl + [show index] or Alt + U + W**
Show Layers	**Alt + W + L**
Show Master Pages	**Alt + W + M**
Show Styles	**Alt + W + S**
Size	**Alt + T + Z**
Snap to Guides	**Alt + V + S or Ctrl + Shift + ;**
Snap to Rulers	**Alt + V + T or Ctrl + Alt + R**
Sort Pages	**Alt + L + S**
Spelling	**Alt + U + S**
Spelling in story editor	**Ctrl + L**
Story Editor/Layout	**Ctrl + E**
Strikethru	**Ctrl + Shift + /**
Style	**Alt + T + E**
Styles palette	**Ctrl + B**
Subscript	**Ctrl + **
Superscript	**Ctrl + Shift + **
Tab	**Tab**
Text flow, Auto/Manual	**Ctrl + flow text (toggle)**
Text flow, Semi-automatic	**Shift + flow text**
Text link tool	**Ctrl + Shift + Alt + Click**
Text tool	**Alt + Shift + F1**
Text wrap redraw, interrupt	**Hold down spacebar during adjustment**
Text Wrap	**Alt + E + W**
Thin space (¼ em)	**Ctrl + Shift + T**
Tile all open stories	**Shift + [Tile]**
Tile	**Alt + W + I**
To beginning of line	**Home key or keypad 7**
To beginning of sentence	**Ctrl + keypad 7**
To beginning of story	**Ctrl + keypad 9**
To end of line	**End or keypad 2**
To end of sentence	**Ctrl + keypad 1**
To end of story	**Ctrl + keypad 3**

Trademark symbol	**Alt + 0153**
Trigger screen redraw	**Ctrl + Shift + F12**
Type Style	**Alt + T + Y**
Underline	**Ctrl + Shift + U or F8**
Undo	**Alt + E + U**
Ungroup	**Alt + E + U or Ctrl + Shift + G**
Unlock	**Alt + E + N or Ctrl + Alt + L**
Unmask and Ungroup	**Ctrl + Alt + 6**
Unmask	**Alt + E + U**
Up one line	**Up arrow or keypad 8**
Up one paragraph	**Ctrl + Up arrow or Ctrl + keypad 8**
Up one screen	**Page Up or Keypad 9**
Zero Lock	**Alt + V + K**
Zoom In	**Alt + V + I**
Zoom Out	**Alt + V + O**
Zoom To	**Alt + V + Z**

CorelDRAW

Align & Distribute

Align Bottom	B	Aligns selected objects to the bottom
Align Centre to Page	P	Aligns the centers of the selected objects to the page center
Align Horizontal Center	E	Horizontally aligns the centers of the selected objects
Align Left	L	Aligns selected objects to the left
Align Right	R	Aligns selected objects to the right
Align Top	T	Aligns selected objects to the top
Align Vertical Center	C	Vertically aligns the centers of the selected objects
Distribute Bottom	Shift + B	Distributes selected objects to the bottom
Distribute Centers Horizontally	Shift + E	Horizontally distributes the centers of the selected objects
Distribute Centers Vertically	Shift + C	Vertically distributes the centers of the selected objects
Distribute Left	Shift +L	Distributes selected objects to the left
Distribute Right	Shift + R	Distributes selected objects to the right
Distribute Spacing Horizontally	Shift + P	Horizontally distributes the space between the selected objects
Distribute Spacing Vertically	Shift + A	Vertically distributes the space between the selected objects
Distribute Top	Shift + T	Distributes selected objects to the top

Display

Full Screen Preview	F9	Displays a full screen preview of the drawing
Refresh Window	Ctrl + W	Forces a redraw of the drawing window
Toggle Display	Shift + F9	Toggles between the last two used view qualities
Show Non Printing Characters	Ctrl + Shift + C	Shows non-printing characters

Dockers

Contour	Ctrl + F9	Opens the Contour docker
Envelope	Ctrl + F7	Opens the Envelope docker
Graphic and Text Styles	Ctrl + F5	Opens the Graphic and Text Styles docker
Lens	Alt + F3	Opens the Lens docker
Linear Dimensions	Alt + F2	Contains functions for assigning attributes to linear dimension lines
Object Properties	Alt + Enter	Opens the Object Properties docker
Position	Alt + F7	Opens the Position docker
Rotate	Alt + F8	Opens the Rotate docker
Scale and Mirror	Alt + F9	Opens the Scale and Mirror docker
Size	Alt + F10	Opens the Size docker
Symbols and Special Characters	Alt + F11	Opens the Symbols and Special Characters docker
View Manager	Alt + F12	Opens the View Manager docker

Clipboard and Object Editing Commands

Copy	Ctrl + C	Copies the selection and places it on the Clipboard
Copy	Ctrl + Ins	Copies the selection and places it on the Clipboard
Cut	Ctrl + X	Cuts the selection and places it on the Clipboard
Cut	Ctrl + Del	Cuts the selection and places it on the Clipboard
Delete	Del	Deletes the selected object(s)
Duplicate	Ctrl + D	Duplicates the selected object(s) to offsets
Paste	Ctrl + V	Pastes the clipboard contents into the drawing
Paste	Ctrl + Ins	Pastes the clipboard contents into the drawing
Redo	Ctrl + Shift + Z	Reverses the last undo operation
Repeat	Ctrl + R	Repeats the last operation
Undo	Ctrl + Z	Reverses the last operation
Undo	Ctrl + Backspace	Reverses the last operation

File Commands

Export	Ctrl + E	Exports text or objects to another format
Import	Ctrl + I	Imports text or objects

New Document	Ctrl + N	Creates a new drawing
Open	Ctrl + O	Opens an existing drawing
Print	Ctrl + P	Prints the active drawing
Save	Ctrl + S	Saves the active drawing

Fill Dialogs

Open Fountain Fill Dialog	F11	Specifies fountain fills for objects
Open Uniform Fill Dialog	Ctrl + F11	Specifies uniform colour fills for objects

Find & Replace Using Text Tool

Find Text	Alt + F3	Opens the Find dialog box
Format Text	Ctrl + T	Opens the Text Format dialog box

Font Commands

Bold	Ctrl+ B	Changes the style of text to bold
Font list	Ctrl + Shift + F	Shows a list of all the available/active fonts
Font weights	Ctrl + Shift + W	Shows a list of all the available/active weights
Italics	Ctrl + I	Changes the style of text to italic
Small caps	Ctrl + Shift + K	Changes all text characters to small capital letters
Underline	Ctrl + U	Changes the style of text to underline
Decrease Font size	Ctrl + 2(numericpad)	Decreases font size to previous point size
Font size	Ctrl + Shift + P	Shows a list of all the available/active font sizes
HTML Font size	Ctrl + Shift + H	Shows a list of all the available/active HTML font sizes
Increase Font size	Ctrl + 8(numericpad)	Increases font size to next point size
Next Font Combo Size	Ctrl + 6(numericpad)	Increases font size to next setting in Font size list
Previous Font Combo Size	Ctrl + 4(numericpad)	Decreases font size to previous setting available in the Font size list
Change case	Shift + F3	Changes the case of selected text

Grid, Guidelines & Snap

Snap to Grid	Ctrl + Y	Snaps objects to the grid (toggle)

Grouping/Combining Objects

Break Apart	Ctrl + K	Breaks apart the selected object
Combine	Ctrl + L	Combines the selected objects
Convert Outline to Object	Ctrl + Shift + Q	Converts an outline to an object
Convert to Curves	Ctrl + Q	Converts the selected object to a curve
Group	Ctrl + G	Groups the selected objects
Ungroup	Ctrl + U	Ungroup the selected objects or group of objects

Help

Help	Shift + F1	Displays What's This? Help

Object Nudge

Nudge down	Dn Arrow	Nudges the object downward
Nudge left	Lft Arrow	Nudges the object to the left
Nudge right	Rt Arrow	Nudges the object to the right
Nudge up	Up Arrow	Nudges the object upward
Super Nudge Down	Shift + Dn Arrow	Nudges the object downward by the Super Nudge factor
Super Nudge Left	Shift + Lft Arrow	Nudges the object to the left by the Super Nudge factor
Super Nudge Right	Shift + Rt Arrow	Nudges the object to the right by the Super Nudge factor
Super Nudge Up	Shift + Up Arrow	Nudges the object upward by the Super Nudge factor
Super Nudge Down	Shift + Dn Arrow	Nudges the object downward by the Super Nudge factor
Micro Nudge Down	Ctrl + Dn Arrow	Nudges the object downward by the Micro Nudge factor
Micro Nudge Left	Ctrl + Lft Arrow	Nudges the object to the left by the Micro Nudge factor
Micro Nudge Right	Shift + Rt Arrow	Nudges the object to the right by the Micro Nudge factor
Micro Nudge Up	Shift + Up Arrow	Nudges the object upward by the Micro Nudge factor

Options

Workspace Options dialog	Ctrl + J	Opens the dialog for setting CorelDRAW options

Object Ordering

Back one	Ctrl + PgDn	Places the selected object(s) back one position in the object stacking order
Forward one	Ctrl + Pg Up	Places the selected object(s) forward one position in the object stacking order
To Back	Shift + Pg Dn	Places the selected object(s) to the back
To Front	Shift + Pg Up	Places the selected object(s) to the front

Object Outline Pen

Open Outline Color Dialog	Shift + F12	Specifies outline color of objects
Open Outline Pen Dialog	F12	Specifies outline pen properties for objects

Document Navigation

Next page	Pg Dn	Goes to the next page
Previous page	Pg Up	Goes to the previous page

Select All

Objects	Ctrl + A	Selects all objects in the entire drawing

Styles

Graphic and Text Styles	Ctrl + F5	Opens the Graphic and Text Styles docker

Text Formatting Using Text Tool

Bullet Text	Ctrl + M	Adds/removes bullets for the text object (toggle)
Center Justify	Ctrl + E	Changes the alignment of text to center alignment
Convert text style	Ctrl + F8	Converts Artistic Text to Paragraph Text or vice versa
Apply Drop Cap	Ctrl + Shift + D	Adds/removes a Drop Cap for the text object (toggle)
Edit Text	Ctrl + Shift + T	Opens the Edit Text dialog box
Force Justification	Ctrl + H	Changes the alignment of text to force last line full alignment
Format Text	Ctrl + T	Formats the properties of text
Full Justify	Ctrl + J	Changes the alignment of text to full alignment
Horizontal Text	Ctrl + ,	Changes the alignment of text to horizontal direction
Left Justification	Ctrl + L	Changes the alignment of text to left alignment
No Justification	Ctrl + N	Changes the alignment of text to have no alignment
Right Justification	Ctrl + R	Changes the alignment of text to right alignment
Vertical Text	Ctrl + .	Changes the text to vertical (toggle)

Text Editing and Cursor Moves Using Text Tool

Deleted Character to Right	Del	Deletes character to the right of the text Cursor
Delete Word to Right	Ctrl + Del	Deletes word to the right of the text Cursor
Cursor Down 1 Frame	Pg Dn	Moves Cursor down 1 frame
Cursor Down 1 Line	Dn Arrow	Moves Cursor down 1 line
Cursor Down 1 Para	Ctrl + Pg Dn	Moves Cursor down 1 paragraph
Cursor left 1 character	Lft Arrow	Moves Cursor left 1 character
Cursor left 1 word	Ctrl + Lft Arrow	Moves Cursor left 1 word
Cursor right 1 character	Rt Arrow	Moves Cursor right 1 character
Cursor right 1 word	Ctrl + Rt Arrow	Moves Cursor right 1 word
Cursor up 1 Frame	Pg Up	Moves Cursor up 1 frame
Cursor up 1 Line	Up Arrow	Moves Cursor up 1 line
Cursor up 1 Paragraph	Ctrl + Up Arrow	Moves Cursor up 1 paragraph
Cursor to Start of Frame	Ctrl + Home	Moves Cursor to the Start of the Frame
Cursor to Start of Line	Home	Moves Cursor to the Start of Line
Cursor to Start of Text	Ctrl + Pg Up	Moves Cursor to the Start of the Text
Cursor to End of Frame	Ctrl + End	Moves Cursor to the end of the Frame
Cursor to End of Line	End	Moves Cursor to the end of the line
Cursor to End of Text	Ctrl + Pg Dn	Moves Cursor to the end of the Text

Select all Text	Ctrl + A	Selects all text in Paragraph Frame or Artistic Text Object
Select Character to Left	Shift + Lft Arrow	Selects the character to the left of the Cursor
Select Character to Right	Shift + Rt Arrow	Selects the character to the right of the Cursor
Select Down 1 Frame	Shift + PgDn	Selects text downwards 1 frame
Select Down 1 Line	Shift + Dn Arrow	Selects text downwards 1 line
Select Down 1 Paragraph	Ctrl + Shift + Dn Arrow	Selects text downwards by 1 paragraph
Select up 1 Frame	Shift + PgUp	Selects text upwards 1 frame
Select up 1 Line	Shift + Up Arrow	Selects text upwards 1 line
Select Up 1 Paragraph	Ctrl + Shift + Up Arrow	Selects text upwards by 1 paragraph
Select Word to Left	Ctrl + Shift + Lft Arrow	Selects the word to the left of the text Cursor
Select Word to Right	Ctrl + Shift + Rt Arrow	Selects the word to the right of the text Cursor
Select to Start of Frame	Ctrl + Shift + Home	Selects text to the Start of the Frame
Select to Start of Line	Shift + Home	Selects text to the Start of the Line
Select to Start of Text	Ctrl + Shift + Pg Up	Selects text to the Start of the Text
Select to End of Frame	Ctrl + Shift + End	Selects text to the End of the Frame
Select to End of Line	Shift + End	Selects text to the End of the Line
Select to End of Text	Ctrl + Shift + Pg Dn	Selects text to the End of the Text

Text Placement

Align to Baseline	Alt + F12	Aligns text to the baseline

Text Tools

Change Case	Shift + F3	Changes the case of selected text
Show Non-printing Characters	Ctrl + Shift + C	Shows non-printing characters
Spell Check	Ctrl + F12	Opens the Spell Checker; checks the spelling of the selected text

Toolbox Tool Selections

Artistic Media Tool	I	Draws curves and applies Preset, Brush, Spray, Calligraphic, or Pressure Sensitive effects to the strokes
Ellipse Tool	F7	Draws ellipses and circles; double-clicking the tool opens the Toolbox tab of the Options dialog box
Eraser Tool	X	Erases part of a graphic or splits an object into two closed paths
Freehand Tool	F5	Selects the last used curve-drawing tool
Graph Paper Tool	D	Draws a group of rectangles; double-clicking opens the Toolbox tab of the Options dialog box
Hand Tool	H	Pan around the drawing by clicking and dragging using this tool

Interactive Fill Tool	G	Adds a fill to object(s); clicking and dragging on object(s) applies a fountain fill
Mesh Fill	M	Converts an object to a Mesh Fill object
Polygon Tool	Y	Draws symmetrical polygons; double-clicking opens the Toolbox tab of the Options dialog box
Rectangle Tool	F6	Draws rectangles; double-clicking the tool creates a page frame
Shape Tool	F10	Edits the nodes of an object; double-clicking the tool selects all nodes on the selected object
Spiral Tool	A	Draws spirals; double clicking opens the Toolbox tab of the Options dialog box
Text Tool drag	F8	Adds text; click on the page to add Artistic Text; click and to add Paragraph Text
Toggle Pick State	Spacebar	Toggles between the current tool and the Pick tool

Visual Basic

Open VBA Editor	Alt + F11	Launches Visual Basic for Applications Editor

Workspace

Display Property Bar	Ctrl + Return	Selects the Property Bar and highlights the first visible item that can be tabbed to

Zoom & Pen

Navigator	N	Brings up the Navigator window allowing you to navigate to any object in the document
Hand Tool	H	Pans around the drawing by clicking and dragging using this tool
Pen Down	Alt + Dn Arrow	Pans the drawing downward
Pen Left	Alt + Lft Arrow	Pans the drawing to the left
Pan Right	Alt + Rt Arrow	Pans the drawing to the right
Pan Up	Alt + Up Arrow	Pans the drawing upward
View Manager	Ctrl + F2	Opens the View Manager docker
Zoom One Shot	F2	Performs one zoom operation and then returns to the previous tool
Zoom out	F3	Zooms out
Zoom To All Objects	F4	Zooms in on all objects in the drawing
Zoom To Page	Shift + F4	Displays the entire printable page
Zoom to Selection	Shift + F2	Zooms in on selected objects

Illustrator

The working in a software become much easy if you know the various keyboard shortcuts of the commands. Various commands in Illustrator are given below with their respective keyboard combinations.

The Tool Selection Commands

Function	*Shortcut*
Select the next pop-up tool	Drag to the right and release on desired tool Alt + click on a tool
Open tool dialog box	Double click on the tool
Hide toolbox and palettes	Tab
Selection tool	V or
	Ctrl + Tab with Direct Selection tool, and then hold Ctrl or
	Ctrl with all other tools if Selection tool was the last tool used
Direct Selection tool	A or
	Ctrl + tab with Selection tool, and then hold Ctrl + Alt with Group Selection tool
	Ctrl with all other tools if Direct Selection tool was the last tool used
Group Selection tool	Alt with Direct Selection tool
	Ctrl + Alt with all other tools if Direct Selection tool was the last tool used
Magic Wand tool	Y
Direct Select Lasso tool	Q

Function	*Procedure*
Select one point	Click with Direct Selection tool
Select one segment	Click with Direct Selection tool
Select one path	Click with Group Selection tool
Select next group up	Click selected path again with Group Selection tool
Select to-level group	Click with Selection tool
Select addtional	Shift + Click
Select specific points	Drag with Direct Selection tool
Select specific paths	Drag with Selection tool
Deselct selected	Shift + click selected
Move selection	Drag
Duplicate selection	Alt + Drag
Constrain to 45^0 movement	Shift + Drag
Duplicate and constrain	Alt + Shift + Drag

Proportionatel resize object — Shfit + drag Bounding Box handle

Resize from center — Alt + drag Bounding Box handle

Resize proportionately from center — Alt + Shift + drag Bounding Box handle

Select all — Ctrl + A

Deselect all — Ctrl + Shift + A

Select all objects with similar Fill, Stroke, Opacity and/or Blending Mode — Click with Magic Wand tool

Add similar colored and stroked objects from the current selection — Alt + Magic Wand tool

Set Magic Wand options — Double click on Magic Wand tool to open the Magic Wand palette

Path Tools

Tool	*Shortcut*
Pen tool	P
Add Anchor Point tool	Alt + Delete Anchor Point tool
	Alt + Scissors tool
Delete Anchor Point tool	-
	Alt + Add Anchor Point tool
Convert Anchor Point tool	Shift + C
	Alt + Pen tool
Pencil tool	N
Smooth tool	Alt + Pencil tool
	Alt + Erase tool
	Alt + Paintbrush tool
Paintbrush tool	B
Scissors tool	C

Function	*Procedure*
Create a straight corner point	Click with Pen tool
Create a smooth point	Drag with Pen tool
Continue existing open path	Click + drag with Pen tool on end point of existing path
Close open path	While drawing, click + drag with Pen tool on the initial end point
	Click + drag with Pen tool on each end point in succession
	Select path and join (Ctrl + J)
Constrain new point to 45 degrees from last point	Shift + drag with Pen tool
Constain control handles to 45 degrees	Shift while dragging handle with Pen tool
Create a path	Click + drag a succession of points with Pen tool

Add anchor points to existing path	Click with the Pen tool on path
Delete achor points from existing path	Shift + click with Pen tool on an anchor point
Convert anchor point to smooth point	Drag with Convert Direction Point tool on existing point
Convert smooth point to corner point	Click with Convert Direction Point tool on smooth point
Convert smooth corner to combination corner	Drag one handle with Direct Selection tool back into the anchor point
Convert somooth corner to curved corner	Drag one handle with Convert Direction Point tool
Draw freestyle paths	Drag with Pencil tool
View Paintbrush options	Double click Paintbrush tool in toolbox
Reshape a path	Select points with Direct Selection, and then drag with Reshape tool
Split path	Click with Scissors tool
Slic multiple paths	Drag wth Knife tool
Constrain Knife slice to straight lines	Alt + drag with Knife tool
Constain Knife slice to 45^0	Shift + Alt + drag with Knife tool

Type Tools

Tool	***Shortcut***
Type tool	T
	Shift + Vertical Type tool
Area Type tool	Alt + Path Type tool
	Shift + Vertical Area Type tool
	Alt + Shift Vertical Path Type tool
Path Type tool	Alt + Area Type tool
	Shift + Vertical Path Type tool
	Alt + Shift + Vertical Area Type tool
Vertical Type tool	Shift + Type tool
Vertical Area Type tool	Alt + Vertical Path Type tool
	Shift + Area Type tool
	Alt + Shift + Area Type tool
Verical Path Type tool	Alt + Vertical Area Type tool
	Shift + Path Type tool
	Alt + Shift + Area Type tool

Function	***Procedure***
Create point type	Click with Type tool
Create rectangle type	Drag with Type tool
Place path type on closed path	Click path with Path Type tool

	Alt + click path with Type tool
	Alt + click path with Area Type tool
Place path type on an open path	Click path with Path Type tool
	Click path with Type tool
	Alt + click path with Area Type tool
Place area type on a closed path	Click path with Area Type tool
	Click path with Type tool
	Alt + click path with Path Type tool
Place area type on an open with	Click path with Area Type tool
	Alt + click path with Type tool
	Alt + click path with Path Type tool
Change vertical type to horzontal type	Choose Type>>Type Orientation>>Horizontal
Change horizontal type to vertical type	Choose Type>>Type Orientation>>Vertical
Select entrie text block	Click text block with Selection tool
Select one character	Drag across character with any Type tool
Select one word	Double click word with any Type tool
Select one paragraph	Triple-click paragraph with any Type tool
Select all text in text block	Click in text block with any Type tool, and then press Ctrl + A.
Flip type on a path	Double clikc the I-bar with any selection tool or just drag it to the opposite side

Line Tools

Tool	*Shortcut*
Line Segment tool	\

Function	*Procedure*
Create line segments using numbers	Click with Line Segment tool
Draw a line segment	Draw with Line Segment tool
Constrain line segments to 45^0	Shift + Drag with Line Segment tool
Create line segment from midpoint using numbers	Alt + click with Line Segment tool
Draw line segment from midpoint	Alt + drag with Line Segment tool
Move line segment while drawing	Spacebar + drag with Line Segment tool
Create multiple line segments	- + drag with Line Segment tool
Create arc segments using numbers	Click with the Arc tool
Draw an arc segment	Draw with Arc tool
Constrain arc segments to circular sections	Shift + drag with Arc tool
Create arc segment from the center	Alt + click with Arc tool

Draw arc segment from the center	Alt + drag with Arc tool
Move arc segment while drawing	Spacebar + drag with Arc tool
Create multiple arc segments	- + drag with Arc tool
Toggle arc between concave and convex	X + drag with Arc tool
Toggle between open and closed arcs	C + drag with Arc tool
Flip the arc	F + drag with Arc tool
Increase arc slope	Up Arrow + drag with Arc tool
Decrease arc slope	Down Arrow + drag with Arc tool
Create spiral using numbers	Click with Spiral tool
Draw spiral	Drag with Spiral tool
Constrain spiral angle	Shift + drag with Spiral tool
Move spiral while drawing	Spacebar + drag with Spiral tool
Create multiple spirals	- + drag with Spiral tool
Decrease spiral decay	Ctrl + drag with Spiral tool
Increase spiral length and size	Alt + drag with Spiral tool
Increase spiral length	Up Arrow + drag with Spiral tool
Decrease spiral length	Down Arrow + drag with Spiral tool
Create a rectangular grid using numbers	Click with the Rectangular Grid tool
Draw an rectangular grid	Drag with Rectangular Grid tool
Constrain rectangular grid to a square	Shift + Drag with Rectangular Grid tool
Create a square rectangular grid	Alt + click with Rectangular grid tool
Draw rectangular grid from the cente	Alt + drag with Rectangular Grid tool
Move rectangular grid while drawing	Spacebar + drag with Rectangular Grid tool
Create multiple rectangular grid	~ + drag with Rectangular Grid tool
Skew horizontal dividers to the left	X + drag with Rectangular Grid tool
Skew horizontal dividers to the right	C + drag with Rectangular Grid tool
Skew vertical dividers to the top of the rectangular grid	F + Drag wtih Rectangular Grid tool
Skew vertical dividers to the bottom of the rectangular grid	V + drag Rectangular Grid tool
Increase vertical dividers	Up Arrow with Rectangular Grid tool
Decrease vertical dividers	Down Arrow + drag with Rectangular Grid tool
Increase horizontal dividers	Right Arrow + drag with Rectangular Grid tool
Decrease horizontal dividers	Left Arrow + drag with Rectangular Grid tool
Create a polar grid using numbers	Click with the Polar Grid tool
Draw an polar grid	Drag wth Polar Grid tool
Constrain polar grid to a circle	Shift + drag with Polar Grid tool
Create a circular polar grid	Alt + click with Polar Grid tool
Draw polar grid from the center	Alt + drag with Polar Grid tool

Move polar grid while drawing	Spacebar + drag with Polar Grid tool
Create multiple polar grid	~ + drag with Polar Grid tool
Skew concentric dividers inward	X + drag with Polar Grid tool
Skew concentric dividers outward	C + drag with Polar Grid tool
Skew radial dividers counterclockwise	F + drag with Polar Grid tool
Skew radial dividers clockwise	V + drag with Polar Grid tool
Increase concentric dividers	Up Arrow + drag with Polar Grid tool
Decrease concentric dividers	Down Arrow + drag with Polar Grid tool
Increase radial dividers	Right Arrow + drag with Polar Grid tool
Decrease radial dividers	Left Arrow + drag with Polar Grid tool

Shape Tools

Tool	*Shortcut*
Rectangle tool	M
Ellipse tool	L

Function	*Procedure*
Create rectangle using numbers	Click with Rectangle tool or Rounded Rectangle tool
Draw rectangle	Drag with Rectangle tool
Draw square	Shift + drag with Rectangle tool
Create centered rectangle using numbers	Alt + click with Rectangle tool
Draw centered rectangle	Alt + drag with Rectangle tool
Draw square from center	Alt + Shift + drag with Rectangle tool
Move rectangle while drawing	Spacebar + drag with Rectangle tool
Create multiple ectangles	~ + drag with Rectangle tool
Create rounded rectangle using numbers	Click with Rounded Rectangle tool
Draw rounded rectangle	Drag with Rounded Rectangle tool
Draw square with rounded corners	Shift + drag with Rounded Rectangle tool
Create centered rounded rectangle	Alt + click with Rounded Rectangle tool
Draw centered rounded rectangle	Alt + drag with Rounded Rectangle tool
Draw square from center with rounded corners	Alt + Shift + drag with Rounded Rectangle tool
Move rounded rectangle while drawing	Spacebar + drag with Rounded Rectangle tool
Create multiple rounded rectangles	~ + drag with Rounded rectangle tool
Create ellipse using numbers	Click with Ellipse tool
Draw ellipse	Drag with Ellipse tool
Draw circle	Shift + drag with Ellipse tool
Create centered ellipse using numbers	Alt + click with Ellipse tool

Draw centered ellipse	Alt + drag with Ellipse tool
Move ellipse while drawing	Spacebar + drag with Ellipse tool
Create multiple ellipses	~ + drag with Ellipse tool
Create polygon using numbers	Click with Polygon tool
Draw polygon	Drag with Polygon tool
Constrain polygon angle	Shift + drag with Polygon tool
Create centered polygon using numbers	Alt + click with Polygon tool
Draw centered polygon	Alt + drag with Polygon tool
Increase polygon sides	Up Arrow + drag with Polygon tool
Decrease polygon sides	Down Arrow + drag with Polygon tool
Move polygon while drawing	Spacebar + drag with Polygon tool
Create multiple polygons	~ + drag with Polygon tool
Create star using numbers	Click with Star tool
Draw star	Drag with Star tool
Constrain star angle	Shift + drag with Star tool
Draw even-shouldered star	Alt + drag wityh Star tool
Move outer points only	Ctrl + drag with Star tool
Increase star points	Up Arrow + drag with Star tool
Decrease star points	Down Arrow + drag with Star tool
Move star while drawing	Spacebar + drag with Star tool
Create multiple stars	~ + drag with Star tool

Transformation Tools

Tool	*Shortcut*
Rotate tool	R
Reflect tool	O
Scale tool	S
Free Transform tool	E

Function	*Procedure*
Moving objects	Drag with the Selection or Free Transform tool
Constrain movements along 45 degrees axis	Shift + drag tool with the Selection or Free Transform tool
Rotate using numbers	Alt + click with Rotate tool
Rotate from center of selection with numbers	Double click with Rotate tool
Free Rotate	Click with Rotate to set Origin, and then drag with Rotate tool
Fre Rotate around selection center	Drag with Rotate tool
Rotate a copy	Alt + drag with Rotate tool

Rotate pattern only	~ + drag with Rotate tool
Scale using numbers	Alt + click with Scale tool
Scle from center of selection with numbers	Double click with Scale tool
Free Scale	Click with Scale to set Origin, and then drag with Scale tool
Free Scale around selection center	Drag with Scale tool
Constrain scaling to 45 degrees	Shift + drag with Scale tool
Scale a copy	Alt + drag with Scale tool
Scale pattern only	~ + drag with Scale tool
Reflect using numbers	Alt + click with Reflect tool
Reflect from center of selection with numbers	Double click with Reflect tool
Free Reflect	Click with Reflect to set Origin, and then drag with Reflect tool
Free Reflect around selection center	Drag with reflect tool
Constrain reflecting angle to 45 degrees	Shift + drag with Reflect tool
Reflect a copy	Alt + drag with Reflect tool
Reflect Pattern only	~ + drag with Reflect tool
Shear using numbers	Alt + click with Shear tool
Free Shear with Shear	Click with Shear to set Origin, and then drag
Free Shear around selection center	Drag with Shear
Constrain shearing to 45 degrees	Shift + drag with Shear tool
Shear a copy	Alt + drag with Shear tool
Shear pattern only	~ + drag with Shear tool

Distortion Tools

Tool	*Shortcut*
Warp tool	Shift + R

Function	*Procedure*
Twirl using numbers	Alt + click with Rotate tool
Free Twirl	Drag with Twirl tool
Reshape distortion brush	Alt + drag with Warp, Twirl, Pucker, Bloat, Scallop, Crystallize or Wrinkle tool
Constrain brush to horizontal or vertical movement	Shift + drag with Warp, Twirl, Pucker, Bloat, Scallop, Crystallize or Wrinkle tool
Set distortion options	Double click on the selected distortion tool

Symbol Tools

Tool	*Shortcut*

Symbol Sprayer tool	Shift + S
Function	***Procedure***
Add a single symbol	Click + Symbol Sprayer tool
Add multiple symbols	Drag + Symbol Sprayer tool
Remove symbols from set	Alt + Symbol Sprayer tool
Move the symbols in a set	Drag with the Symbol Sprayer tool
Change the stacking order of the symbols	Alt + Symbol Sprayer tool
Scrunch the symbols closer together	Drag with the Symbol Sprayer tool
Move the symbols farther apart	Alt + Symbol Sprayer tool
Increase the symbol size	Drag with the Symbol Sprayer tool
Decrease the symbol size	Alt + Symbol Sprayer tool
Rotate the symbols	Drag with the Symbol Sprayer tool
Increase the symbol's transparency	Drag with the Symbol Sprayer tool
Decrease the symbol's transparency	Alt + Symbol Sprayer tool
Change the symbol's colour	Drag with the Symbol Sprayer tool
Restore the symbol's original colour	Alt + Symbol Sprayer tool
Apply a style to the symbol	Drag with the Symbol Sprayer tool
Remove the style from a symbol	Alt + Symbol Sprayer tool

Graph Tools

Tool	*Shortcut*
Column Graph tool	J
Function	***Procedure***
Create a Graph sized by numbers	Click with any Graph tool
Create a Graph sized by dragging	Drag with any Graph tool
Create a square or circular graph	Shift + drag with any Graph tool
Create a Graph from the center	Alt + drag with any Graph tool

Paint Tools

Tool	*Shortcut*
Gradient tool	G
Gradient Mesh tool	U
Paint Bucket tool	K Alt + Eyedropper tool
Eydropper tool	I Alt + Paint Bucket tool

Function	*Procedure*
Change Linear Gradient direction and/or length	Drag with Gradient tool
Constrain Gradient Direction to 45^0 angles	Shift + drag with Gradient tool
Change Radial Gradient size and/or location	Drag with Gradient tool
Change Radial Gradient origin point	Click with Gradient tool
Sample colour to Colour palette	Click with Eyedropper tool
Change Paint Style of selected objects	Double-click with Eyedropper tool on an object with the desired style
Paint unselected objects	Click objects with the Paint Bucket tool
Measure a distance	Click the start and end location with the Measure tool
Measure a distance by 45^0 angles	Shift + click the start and end location with the Measure tool

Blend, Auto Trace and Slice Tools

Tool	*Shortcut*
Blend tool	W
Slice tool	Shift + K

Function	*Procedure*
Blend between two paths	Click corresponding selected points on each path with Blend tool
Set Blend options	Double click on the Blend tool
Auto Trace Images	Click area to be traced with Auto Trace tool
Divide artwork into slices	Drag + Slice tool
Constrain slice to a square	Alt + drag with the Slice tool
Slice selected objects	Drag + Slice Selected tool

Viewing Tools

Tool	*Shortcut*
Hand tool	H
	Spacebar (when not enterin text)
Zoom tool	Z
	Ctrl + spacebar
Zoom Out tool	Ctrl + Alt + spacebar
	Alt + Zoom tool

Function	*Procedure*
Reposition the page	Drag with the Hand tool
Fit the page within the document window	Double click on the Hand tool
Moving page boundaries	Drag with the Page tool

Reset page boundaries	Double click on the Page tool
Zoom in	Click with the Zoom tool
	Ctrl + Plus Sign (+)
Zoom Out	Alt + click with the Zoom tool
	Ctrl + Hyphen (-)
Zoom in to a specific area	Drag with the Zoom tool
Move the Zoom Marquee while drawing	Spacebar while dragging with the Zoom tool
Draw the Zoom Marquee from its center	Ctrl + drag with the Zoom tool

TYPE COMMANDS

Type Shortcuts

Action	*Shortcut*
Copy type on a path	Alt + drag the I-bar using any selection tool.
	Spacebar (when not enterin text)
Flip type on a path	Double click the I-bar with any selection tool or just drag it to the opposiete side of the path
Move insertion point to next character	Right Arrow
Move insertion point to previous character	Left Arrow
Move insertion point to next line	Down Arrow
Move insertion point to previous line	Up Arrow
Move insertion point to next word	Ctrl + Right Arrow
Move insertion point to previous word	Ctrl + Left Arrow
Move insertion point to next paragraph	Ctrl + Down Arrow
Move insertion point to previous paragraph	Ctrl + Up Arrow
Select all type in stroy	Ctrl + A when the insertion point is in the story
Select all type in document	Ctrl + A when any tool but the Type tools are selected
Select next character	Shift + Right Arrow
Select previous character	Shift + Left Arrow
Select next line	Shift + Down Arrow
Select previous line	Shift + Up Arrow
Select next word	Ctrl + Shift + Right Arrow
Select previous word	Ctrl + Shift + Left Arrow
Select next paragraph	Ctrl + Shift + Down Arrow
Select previous paragraph	Ctrl + Shift + Up Arrow
Select word	Double click word
Select paragraph	Triple click paragraph

Deselect all type	Ctrl + Shift + A
Duplicate column outline and flow text	Alt + drag column outline with Direct Selection tool
Insert discretionary hyphen	Ctrl + Shift + Hyphen (-)
Insert line break	Press Enter

Paragraph Formatting

Action	*Shortcut*
Display Paragraph palette	Ctrl + Shift + M
Align paragraph flush left	Ctrl + Shift + L
Align paragraph flush right	Ctrl + Shift + R
Align paragraph flush cente	Ctrl + Shift + C
Align paragraph justified	Ctrl + Shift + J
Align paragraph force justified	Ctrl + Shift + F
Display Tab Ruler palette	Ctrl + Shift + T
Align Tab palette to selected paragraph	Click Tab palette size box
Cycle through tab stops	Alt + click tab stop
Move multiple tab stops	Shift + drag tab stops
Cycle tab measurements	Click

Character Formatting

Action	*Shortcut*
Display Character palette	Ctrl + T
Highlight font	Ctrl + Alt + Shift + M
Increase type size	Ctrl + Shift + >
Decrease type size	Ctrl + Shift + <
Increase type to next size on menus	Ctrl + Alt + >
Decrease type to next size on menus	Ctrl + Alt + <
Highlight size	none
Set leading to Solid	Double click Leading symbol in Character palette
Highlight leading	none
Increase Baseline Shift	Alt + Shift + Up Arrow
Decrease Baseline Shift	Alt + Shift + Down Arrow
Increase Baseline Shift x5	Ctrl + Alt + Up Arrow
Decrease Baseline Shift x5	Ctrl + Alt + Shift + Down Arrow
Kern/Track closer	Alt + Left Arrow
Kern/Track apart	Alt + Rigth Arrow
Kern/Track closer x5	Ctrl + Alt + Left Arrow

Kern/Track apart x5	Ctrl + Alt + Right Arrow
Reset Kerning/Tracking to 0	Ctrl + Shift + Q
Highlight Kerning/Tracking	Ctrl + Alt + K
Reset Horizontal Scale to 100%	Ctrl + Shift + X

COLOUR COMMANDS

Colour Palette

Action	*Shortcut*
Show/Hide Colour palette	F6
	Ctrl + I
Rever to default colours	D
Toggle focus between Fill and Stroke	X
Choose current colour in Color palette	Comma (,)
Chang paint to None	/
Apply to inactive Fill/Stroke	Alt + click in colour ramp on Color palette
Apply colour to unselected object	Drag colour swatch from Colour palette to object
Apply colour to selected object	Click swatch in Colour palette
Copy Paint Style from any (source) object to all selected objects	Click source object with Eyedropper
Tint process colour	Shift + drag any Colour palette slider
Cycle through Colour modes	Shift + click Colour Ramp

Swatch Palette

Action	*Shortcut*
show/Hide Swatches palette	F5
Toggle focus between Fill and Stroke	X
Add Swatch	Click the New Swatch icon
	Drag from Colour or Gradient palette into swatches
Replace swatch	Alt + drag from Colour or Gradient palette into swatches
Duplicate swatch	Alt + drag swatch onto New Swatch icon in Swatches palette
Delete swatch	Drag to Trash icon in Swatches palette
	Click Tash icon with swatches selected
Select contiguous swatches	Shift + click first and last swatches
Select noncontiguous swatches	Ctrl + click each swatch
Switch keyboard focus to Swatches palette	Ctrl + Alt + click in swatches palette
Apply colour to unselected object	Drag colour swatch from Swatches palette to object
Apply colour to selected object	Click swatch in Swatches palette

Gradient Palette

Action	*Shortcut*
Choose current gradient in Gradient palete	Period (.)
Show/Hide Gradient palette	F9
Apply swatch to selected colour stop on gradient palette	Alt + click swatch
Add new colour stop	Click below gradient ramp
Duplicate colour stop	Alt + drag colour stop
Sqp colour stops	Alt + drag colour stop on top of another
Suck colour for colour stop with Eyedropper	Shift + click with Eyedropper
Reset Gradient to default Black, White	Ctrl + click in gradient swatch
Apply colour to unselected object	Drag colour swatch from Gradient palette to object
Apply colour to selected object	Click swatch in Gradient palette

Stroke Palette

Action	*Shortcut*
Show/Hide Stroke palette	F10
Increase/decrease Stroke weight	Highlight Stroke field, use up or down arrows, press Enter when finished
Increase/decrease Miter account	Highlight Miter field, use up or down arrows, press Enter when finished

OTHER PALETTES

Miscellaneous Palette Commands

Action	*Shortcut*
Collapse/display Palette	Click box in upper-right corner
Cycle through Palette views	Double click palette tab
Apply settings	Enter
Apply settings while keeping last text field highlighted	Shift + Enter
Highlight Next Text field	Tab
Highlight Previous Text field	Shift + Tab
Highlight any text field	Click label or double click current value
Increase value by base increment	Highlight field, Up Arrow
Decrease value by base increment	Highlight field, Down Arrow
Increase value by large increment	Highlight field, Shift + Up Arrow
Decrease value by large increment	Highlight field, Shift + Down Arrow
Combine palettes	Drag palette tab within other palette
Dock palette	Drag palette tab to bottom of other palette
Separate palette	Drag palete tab from current palette

Transform Palette

Action	*Shortcut*
Show/Hide Transform palette	none
Copy object while transforming	Alt + Enter
Scale proportionately	Ctrl + Enter
Copy object while scaling proportionate	Ctrl + Alt + Enter

Layers Palette

Action	*Shortcut*
Hide/Show	F7
New Layer	Click New Layer icon
New Layer with Options dialog box	Alt + Click New Layer icon
New layer above active layer	Ctrl + Alt + click New Layer icon
New layer below active layer	Ctrl + click New Layer icon
Duplicate layer(s)	Drag layer(s) to New Layer icon
Change layer order	Drag layers up and down within layer list
Select all objects on a layer	Alt + click that layer
Select all objects on several layers	Shift + Alt + click each layer
Select contiguous layers	Shift + click layers
Select noncontiguous layers	Ctrl + click layers
Move objects to a different layer	Drag coloured square to a different layer
Copy objects to a different layer	Alt + drag colour square to a different layer
Hide/Show layer	Click Eyeball icon
View layer while hiding others	Alt + click Eyeball icons
View layer in Artwork mode	Ctrl + click Eyeball icon
View layer in Preview while others are artwork	Ctrl + Alt + click Eyeball icon
Lock/Unlock layer	Click Pencil tool
Unlock layer while locking others	Alt + click Pencial icon
Delete layer	Drag layer to Trash icon
	Select layer and click Trash icon
Delete layer without warning	Alt + drag layer to Trash icon
	Select layer and Alt + click Trash icon

MISCELLANEOUS COMMANDS

Viewing Shortcuts

Action	*Shortcut*
Zoom In	Ctrl + Plus Sign (+)

	Click with Zoom tool
Zoom Out	Ctrl + Hyphen (-)
	Alt + click with Zoom tool
Fit Document in Window	Ctrl + 0
	Double click Hand tool
View at Actual size (100%)	Ctrl + 1
	Double click Zoom tool
Artwork/Preview mode	Ctrl + Y
Preview Selection mode	Ctrl + P + Alt + Y
Custom view recall	Ctrl + Alt + Shift + 1 through Ctrl + Alt + Shift + 0
Show/Hide edges	Ctrl + H
Show/Hide guides	Ctrl + ;
Show/Hide grid	Ctrl + '
Show/Hide rulers	Ctrl + R
Hide selected objects	Ctrl + 3
Hide unselected objects	Ctrl + Alt + 3
Show all hidden objects	Ctrl + Shift + 3
Window mode	F (when in Full Screen mode)
Full Screen mode with menu	F (when in Window mode)
Full Screen mode	F (when in Full Screen mode with menu)

Miscellaneous Commands

Action	*Shortcut*
Nudge selection	Arrow keys
See special Status Line categories	Alt + click status bar
Cycle through units	Ctrl + U
View anagram of credits	Alt + click illustrator click toolbox
Speed up credits in About box	Alt
Display context-sensitive menus	Ctrl + Right click
Highlight last active text field	Ctrl + ~

Generic Dialog Box Commands

Action	*Shortcut*
Cancel	Esc
OK	Enter
Highlight next text field	Tab
Highlight previous text field	Shift + Tab
Highlight any text filed	Click label or double click current value

7 Projects

Windows XP

Booting of the System

Boot the computer from the very beginning and see the desktop and icons on the screen.

Using the Help

Click at Help from the Start button and see the topics covered under it.

Using the Recycle Bin

Delete an icon from desktop. Now, go to the Recycle Bin and restore it.

Creating Folders

As the method of creating folders mentioned in an earlier chapter, create folders with the names of CLASS IX, CLASS X, CLASS XI and CLASS XII.

Renaming Folders

Rename a folder with a different name.

Using Paint

Create a drawing in Paint. Open the same picture in Image and make changes in it and give captions.

Using Word Pad

Create a letter in Word Pad and print it.

Using Calculator

You must have used ordinary calculator, try using the scientific calculator of Windows specially for calculating the value of various Sine/Cosine value in radians.

Photoshop

Creating a File in Photoshop

Open Photoshop and create a new file in it.

Opening an Existing File in Photoshop

Open an existing file in Photoshop.

Using Rectangular Marquees

Open an image in photoshop and draw an marquees over it.

Using Move Tool

Using move tool move an image to different location.

Using Lasso Tool

Using lasso tool create a lasso over the image.

Using Magic Wand Tool

Using magic wand tool select an area of the image.

Using Croping Tool

Use crop tool to get rid of unwanted parts of the picture.

Using Slice Tool

Open an image and create slices of it.

Using Airbrush Tool

Using airbrush tool spray the image with different colours.

Using Paintbrush Tool

Use paintbrush tool and create a drawing.

Using Clone Stamp Tool

Use clone stamp tool take out a sample of the picture and apply it to another image.

Using History Brush Tool

Use history brush tool to paint a copy of one image into another image.

Using Eraser Tool

Use eraser tool and erase a part of the drawing.

Using Paint Bucket Tool

Select a portion of an image and fill colour in it using Paint Bucket tool.

Using Blur and Sharpen Tool

Use blur and sharpen tools to soften and harden the edges of the image.

Using Dodge Tool

Use dodge tool to darken a portion of the drawing.

Using Path Component Selection Tool

Use this tool to select a portion of the image.

Using Type Tool

Use type tool to write your name on the drawing.

Using Pen Tool

Use pen tool to draw lines on the screen.

Using Notes Tool

Use notes tool to write notes on the drawing.

Using Eyedropper Tool

Use eyedropper tool to pick a particular colour from a drawing.

Using Hand Tool

Use hand tool to see the various portions of the image.

Using Zoom Tool

Use zoom tool to see the image in various sizes.

Create a New Layer

Using the layer option create a new layer in the image.

Hide the Layer

Make the layer disappear by hiding it.

Showing the Layer

After hiding the layer show it again.

PageMaker

Create a New Page

Create a new page of the size 6" x 8.5" and place the text shown on the new page.

Formatting

Format it according to the options of PageMaker.

Spell Checking

Spell check it.

Editing

Edit it for corrections if any.

Creating Style Sheets

Try creating Style Sheet for the Text and Headings.

5th March, 2005

To,

The General Manager
Unit Trust of India
Gulab Bhawan
New Delhi - 110 002

Ref: Non-receipt of Dividend Warrant againt Folio no. 4000245497

Sir,

I am holder of the 100 units under the above folio number. For the last so many years I have been receiving the dividend againt it during the month of January itself. But, this year so far I have not received any intimtion. In fact, I have received dividend for my other units in January itself.

I hope that you would try to search for my dividend warrant and send the same to me at the earliest.

In case it is lost in post, please send me the replacement.

Hoping for an early action,

Thanking you,

Yours faithfully,

A K Hangal
T-391 Ahata Kidara
Delhi - 110 006

Printing

Print it on your printer.

Changing Font and Size

Change the font and its size to see how it looks.

Changing Alignment

Try changing the alignment of the text.

Putting Line in the Text

Try putting a 1pt line after the text.

CorelDRAW

Drawing Lines

Draw a straight line.

Formatting the Text

Increase the line spacing and word spacing in the Text.

Changing Font of the Text

Change the Font and Size of the font in the text.

Moving Text

Move text from one place to another.

Rotate Text

Rotate a line of text to 60^0.

Fill Colours

Assign a fill colour to the text.

Fitting Text to a Path

Draw a line. Fit text on it.

Creating Rectangles

Create rectangles and squares.

Creating Circles and Ellipses

Draw circles and ellipses using the tools provided by CorelDRAW.

Drawing Polygons

Draw polygons, stars and spirals.

Select Objects

Select objects using Tab key. Try Multiple selection too.

Combining Objects

Place two objects in the drawing and combine them.

Intersecting Objects

Create an intersection of two objects in a drawing.

Copying Objects

Try copying object from one place and placing it at another.

Creating Symbols

Create various type of symbols.

Aligning Objects

Place two objects in a drawing and align them.

Object

Format it according to the options of PageMaker.

Locking Objects

Place two objects in a drawing and lock them.

Find and Replace Objects

Use Find and Replace Objects options to find and replace objects.

Illustrator

Perform the Following Operations in Illustrator

Opening an Existing File

Place an Image

Drawing a Rectangle

Create a Live Rounded Rectangle

Draw an Ellipse

Draw Polygons, Stars and Spirals

Draw a Regular Polygon

Draw a Star

Create a Double Star

Create a Spiral

Draw Curves using pen

Convert Points between Corner and Smooth

Create Text Objects

Resize and Reshape Text Blocks

Add Text to the existing one

Select a Typeface for the text

Reduce/Enlarge Type of the text

Change distance between lines

Make Superscript and Subscript

Create Various Text Effects